Professional Software Development with Visual C++ 6.0 & MFC

Professional Software Development with Visual C++ 6.0 & MFC

Chao C. Chien

CHARLES RIVER MEDIA, INC.
Hingham, Massachusetts

Acquisitions Editor: Brian J. Sawyer
Production: Publishers' Design & Production Services
Cover Design: The Printed Image

CHARLES RIVER MEDIA, INC.
20 Downer Avenue, Suite 3
Hingham, Massachusetts 02043
781-740-0400
781-740-8816 (FAX)
info@charlesriver.com
www.charlesriver.com

This book is printed on acid-free paper.

Chao C. Chien. *Professional Software Development with Visual C++ 6.0 & MFC.*
ISBN: 1-58450-097-2

Library of Congress Cataloging-in-Publication Data

Chien, Chao.
Professional software development with visual C++ 6.0 & MFC / Chao C. Chien.
p. cm.
ISBN 1-58450-097-2
1. Computer software—Development. 2. C++ (Computer program language) 3. Microsoft Visual C++. I. Title.
QA76.76.D47 C49 2001
005.26'8—dc21
2001005089

Printed in the United States of America
01 02 7 6 5 4 3 2 First Edition

Contents

Acknowledgments

Many people made it possible for me to write this book, and they deserve my thanks.

A project such as this isn't trivial; it takes time away from life and work. For that, I thank my wife Rodi for understanding the drive behind such an enterprise, and providing the space and encouragement for its completion. It certainly made the effort enjoyable and worthwhile.

I also would like to express my appreciation for the support from Charles River Media's Acquisitions Editor, Mr. Brian Sawyer, who had faith in this venture ever since he saw the first 50 pages of the first draft. His continued assistance and accommodation in times of difficulty made the project a success.

Preface

The purpose of this book is to teach you to use Microsoft's Visual C++ language and tool sets to develop commercial-grade software products. The book will guide you from the fundamentals through application deployment, covering the complete life cycle of Windows desktop and component application development. With this goal in mind, the book structures itself into three distinct areas.

THE STRUCTURE OF THE BOOK

The first area of study shows you how to use Microsoft's Visual Studio's rapid development facilities to quickly generate application frameworks, organize an application's data, class objects, and processing functions, and manage projects. In the process we will learn about the Windows application frameworks and develop a systematic working approach to application development that will enable you to build Windows software efficiently with the highest quality; that is, minimum bugs. This is the *visual* and preparatory phase of our mission.

The second area of concentration introduces you to the rich collection of Microsoft's foundation classes, MFC, and demonstrates how you can use them as the cornerstone to different application requirements that can range from desktop client/server programs to Internet browsers and code components, depending on your specialization. This is the MFC phase of our mission.

In the third area of the book, you learn how to produce professional-quality applications. You experience those elements that will elevate your program products from being mere exercises to commercially viable projects.

HOW TO USE THIS BOOK

This book emphasizes the action of program development as opposed to the discussion of C++ theories. However, when understanding the theories is essential to the goal of applications, they are explored in detail. The bulk of the book consists of clearly stated programming procedures supported by guided hands-on examples. Therefore, when you use this book you should be ready to do work, because illustrations and exercises are really what teach programming.

The sample programs are small and to the point. You can think of the book as a collection of unit tests—bite-size morsels that hit the spot. For that, this book can also serve you well as a reference to VC++ and MFC.

WHAT YOU NEED

To use this book you need two things: a PC and Microsoft's Visual C++ 6.0, preferably the Enterprise Edition, which offers the widest range of support materials. If you cannot get the Enterprise Edition, at least use the Professional Edition to make the journey worth your while. The Standard Edition will work, but you miss out on goodies such as remote database controls, static linking to the MFC library, code optimization, and InstallShield®, which helps you create software installation packages. You can compare the detailed features of these editions on the Microsoft Web site.

This book was written using the Enterprise Edition.

CONTENTS AT A GLANCE

Part I: The Visual C++ Developer Studio

Work with the Visual Studio, use the AppWizard to develop VC++ Windows applications, and learn C++ along the way.

Part II: MFC GUI

Learn all about windows controls, including the static control, text box, command button, check box, radio button, group control, combo box, list box, slider, spin control, progress bar, picture control, and animation control. In addition, learn to work with the modal and modeless dialogs, SDI, and MDI application frameworks.

Part III: VC++ Projects

Learn to handle errors and use the Integrated Development Environment to manage application-programming projects.

Part IV: The Document/View Paradigm

Learn about the architectures of a Windows application, including the basic CMainFrame, CDocument, and CView Classes and how their variations enable you to produce split-screen windows and multiple views. Understand how the device context helps you display on the screen, and use the application framework's built-in printing and print preview facilities.

Part V: Working with MFC Data Classes

Dig into such fundamental MFC data members as CString, date and time, lists, and arrays. Then, persist them to files.

Part VI: Database Processing

Apply the MFC to dealing with databases, including ODBC, SQL, DAO, OLE DB, and ADO. In addition, learn to display complex data with grids, image lists, and list and tree views.

Part VII: Component Programming

Become skilled in creating program dynamic link libraries and ActiveX components.

Part VIII: Professional Software Development

Study what makes a professional-quality software application, including manipulating the toolbar, status bar, menus, common dialog boxes, building property sheets and wizards, applying a timer control, and interfacing with the command line and Windows' registry. Add bells and whistles such as tooltips, pop-up menus, splash screens, tips of the day, and system information to jazz up your software products. Construct onscreen help and package your software for distribution.

Part IX: Beyond VC++ 6.0

Take a long-range view on where your programming education will take you, and preview the new Microsoft .NET application platform and its new languages, including VC++ 7.0, managed VC++ (VC++.NET), and C#.

PART I

The Visual C++ Developer Studio

A great advantage of working with Visual C++ compared to other C++ languages is the rapid development tool sets offered by Visual Studio[1], Microsoft's IDE (*integrated development environment)*. In fact, many Windows software developers consider the visual development environment the sole reason for using it, besides working with MFC. Therefore, virtually all studies of VC++ begin with a look at Visual Studio. This book agrees with this approach, and goes one step further and makes it the backbone of our learning. In this first part of the book, you will learn to employ the IDE's wealth of features to generate basic application frameworks quickly and develop your fundamental application development skills.

[1] Strictly speaking, Visual Studio is the environment for all of Microsoft's Visual products, including Visual Basic and others. Here, the terms Visual Studio, Developer Studio, IDE, and other colloquial references all mean the same thing: the compiler programming environment in which you do Visual C++ work.

1 Rapid Application Development

The main concern of our first outing in the Visual C++ programming arena is becoming familiar with the work environment rather than learning C++ programming. Therefore, as your first experience with Visual C++, you will create a Windows application that will do nothing more than appear with a dialog box as its main window. To learn the process, simply follow the instructions here.

It is assumed that you have started Visual C++ (Figure 1.1).

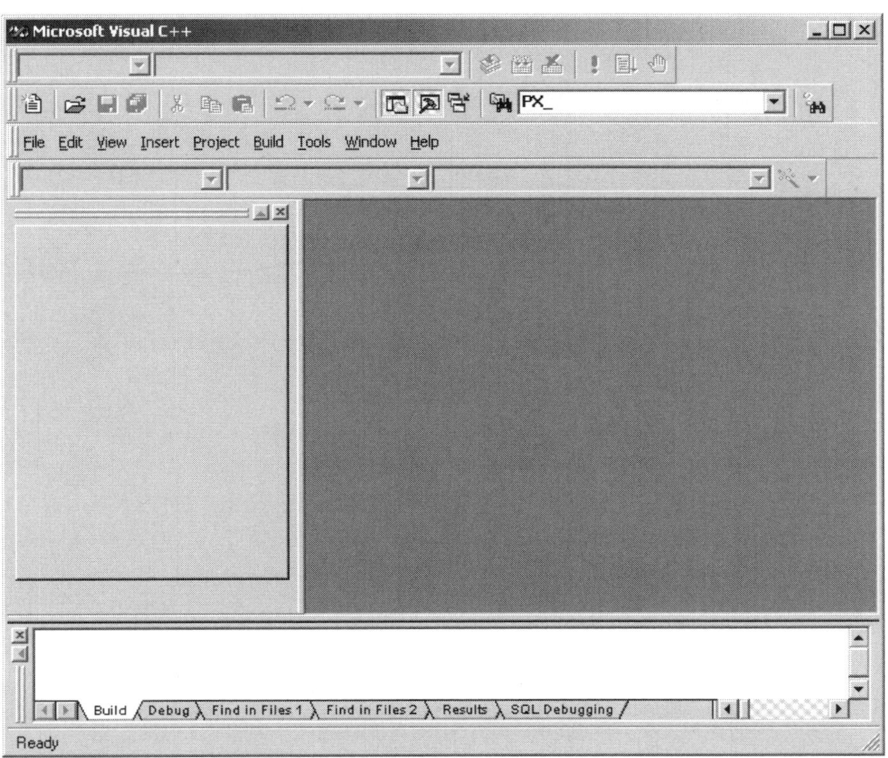

FIGURE 1.1 VC++ opening screen.

WORKING WITH APPWIZARD

1. Choose the File->New command (Figure 1.2).

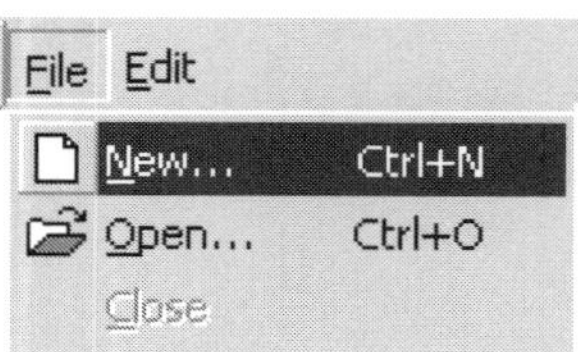

FIGURE 1.2 The File->New command.

2. Choose MFC AppWizard with the Project name (**DialogDemo**) and location entered as shown in (Figure 1.3). Then, click OK to activate AppWizard.

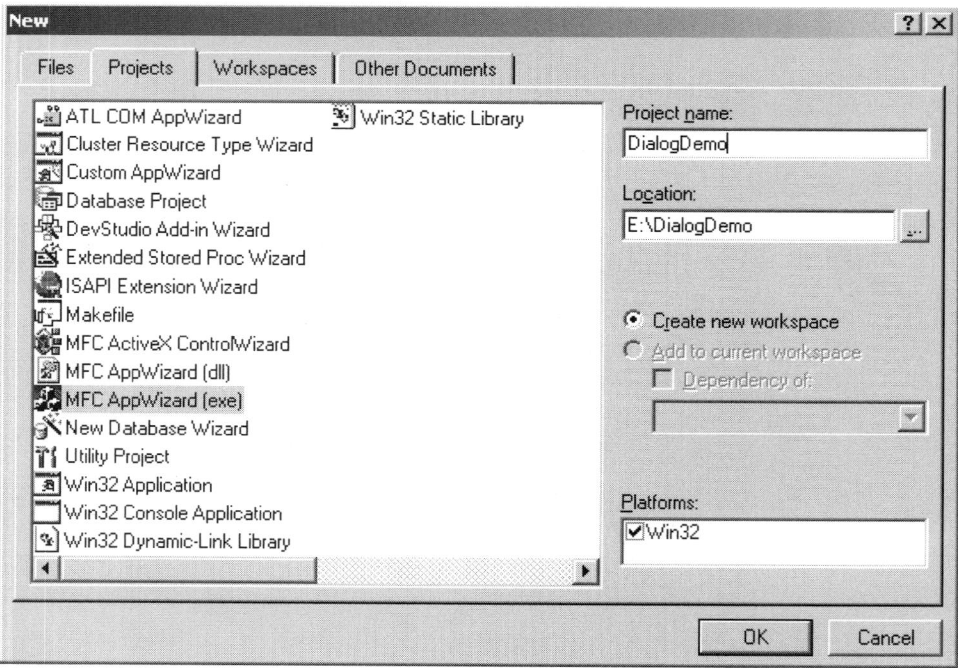

FIGURE 1.3 The VC++ IDE File->New Screen.

3. In Step 1 of AppWizard, select "Dialog based" (Figure 1.4), and then click Next.

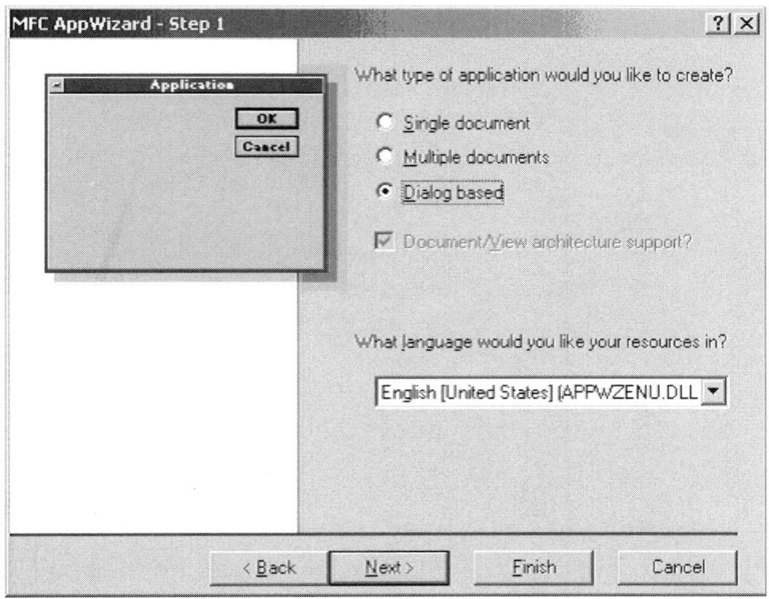

FIGURE 1.4 AppWizard Step 1.

4. Accept Step 2 as is (to generate an application that will have an About box with no context-sensitive onscreen help and capable of accepting ActiveX controls, as in Figure 1.5) and use the next button to move on to Step 3.
5. Accept Step 3 so we'll have code comments, and proceed to Step 4 (Figure 1.6).
6. Accept Step 4 as is, and click Finish to complete the AppWizard.

A project information summary is presented for your review (Figure 1.7).

7. When you are finished reviewing the summary, click OK to generate the project (Figure 1.8).
8. Select "TODO: Place dialog controls here" by clicking it with the mouse, and remove it by pressing the [Delete] key on the keyboard.

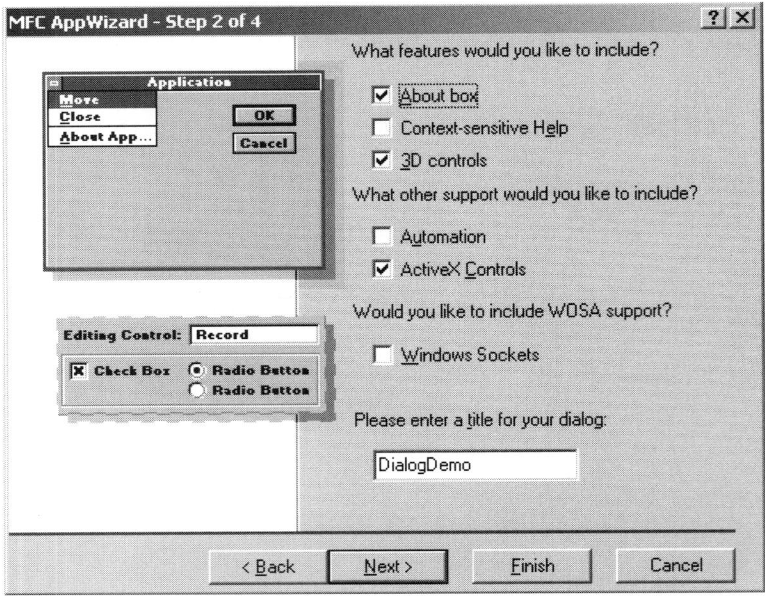

FIGURE 1.5 AppWizard Step 2.

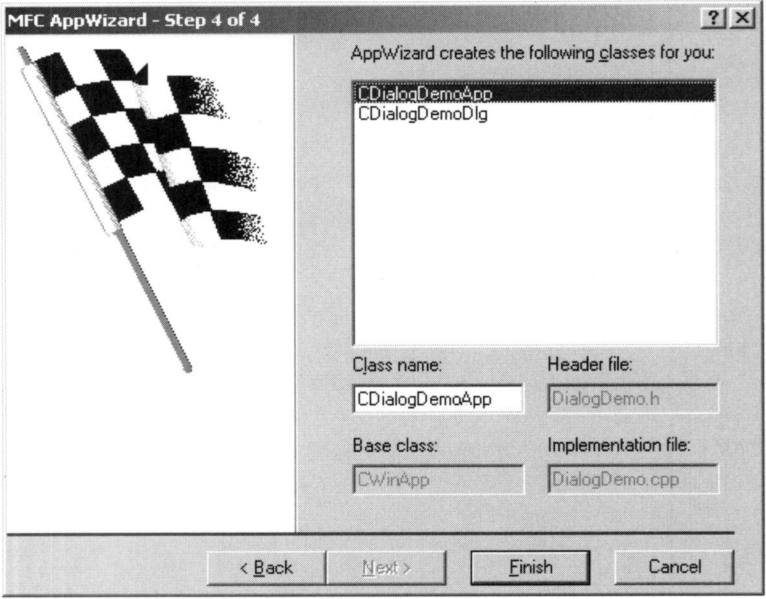

FIGURE 1.6 AppWizard Step 4.

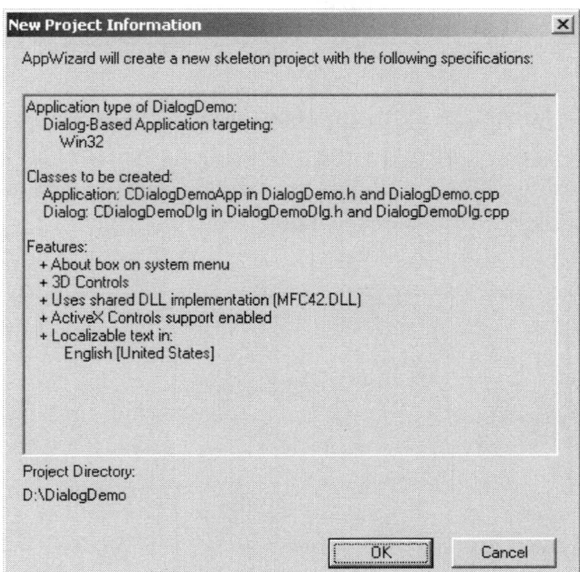

FIGURE 1.7 AppWizard new project summary.

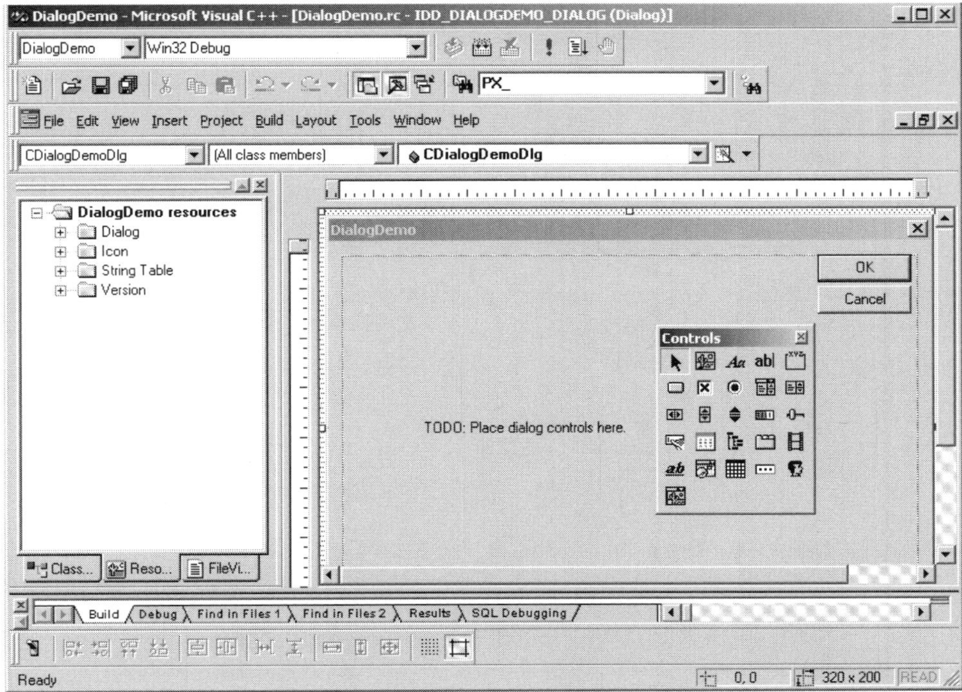

FIGURE 1.8 The new project.

COMPILING AN APPLICATION

Compiling an application in VC++, as compared to earlier C and C++ compilers in which you must compose the command line by specifying switches and options, is a simple matter of choosing a command. For the following exercise, you may use the D:\Chapter01\CompilingAnApplication\DialogDemo example.

1. To compile the new application, choose Build->Build All(Figure 1.9).

FIGURE 1.9 The Build->Rebuild All command.

Alternatively, you can click Build or press [F7] (Figure 1.10).

FIGURE 1.10 The Build toolbar.

The application is compiled, and an executable is produced (Figure 1.11).

```
--------------------Configuration: DialogApp - Win32 Debug--------------------
Compiling resources...
Compiling...
StdAfx.cpp
Compiling...
DialogApp.cpp
DialogAppDlg.cpp
Generating Code...
Linking...

DialogApp.exe - 0 error(s), 0 warning(s)
```

Build | Debug | Find in Files 1 | Find in Files 2

FIGURE 1.11 Compilation log.

EXECUTING AN APPLICATION

With VC++, you also can execute a compiled application right in the development environment.

1. To run the newly compiled application, choose Build->Execute DialogDemo.exe (Figure 1.12)

FIGURE 1.12 The Execute command.

Alternatively, click Run or press [Ctrl-F5] (Figure 1.13). A dialog window appears as shown in (Figure 1.14).

FIGURE 1.13 The Execute toolbar.

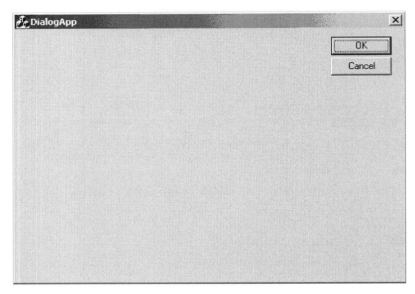

FIGURE 1.14 The DialogDemo main window.

2. Click OK or Cancel to terminate the application.
3. Close the project with the File->Close Workspace command (Figure 1.15).

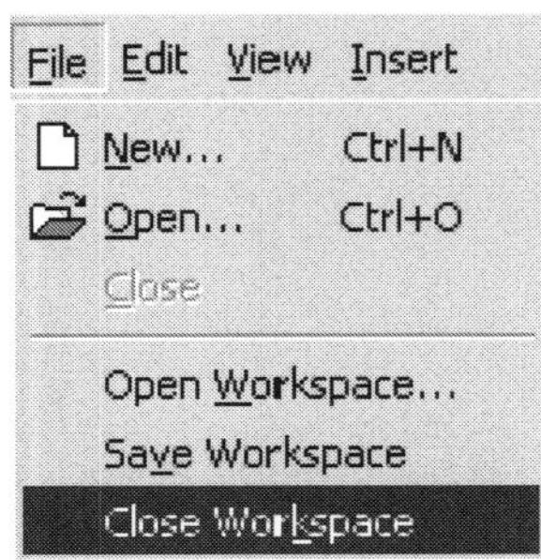

FIGURE 1.15 The Close Workspace command.

AN SDI APPLICATION

Next, we'll turn to the second type of desktop Windows application that you can quickly generate using AppWizard, a Windows application with a "child window," just like the Windows accessory Notepad program.

1. Use the File->New command to start a new application named SDIApp, as illustrated in Figure 1.16.

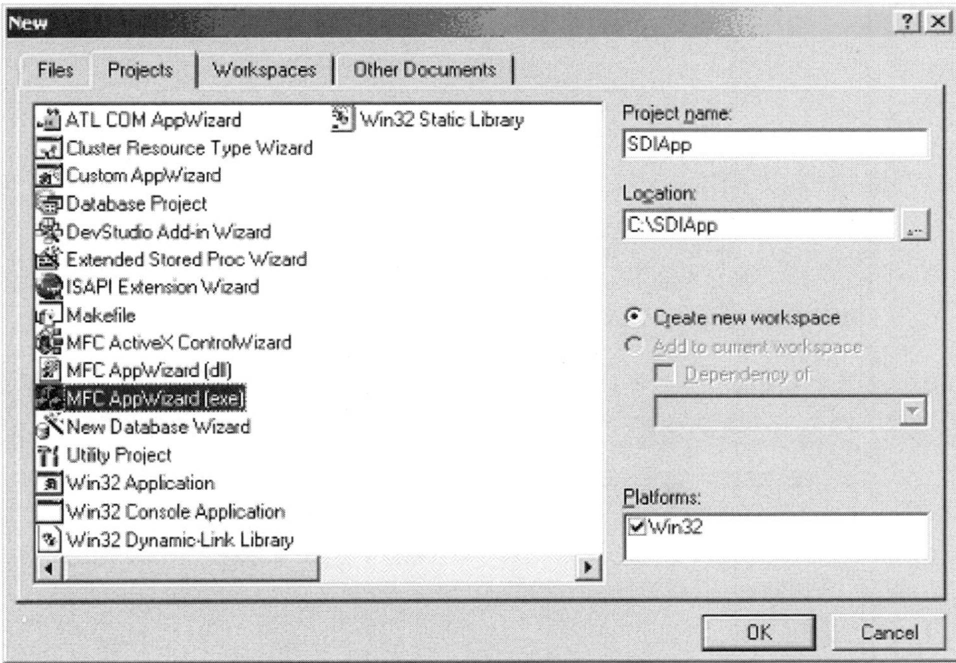

FIGURE 1.16 New SDIApp Project

2. In Step 1 of AppWizard, select Single document (Figure 1.17).
3. Accept all the remaining steps (Figure 1.18, Figure 1.19, Figure 1.20, and so on) until the project is generated.
4. Compile and execute the new application as in the last example.

A new application with a child window appears (Figure 1.21).

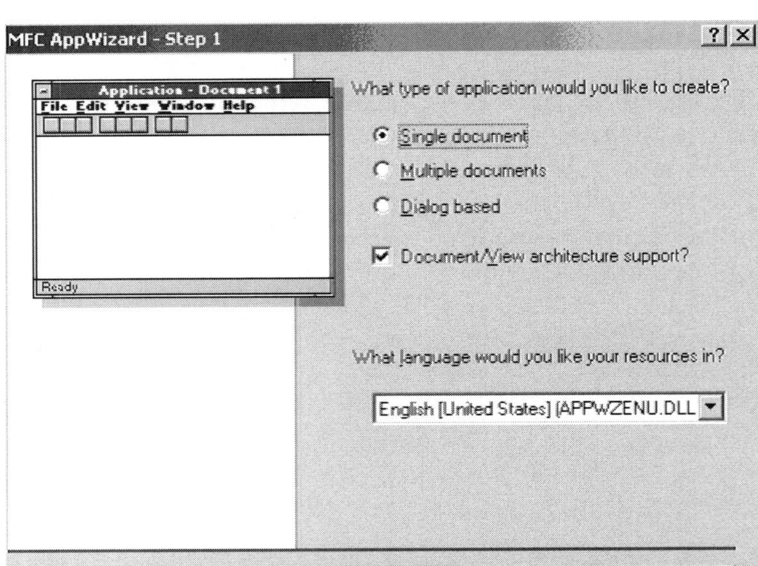

FIGURE 1.17 AppWizard Step 1—Single document model.

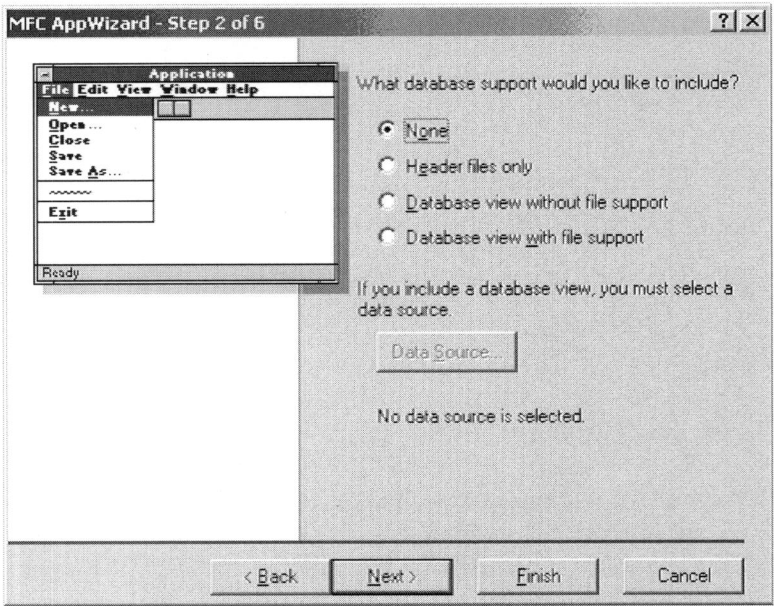

FIGURE 1.18 AppWizard Single document model Step 2.

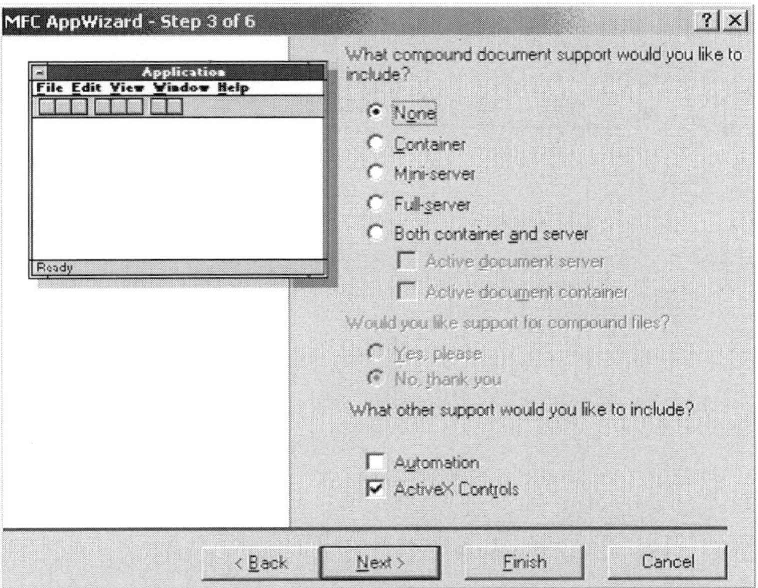

FIGURE 1.19 AppWizard Single document model Step 3.

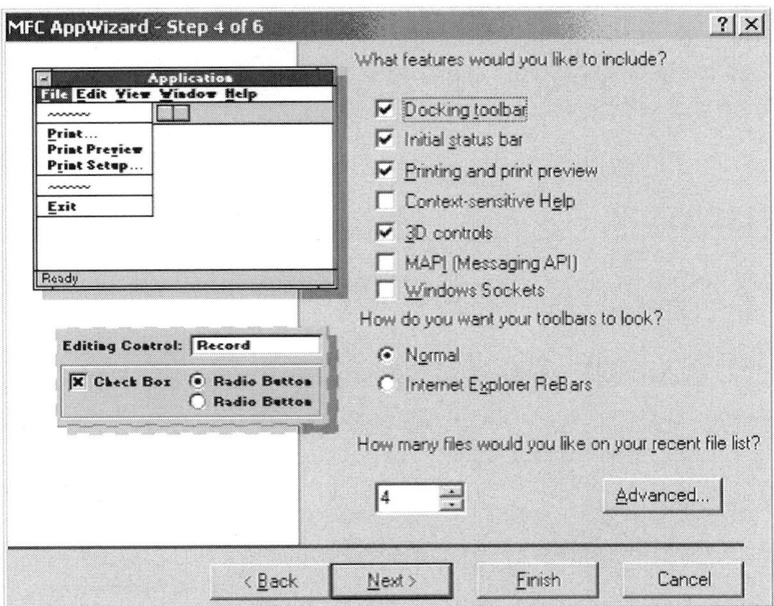

FIGURE 1.20 AppWizard Single document model Step 4.

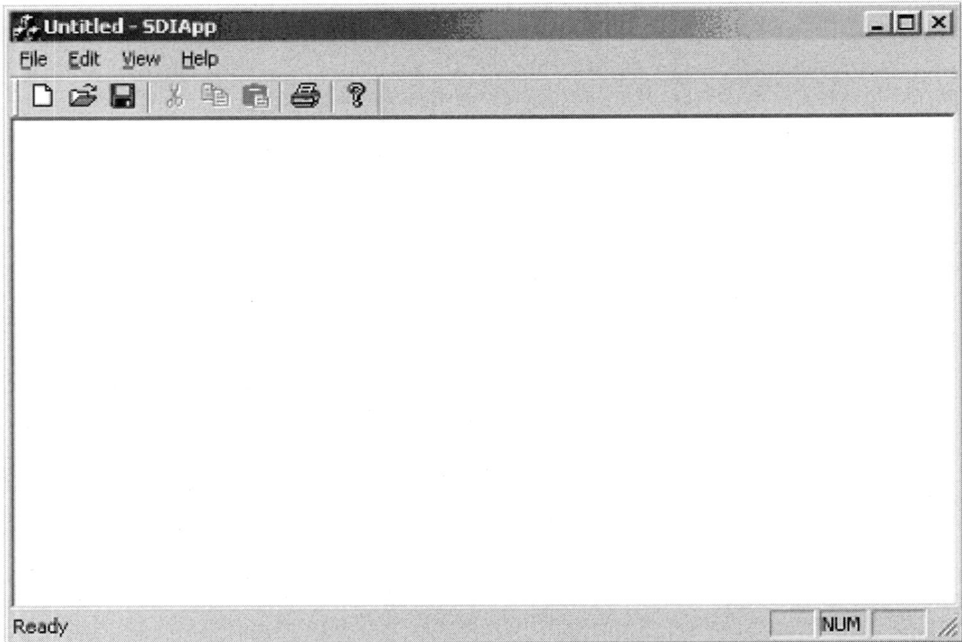

FIGURE 1.21 The SDIApp main window.

5. Use the File->Exit command to terminate the SDIApp application, and then close its project workspace.

AN MDI APPLICATION

As a third illustration, we'll generate an MDI application, an application that can have multiple child windows.

1. Again, use the File->New command to start AppWizard. This time, set the project name to MDIApp (Figure 1.22).
2. In Step 1, select Multiple document (Figure 1.23).
3. For the rest of the steps, accept the defaults and finish the AppWizard steps. Compile the generated program and execute it. The MDIApp main window should appear as shown in (Figure 1.24).

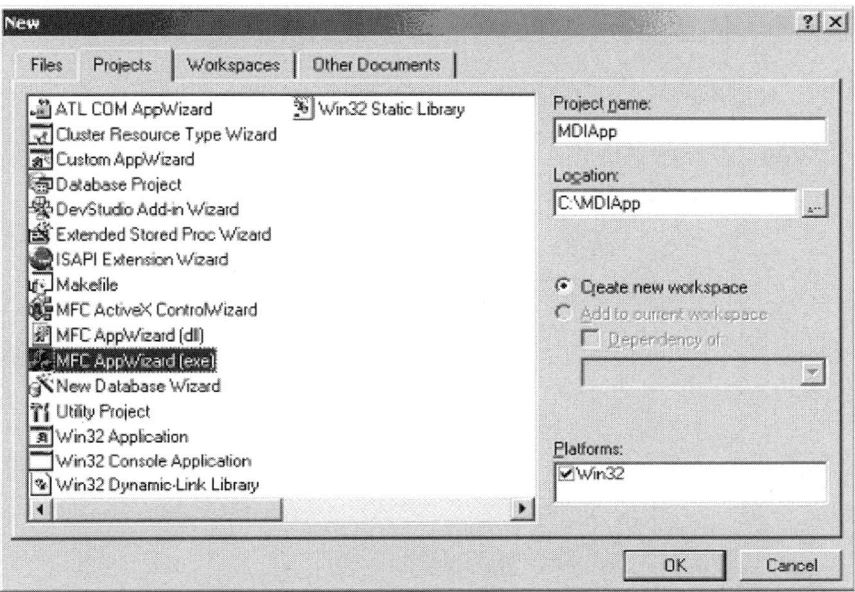

FIGURE 1.22 The New MDIApp project.

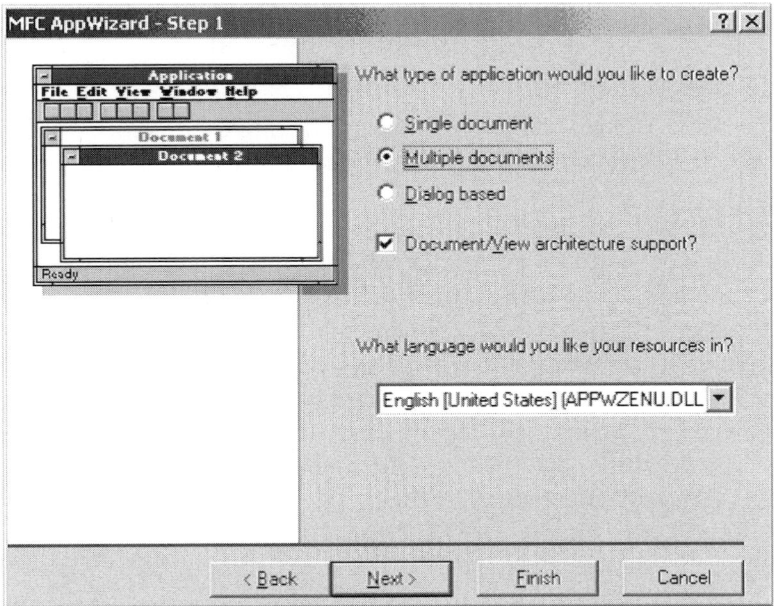

FIGURE 1.23 MDIApp AppWizard Step 1.

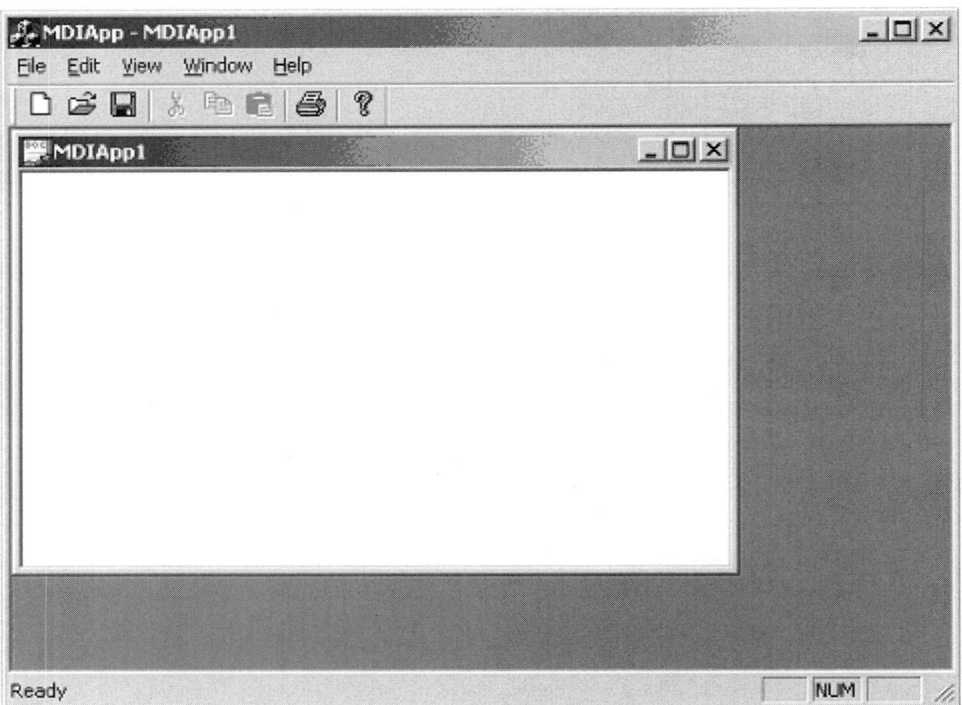

FIGURE 1.24 The MDIApp main window.

4. Try the Window->New window command to create more child windows, then terminate the application and close the workspace.

The preceding three examples showed us how we can use AppWizard to quickly generate three types of desktop Windows applications: the dialog-based application that has but a main dialog as the user interface; the SDI, or single document interface application that comes with a single child window; and the MDI, multiple document interface application that is capable of having many child windows. Each of these types of applications represents an application *framework* that you can use to showcase your program logics. Mind you that we have yet to write a single line of C++ program code, which brings home the advantage of using a Visual environment to develop Windows applications.

Next, we will examine the C++ language.

2 A Quick C++ Review

At this point, let's take time out to quickly review the C++ language, which is at the core of our subject matter. Although this book presupposes that you are at least somewhat familiar with the C++ language (so that we can concentrate on the Visual environment, MFC, and professional software development topics), it is prudent, even for the experts among us, to briefly review the subject.

For the uninitiated, this is a first exposure to the subject, so, technically, we also can call it a preview. You can regard this chapter as a quick start to a new subject that is essential for understanding the materials in this book.

Because this chapter is but a brief discussion of the key language elements pertinent to the materials covered in this book, do not entrust your learning of the C++ language solely to this chapter. You should also have a comprehensive reference for C++ related issues on which you can depend. This is especially true if you are new to the language and are trying to learn it along with Visual C++ and MFC.

Moreover, because C++ is an extension of C, some C elements may be mentioned, but a discussion of C is not in the present agenda. If you're unfamiliar with C, you should have access to a source for its features, as they can be used in VC++ programming.

DATA

The fundamental purpose of a computer language is to manipulate data, whether numeric values, text, graphical information, or communication code. When being processed, data are held in the computer's memory and are identified by mnemonic names called *identifiers* or *variables*.

When you declare a variable, you precede it with its type, such as:

```
BOOL     bSave;
```

Value versus Reference

In C++, a data item that occupies computer memory can be referred to by its identifier or memory address. The memory address is called a *pointer*, and is denoted by the symbol "&." For example, if the variable name is **MyName**, its pointer is **&MyName**.

You can declare a variable as a pointer, such as:

```
char*     pName;
```

In this case, a variable is declared to point to a character data item in memory.

When communicating between program code members, an identification of the item *by reference* means the item's pointer, or memory address, is referred to. By having knowledge of the memory address, the code members can access the same, real data at that memory location.

In contrast, when the actual item's name is used, a copy of the data item is passed. Consequently, different code parts end up working on different copies of the item. In such a case, we refer to the identification as *by value*.

Data Types

To enable processing, variables are classified by type. Table 2.1 lists the data types recognized in C++, with the last two being unique to MFC.

TABLE 2.1 C++ DATA TYPES

Data Type	*Description*
BOOL	A Boolean value.
BSTR	A 32-bit character pointer.
BYTE	An 8-bit integer that is not signed.
COLORREF	A 32-bit value used as a color value.
DWORD	A 32-bit unsigned integer or the address of a segment and its associated offset.
LONG	A 32-bit signed integer.
LPARAM	A 32-bit value passed as a parameter to a window procedure or callback function.
LPCSTR	A 32-bit pointer to a constant character string.
LPSTR	A 32-bit pointer to a character string.

TABLE 2.1 *(Continued)*

Data Type	Description
LPCTSTR	A 32-bit pointer to a constant character string that is portable for Unicode and DBCS.
LPTSTR	A 32-bit pointer to a character string that is portable for Unicode and DBCS.
LPVOID	A 32-bit pointer to an unspecified type.
LRESULT	A 32-bit value returned from a window procedure or callback function.
UINT	A 16-bit unsigned integer on Windows versions 3.0 and 3.1; a 32-bit unsigned integer on Win32.
WNDPROC	A 32-bit pointer to a window procedure.
WORD	A 16-bit unsigned integer.
WPARAM	A value passed as a parameter to a window procedure or callback function: 16 bits on Windows versions 3.0 and 3.1; 32 bits on Win32.
POSITION	A value used to denote the position of an element in a collection; used by MFC collection classes.
LPCRECT	A 32-bit pointer to a constant (nonmodifiable) RECT structure.

Arrays

An array is an indexed set of data that occupy contiguous memory locations. For example, "int n[10]" represents an integer array of 10 elements.

A string of the *char* type is by definition an array of characters.

In addition, when an array is referenced, it is not by value but by memory address.

Type Casting

If you assign values between two variables that are of different types but the assignment actually makes sense, you can force the operation by typecasting the value of one into the other. For example, if x is of the double type, and y is of the float type, you can pass the value of y to x if you typecast y, as in:

```
x = (double) y;
```

STATEMENTS AND BLOCKS

The operations to be performed in a program are expressed as instructions, which are called *statements* in C++. A statement in C++ is an expression that ends in ";"—the semicolon. A typical C++ statement looks like this:

```
int     n;
```

This statement establishes a data variable of the indigent type (int) named n. The next statement takes the value in the variable, adds 1 to it, and puts the result back in the same memory location occupied by the variable.

```
n = n + 1;
```

The preceding statement can also be expressed as:

```
n++;
```

A group of statements that must be performed as a single unit to achieve a specific purpose is enclosed in a pair of braces to form a code block, such as:

```
{
     n = n + 1;
     j = n * 3;
}
```

FUNCTIONS

A function can loosely be defined as a block of code that can be uniquely identified by a name and has a type. For example, the following function is called *GetTax()*, and it is of the float type because it computes a float value as a result:

```
float     GetTax( float price, float rate )
{
     float tax;
     tax = price * rate;
     return tax;
}
```

The *GetTax()* function is passed two values: price and rate, both of the float type. A tax value is computed based on these two input values called *parameters*, and the resultant tax value is *returned* by the function. This returned value is the value of the function, enabling the function to be used in the following fashion:

```
float     salesTax = GetTax( 100, 0.08 );
```

The returned value is equivalent to the function.

In this example the parameters are supplied to the function by value; that is, the function obtains copies of the parameters' values with which to work. If the actual parameters were to be worked on, the function would have been:

```
float     GetTax( float* price, float* rate )
```

The form of a function is:

```
type     function_name( parameters, …)
{
     return value;
}
```

Understanding functions is paramount for the C, C++, and VC++ programmers because the function is the backbone of the languages. Virtually every code module is a function. There is no such thing as a subroutine as in many other languages. In fact, a main program module itself is a function.

Because the basic language offers only the fundamental syntax and constructs that are used to build all available program operations, the capabilities of a program are derived from functions. The power of MFC is precisely the richness of the library of functions that it contains.

LOGIC FLOW CONTROL

As other languages, C++ has logic flow control devices that will enable the expression of choices and iteration.

if-else

The *if* structure evaluates an expression for truthfulness and routes the program logic accordingly. For example:

```
if ( Purchase > 1000 )
     Discount = Purchase * 0.15;
else
     Discount = 0;
```

switch

The switch mechanism routes the program logic according to a given value. For example:

```
switch( GroupSize )
{
     case 1: Do something;
          break;
     case 2: Do something else;
          break;
     Default: Do nothing;
}
```

In this example, the value in the variable *GroupSize* determines what the next processing action will be. If the value is 1, the program will do something and move on to beyond the *switch* code block or the scope of the switch construct—the *break* keyword breaks out of the code block. If the value is 2, the program will do something else. Otherwise, the Default action will be taken.

for

The *for* loop will iterate an action (statement or code block) as many times as dictated by the counting scheme enacted in the structure. For example:

```
for ( int n = 0; n < 10; n++ )
{
     Do something;
}
```

In this example, an integer variable is declared for use in a loop. The loop action is enclosed inside a block; that is, everything between the braces is to be iterated. The integer is initialized to a value of 0. As the program logic iterates, this value is incremented by 1 (n++). The iteration stops when n has been incremented to 10, which will put it over the termination criteria of n < 10.

while

The *while* structure enforces a loop as long as an evaluation condition holds true, such as:

```
int     n = 0;
while ( n < 10 )
```

```
{
     Loop action;
     Something that makes the value in n change;
}
```

do

A different form of the *while* loop is the *do* loop, which evaluates the loop condition at the end of the loop rather than at the beginning, thus causing the loop to execute at least once. For example:

```
int     n = 0;
do
{
     Loop action;
     Something that makes the value in n change;
} while ( n < 10 )
```

CLASSES AND OBJECTS

We now come to perhaps the most prominent of the C++ languages features: classes and objects.

Let's reexamine the declaration of a variable. Specifically, look at the following sample statements:

```
int     iAge;
int     iGrade;
```

Here we have two data items, both of the integer type. What does this mean in terms of computer operations? What really happens here is that the computer language has a built-in set of definitions governing the construction and behavior of an integer, including how much memory such a data item would consume, and the rules prescribing its operations. For example, the language knows that an integer does not carry with it a fraction. That is how computers work: by rules and built-in regulations called language syntax. For example, when you place a + operator between two numeric values, the rules dictate that the values are to be added together, whereas if the same symbol is placed between two character strings, the language knows that the sign means concatenation and not addition.

As you can see, you can use a built-in set of definitions to produce multiple instances of data items with similar characteristics. In C++ lingo, that declaration of an item, or *object*, is called *instantiation*.

Let's carry this concept one step further. Suppose according to the data type specifications, an integer has an extra built-in operation represented by some symbol that will automatically produce the square of its value. The effect of this is that every time you create a new integer, you can automatically use this symbol or operation to obtain its square. Further, if this square is retained in another variable internal to the integer, you can directly go to that variable to obtain the square without running the squaring operation.

To really appreciate this concept, let's push the hypothesis one more step. Let's say the language not only comes with built-in data types such as integers and floating points and strings, but allows you to define your own data type with all the trimmings such as those just described as long as you furnish the data's operational definitions. What you have is called a *class*.

In C++, a class is a "blueprint" or a set of definitions on which you can create things called *objects*. An object instantiated from a class will have a name just like a data item. In fact, we often call such an object a *variable* of a particular class. To bring home the point, if we call int an integer class, then an integer variable would be an integer object. Thus, a class is tantamount to our reaching beyond the confines of predesigned data types and being able to definine our own object types. Before the concept of class, programmers did not regard data types as classes because the data types' definitions or "blueprints" were hidden inside the language compiler and could not be seen.

A class has built-in operations expressed as functions called *methods* or just *member functions*. It also can have built-in data items called the *members* or *member variables*. These member functions and member variables are identified as extensions of the object. For example, suppose CMyClass is the name of a class. The following statements create an object based on this class, invoke the member function called *GetSource()*, and assign the value of 5 to its member integer named **m_iAge**:

```
CMyClass     item;
item.GetSource();
item.m_iAge = 5;
```

The best way to visualize a class is to create one. Go to Visual C++ IDE's ClassView, bring up the context menu, and choose the New Class command as shown in Figure 2.1. In the New Class dialog, select Generic Class and enter the name of the class that you want to create, such as **CMyClass**, as shown in Figure 2.1. When you click OK, a new class will be created for you in which you can study its form.

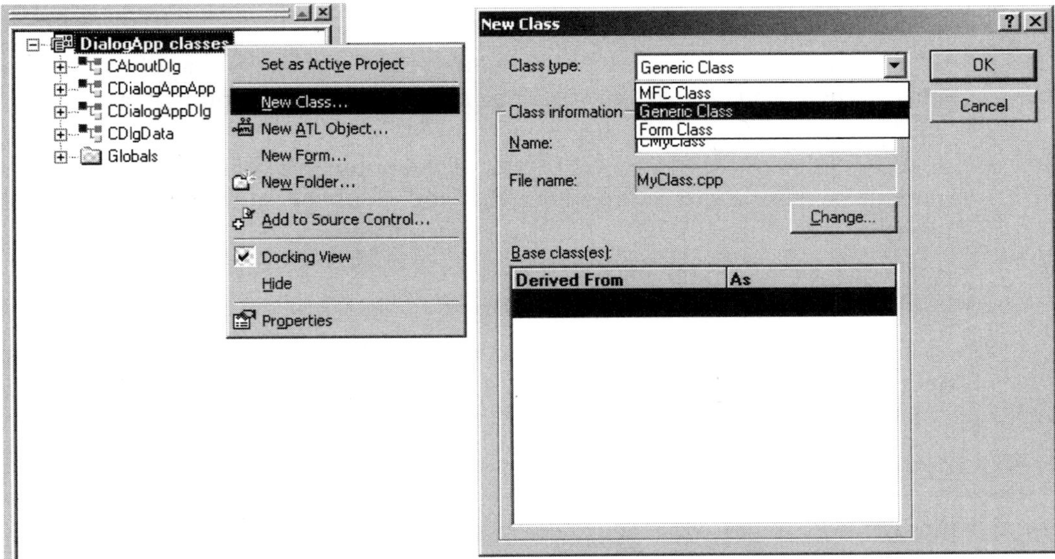

FIGURE 2.1 Defining a new generic class.

Constructor and Destructor

A basic class such as CMyClass is quite simple. In the header file MyClass.h, you'll see that the class is defined as:

```
class CMyClass
{
public:
     CMyClass();
     virtual ~CMyClass();

};
```

This class has two member functions. The first, CMyClass(), which bears the class's name, is the class's *constructor*. The constructor is the function that will be invoked when an object is instantiated (or when a variable is declared) from the class. The second function with a preceding ~ is the *destructor*. The destructor function is called when an object of the class is destroyed and removed from the computer's memory. The bodies of the function are contained in the source file, MyClass.cpp.

Instantiating an Object

As mentioned, the idea of instantiating an object is similar to that of declaring a data variable—you create a real object by following the prescription of a blueprint called a class.

In C++, there are two ways to instantiate an object. One is to create it on the operating system's stack, using a form that you should be intimately familiar with (compare it to "int nSize"):

```
CMyClass     myObject;
```

The second way is to create it on the heap, which is to first identify the object's memory address location, and then subscribe memory for it. The coding form is:

```
CMyClass*     pMyObject;
pMyObject = new CMyClass;
```

The first statement creates a pointer to an object (but no object yet). The second statement creates the object with the *new* keyword.

When the object is ready to go out of scope—that is, when the domain in which it exists is about to vanish, such as when a function ends—you will remove the object pointer from the heap with the *delete* keyword, such as:

```
delete pMyObject;
```

You will encounter this many times in this book.

Class Members

A class can have built-in functions and objects (such as data variables), and they can be of different scopes.

public

A public class member is one that can be accessed by external parties, such as the previous *GetSource()* and **m_iAge** examples.

private

A private member is one that can be accessed by members within the same object. It is inaccessible and transparent to an external party.

protected

There is a third member scope known as *protected*, which we discuss after *inheritance*.

Inheritance

Another property of a class is that it can be used as a base to engender other classes.

Suppose you're in a department store shopping for a microwave oven. You ask the salesperson what model 1000 can do, and she informs you that it can be programmed, has a certain volume capacity, and so forth. Then you ask what model 1000A is, and she tells you that it is the same as model 1000, but comes with a rotating tray. What she has said is equivalent to the statement that "the model 1000A design is inherited from model 1000." In other words, she doesn't have to say that "model 1000A can be programmed, has volume capacity of..." all over again—that is implied.

In C++, a class can be derived from another class. Such a *derived class inherits* the properties of the *base class*, plus whatever new members it defines. If you use the same procedure described previously in VC++ to create a new class by deriving it from another class, it would appear as shown in Figure 2.2 and here:

```
class CHerClass : public CMyClass
{
public:
     CHerClass();
     virtual ~CHerClass();

};
```

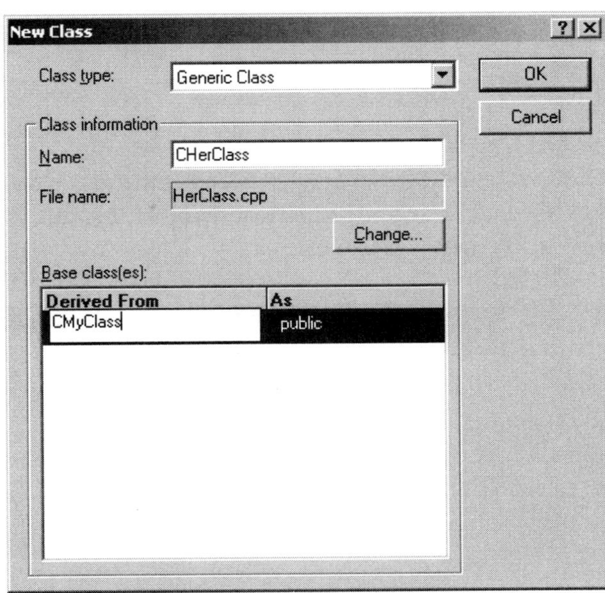

FIGURE 2.2 Deriving a new class.

Derived classes allow us to create new objects that have the basic properties of an existing class plus more, thus saving us the work of having to define the same things over again.

The entire MFC library of classes, with the exception of the CCreateContext class, is derived from one ancestor, the CObject class.

Protected

A private member by definition has a scope that is private to the domain in which it is defined. Therefore, whereas other members of the same class can access a private member, it is inaccessible to members of a derived class. However, if a member is scoped as *protected*, it can be accessed, but not by an external party.

Member Functions

While member objects have the public, private, and protected properties, member functions have more variations, which we'll quickly summarize here.

Overloading

In C++, you can have different member functions in the same class having the same name, yet taking on different parameters. These are *overloaded* functions. This language feature allows us the flexibility of providing diverse functional forms to accommodate diverse input and usage requirements, yet producing a unified result. For example, the following two member functions can coexist:

```
long     GetRecNum( char* cID );
long     GetRecNum( int nID );
```

With the first function, you can obtain a data record number by providing a data ID as a character string. In the second function, you can produce the same record number by providing the data ID as an integer. With these overloaded functions you can obtain the database record number by producing an ID in either numeric or character form.

Virtual Functions

A virtual function is a function that can be (and is expected to be) redefined in the derived class. This feature allows a function with a predetermined name to acquire local, distinct behavior. In addition, because of the virtual function's flexibility, when you derive classes from a same base class, you end up with diverse behaviors for the same function. This is known as *polymorphism*.

The idea is like a certain PC line having a hardware bay reserved at a certain location in the computer case. Model A has a RW-CD-ROM unit there, but in Model B it is a DVD player—same basic design, but different implementations—and you can include both models in one description: that both have built-in mass storage devices.

Accessing Members

In accessing members, you use different notations depending on how the object is created. If the object is instantiated on the stack, you use the dot "." to extend the member. For example, to invoke the *Initialize()* function of the myObject object, you code:

```
myObject.Initialize();
```

If the object is a pointer and is instantiated on the heap (with the *new* keyword), you use the *indirection* operator:

```
pMyObject->Initialize();
```

COMMENTS

In C and C++ text preceded by "//" is meant to be a comment and not code, such as:

```
// TODO: Add your specialized code here and/or…
```

After "//", all the text up to the end of a line will be ignored by the compiler.

If a group of text, whether it is a partial line or it spans multiple lines, is meant to be comments, it should be enclosed between "/*" and "*/", such as:

```
OnCreateClient(LPCREATESTRUCT /*lpcs*/, CCreateContext* pContext)
```

This chapter is obviously by no means an exhaustive discourse on the subject of C++, but it covers most of the topics that we will come across in the remainder of the book. Therefore, even if you have no background in C or C++, you should be able to handle the materials to come. If you are indeed a true C++ novice, you might have found the pace of this chapter a bit fast and the coverage overwhelming. That's all right. Later, as we go over the features in context, you can come back and revisit the chapter.

Of all the matters discussed, perhaps the most prominent one are classes and objects, the core of the OOP (*object-oriented programming*) school of thought and the C++ language as distinguished from C. Indeed, the use of objects, instantiated from classes, greatly helps a programmer modularize her design and organize her thought processes. More important, we must have a good grasp of it if we are to learn MFC, *Microsoft Foundation Classes.*

3 Working with Visual Developer Studio

As you have just experienced, the Visual C++ Developer Studio allowed us to quickly create three Windows applications, using AppWizard to help us accomplish the tasks by merely making a few feature choices. This is the benefit of working in an *IDE*, or *integrated development environment*. Granted, these applications don't do much (but then, that's why we need to program); however, the *application framework* saves us hours in coding that used to be done manually.

Besides AppWizard, Developer Studio actually does much more toward helping us create applications without coding. We will now explore these facilities.

1. Bring back the **SDIApp** project for illustration purposes using the File->Open Workspace command (Figure 3.1).

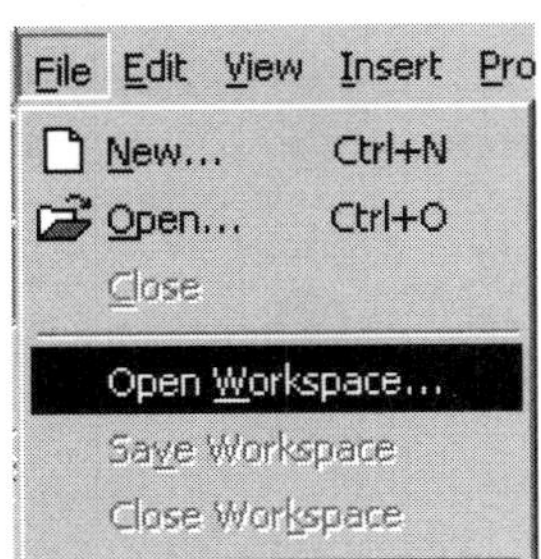

FIGURE 3.1 The Open Workspace command.

Alternatively, better yet, use the File->Recent Workspaces command (Figure 3.2).

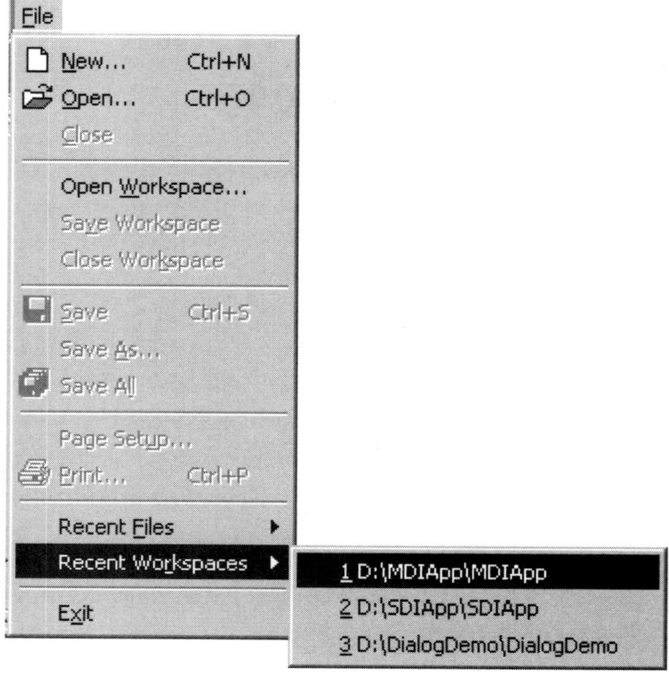

FIGURE 3.2 Recent projects.

RESOURCEVIEW

One of the most powerful features of the VC++ IDE is the organization of resources that are visually rendered. To experience working with VC++ resources, open the D:\Chapter03\SDIApp project.

1. Select the ResourceView tab (Figure 3.3). Here you'll find the *resources* consumed by the project visually represented.
2. Expand the resource tree (Figure 3.4). You should see seven resource categories from Accelerator to Version. These categories allow you to customize an application without coding. We will investigate each.

Menu

1. Expand the Menu tree as in Figure 3.5.

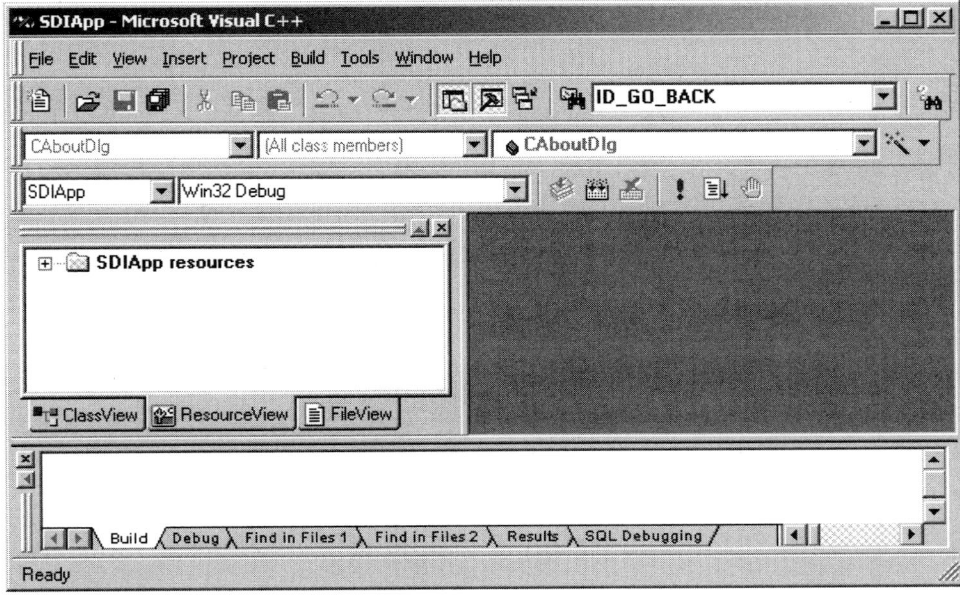

FIGURE 3.3 ResourceView.

SDIApp resources
Accelerator
Dialog
Icon
Menu
String Table
Toolbar
Version

FIGURE 3.4 The resource tree.

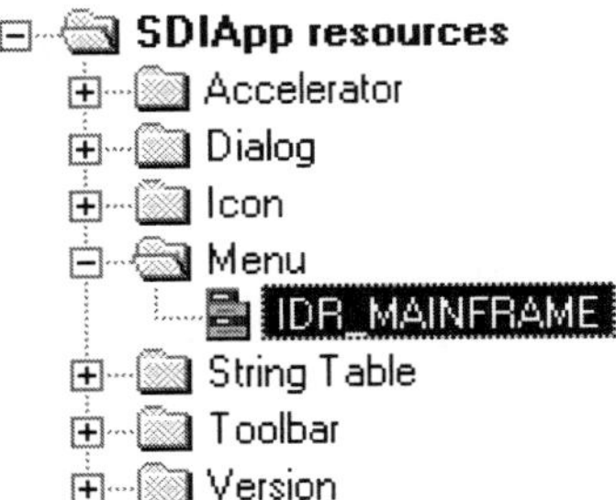

FIGURE 3.5 The IDR_MAINFRAME menu resource listing.

Here we have one menu resource with the *ID* IDR_MAINFRAME.

2. Use the Open command from the Menu resource's context menu (Figure 3.6), or just double-click on IDR_MAINFRAME to bring up the menu resource (Figure 3.7).

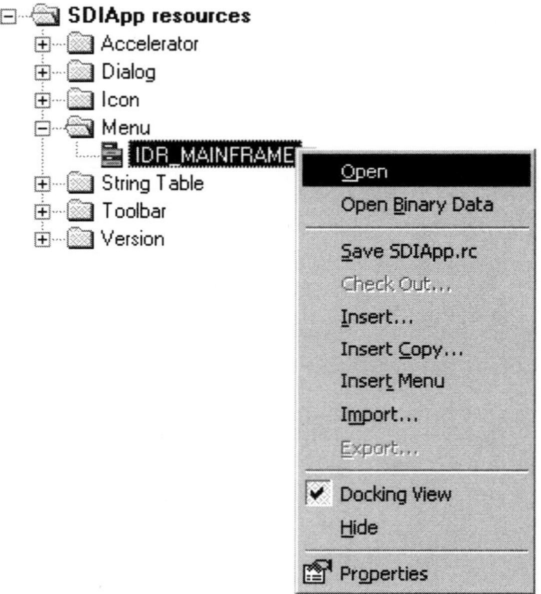

FIGURE 3.6 Opening a resource.

This menu represents visually the menu used in the **SDIApp** project.

Adding Menu Items

To add a new menu item, follow these steps:

1. Select the new, empty menu entry as in Figure 3.8.
2. Begin typing the new menu command, say, "&Customer," as shown in Figure 3.9.

Note the ampersand (&) in front of the letter C. This is what makes the letter C the *hot key* in the command.

FIGURE 3.7 The menu resource.

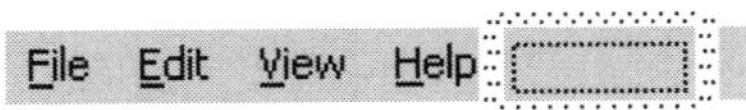

FIGURE 3.8 Empty menu command.

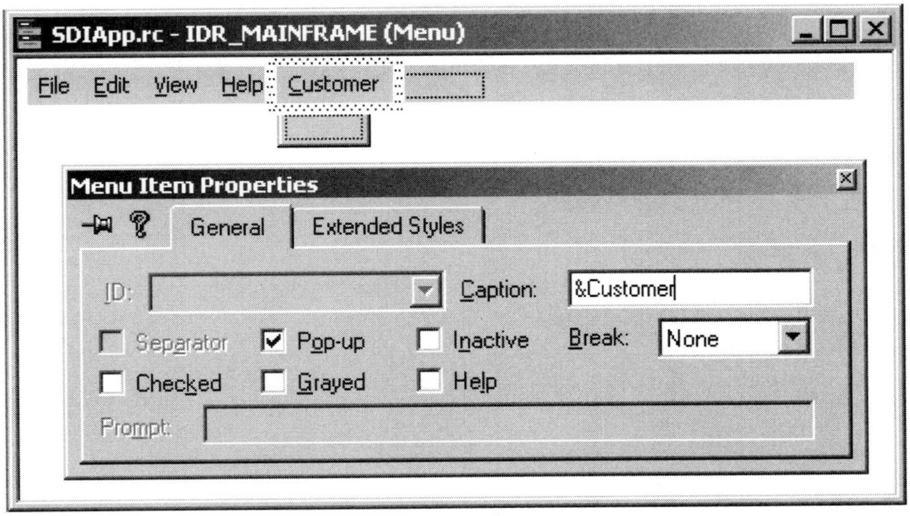

FIGURE 3.9 A Menu Properties dialog.

Note also that you could have brought up the Menu Items Properties dialog box by using the Open command in the context menu instead of just beginning to type.

When you're finished, close the Menu Item Properties dialog box. You should see a new menu entry added to the menu resource.

3. Apply the same procedures and add three more entries under "Customer" (Figure 3.10).

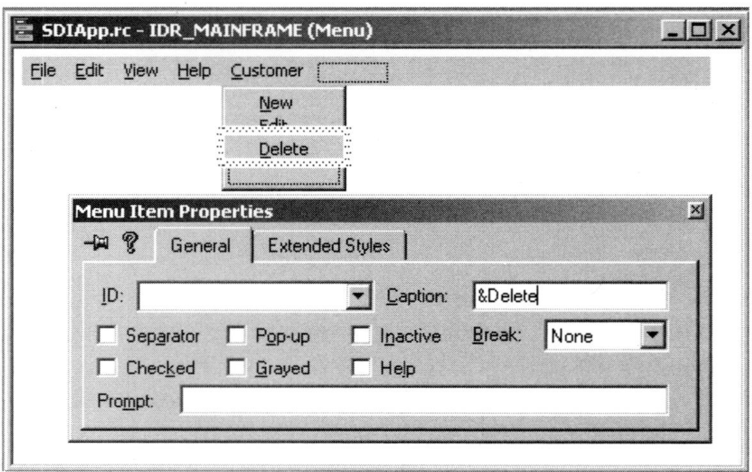

FIGURE 3.10 The Customer menu resource.

4. Bring back the Properties dialog box for any of the new menu entries and you should see that Developer Studio's IDE has generated IDs for each new menu entry (Figure 3.11).

The IDE will use the IDs to manage the resources.

5. Close the menu resource window.

Editing Menu Items

To edit an existing menu entry, just bring up its Properties dialog box and make the modifications.

Deleting Menu Items

To remove a menu entry, select it and press the [Delete] key on the keyboard.

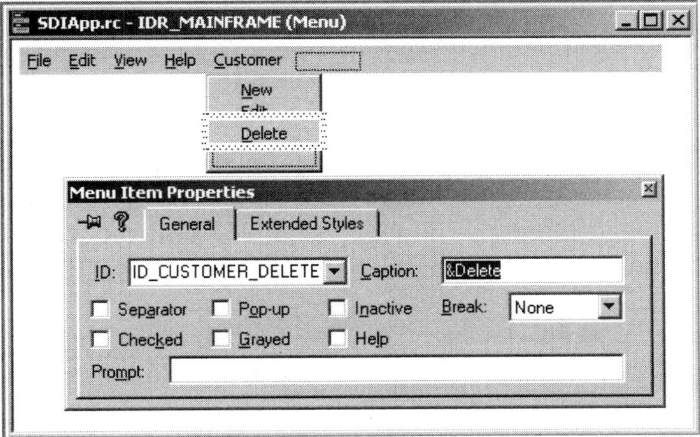

FIGURE 3.11 The Menu command ID.

Relocating Menu Items

To relocate a menu item, grab it and drag it to the new location.

Accelerator

The accelerator helps you organize the hot keys—quick key presses to activate commands.

1. Bring up the IDR-MAINFRAME accelerator in the usual manner (Figure 3.12).

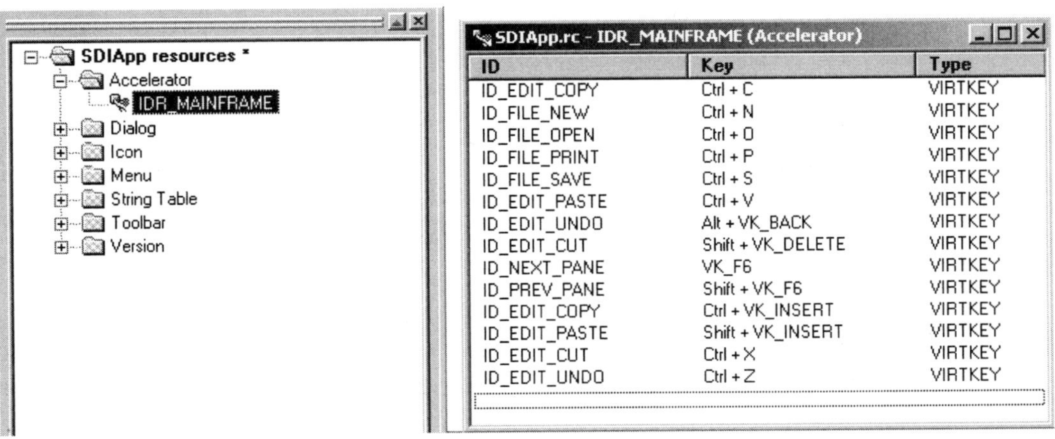

FIGURE 3.12 The accelerator resource.

For example, in **SDIApp** you can press [Ctrl+C] to invoke the Edit->Copy command.

Adding a Hot Key

To add a hot key, say [Ctrl-A] for the New Customer command, follow these steps:

1. Choose the New Accelerator command from the context menu (Figure 3.13).

SDIApp.rc - IDR_MAINFRAME (Accelerator)

ID	Key	Type
ID_EDIT_COPY	Ctrl + C	VIRTKEY
ID_FILE_NEW	Ctrl + N	Y
ID_FILE_OPEN	Ctrl + O	Y
ID_FILE_PRINT	Ctrl + P	Y
ID_FILE_SAVE	Ctrl + S	Y
ID_EDIT_PASTE	Ctrl + V	Y
ID_EDIT_UNDO	Alt + VK_BA	Y
ID_EDIT_CUT	Shift + VK_D	Y
ID_NEXT_PANE	VK_F6	Y
ID_PREV_PANE	Shift + VK_F	Y
ID_EDIT_COPY	Ctrl + VK_INSERT	VIRTKEY
ID_EDIT_PASTE	Shift + VK_INSERT	VIRTKEY
ID_EDIT_CUT	Ctrl + X	VIRTKEY
ID_EDIT_UNDO	Ctrl + Z	VIRTKEY

Cut
Copy
Paste
New Accelerator
ClassWizard...
Properties

FIGURE 3.13 Adding a new accelerator.

The Accel Properties dialog box appears (Figure 3.14).

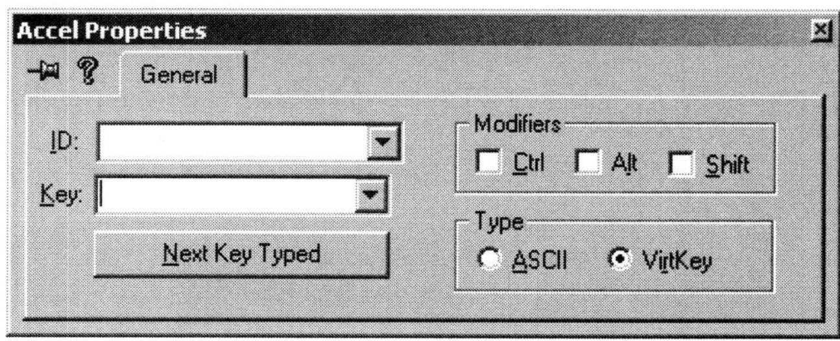

FIGURE 3.14 The Accel Properties dialog.

2. Click Next Key Typed.

You'll be instructed to press the key that will be used as the hot key (Figure 3.15).

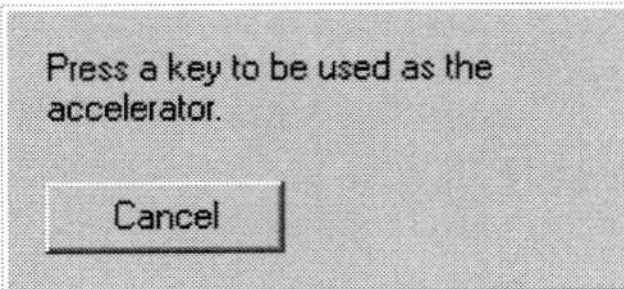

FIGURE 3.15 Defining a hot key.

3. Press [Ctrl-A] and the key is captured for you (Figure 3.16).

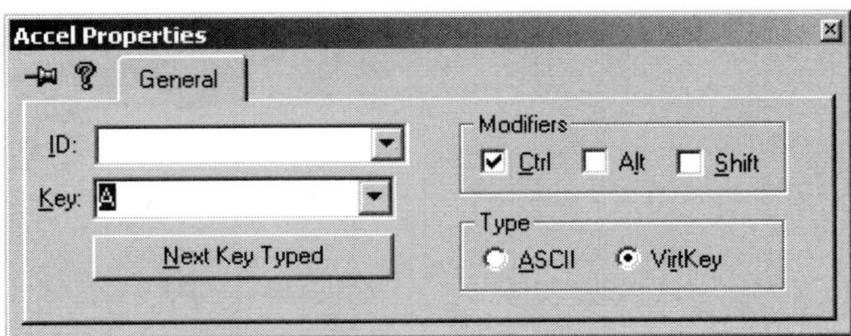

FIGURE 3.16 Recording a hot key.

4. Next, provide a unique ID for the hot key, and close the Properties dialog box (Figure 3.17).

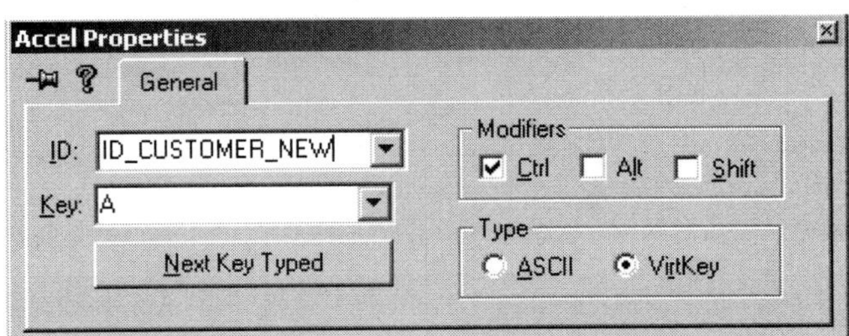

FIGURE 3.17 Hot key ID.

A new accelerator entry is created (Figure 3.18).

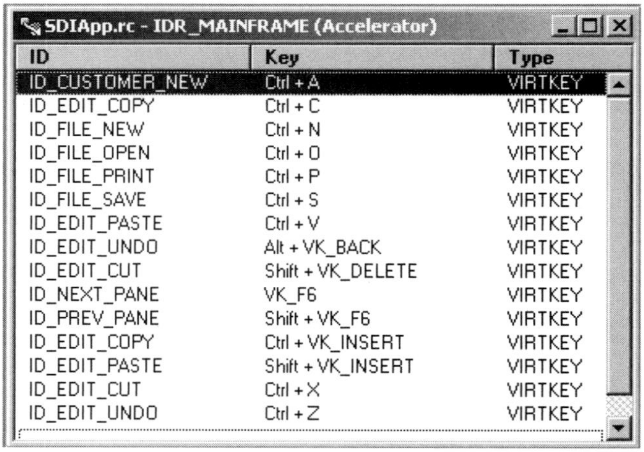

SDIApp.rc - IDR_MAINFRAME (Accelerator)

ID	Key	Type
ID_CUSTOMER_NEW	Ctrl + A	VIRTKEY
ID_EDIT_COPY	Ctrl + C	VIRTKEY
ID_FILE_NEW	Ctrl + N	VIRTKEY
ID_FILE_OPEN	Ctrl + O	VIRTKEY
ID_FILE_PRINT	Ctrl + P	VIRTKEY
ID_FILE_SAVE	Ctrl + S	VIRTKEY
ID_EDIT_PASTE	Ctrl + V	VIRTKEY
ID_EDIT_UNDO	Alt + VK_BACK	VIRTKEY
ID_EDIT_CUT	Shift + VK_DELETE	VIRTKEY
ID_NEXT_PANE	VK_F6	VIRTKEY
ID_PREV_PANE	Shift + VK_F6	VIRTKEY
ID_EDIT_COPY	Ctrl + VK_INSERT	VIRTKEY
ID_EDIT_PASTE	Shift + VK_INSERT	VIRTKEY
ID_EDIT_CUT	Ctrl + X	VIRTKEY
ID_EDIT_UNDO	Ctrl + Z	VIRTKEY

FIGURE 3.18 A new accelerator entry.

Editing a Hot Key

To edit a hot key, select it and open its Properties dialog box, or just double-click on it or press [Enter] when it is selected, and make the intended modifications.

Deleting a Hot Key

To delete a hot key, select it and press [Delete], or use the Cut command from its context menu.

1. Close the Accelerator resource dialog box.

String Table

String Table is where string data resources are organized. Collecting strings in a table away from the actual program code will allow you to replace them collectively or convert them into other languages easily. You add, edit, and delete string entries exactly as you would other resources, such as accelerators and menus, as you have learned. Here, you'll see how a typical string is used.

1. Bring up the IDR_MAINFRAME string resource and modify it as shown in Figure 3.19.
2. Close the String Table Resource dialog box and compile the application. Execute it and you should see a new application window title (Figure 3.20).

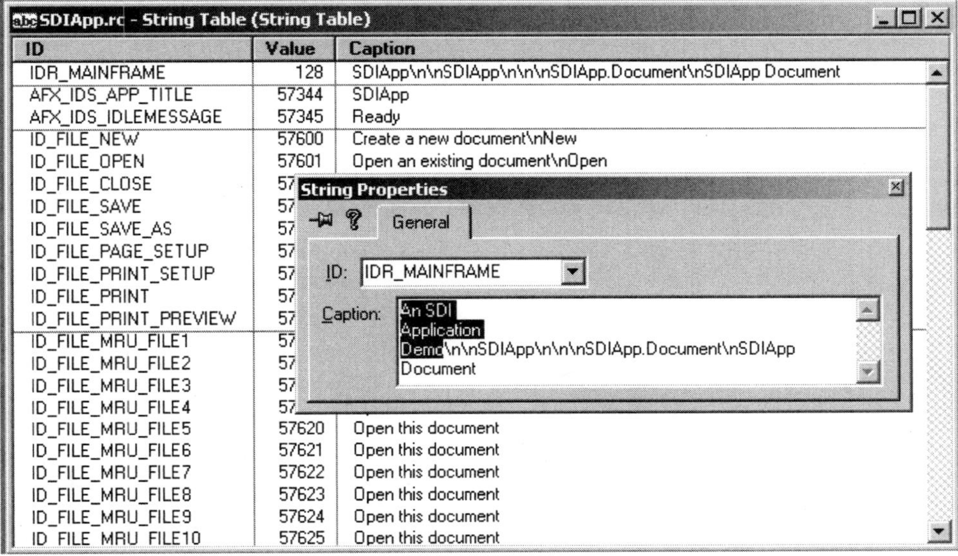

FIGURE 3.19 Modifying a string resource.

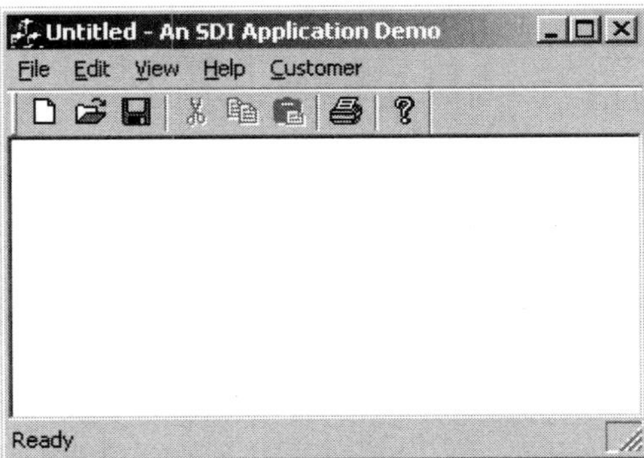

FIGURE 3.20 Main window title.

Obviously, because we had not yet written any code, Visual C++ Developer Studio's IDE is doing work behind the scene to use these resources and make use of them in the appropriate places.

As you have seen, the resource ID IDR_MAINFRAME has been applied to more than one resource. This is because for a particular application *paradigm*, such as the SDI model, a certain built-in mechanism is used to harness the resources of a particular resource ID and build the application with it. This is the beauty of using such an integrated environment—it reduces the overhead work that we have to do. Later, we will investigate the mechanics behind some of these mechanisms.

Icon

The icons used by the application are organized under Icon (Figure 3.21).

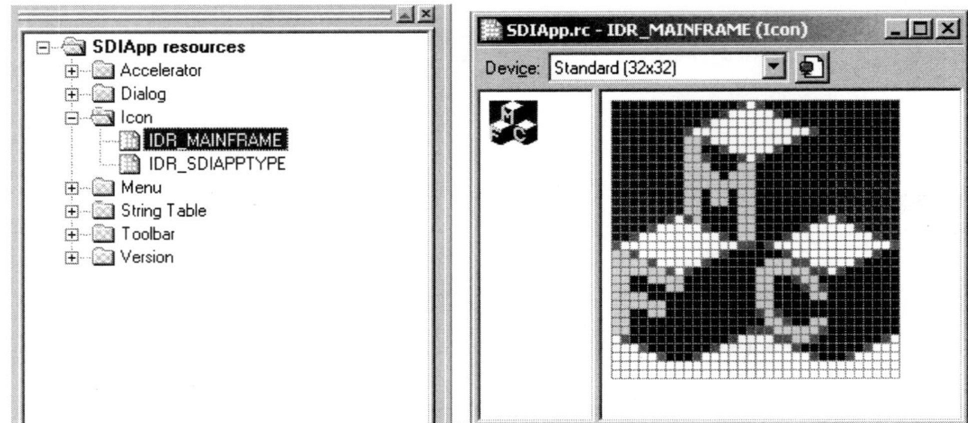

FIGURE 3.21 The Icon resource.

Working with icons is like working with the Paint graphics program. The important issue is that the icons must be carefully IDed and saved.

Application Icon

For example, to change an application's icon, follow these steps:

1. Select the IDR_MAINFRAME icon and remove it by pressing the [Delete] key on the keyboard.
2. Insert a new, blank icon: (Figure 3.22).
3. Draw the new icon (Figure 3.23).
4. When the icon is in focus, press [Enter] to bring up the Properties dialog box (Figure 3.24).
5. Change the ID to IDR_MAINFRAME, the same ID that is used by the application framework.

FIGURE 3.22 The Insert Icon command.

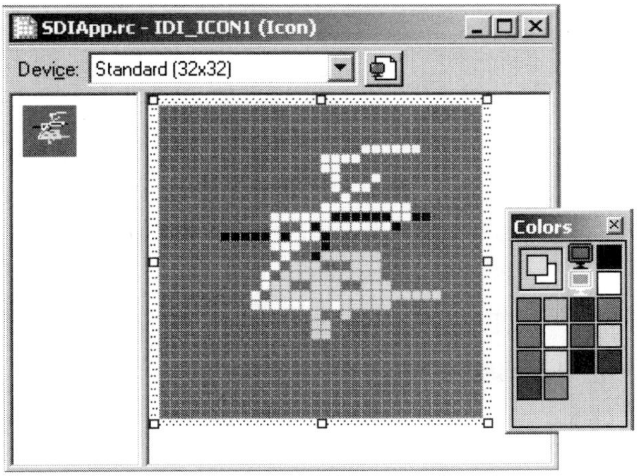

FIGURE 3.23 Drawing a new icon.

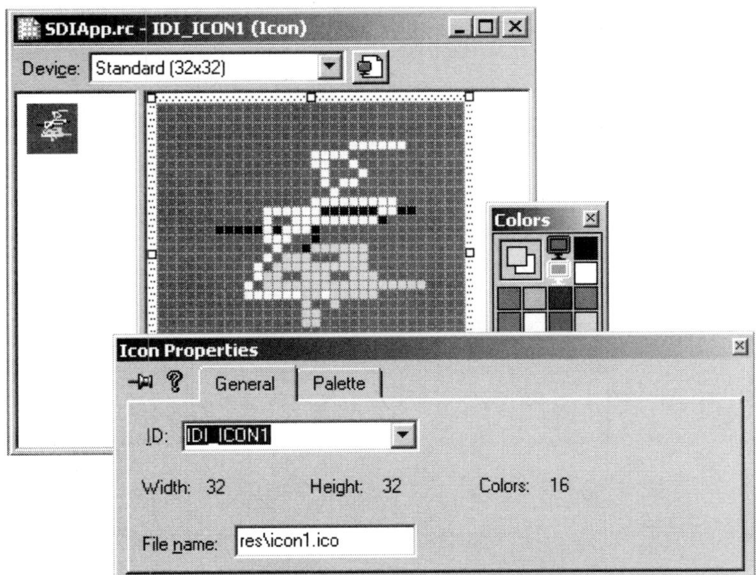

FIGURE 3.24 Icon Properties dialog.

6. Change the icon's filename to an appropriate one, such as "res\app.ico" as in Figure 3.25.

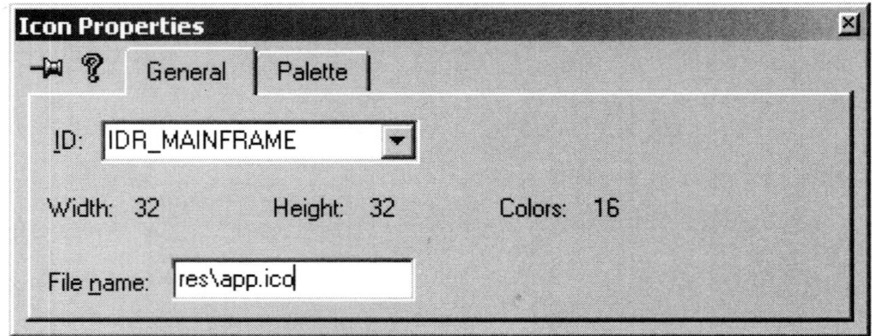

FIGURE 3.25 Icon Properties.

7. Close the Properties dialog box.
8. Save the updates (Figure 3.26).

FIGURE 3.26 The Save All toolbar.

9. Recompile the application.

The application's main window now has a new icon.

10. Choose the Help->About command.

You should see the new icon used in the About dialog box as well (Figure 3.27).

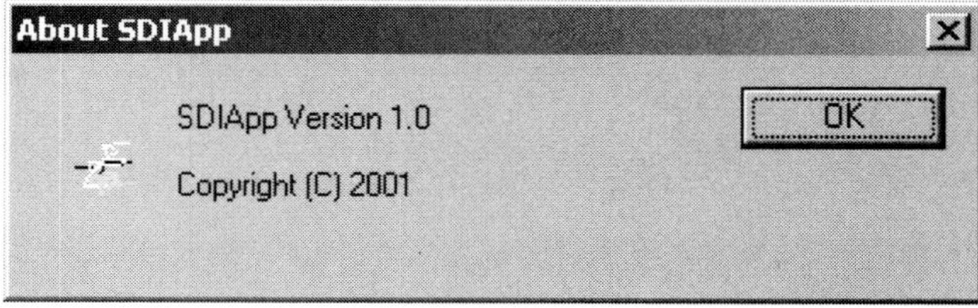

FIGURE 3.27 New icon in About dialog.

Toolbar

Working with toolbar resources takes on techniques developed in working with menus and icons. You add new toolbar buttons just as you do with menus—simply work with a new, blank button (Figure 3.28).

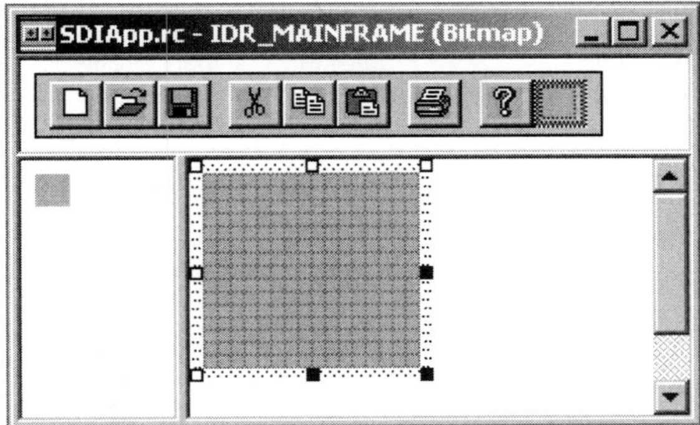

FIGURE 3.28 New toolbar button.

Every time you create a new toolbar button, the system generates a new, blank one for you.

Relocating a Toolbar Button

To relocate a toolbar button, grab it and drag it to its destination.

To separate a button from its neighbor, grab it and "nudge" it away from its neighbor and literally bump into the neighbor on the other side before releasing the mouse.

Toolbar ID

In working with toolbars, it is important that you manage the button IDs correctly. Look at the pair of menu command and toolbar button IDs shown in Figure 3.30. They are the same ID (Figure 3.29).

The reason the menu File->Open command and the toolbar Open command have the same ID is because they do the same thing. In other words, they trigger the same command. Windows processes commands through *messages*, which you will learn in this book, and messages are identified through IDs.

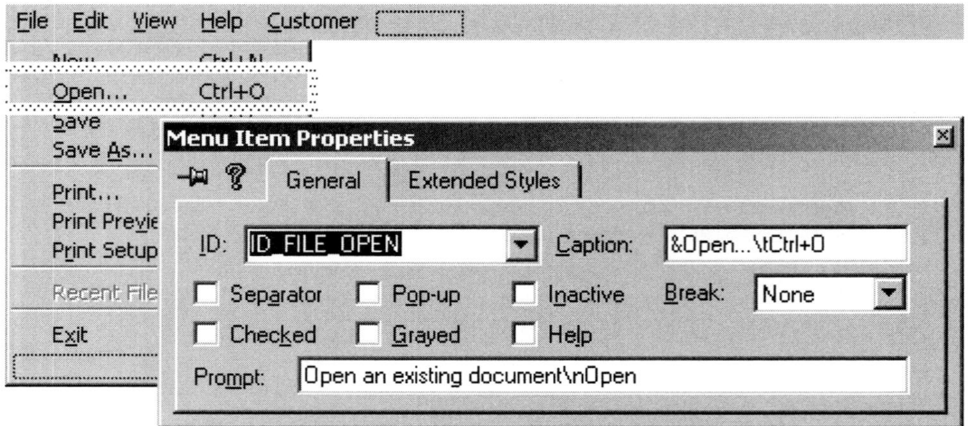

FIGURE 3.29 File->Open command ID.

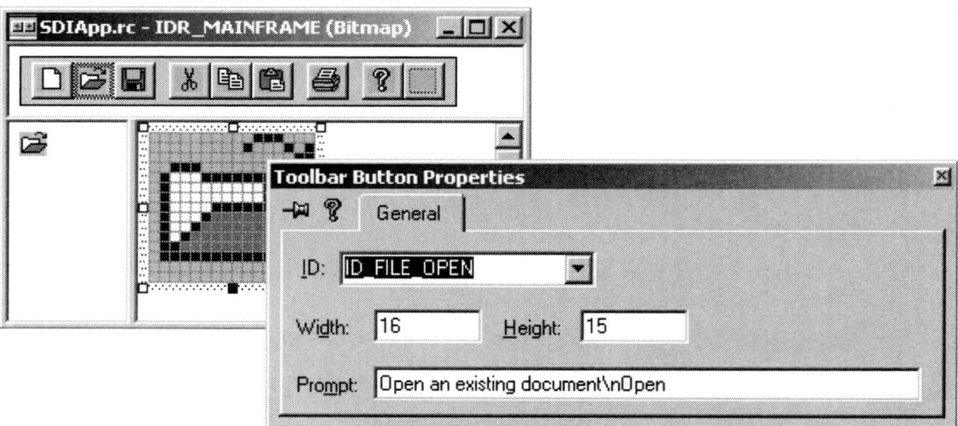

FIGURE 3.30 Command and toolbar button IDs.

Version

Version maintains the application's versioning information, and the mechanism is self-evident (Figure 3.31).

When you show the properties of an executable, such as from the Windows Explorer program, you'll be able to check the application's version. By failing to update the version information, your application will always assume the same version number, and users will not be able to tell an updated version from an old one.

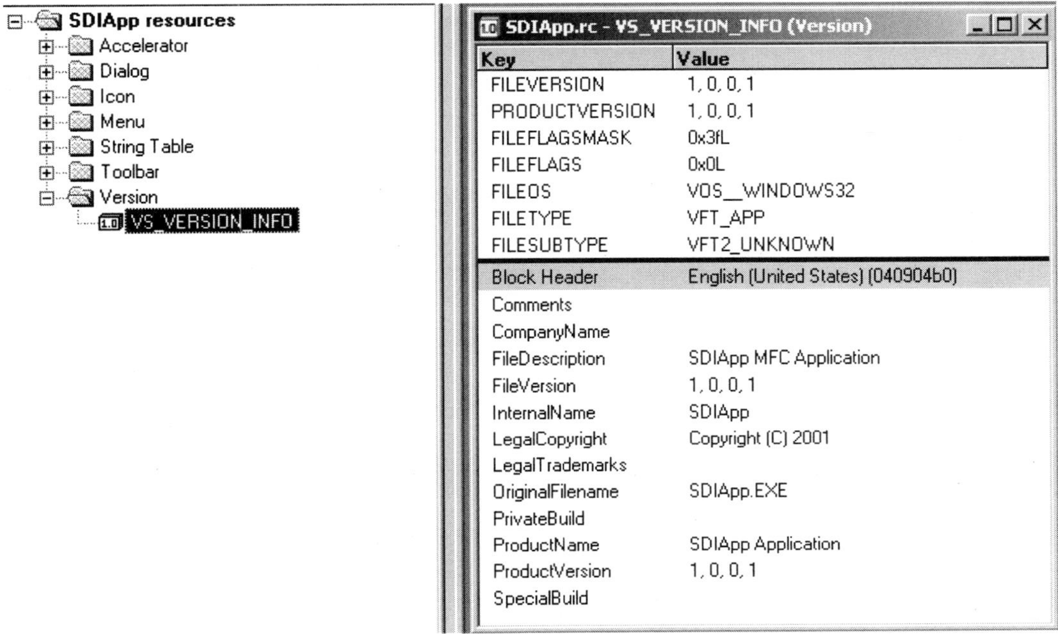

FIGURE 3.31 Program versioning.

Prompt Messages

Although not officially a component of ResourceView, prompt messages are managed here, too.

1. Execute the **SDIApp** and place the mouse pointer over the Open toolbar button.

You should see the "Open" tooltip and the corresponding prompt message at the status bar (Figure 3.32). The same status bar message appears if you were to scan down to the File->Open menu command.

If you try it with the Customer commands, however, no messages will display. This is because we have yet to provide any.

2. Bring up the File->Open Properties dialog box (Figure 3.33).

You should see the Prompt entry.

A Prompt message entry has two parts, one for use at the status bar, and one as a tooltip. They are separated by the new-line character "\n." Therefore, if you were

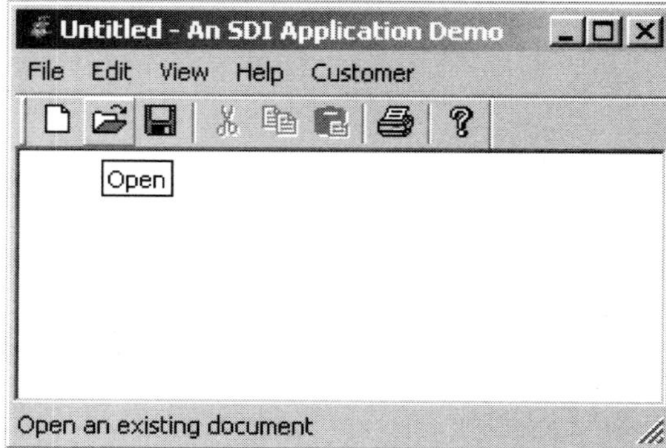

FIGURE 3.32 The "Open" tooltip.

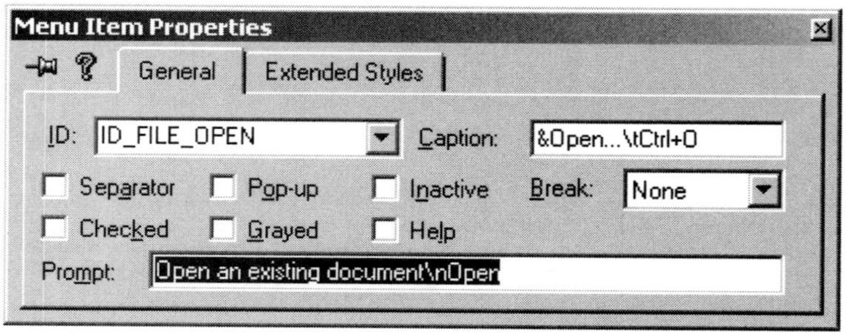

FIGURE 3.33 The command prompt.

to provide similar messages for the Customer->New command, you would enter something like what is shown in Figure 3.34.

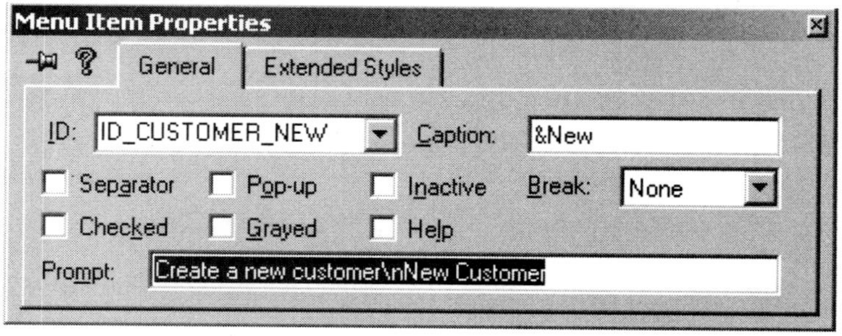

FIGURE 3.34 New customer prompt message.

3. Create a new customer\nNew customer.
4. Close the **SDIApp** workspace.

FILEVIEW

Now let's leave ResourceView (but return soon to look at Dialog) and take a brief look at FileView (Figure 3.35).

FileView is where you get to work directly with the application program project's files. As shown in Figure 3.35, the program files are organized into source files,

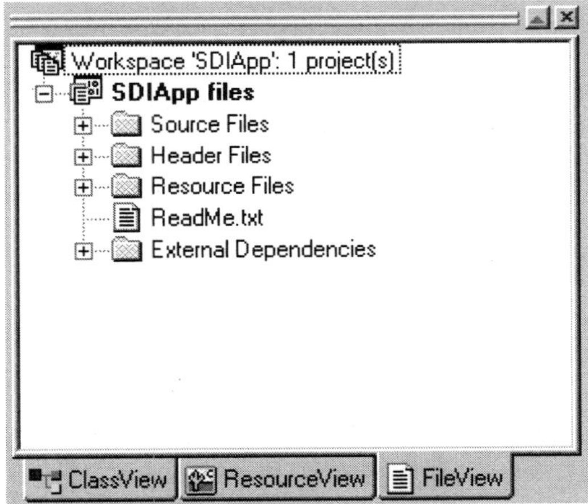

FIGURE 3.35 FileView.

header files, resource files, and other support categories. For the coder/programmer, the categories of the most interest are the source files and header files. Source files, with the filename extension .cpp (Figure 3.36), contain program logic. Header files, with the filename extension .h (Figure 3.37), contain definitions and logic *prototypes*. You will become familiar with these concepts soon.

1. Open the **SDIApp.cpp** file in the usual manner, and take a quick look at the code in it (Figure 3.38).

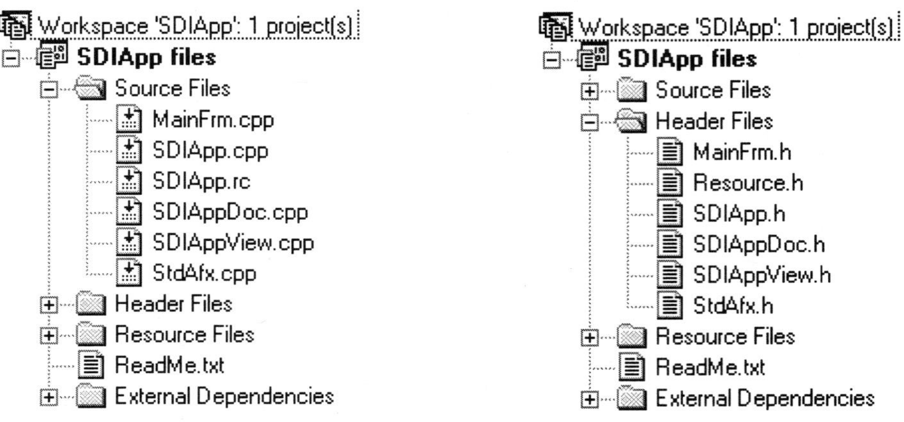

FIGURE 3.36 The Source Files listing.

FIGURE 3.37 The Header Files listing.

```
// SDIApp.cpp : Defines the class behaviors for the application.
//

#include "stdafx.h"
#include "SDIApp.h"

#include "MainFrm.h"
#include "SDIAppDoc.h"
#include "SDIAppView.h"

#ifdef _DEBUG
#define new DEBUG_NEW
#undef THIS_FILE
static char THIS_FILE[] = __FILE__;
#endif

/////////////////////////////////////////////////////////////////////////////
// CSDIAppApp

BEGIN_MESSAGE_MAP(CSDIAppApp, CWinApp)
    //{{AFX_MSG_MAP(CSDIAppApp)
    ON_COMMAND(ID_APP_ABOUT, OnAppAbout)
        // NOTE - the ClassWizard will add and remove mapping macros here.
        //    DO NOT EDIT what you see in these blocks of generated code!
    //}}AFX_MSG_MAP
    // Standard file based document commands
    ON_COMMAND(ID_FILE_NEW, CWinApp::OnFileNew)
    ON_COMMAND(ID_FILE_OPEN, CWinApp::OnFileOpen)
    // Standard print setup command
    ON_COMMAND(ID_FILE_PRINT_SETUP, CWinApp::OnFilePrintSetup)
END_MESSAGE_MAP()

/////////////////////////////////////////////////////////////////////////////
// CSDIAppApp construction
```

FIGURE 3.38 SDIApp.cpp code sample listing.

As a newcomer to VC++, you should find the coding intimidating. However, after the next chapter, you will be able to discern its contents quite comfortably.

2. Close all windows and close the **SDIApp** workspace.

When you use the Visual C++ Developer Studio IDE to generate application frameworks, you do a great deal toward developing complex Windows applications before writing the first line of code. However, the fact remains that application functionalities are derived from programming. Therefore, we will now officially begin to learn C++ programming, while attempting to have the IDE do as much work for us as possible.

PART II MFC GUI

The MFC, Microsoft Foundation Classes, library is a collection of pre-written C++ classes designed to provide you with the wherewithal to develop Windows applications. Using MFC is therefore an efficient way to go about designing Windows programs, desktop or otherwise.

In this part of the book, you'll learn to work with the MFC library classes that are considered fundamental to the development of Windows desktop applications or modules that provide GUI, or *graphical user interface*. These classes are also relatively easy to learn; therefore, they make great candidates as topics for easing into a subject that is at times considered difficult.

The first set of classes that we'll explore produces visual results, which makes it fun to learn. Because these classes are straightforward, we can afford to take advantage of the situation and hone our skills working with visual IDE features at the same time.

As our official venture into MFC, we'll learn to work with the dialog box, based on the CDialog class. Because a dialog box, or simply dialog, is visual and has a "surface"—it appears as a window on the screen with a solid background—you can "place" objects, called controls[1], on it using drag-and-drop techniques as opposed to coding, thus allowing us to explore the IDE and its toolsets. These controls include familiar entities such as the drop-down box and radio buttons. In the illustrations that follow, you'll learn to craft these controls using the VC++ IDE facilities.

Controls are important because they simplify and facilitate user interfacing. In the DOS days, interactions between applications and users were text based. For

[1] The controls introduced here are known as Windows '95 controls, because they were first introduced under that version of Windows.

instance, a user must enter a "Y" to indicate "Yes," and "N" to indicate "No." The Windows graphical user interface changed all that. As a result, Windows application development involves a great deal of GUI control usage. Needless to say, it is to our advantage to become familiar with them. The skillful use of controls often spells the difference between amateur and expert programming. Therefore, a heavy dose of control programming is helpful in getting started with Windows application development.

There are two types of dialog boxes or dialogs: the modal dialog and the modeless dialog. Traditionally, they are discussed together for categorical reasons. In this book, we'll first talk about the modal dialog, then branch off to learn the controls, and come back to deal with the more complex modeless dialog, because this path represents a learning curve that increases with difficulty.

4 The CDialog Class

The main dialog in the **DialogDemo** application has a gray surface. It is constructed based on a class named CDialog. The CDialog is one of the easiest classes with which to work. In this chapter, we'll illustrate its basic workings.

In the demonstration exercises that follow, continue to work with the **DialogDemo** project that you have been developing, or open the **DialogDemo** project from the accompanying CD-ROM for Chapter 4 and work from it.

In this example, we'll use a button in the main dialog window of the application to bring up a new dialog box, and then use a button in the new dialog box to close it.

First, we'll create a new dialog for us to open.

1. In ResourceView, select the Insert Dialog command as shown in Figure 4.1.

FIGURE 4.1 The Insert Dialog command.

A new dialog appears with the ID of IDD_DIALOG1.

2. Change the new dialog ID to IDD_DATA_DIALOG through its properties.

CREATING A DIALOG CLASS

What we've created so far is not a dialog, but a visual resource in the VC++ environment. This resource is unknown to C++ and is of no coding relevance. What we want to do is create a class based on this resource so that we can create a dialog object from it. The ClassWizard can help us do that.

1. With the IDD_DATA_DIALOG resource open and selected, choose the View->ClassWizard command.
2. When prompted, choose the "Create a new class" radio button as in Figure 4.2.

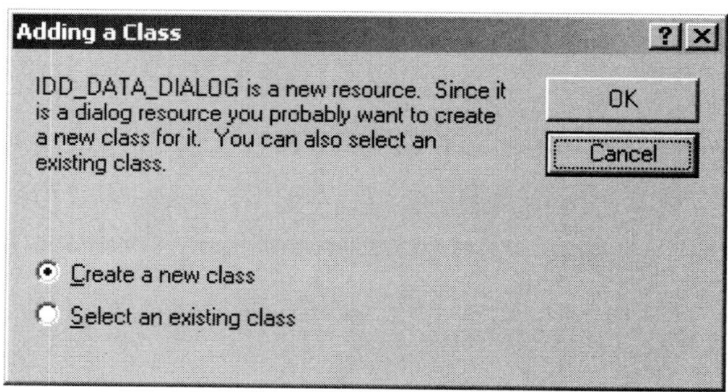

FIGURE 4.2 Creating a new class.

Enter the new class name of CDataDlg as in Figure 4.3.

3. Click OK to close the ClassWizard window.

A new class named CDataDlg appears in ResourceView. ClassWizard has created a new class named CDataDlg based on the CDialog class for us. We can now instantiate a new dialog object from it and deploy it. However, first, we will create a button to launch it with. As it turns out, since both the OK button and the Cancel button in the main dialog do pretty much the same thing, we only need one of

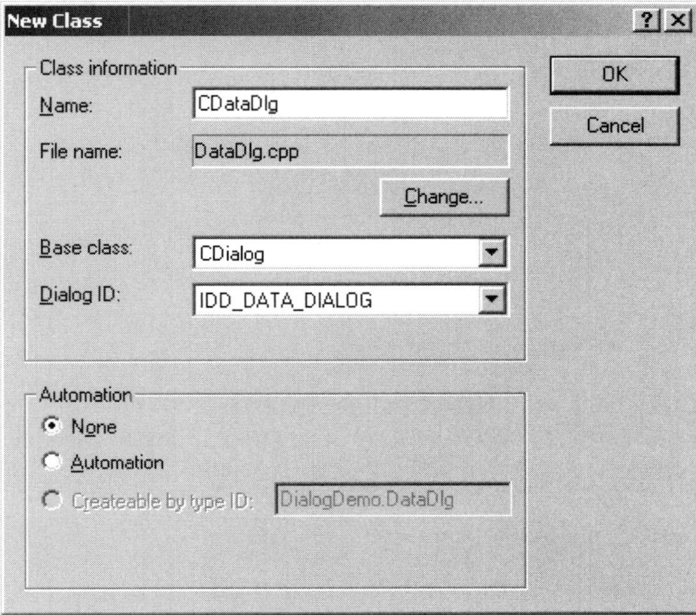

FIGURE 4.3 Creating CDataDlg class.

them to terminate the application. The other we can "borrow" and turn into the button we need to open the new dialog.

4. In the **DialogDemo** project, open the IDD_DIALOGDEMO_DIALOG resource.

You should see two buttons on the dialog box, one labeled "OK," the other "Cancel." They both close the window (although reporting different operational statuses, as you will soon learn).

5. Click Cancel (Figure 4.4)

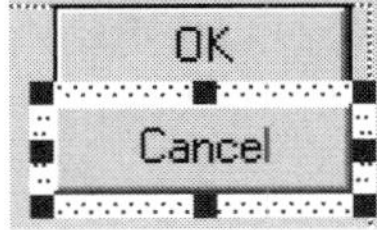

FIGURE 4.4 The Cancel button.

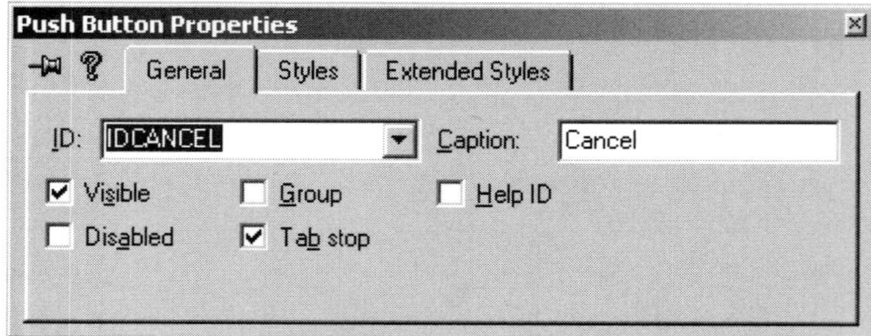

FIGURE 4.5 The Cancel Button Properties dialog.

6. Bring up its Properties dialog box (Figure 4.5).
7. Change its ID to ID_DATA_DIALOG, and the caption to Data Dialog as in Figure 4.6.

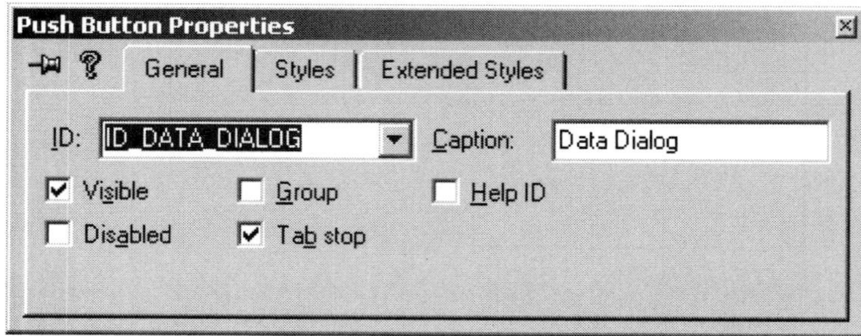

FIGURE 4.6 Button ID.

8. Close the Properties dialog box.

ADDING FUNCTIONS WITH CLASSWIZARD

A C++ function is code that you can type into a program as text, and that's what programmers used to do until the introduction of integrated development environments such as VC++. The advantage of using such a tool that normally has a built-in code editor is that the development environment implicitly handles much of the housekeeping chores that a programmer must otherwise contend with, thus reducing the possibility of human errors. When you use VC++'s ClassWizard to create new program functions, you can concentrate on the function's logic and not worry so much about the placement of the code and the pairing of the function with its prototype—ClassWizard handles all the code organization issues for us. The following exercise brings home the point.

Again, we are using the **DialogDemo** project as our example platform.

1. With the "Data Dialog" button selected, bring up ClassWizard (View->ClassWizard).

The screen shown in Figure 4.7 appears.

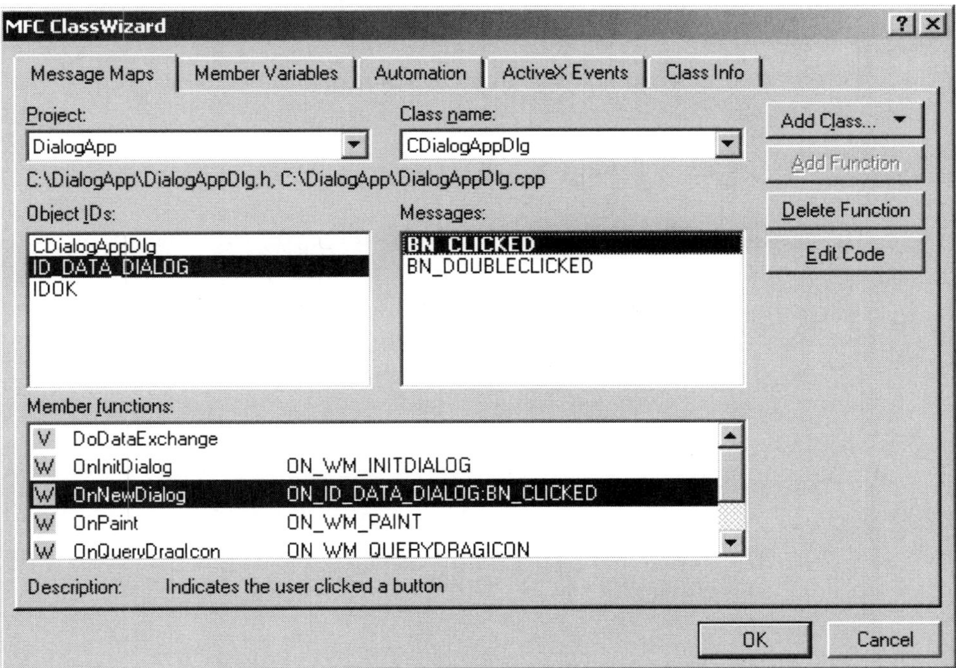

FIGURE 4.7 ClassWizard for button-click message.

Note that ID_DATA_DIALOG is already selected in Object IDs, and the corresponding *messages* are listed to its right.

When a button is chosen, Windows generates a message for it. A message is merely a number of identification. It is deposited with a Windows *message queue*—a list—to await handling. When its turn comes up, Windows knows that the button has been chosen and implements the action that is to be executed. It is up to us to specify what that action is.

2. Select the BN_CLICKED message and click Add Function.
3. In the Add Member Function dialog box, accept the proposed function name (because it expresses the correct action) as in Figure 4.8.

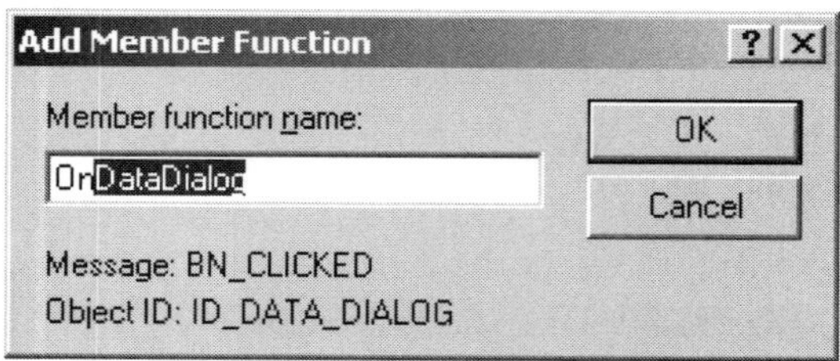

FIGURE 4.8 ClassWizard-generated function name.

4. Click Edit Code in ClassWizard.

The DialogDemoDlg.cpp file is opened for you with the cursor located at the *OnDataDialog()* function so you can immediately go to work.

5. Below the "// TODO: Add your control notification handler code here" line, enter the following code (your true first time coding):

```
// TODO: Add your control notification handler
CDlgData        dlg( this );
```

6. At the end of this line press [Enter].
7. The cursor will be placed immediately below this line, flush with the start of the first code line.

INTELLISENSE

We'll now experience a helpful coding feature that comes with VC++ exclusively: *IntelliSense.*

1. Continuing from the last exercise, type "dlg" without pressing any other key.

You should see the display shown in Figure 4.9.

VC++ knows that you are about to enter a member function of the CDialog class (because **dlg** is of the CDlgData class, which is derived from CDialog), and automatically provides you with the available functions to select.

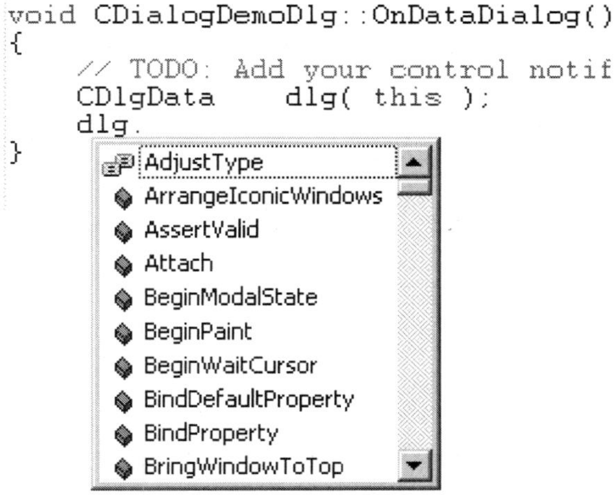

```
void CDialogDemoDlg::OnDataDialog()
{
    // TODO: Add your control notif
    CDlgData    dlg( this );
    dlg.
}
```

AdjustType
ArrangeIconicWindows
AssertValid
Attach
BeginModalState
BeginPaint
BeginWaitCursor
BindDefaultProperty
BindProperty
BringWindowToTop

FIGURE 4.9 IntelliSense.

2. Type "do" and you should see "DoModal." Select it in any way you want, such as clicking it with the mouse and pressing [Enter].

"DoModal" is installed in your code.

3. Complete the statement by typing "();" to achieve:

```
CDlgData       dlg( this );
dlg.DoModal();
```

4. Next, use [Ctrl-Home] to move the cursor to the top of the source file, and then enter the line in bold:

```
#include "stdafx.h"
#include "DialogDemo.h"
#include "DialogDemoDlg.h"
#include "DlgData.h"
#ifdef _DEBUG
#define new DEBUG_NEW
#undef THIS_FILE
static char THIS_FILE[] = __FILE__;
#endif
```

5. Save the files, compile the program, and then execute it. Click the Data Dialog button to launch the new dialog box, and then click either OK or Cancel to close it. When you're done, terminate the application.

This is what we've done.

In the *OnDataDialog()* function, we instantiated an object named "dlg" based on the CDlgData class—and if you like, in traditional parlance, we declared a variable named "dlg" of the type CDlgData.

However, by the DialogDemoDlg.cpp file alone, the compiler wouldn't know what this CDlgData class is. Therefore, we assist the process by including the header file "DlgData.h," which contains the class' definitions. This way, the compiler knows what to do with the class and creates the object for us.

THE MODAL DIALOG

DoModal() is the CDialog class function that "launches" the dialog box. You'll get to know much more about it soon.

A *modal* dialog stays on the screen and forces all actions to be focused on the dialog until it is closed. The antithesis of the modal dialog is the *modeless* dialog, which allows you to work with elements other than the dialog while the dialog is open on the screen. The workings of a modeless dialog are quite a bit more involved than a modal dialog. Therefore, we'll table its discussion until we have some experience working with C++ and MFC.

5 The Static Box, Edit Box, and Button

The institution of the CDialog class as a fundamental MFC member has a significant purpose: it provides a platform or "surface" on which you can visually implement objects that are visible—controls, the visual part of Visual C++. Doing work visually (dragging and dropping picture objects) decreases the need for coding (typing), thus increasing work efficiency. This is the underpinning of the concept of *rapid application development*, or *RAD*.

Everybody who works with Windows has seen a dialog such as the one depicted in Figure 5.1. This dialog is used for data entry and contains a label, an edit box, and a button for closing the dialog. Not only is this setup simple and common, it is easy to construct. Therefore, we'll officially begin our study of Windows controls (*Visual C++*) by learning to implement labels (static controls), edit boxes, and buttons.

FIGURE 5.1 A typical data entry dialog.

THE STATIC CONTROL

A static control (Figure 5.2) is also called a *label*. It is based on the MFC's CStatic class and is used to display a text element with no user editing capabilities. Its application can be borne out by the following implementation example.

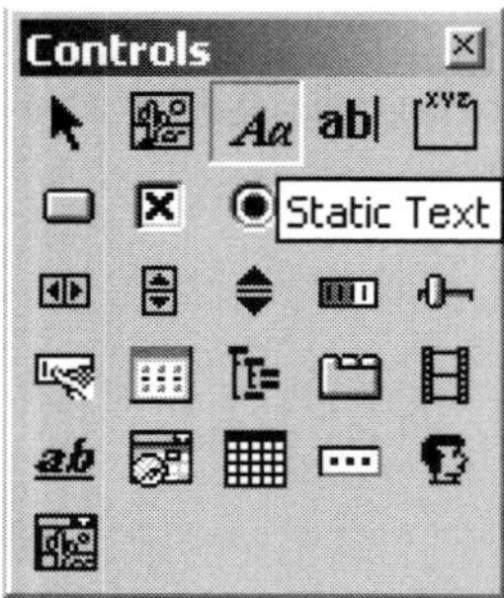

FIGURE 5.2 The Static Control tool.

1. In the **DialogDemo** project, open the new dialog resource. Then, select the static control from the toolbox and drag it onto the dialog box.

When you release the mouse, the static control will be selected and has the label "Static."

2. Type the intended label, such as "&Last name:" to set the caption and leave the ID unchanged (Figure 5.3).

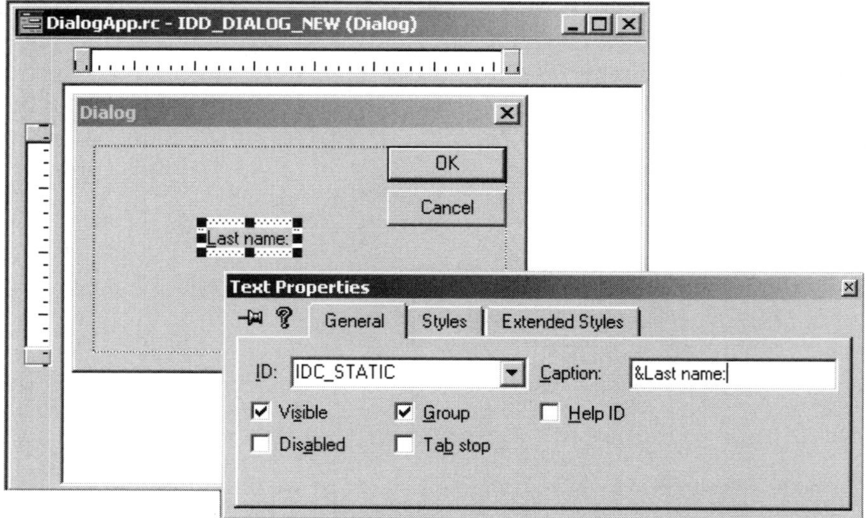

FIGURE 5.3 Static Control properties.

Static controls are seldom active in applications, so we usually don't bother to assign unique IDs to them. Therefore, in most applications, static control IDs are virtually all IDC_STATIC. You do assign a unique ID to a static control, though, if you intend to "do" something with it, such as changing its caption programmatically.

3. Close the Properties dialog box.

THE TEXT BOX CONTROL

The text box, or edit box, based on the MFC CEdit class, allows a user to enter (and retrieve) data, and you can implement it on a dialog surface using the drag-and-drop approach just as you would with a static control. To see how, follow these instructions based on the **DialogDemo** project.

1. With the new dialog box open, from the Controls toolbox select the Edit Box tool (Figure 5.4) and drag it onto the dialog box, placing it next to the "Last name" static text control (Figure 5.5).

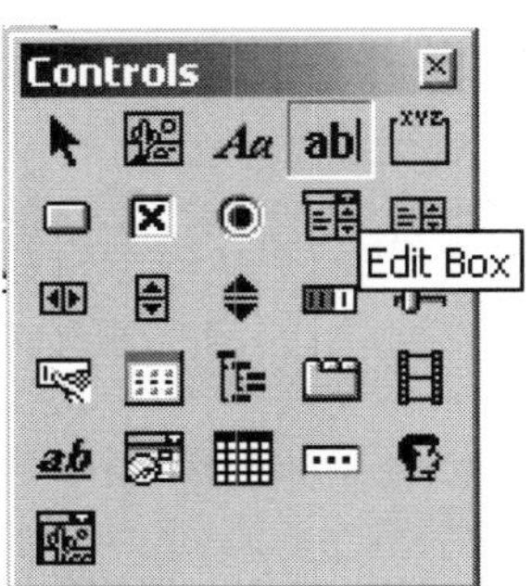

FIGURE 5.4 The Edit Box tool.

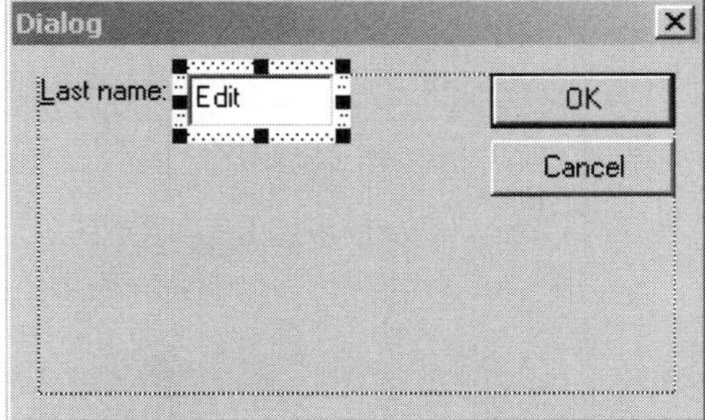

FIGURE 5.5 Edit Box on form.

2. Bring up the Properties dialog box for the edit box. Set its ID as shown in Figure 5.6, and then close it.

We assign the edit box a unique ID because we intend to do something with it; therefore, we need to provide VC++ an identifier for it.

3. Similarly, create a new edit box (with an appropriate static box) and give it the ID of IDC_EDIT_FIRSTNAME.

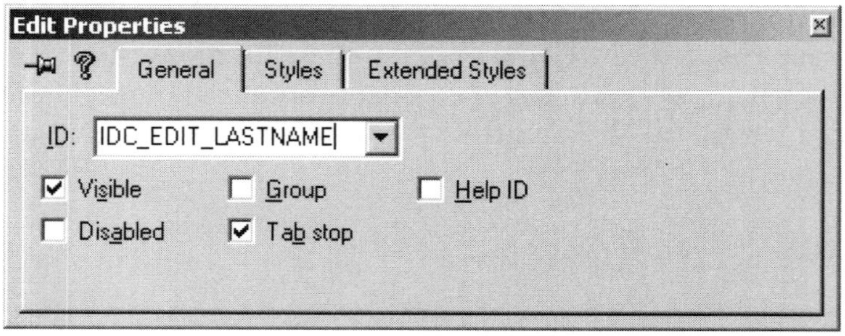

Edit Properties
General | Styles | Extended Styles
ID: IDC_EDIT_LASTNAME
Visible | Group | Help ID
Disabled | Tab stop

FIGURE 5.6 Edit box ID

4. Save the change.

The CEdit Class

In order to work with the edit box as opposed to it just being there, we need to identify it. That means we need to create a variable that represents it. Technically speaking, we're going to instantiate an object of the CEdit class.

1. Select the Last Name edit box and bring up ClassWizard.
2. Select the Member Variables pane (Figure 5.7).

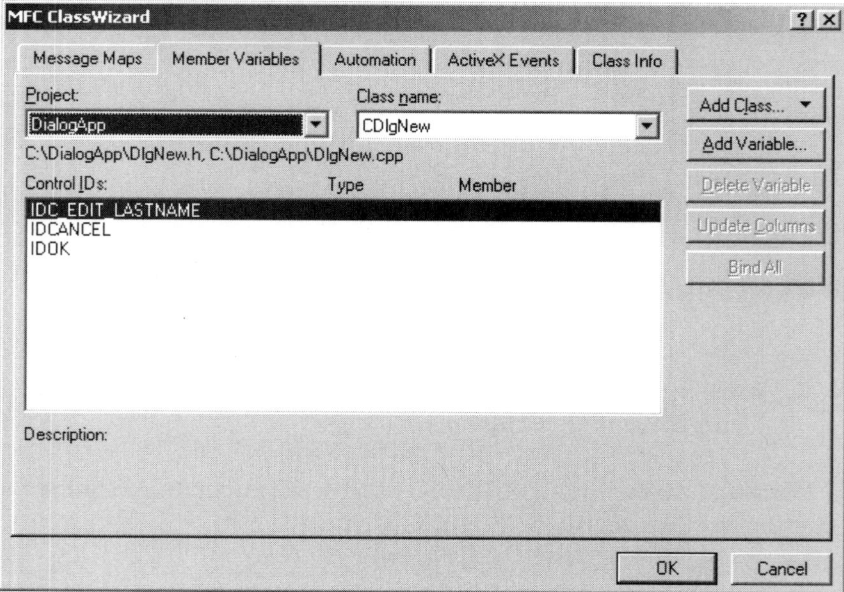

FIGURE 5.7 ClassWizard Member Variables pane.

3. Click the Add Variable button so we can define a variable for the edit box.

As you can see, ClassWizard already populated virtually everything for us, including the variable prefix "m_," which is by convention used to start a class' *member variable.*

4. Use ClassWizard to create a variable of the control type for it (Figure 5.8).

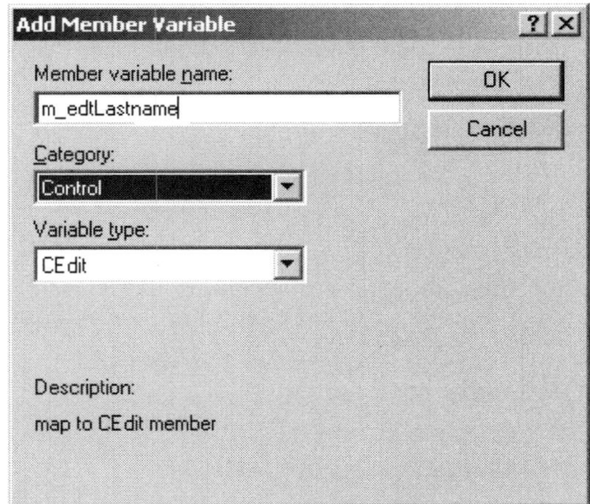

FIGURE 5.8 Adding a Control Member variable.

I choose to prefix my variables with abbreviations that tell me what type the variable is. "edt" is my way of saying that it is of the CEdit class.

5. Close the ClassWizard window.
6. Examine the resultant code in the DlgData.h file:

```
enum { IDD = IDD_DIALOG_NEW };
CEdit     m_edtLastname;
```

Windows Messages

Now, we'll write some code to process the edit box data. What we want to do in this example is display some data in the edit box the moment the new dialog box is displayed. We will let the user edit it, and retrieve the data when the user clicks OK to close the new dialog window.

1. From ClassView, select **CDlgData.**
2. Choose Add Windows Message Handler from the context menu (Figure 5.9).

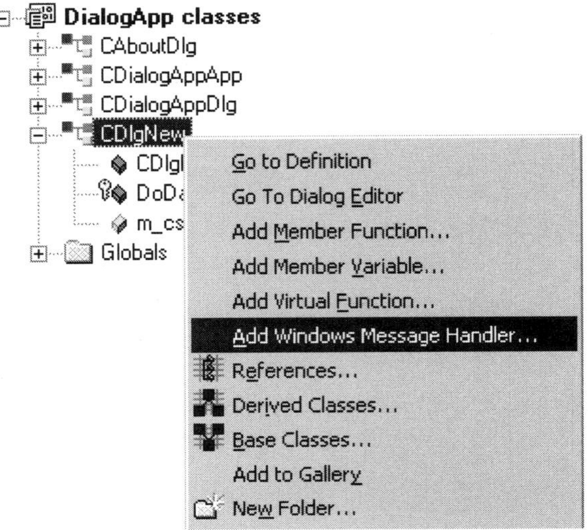

FIGURE 5.9 Add Windows Message Handler command.

The New Message dialog window appears (Figure 5.10).

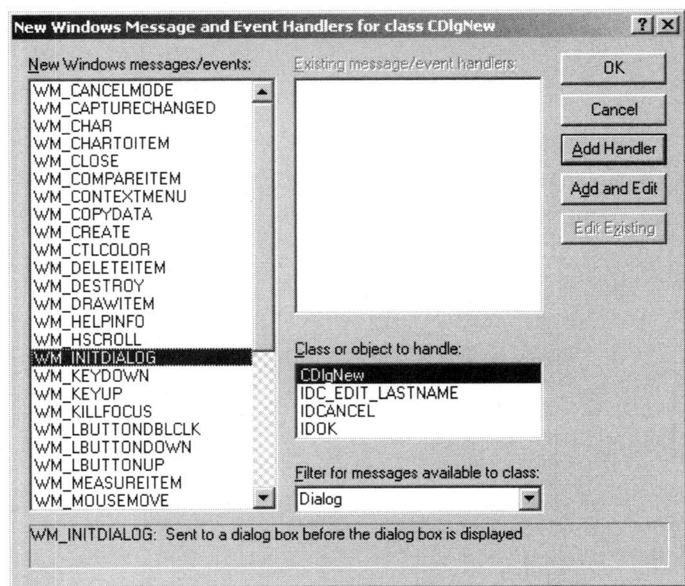

FIGURE 5.10 Windows Message and Event Handler listing.

3. Select the **WM_INITDIALOG** message, and click Add and Edit.

You are now in the DlgData.cpp source file ready to implement the logic in the overridden virtual function *OnInitDialog()*. You can tell that it is a local version of the function because it first calls the parent class' virtual function "CDialog:: OnInitDialog()."

To work with the **m_edtLastname** variable, such as to give the object data, we'll use one of the CEdit functions.[1]

1. Modify CDlgData's *OnInitDialog()* function as follows:

```
BOOL CDlgData::OnInitDialog()
{
     CDialog::OnInitDialog();

     // TODO: Add extra initialization here
     m_csLastname = "Jones";
     m_edtLastname.SetWindowText( "Jones" );
```

2. Compile the program and test it.

When you open the data dialog, you should see the text "Jones" in the Last Name edit box.

To retrieve data from the edit control, we need to generate a function for the OK button so that when it is clicked, code is invoked to read the control data.

3. Generate a BN_CLICKED message for the OK button in the data dialog and name it **OnOK**.
4. Edit the *OnOK()* function in CDlgData to:

```
void CDlgData::OnOK()
{
     // TODO: Add extra validation here
     CString     csLastname;
     m_edtLastname.GetWindowText( csLastname );
     MessageBox(csLastname, "Last Name", MB_OK);
     CDialog::OnOK();
```

[1] Actually CWnd functions. CWnd is CEdit's parent class, and CEdit inherits its parent's member functions.

5. Compile the program and test it.

Can you tell what the *MessageBox()* function does?

What we're doing in this case is creating a CString variable named **csLastname** to receive the results of the editing, then using the *GetWindowText()* function to extract the results, and it all happened when the OK button was clicked to close the data entry dialog.

Note in the last code example that the **csLastname** variable does not begin with "m_" because it is a variable local to the *OnOK()* function and not a member variable of a class.

Adding a String Variable

There is another way to give an edit box data, and it involves using a text variable directly without going through the object itself. Let's see how this is done.

1. While the edit box is selected, bring up ClassWizard.
2. Select the Member Variables pane.
3. Click the Add Variable button so we can define a variable for the edit box.
4. Enter the variable name **m_csLastname.**
5. Set variable type to "CString" as shown in Figure 5.11, and then click OK in the dialog box.

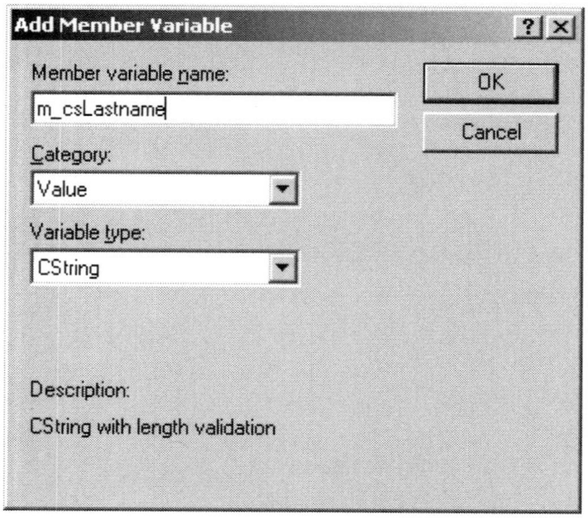

FIGURE 5.11 Adding a member variable.

You should see a new variable of the MFC CString class defined. CString is the MFC that provides services for character or text data. (CString is discussed in detail in Chapter 20.) "cs" is a way of saying that the variable is of the CString type.

6. Close the ClassWizard dialog box. (You may want to return to the Message Maps pane before doing so.)

Nothing seems to have changed. However, if you were to select ClassView, you should see the new entry **m_csLastname** (Figure 5.12).

FIGURE 5.12 ClassWizard-generated variable.

If you like, you can double-click on **m_csLastname** or use the Go To Definition command from the context menu to view the code behind it. Again, VC++ IDE has already generated the pertinent code for us.

We're now ready to use the new CString variable to do business.

Data Exchange

The action here is rather convoluted; therefore, go slow on it. However, as long as you work in the VC++ IDE it is not necessary for you to understand it all immediately to see the whole thing work. Therefore, just proceed to observe what the demonstration does.

1. Enter the code in bold (and remove the *SetWindowText()* function there):

```
BOOL CDlgData::OnInitDialog()
{
    CDialog::OnInitDialog();

    // TODO: Add extra initialization here
    m_csLastname = "Jones";
    UpdateData( FALSE );
```

2. Save the program changes, compile it, and execute it. Bring up the new dialog window and see if any data went into it. Then exit the application.

The first statement assigns the value "Jones" to the CString variable. The second statement causes the data to show up in the edit box when the new dialog box is initialized.

Just a bit above the *OnInitDialog()* function in the DlgData.cpp source file, you should find the following code function:

```
void CDlgData::DoDataExchange(CDataExchange* pDX)
{
	CDialog::DoDataExchange(pDX);
	//{{AFX_DATA_MAP(CDlgData)
	DDX_Control(pDX, IDC_EDIT_LASTNAME, m_edtLastname);
	DDX_Text(pDX, IDC_EDIT_LASTNAME, m_csLastname);
	//}}AFX_DATA_MAP
}
```

In the *DoDataExchange()* function is a *DDX_Text()* function. This *DDX_Text()* function sets a relationship between a resource (ID) and its associated variable. The *UpdateData()* function then causes data to be placed in the resource or to be retrieved from it.

DataUpdate(FALSE) causes data to be entered in the resources (due to the behind-the-scene actions of the DataExchange mechanism). *DataUpdate(TRUE)*, on the other hand, retrieves the data from the resources and copies it into the corresponding variable.

Now we'll retrieve the data from the edit box. The constraint is that data will be accepted only if the user closes the new dialog box by clicking OK. Clicking Cancel will forgo any changes.

3. Enter the code in bold in the *OnOK()* function of the CDlgData class as shown (with the *GetWindowText()* function removed):

```
void CDlgData::OnOK()
{
	// TODO: Add extra validation here
	// CString     csLastname;
	// m_edtLastname.GetWindowText( csLastname );
	// MessageBox(csLastname, "Last Name", MB_OK);
UpdateData(TRUE);
	CDialog::OnOK();
}
```

4. Save the changes and close the DlgData.cpp file.
5. Modify the *OnDataDialog()* function in the CdialogAppDlg class as shown (typing slowly so you can take advantage of IntelliSense):

```
void CDialogDemoDlg::OnDataDialog()
{
     // TODO: Add your control notification handler code here
     CDlgData     dlg( this );
     dlg.DoModal();
     MessageBox(dlg.m_csLastname, “Last Name”, MB_OK);
}
```

6. Save the changes, compile the program, and execute it. Try modifying the last name in the new dialog box and exit by clicking either OK or Cancel to study the respective effects.

In this example, the data editing dialog box is displayed and held on the screen (*DoModal()*). After the dialog box is closed, the data from its **m_csLastname** variable (**dlg.m_csLastname**) is then displayed in a message box titled “Last Name” with an OK button.

Edit Box with Numeric Data

The edit box can handle many different types of data. Here, we’ll try working with numbers.

1. Create a new edit box in the new dialog box and set its ID to IDC_EDIT_AGE.
2. In the edit box’s Properties dialog, check the Number Check box in the Styles tab and close it (Figure 5.13).

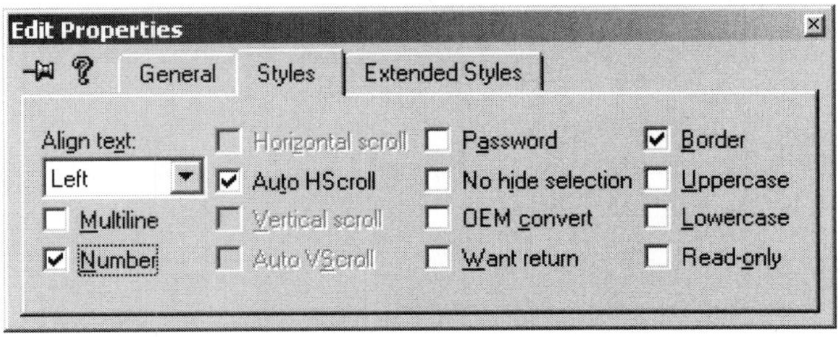

FIGURE 5.13 The Number edit box properties.

3. In ClassWizard, create a variable for IDC_EDIT_AGE named **m_iAge** of the **int** type (Figure 5.14).

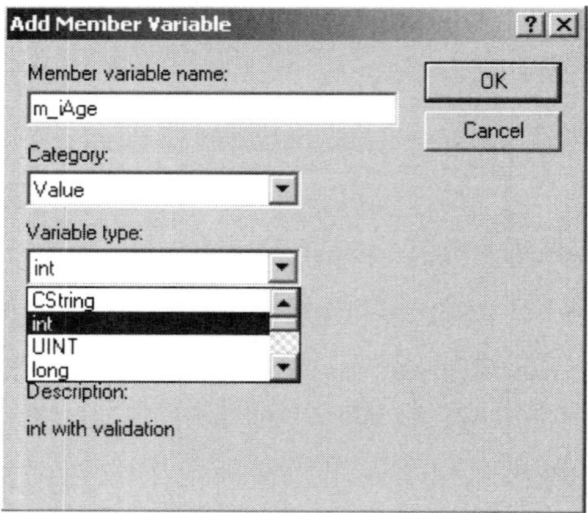

FIGURE 5.14 Adding an integer variable.

4. Set the variable's minimum and maximum values in ClassWizard as shown in Figure 5.15.

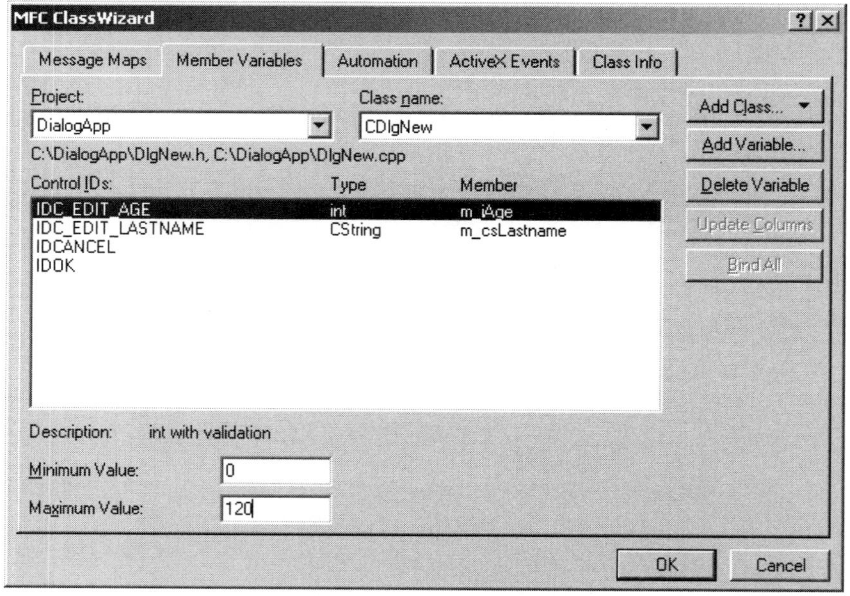

FIGURE 5.15 Setting a control variable's minimum and maximum values.

5. Close ClassWizard and compile the program. Test it with various age values and observe the results.
6. Examine the source code.

Disabling Editing

You can use an edit box for more than just data editing. It can be used as a data-displaying device just as the static control. To do so, you simply disable editing from the edit box's properties (Figure 5.16).

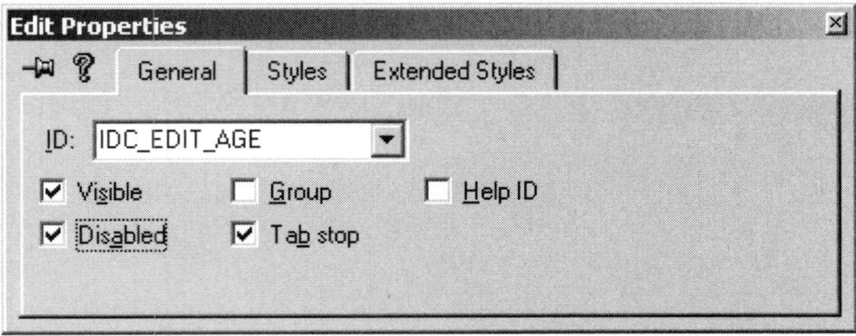

FIGURE 5.16 Disabling the edit box.

If you need to control this property at runtime, such as disabling an edit box by default but enabling it for editing when certain conditions are met, you will create an object for the edit box and then use the *SetReadOnly()* member function. *SetReadOnly(TRUE)* causes the edit control to be read only, or uneditable. *SetReadOnly(FALSE)* reverses the effect. For example, to cause the edit box to be read-only:

```
edtFirstname.SetReadOnly( TRUE );
```

Styling the Edit Box

You can also cause an edit box to assume different looks, or accept data in uppercase or lowercase. Again, you do it through the properties (Figures 5.17 and 5.18). Try the various options and observe the intended effects.

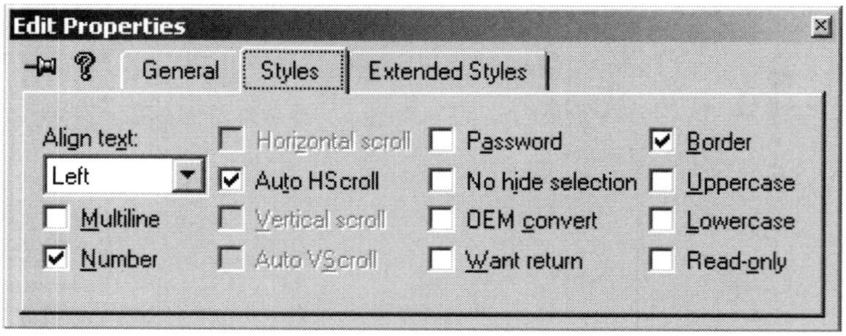

FIGURE 5.17 The edit box Style properties.

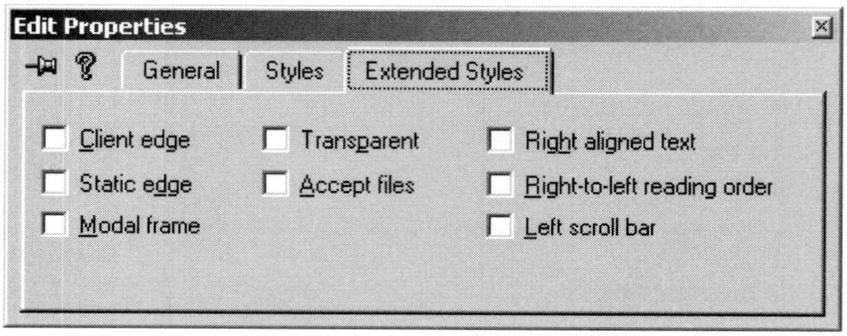

FIGURE 5.18 The edit box Extended Style properties.

THE BUTTON CONTROL

The last of the triumvirate of controls that we are introducing in this chapter is the button control, as encapsulated in the CButton class. A button control allows us to issue action commands.

To install a button control on a form, either select the Button tool (Figure 5.19) and then draw it with the mouse, or select it and drag it onto the form. Once a button is created visually, you can use its properties to set its look and feel (Figure 5.20).

Implementing a Command Button

The most basic function of a button is to provide a means for the user to invoke a command. The procedure for implementing a button on a form is as follows.

1. Install a button on a form or "surface."
2. Assign a unique ID to the button, and provide a meaningful caption for display, such as shown in Figure 5.21.

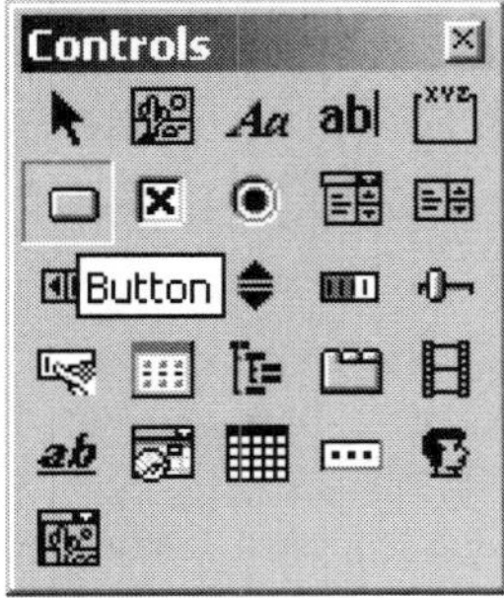

FIGURE 5.19 The Button Control tool.

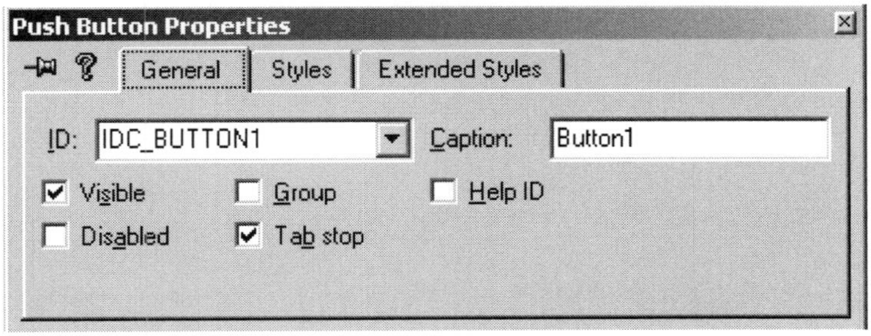

FIGURE 5.20 Button properties.

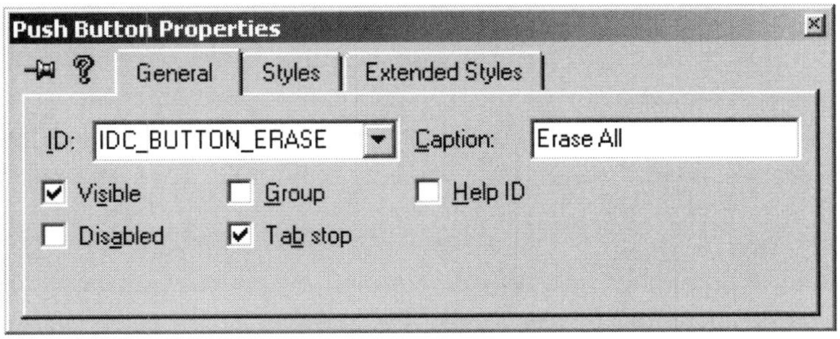

FIGURE 5.21 Erase All button properties.

3. Size the button and position it.
4. Use ClassWizard to add a command message support for the button, as in Figure 5.22, and use the Add Function button to generate the skeleton of a support function for the command message.

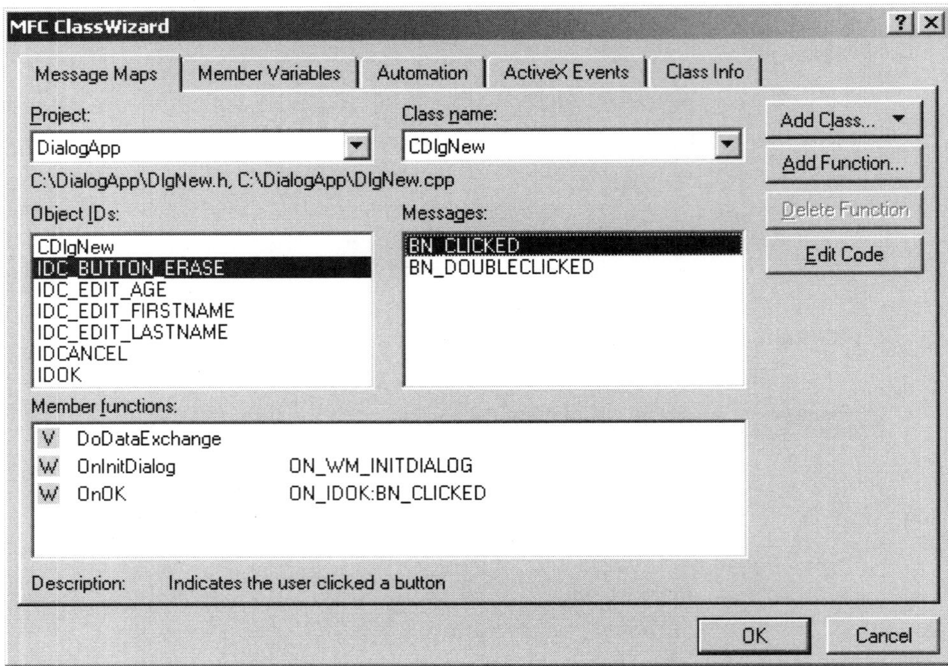

FIGURE 5.22 Generating a button event message handler function.

5. Use the Edit Function button in ClassWizard to get to the function source code and add your command processing function.

As with edit controls, you can set a number of properties to render a button's behavior differently. We'll discuss these features in later sections in context.

6 The Check Box, Radio Button, and Group Control

When you need to provide user interfaces for textual or numeric data, you use the edit control, as illustrated in the last chapter. When it comes to data that have finite value options such as yes or no, or data choices that can be easily represented by a set of values such as 1, 2, and 3, the check box and the radio button are the better controls to use. In this chapter, we'll explore their behaviors, and understand under what circumstances one should be used over another.

THE CHECK BOX CONTROL

A check box, or checkbox, also from the CButton class, is commonly used to communicate a yes or no (or true or false) data value. For example, when a check box is checked, it might indicate that a certain condition is set, while an unchecked box might indicate the opposite.

You install a check box the same way you do other controls: by selecting the Check Box tool (Figure 6.1) from the toolbox and drawing it on a surface, or by dragging the tool to the destination. Once the visual check box is in place, you use the Properties dialog to condition it. Most notably, you assign it a unique ID and a proper caption, such as shown in Figure 6.2.

When you have a visual check box resource, you use ClassWizard to generate a BOOL type variable for it with which you can then set its value to TRUE or FALSE. The following is an illustration of the working of a check box.

FIGURE 6.1 The Check Box tool.

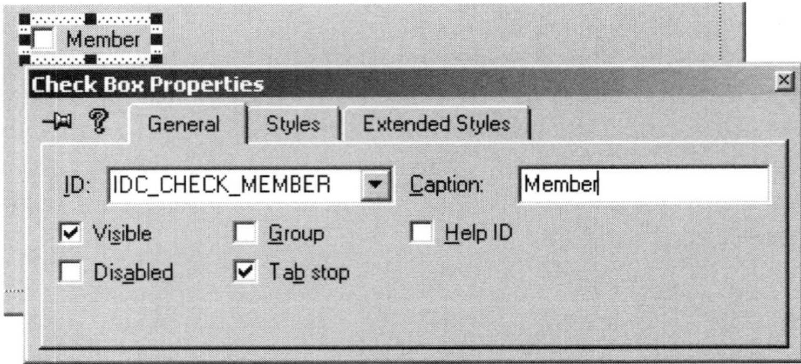

FIGURE 6.2 Check Box Properties dialog.

Reading the Check Box

First, we illustrate how you would obtain the data from a check box.

1. In the **DialogDemo** project (or using the one from the CD-ROM), create a check box resource as shown in Figure 6.2.
2. With ClassWizard, add a variable named **m_bMember** for the new check box (Figure 6.3), with "m_b" denoting the variable as a class member variable of the Boolean type.
3. To receive the edited value of the check box, add the following code to the *OnDataDialog()* function in DialogDemoDlg.cpp:

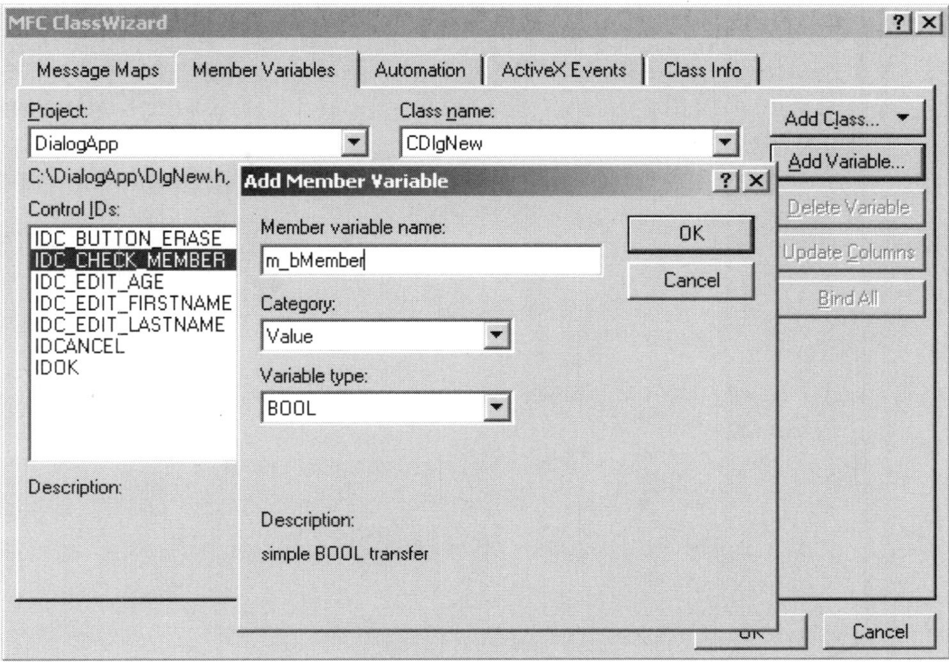

FIGURE 6.3 Adding a Boolean member variable.

```
void CDialogDemoDlg::OnDataDialog()
{
    // TODO: Add your control notification handler code here
    CDlgData    dlg( this );
    dlg.DoModal();
    MessageBox( dlg.m_csLastname, "Last Name", MB_OK );
    if ( dlg.m_bMember )
        MessageBox( "Is member.", "Edit", MB_OK );
    else
        MessageBox( "Is not a member.", "Edit", MB_OK );
}
```

4. Compile and test the check box.

Because m_bMember is of the BOOL type, it can have values of TRUE or FALSE. The statement "*if (dlg.m_bMember)*" inspects this value and determines what follow-up logic to execute.

Setting the Check Box

Likewise, to report (display) a yes or no status through a check box you first assign the status value to the check box's variable, and then use the *UpdateData(FALSE)* function to load the check box.

To test this using the **DialogDemo** project, modify CDlgData's *OnInitDialog()* function per the bold text shown here:

```
BOOL CDlgData::OnInitDialog()
{
     CDialog::OnInitDialog();

     // TODO: Add extra initialization here
     m_csLastname = "Jones";
     m_bMember = TRUE;
     UpdateData( FALSE );
```

You can also do it in the *OnDataDialog()* function before the new dialog is deployed as follows:

```
void CDialogDemoDlg::OnDataDialog()
{
     // TODO: Add your control notification handler…
     CDlgData     dlg( this );
     dlg.m_bMember = TRUE;
     dlg.DoModal();
```

THE RADIO BUTTON

In contrast with the check box, which represents a different data value and is independent from each other, the radio button (Figure 6.4), also of the CButton class, is used to express a selected value among many possibilities. In other words, of a group of radio buttons only one can be selected at any time. For example, let's say a club member might be of the types "Permanent," "Temporary," or "Guest." A set of radio buttons can be used to indicate which type a member is by selecting the radio button that represents that value (Figure 6.5), and each member can only be of one particular type.

Follow these steps to see how radio buttons are implemented:

1. Assuming that we are still working with the **DialogDemo** project, install three radio buttons on the new dialog box as shown in Figure 6.5. (If the

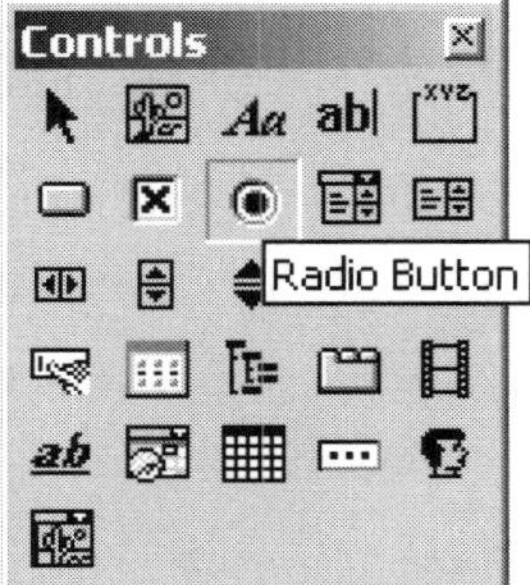

FIGURE 6.4 The Radio Button tool.

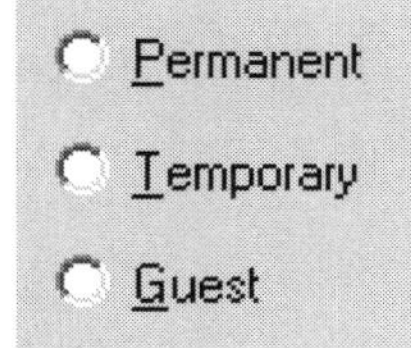

FIGURE 6.5 A radio button set.

screen is too crowded, use the View->Full Screen command to work in an expanded view.)

2. Set their resource IDs to those listed in Table 6.1.

TABLE 6.1 ID Settings for Radio Buttons

Resource	ID
Permanent	IDC_RADIO_PERM
Temporary	IDC_RADIO_TEMP
Guest	IDC_RADIO_GUEST

3. Make sure that you set all the radio buttons to be tab stops and, in particular, the "Permanent" type radio button to be a group (Figure 6.6).

FIGURE 6.6 Radio button properties.

4. Use ClassWizard to create an integer member variable (to hold the various discrete membership types) for the permanent member type radio button as shown in Figure 6.7.

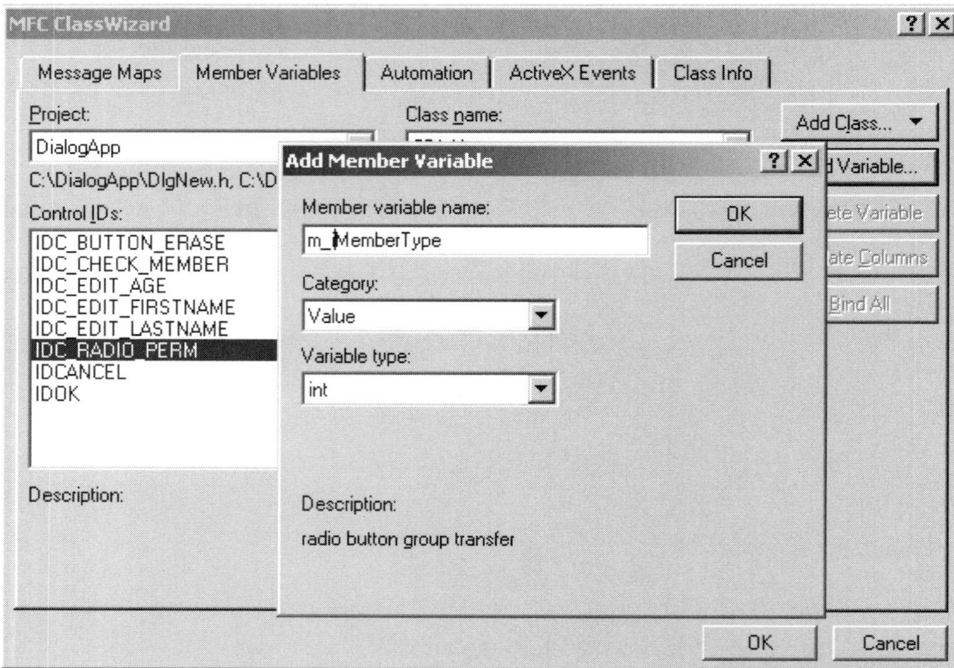

FIGURE 6.7 New m_iMemberType variable.

In fact, you should see the radio buttons unlisted in ClassWizard except the one designated as the "group." This is because actually you don't have three membership variables. You have one variable that can take on three different values. These values are visually presented as three items on the screen.

Now we impart logic to the scheme.

5. Add the following code shown in bold:

```
BOOL CDlgData::OnInitDialog()
{
     CDialog::OnInitDialog();

     // TODO: Add extra initialization here
```

```
        m_csLastname = "Jones";
        m_iMemberType = 1;
        UpdateData( FALSE );
```

"m_iMemberType = 1;" signifies the initial value of the variable to be 1, and will cause the second radio button to be selected. The first value of a group of radio buttons is 0 (zero).

To capture the user-edited radio button value, add the following code shown in bold:

```
    void CDialogDemoDlg::OnDataDialog()
    {
        // TODO: Add your control notification handler…
        CDlgData     dlg( this );
        dlg.DoModal();
        switch ( dlg.m_iMemberType )
        {
        case 0:
            MessageBox( "Permanent member.", "Membership", MB_OK );
            break;
        case 1:
            MessageBox( "Temporary member.", "Membership", MB_OK );
            break;
        default:
            MessageBox( "Guest member.", "Membership", MB_OK );
        }
```

The switch structure merely responds to the three possible values in **m_iMemberType**.

Good Coding

Of course, if possible, you should not be working with values of 0, 1, and 2, which convey no immediate sense of the membership types. Instead, you always should use the *enumerated* data type for such logical expressions, or at least define the values with mnemonics. Here, we'll illustrate how by defining the values, we make the program source code easy to read.

1. Add the code shown in bold to the **StdAfx.h** file:

```
#if _MSC_VER > 1000
#pragma once
#endif // _MSC_VER > 1000
```

```
#define VC_EXTRALEAN          // Exclude…
#define PERM  0
#define TEMP  1
#define GUEST 2
#include <afxwin.h>         // MFC core and standard components
#include <afxext.h>         // MFC extensions
```

This header file is used to define initial values and will be read by all the code files in the project.

2. Change the initialization code to:

```
BOOL CDlgData::OnInitDialog()
{
     CDialog::OnInitDialog();

     // TODO: Add extra initialization here
     m_iMemberType = TEMP;
     UpdateData( FALSE );
```

3. Change the reporting code to:

```
void CDialogDemoDlg::OnDataDialog()
{
     // TODO: Add your control notification handler…
     CDlgData     dlg( this );
     dlg.DoModal();
     switch ( dlg.m_iMemberType )
     {
     case PERM:
          MessageBox( "Permanent member.", "Membership", MB_OK );
          break;
     case TEMP:
          MessageBox( "Temporary member.", "Membership", MB_OK );
          break;
     default:
          MessageBox( "Guest member.", "Membership", MB_OK );
     }
```

Indeed, professional programmers would urge you to go one step further and use a string array in favor of the cumbersome switch mechanism:

```
void CDialogDemoDlg::OnDataDialog()
{
```

```
    // TODO: Add your control notification handler…
    CDlgData     dlg( this );
    dlg.DoModal();
    CString     csMemberType[] =
  { "Permanent member.",
    "Temporary member.",
    "Guest member." };
    MessageBox(csMemberType[dlg.m_iMemberType], "Membership", MB_OK );
```

THE GROUP CONTROL

Controls, if allowed to scatter on a display, look bad and confuse the user. When controls exhibit group characteristics, they should be visually collected as collections using the group control.

To use the group control (Figure 6.8), simply render it on the display, enclosing the controls that it is meant to group, as in Figure 6.9.

That is it. The only things you need to make sure are that:

FIGURE 6.8 The Group Control tool.

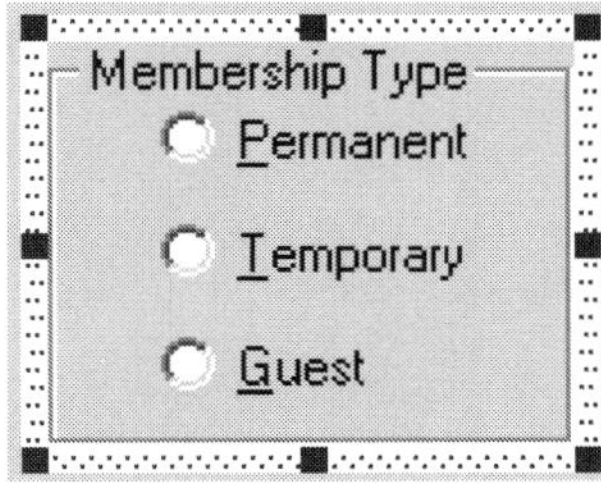

FIGURE 6.9 Group Control enclosing radio buttons.

1. Its caption has no quick-key access (underscored character).
2. It is not set to be a tab stop.
3. It assumes the default ID of IDC_STATIC (the group control is of the CStatic class) unless you specifically have intentions to do something with it, such as programmatically changing its caption.

7 The Combo Box and the List Box

The edit control was designed to facilitate general data entry. Check boxes and radio buttons are graphical means of limited-value data transactions.

We emphasize the graphical aspect because anything graphical is usually better than textual, which is why most people favor Windows over DOS—a picture is worth a thousand words.

The product of this line of thinking is the category of mechanisms that allows a user to choose from data options or lists as opposed to having to type them. In the Windows environment, by far the most widely employed devices in support of the "pickable" approach to data interaction are the combo box and the list box.

THE COMBO BOX CONTROL

The combo box, of the CComboBox class, is most often used as an input device rather than an output device. It is commonly used to allow a user to select values from a relatively large array of values without having to display them all on the screen as with radio buttons, because the combo box can be set to hide its values when inactive.

Rendering a Combo Box

The best way to visually create a combo box is to select the Combo Box tool (Figure 7.1), and then drag the mouse to draw it to the size that the combo box will be when its list drops down. The sequence of events is depicted in Figure 7.2.

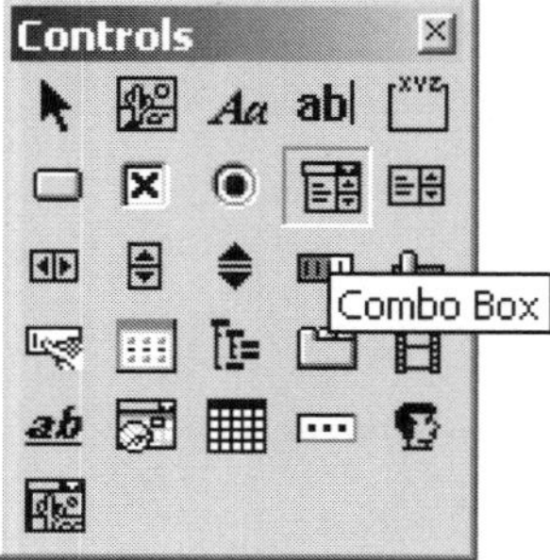

FIGURE 7.1 The Combo Box tool.

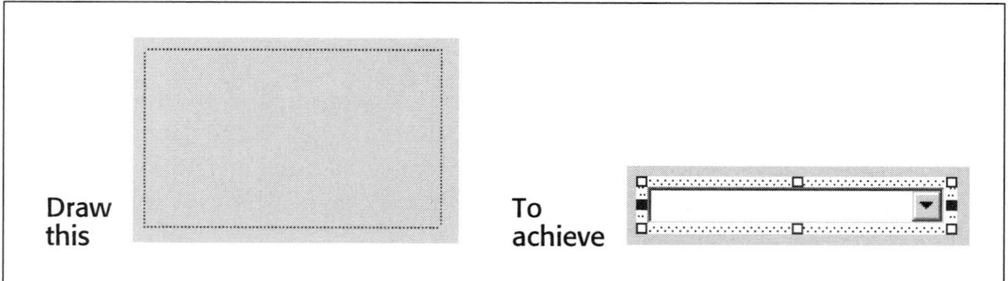

FIGURE 7.2 Creating a combo box.

If you created the combo box by dragging the Control tool directly on to the supporting surface as opposed to actually selecting the tool first and then drawing it with the mouse, the drop-down list might not open during runtime. In such a case, you'll need to redefine its dimensions by editing it in directly in the resource (.rc) file.

To see a combo box work, perform the following:

1. In **DialogDemo**, generate a combo box as described previously.
2. Set its ID to **IDC_COMBO_STATE** and use ClassWizard to create a variable for it (Figure 7.3).

This variable, **m_cboState**, will denote the control object itself.

3. Next, create a CString variable for it (Figure 7.4).

This variable, **m_csState**, will hold the combo box's current text value.

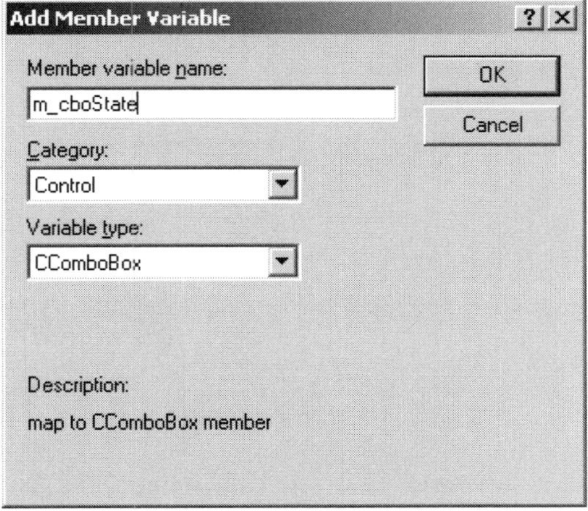

FIGURE 7.3 Adding a combo box control variable.

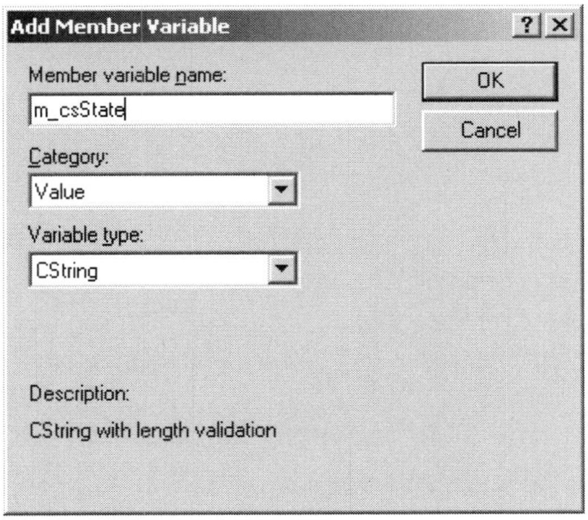

FIGURE 7.4 Adding a CString variable.

Loading Data in a Combo Box

There are several ways to add list contents to a combo box. If you know what the list data are at design time, you can type them into the combo box's Properties dialog directly as shown in Figure 7.5. (Separate the data entries with [Ctrl-Enter].)

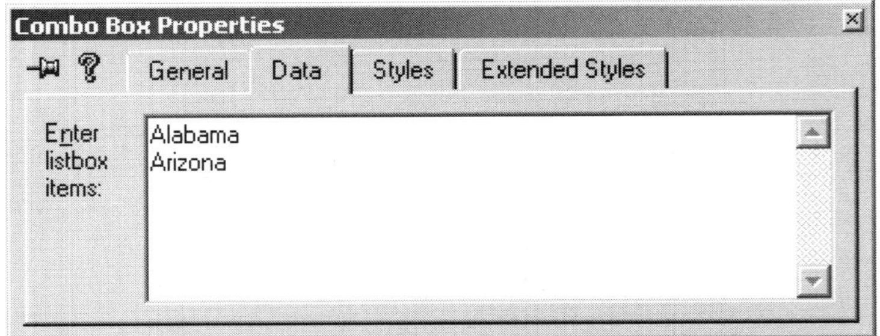

FIGURE 7.5 Loading data in a combo box.

If the data are known only at runtime, as in the case when data are extracted from a database, you would add the data programmatically as follows.

1. Add the combo box initialization code as follows:

```
BOOL CDlgData::OnInitDialog()
{
     CDialog::OnInitDialog();

     // TODO: Add extra initialization here
     m_csLastname = "Jones";
     m_iMemberType = TEMP;
     m_cboState.ResetContent();
     m_cboState.AddString( "Alabama" );
     m_cboState.AddString( "Alaska" );
     m_cboState.AddString( "Arizone" );
     m_cboState.AddString( "California" );
     m_cboState.AddString( "Delaware" );
     UpdateData( FALSE );
```

The *ResetContent()* function clears the combo box of any pre-existing data. The *AddString()* function appends data to the control.

2. Compile the program and test the mechanical workings of the combo box.

As you can see, the combo box is filled with data. The only problem is that it appears empty until you drop the list down. To remedy this, you need to initialize the list selection.

3. Add the code shown in bold, and compile and test the program again. Make sure that you place this initialization function after the *Update-*

Data() function so it can take effect after all data exchange operations are finished.

```
m_cboState.AddString( "Alabama" );
m_cboState.AddString( "Alaska" );
m_cboState.AddString( "Arizone" );
m_cboState.AddString( "California" );
m_cboState.AddString( "Delaware" );
UpdateData( FALSE );
m_cboState.SetCurSel(0);
```

The *SetCurSel()* function sets the combo box's current selection by a data index. 0 (zero) represents the first data element in the list.

Using a Combo Box

Obtaining the selected combo box data is as easy as reading its string variable.

1. Add the code shown in bold to your DialogDemo program:

```
void CDialogDemoDlg::OnDataDialog()
{
     // TODO: Add your control notification handler…
     CDlgData     dlg( this );
     dlg.DoModal();
     MessageBox( dlg.m_csState, "State", MB_OK );
```

Here we merely display the data in **m_csState** (which belong to dlg; hence, "dlg.m_csState") with a message box.

Of course, if you need to use the data elsewhere in the program, you can capture it in a separate variable for future use, such as:

```
CString     csMemberState;
csMemberState = dlg.m_csState;
```

Now we'll demonstrate capturing the data selected by the user.

A string variable makes life easy for obtaining data from a combo box if you're interested primarily in the text data being selected. In real-life programming, often you need the selected data index as opposed to the actual text data. For instance, you might be coordinating the combo box selection with the data in a database table. In such a case you would be better off without the string variable and the interference of data exchange, which flushes the combo box data. For example, the following code shows how you would determine the index of the data selected, and then use the index to obtain the actual data.

```
CString     csState;      // String for selected data.
int     iSelect;      // Index for selected data.
iSelect = m_cboState.GetCurSel();      // Get index.
m_cboState.GetLBText(iSelect,csState);
```

If you want to try the sample code, first remove the string variable through ClassWizard (and any existing involvement of it in the program).

THE LIST BOX

The list box, of the CListBox class, behaves in many ways like the combo box, but also differently in several aspects. For one, the list in a list box does not drop down; you get to see a large portion of the data in its inactive state. If the list box is too small to accommodate all the list data, scroll bars will be provided. When screen display space is not an issue, the list box often is a more pleasant device to work with from the user's perspective than the combo box because the user can see at least some of the data on the screen.

A list box is typically implemented as described here, assuming that we're using the **DialogDemo** project for illustration.

1. Install a list box (Figure 7.6) visually on the DlgData dialog resource.

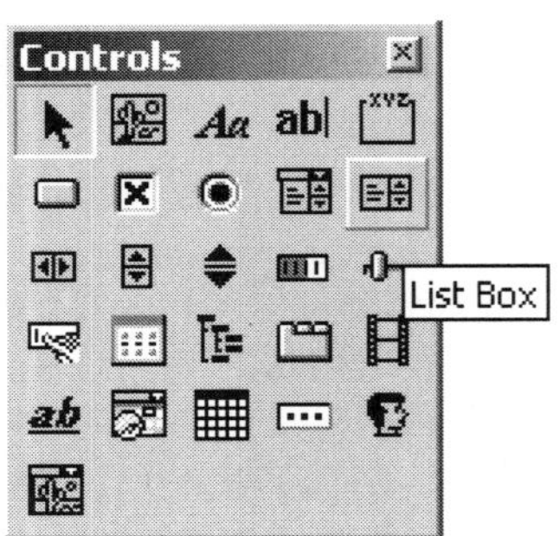

FIGURE 7.6 The List Box tool.

2. Assign an ID for the control, such as IDC_LIST_SITES.
3. Instantiate a CListBox object for it and name it **m_lstSites**.
4. Initialize the list box with:

```
BOOL CDlgData::OnInitDialog()
{
     CDialog::OnInitDialog();

     // TODO: Add extra initialization here
     m_lstSites.ResetContent();
     m_lstSites.AddString( "Central" );
     m_lstSites.AddString( "Eastside" );
     m_lstSites.AddString( "Main Office" );
     m_lstSites.AddString( "Uptown" );
     m_lstSites.AddString( "Westside" );
```

5. Compile the program and see the results.

In short, you implement a list box as follows.

1. Create the list box by normal visual means.
2. Instantiate the object, and one for its string data, if you want to use data exchange to read the selected data.
3. Use *AddString()* to load the list box with string data.
4. Read the list box data via its string variable by way of data exchange.
5. To obtain multiple list box data selections, set up an integer array to receive the indices, and then use the *GetSelCount()* function to get the selection count, and the *GetSelItems()* function to read the indices.

Reading the List Box

To obtain the user-selected text from the list box, you can create a CString member variable and have data exchange fill it for you, with which you are by now familiar. If you prefer (and without the interference of data exchange), you can use the *GetCurSel()* function to determine the selected data's index, and then use it in the *GetLBText()* function to extract the data. For example:

```
CString     csSite;
m_lstSites.GetLBText( m_lstSites.GetCurSel(), csSite );
```

The first parameter in the *GetLBText()* function is the integer index, which we can obtain using the *GetCurSel()* function. The second parameter is the CString object that will hold the selected data.

The list box allows you to make multiple selections (if you have set the list box's "Selection" property to "Multiple"). In such a case, a single CString object will not suffice; you will need an array for that. The following is a sample code that shows how multiple selections are read:

```
int     iSites[5];
int     iSel;
iSel = m_lstSites.GetSelCount();
m_lstSites.GetSelItems( iSel, iSites );
```

Here, an integer variable is set up to hold the number of selections. An integer array is set up to hold the selected indices. The *GetSelCount()* function gets the number of selected items, and the *GetSelItems()* function fills the array with the selected indices. With the indices, you can create a loop to read the selected text if you wish.

8 The Slider Bar, Spin Control, and Progress Bar

The edit control, radio button, check box, combo box, and so on discussed up to now constitute the group of user interface controls that can be described as offering precise data interfacing. A data item can be selected "precisely" from a list of choices. A value is "precisely" identified in a group of radio buttons. There are situations in which the exact value of a data item may not be important as compared to the "quality" of the data value. There exists a group of controls that allow data values to be "estimated," and they include the slider bar, the spin control, and the progress bar.

THE SLIDER OR TRACKBAR CONTROL

The slider bar, or trackbar, allows a user to *estimate* an input value by moving a slider on the screen with the mouse (and, technically, with the keyboard too, as you will see). With a slider, you can visually estimate a numeric value as opposed to entering it by typing.

The slider bar, based on the CSlideCtrl class, is easy to implement. You instantiate an object for it, set the slider range, let the user move it, and then read its resultant value. The following example, using the **DialogDemo** project as the platform, shows you how this is done.

1. Visually install a slider control (Figure 8.1), with ID IDC_SLIDER_SKILL, on the DlgData display as in Figure 8.2.

(A static control was added to label it as well.)

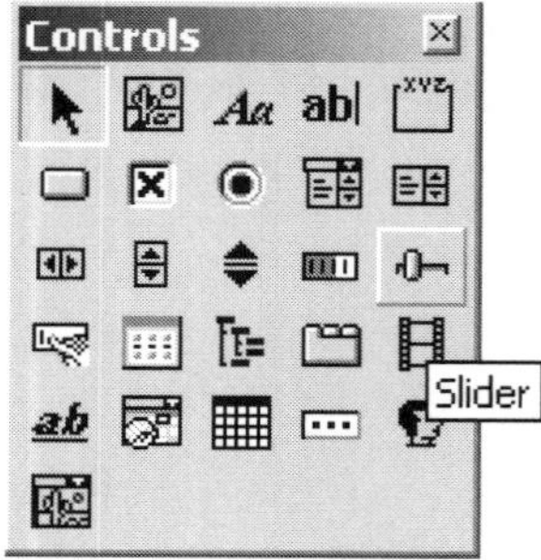

FIGURE 8.1 The slider control.

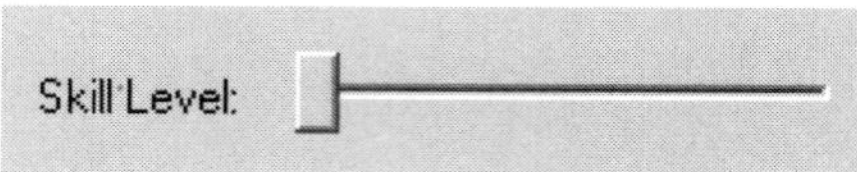

FIGURE 8.2 A slider object.

2. Use ClassWizard to create two variables for the slider, a variable named (CSliderCtrl) **m_slSkill** to denote the control itself, and a variable named (int) **m_iSkill** to hold the position value of the slider used by data exchange.
3. Initialize the slider with:

```
BOOL CDlgData::OnInitDialog()
{
     CDialog::OnInitDialog();

     // TODO: Add extra initialization here
     m_slSkill.SetSelection(0,100);
```

SetSelection(0,100) sets up the slider to range from a value of 0 (zero) to 100.

4. To see the result, add the reporting code as follows:

```
void CDialogDemoDlg::OnDataDialog()
{
     // TODO: Add your control notification handler…
     CDlgData     dlg( this );
     dlg.DoModal();
     CString     csSkill;
     csSkill.Format("%3i", dlg.m_iSkill);
     MessageBox( csSkill, "Skill Level", MB_OK );
```

Here we use a temporary string to accommodate the resultant **m_iSkill** value for display as a string via the *MessageBox()* function. We also introduced a new CString function *Format()*, which formats a string according to a format specification. "%3d" uses the trailing integer value to form a string of three digits.

Because the slider control is set to be a tab stop, you can reach it as a user by tabbing. Once it is in focus, you can use the arrow keys to navigate it.

Reading Slider Values

The (int) **m_iSkill** variable was created to support the data exchange actions. With it, the *UpdateData(TRUE)* function downloads the slider current position value into the variable for us. However, you are not obliged to use this approach. You can read the slider value directly if you prefer. Again, we'll use an illustration to show how it works.

1. Use ClassWizard to generate a handler function for the command message **NM_RELEASEDCAPTURE** (Figure 8.3).

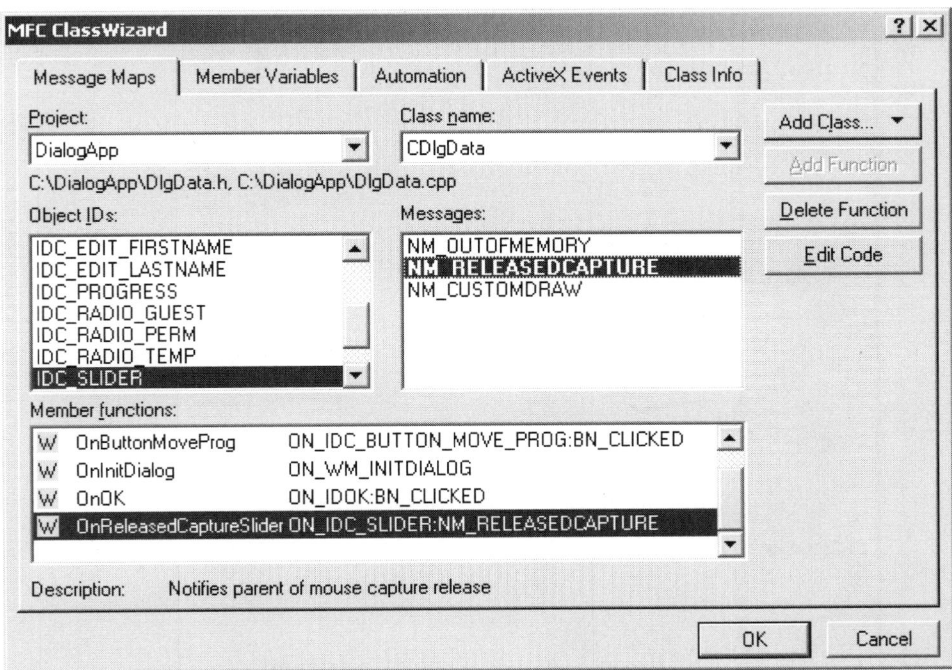

FIGURE 8.3 The slider control's NM_RELEASEDCAPTURE message.

The corresponding coding is:

```
void CDlgData::OnReleasedCaptureSlider(NMHDR* pNMHDR, LRESULT* pResult)
{
     // TODO: Add your control notification handler…
```

```
        int     iSkill;
        iSkill = m_slSkill.GetPos();
        *pResult = 0;
}
```

Here we read the slider position value with the class member function *GetPos()*, which returns an integer. Figure out a way to display this value.

THE SPIN CONTROL

Unlike the slider control, the spin control, which is based on the MFC CSpinButtonCtrl class, allows the user to "dial in" a numeric data item. Unlike the slider control, you can also enter the value precisely if necessary. Its implementation is also relatively straightforward. Again, we use the **DialogDemo** project for its demonstration.

1. Visually install a spin control (Figure 8.4) and an edit box on the DlgData display (a label for them was added too, as in Figure 8.5).

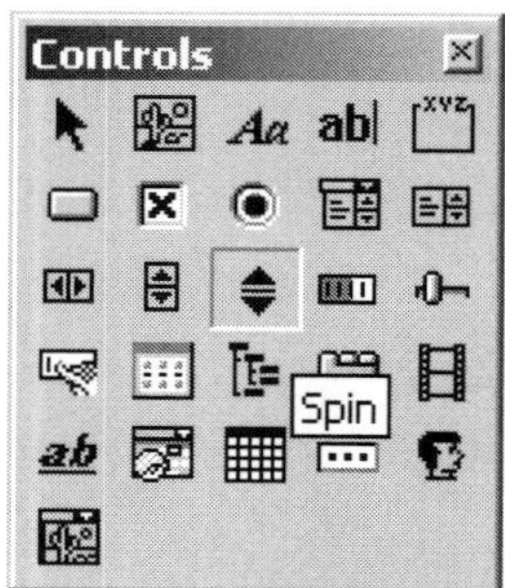

FIGURE 8.4 The spin control.

FIGURE 8.5 The spin control implementation.

The edit box will be used to display the numeric input.

2. Create a variable for the spin control object (i.e., instantiate it) named **m_spAge**.
3. Create a variable for the edit box object (i.e., instantiate it) named **m_edtAge**.
4. Set the spin control properties as shown in Figure 8.6.

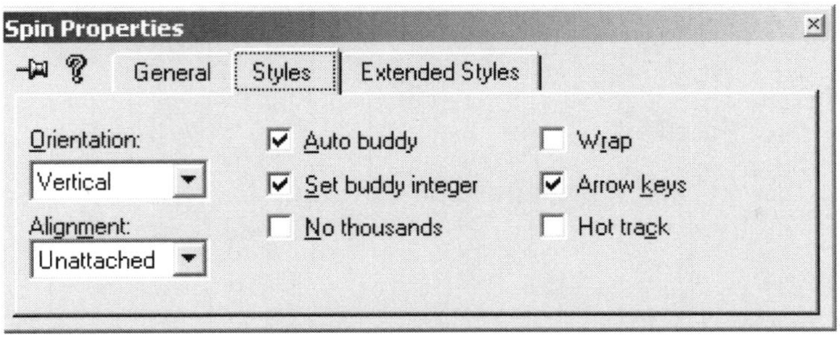

FIGURE 8.6 Spin control properties.

"Auto buddy" indicates that there will be a "buddy" in the form of a CWnd window (here an edit control) for displaying the spin control position value. "Set buddy integer" causes the buddy to display the values (as integers).

4. Add the following initialization code to set up the spin control:

```
BOOL CDlgData::OnInitDialog()
{
    CDialog::OnInitDialog();

    // TODO: Add extra initialization here
    m_spAge.SetBuddy(&m_edtAge);
    m_spAge.SetRange(0,120);
    m_spAge.SetPos(0);
```

The *SetBuddy()* function "attaches" the edit control to the spin control. Note that it uses a pointer to the buddy CWnd object.

5. Compile the program and try the controls.
6. Try different spin control "alignment" property settings to get a feel for its styles.

In summary, to implement spin control, use this procedure:

1. Create the spin control and its buddy edit box visually by normal toolbox means.
2. Set the spin control properties to "Auto buddy" and "Set buddy integer."
3. Instantiate both the controls.
4. Set up the spin control with the *SetBuddy() and SetRange()* function.

5. Read the resultant slider position value with the *GetPos()* function if necessary.

Reading the Spin Control Position

To obtain the current spin control position value, use the *GetPos()* class member function or, if you have an edit box as a buddy, get the value from it.

THE PROGRESS BAR

Not all computer operations result in visual effects. A mathematical computation might take a significant amount of time and yet produces no visual evidence of activity. When this occurs, a user can be tricked into thinking that something has gone wrong; that the computer might be frozen. To prevent such erroneous impressions, you might use a progress bar, represented in MCF by the CProgressCtrl class, to artificially indicate activity.

Almost all of you have seen a progress bar at work at one time or another. A typical example would be during the installation of a program or downloading a file from the Internet. A moving bar on the screen shows how far the file copying operation has advanced

The working of a progress bar is simple. You instantiate a bar object (i.e., create a variable for it), set a display value range, and then reposition the bar's progress point as dictated by certain ongoing events or operation that the bar was designed to track.

As an example of how a progress bar works, we'll use a button to control the bar movements. Every time the user clicks the button, the bar moves a notch. This way, we don't have to cloud the issue by introducing some complicated processes just so that we have something to track.

ON THE CD

Open the **DialogDemo** project if it isn't already open.

1. Use the Progress Bar tool (Figure 8.7) to create a progress bar on the CDlgData display, along with a button as suggested in Figure 8.8.
2. Use ClassWizard to generate a member variable for the progress bar named **m_pgDemo**.
3. Generate a handler function for the button's BN_CLICK command message.
4. Modify the *OnInitDialog()* function as per the following bold code:

```
BOOL CDlgData::OnInitDialog()
{
     CDialog::OnInitDialog();
```

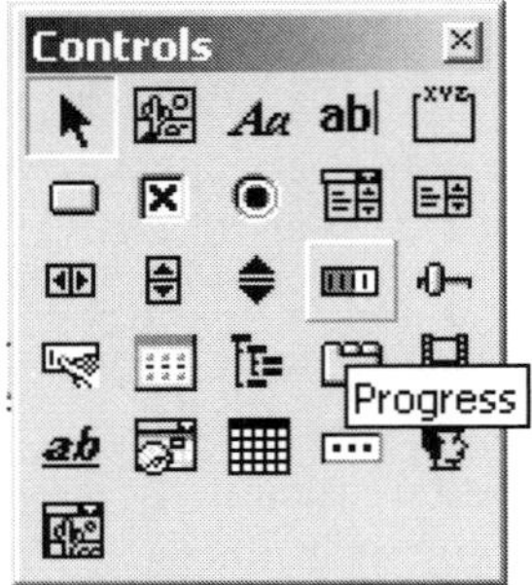

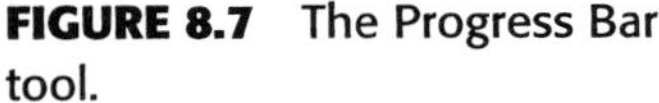
FIGURE 8.7 The Progress Bar tool.

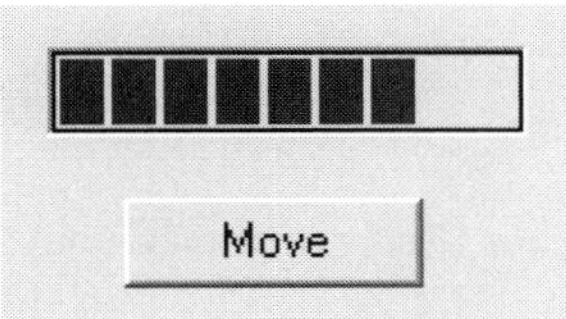

FIGURE 8.8 Progress bar in action.

```
    // TODO: Add extra initialization here
    m_pgDemo.SetRange(1,100);
```

The progress bar's *SetRange()* function defines the incremental range for the progress bar. Here we set the control to start with none of the bar filled, and the potential to increment by 100 steps.

5. Implement the following code for the button click event:

```
void CDlgData::OnButtonMoveProg()
{
    // TODO: Add your control notification handler…
    m_pgDemo.StepIt();
}
```

The *StepIt()* function causes the progress bar to move to the next step. In a real application, it will be triggered by the event the progress bar is tracking.

6. Compile the program and test the progress bar by clicking its control button.

If you wish to control the step amount, use the *SetStep()* progress bar member function, such as "m_pgDemo.SetStep(2)" to increment by two units at a time. By omitting to set the step value, the progress bar will step by increments of 10.

Further, if you like you can set the progress position using the *OffsetPos()* member function by specifying the amount of steps to move, or the *SetPos()* function to directly specify the position to move to. You would use these functions typically when the progress of the operation being monitored must be polled. An example of this would be an event taking place as a separate process in the background. A timer (which you will learn about later) causes the event to be checked at preset time intervals and updates the progress bar according to the real-time advancement of the event.

Let us recap. To implement a progress bar, follow these steps:

1. Create the progress bar visually by normal toolbox means.
2. Set the bar range by specifying the lower and upper limits as integers.
3. Use *SetStep()*, if necessary, to set the bar movement increment step size.
4. Update the bar with the *StepIt()* member function, or *OffsetPos()* or *SetPos()* for discrete control.

9 The Picture and Animation Controls

Not all data are of the textual or numeric type. There are graphical data too; some of them even move. In VC++, two controls exist to make their presentation extremely easy: the picture and animation controls.

THE PICTURE CONTROL

You use the picture control, of the CStatic class, to display pictures, and its implementation procedure is very simple. Again, we'll do an exercise to illustrate it. You'll need to have a picture file in order for it to work. Any file, perhaps a bitmap (.bmp) file from the system will do.

To see how a picture control works, activate the **DialogDemo** project.

1. Install a picture control (Figure 9.1) on the DlgData display.

FIGURE 9.1 The Picture Control tool.

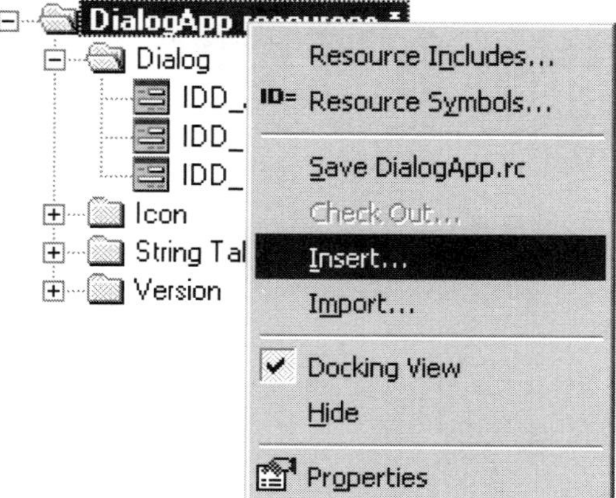

FIGURE 9.2 ResourceView context menu.

2. In ResourceView, bring up the context menu for the **DialogDemo** resources node and choose the Insert command (Figure 9.2).
3. From the Insert Resource dialog, select Bitmap (Figure 9.3) and click the Import button.

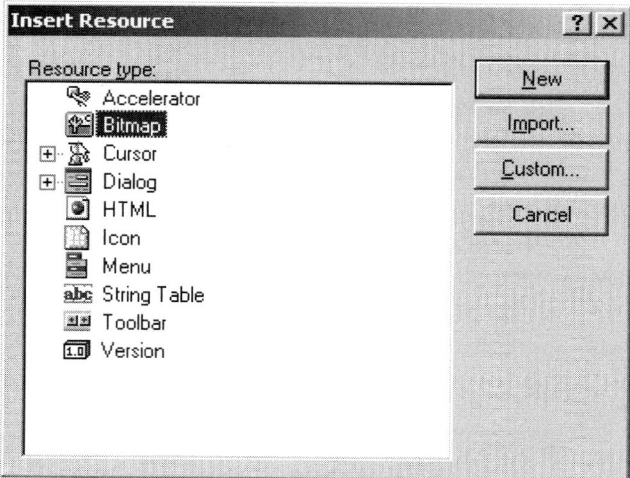

FIGURE 9.3 The Insert Resource list.

4. Select a picture file, such as shown in Figure 9.4.

As you can see, you can work with several different picture types with the picture control.

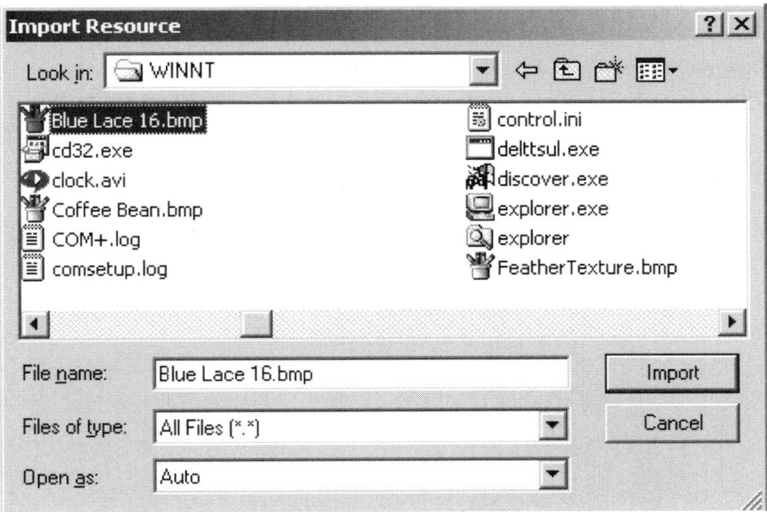

FIGURE 9.4 Importing a resource.

5. When the picture is inserted into the resources, bring up its Properties dialog, change the ID to an appropriate one, such as IDB_BITMAP_DEMO, and close the display.

You should see the resource in the tree listing.

6. Bring up the Properties dialog of the picture control and set its type to Bitmap (Figure 9.5).

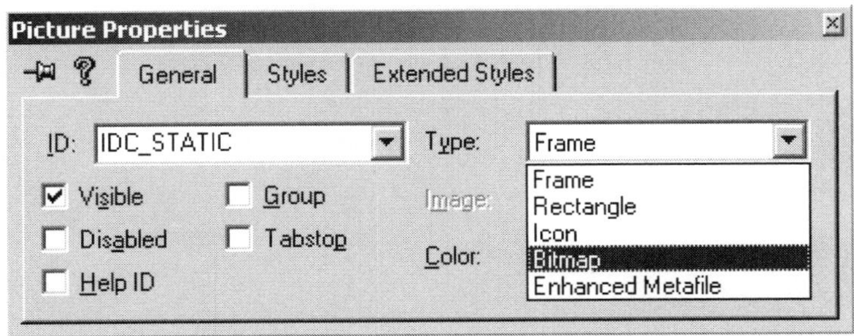

FIGURE 9.5 The Picture Control Properties dialog.

7. Select the image (Figure 9.6).
8. Adjust the picture placement, compile the program, and test it.

FIGURE 9.6 Selecting a picture control image.

The following summarizes the procedure for constructing a picture control.

1. Create the picture control visually by normal toolbox means.
2. Add the picture resource to the project.
3. Set the picture control type property to the appropriate picture type in the Properties dialog.
4. Select the image in the Properties dialog.

THE ANIMATION CONTROL

The operation of the animation control, of the CAnimateCtrl class, which works on .avi files, is just one step beyond that of the picture control. The following exercise, based on the **DialogDemo** project, demonstrates how to set up an animation control.

1. Install an animation control (Figure 9.7) on the DlgData display and ID it properly.

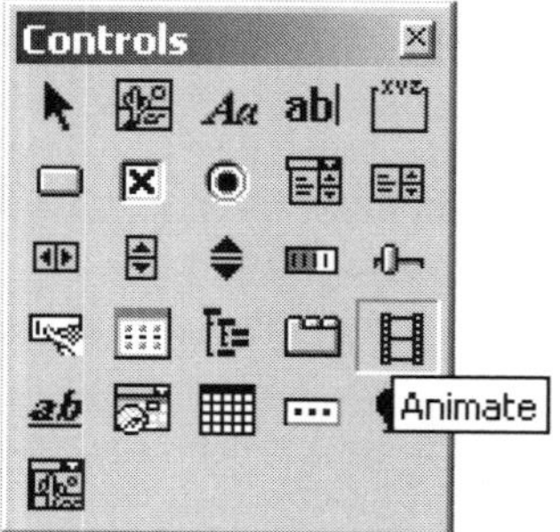

FIGURE 9.7 The Animate Control tool.

2. Instantiate an object based on it, named, say, **m_anDemo**.
3. Add the initialization code as follows:

```
BOOL CDlgData::OnInitDialog()
{
     CDialog::OnInitDialog();

     // TODO: Add extra initialization here
     m_anDemo.Open( "d:\\Program Files\\Microsoft Visual
Studio\\Common\\Graphics\\Videos\\Search.avi" );
```

The animation control's *Open()* class member function opens the target animation file.

For illustration purposes, this exercise uses the searchlight file from Windows. You can use any substitute you like.

4. In the Properties dialog for the animation control, set "Auto play" on (Figure 9.8).

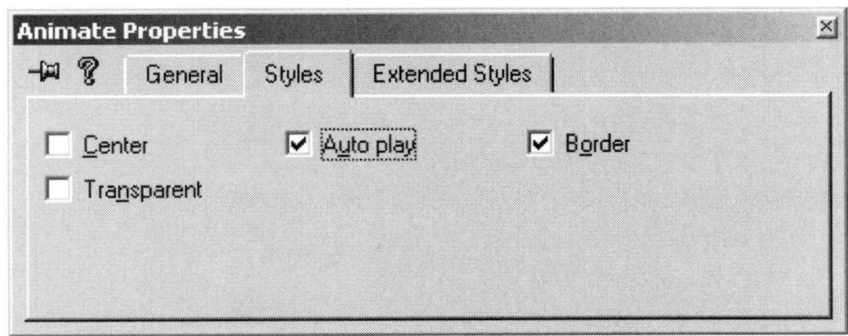

FIGURE 9.8 Auto play.

5. Compile the program and test it.

The use of the animation control to display an .avi file is summarized here:

1. Create the animation control visually by normal toolbox means.
2. Instantiate an object for the control.
3. Set the "Auto play" type property if desired for automatic endless play.
4. Play the animation with the *Play()* function.

Manual Playing

Obviously, the "Auto play" property causes the animation to play by itself. However, you can control the play programmatically if that is what the application requires. For example, you can set up the animation for the user to activate. To do this, you can add a button to the program, whereby when the button is chosen, it triggers the *Play()* class member function.

The *Play()* function takes the form of

```
BOOL Play( UINT nFrom, UINT nTo, UINT nRep );
```

nFrom denotes the first frame position. nTo is the last frame position. nRep indicates the number of times to play. If nRep is –1, that means endless playing.

10 Creating Control Objects from Code

Developing programs visually is fun and efficient. However, you do rely on the IDE to generate a lot of code for you, thereby reducing the flexibility you otherwise would have if you code the whole thing manually. We quickly ran over a gamut of controls, learned many MFC classes and functions, but in reality we did little C++. The emphasis was decidedly on the "visual" aspect of things. Nevertheless, we did what we did for a purpose. The experience gave us a chance to go over the IDE and explore much of its operations.

Using the IDE to implement controls is great, but there comes a time when you must code them without the benefit of the visual aids. One of the most compelling reasons is that to visually implement controls you must have a resource surface on which to visually place them. What do you do when you don't have such a medium to work with? When that happens, the visual approach will no longer work. In this chapter, we'll learn to construct controls through coding.

CREATING AN EDIT BOX

We'll begin our new venture by learning to create an edit box from code.

1. Use MFC AppWizard to generate an SDI application based on the CView class, and call the application **CtrlDemo**.
2. Add a private variable of the CEdit* pointer type in the View class (Figure 10.1).

As a refresher, a pointer is a computer memory address that points to an object. Here we create a pointer named **m_pEditBox** that is meant to point at an edit box;

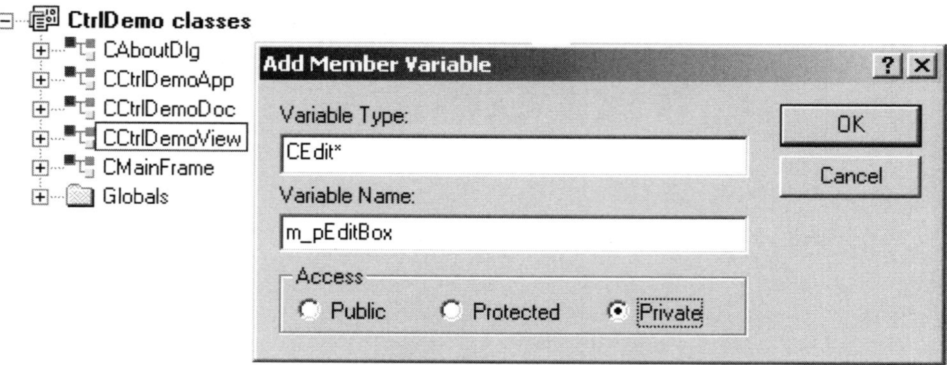

FIGURE 10.1 Adding a private pointer variable.

therefore, the pointer is CEdit*, where "*" denotes "pointer." Obviously, the actual edit box object has yet to be created. All we can do at this time is to reserve a memory address for it. The resultant code generated in the header file is:

```
// Generated message map functions
protected:
     //{{AFX_MSG(CCtrlDemoView)
          // NOTE - the ClassWizard will add and…
          //    DO NOT EDIT what you see in these…
     //}}AFX_MSG
     DECLARE_MESSAGE_MAP()
private:
     CEdit* m_pEditBox;
```

3. In ClassWizard, generate a handler function for the View class' **OnInitialUpdate** command message (Figure 10.2).
4. In the *OnInitialUpdate()* function, enter the code shown in bold:

```
void CCtrlDemoView::OnInitialUpdate()
{
     CView::OnInitialUpdate();

     // TODO: Add your specialized code here and/or…
     // Edit box
     m_pEditBox = new CEdit;
     m_pEditBox->Create( WS_CHILD | WS_VISIBLE | WS_TABSTOP |
WS_BORDER,
```

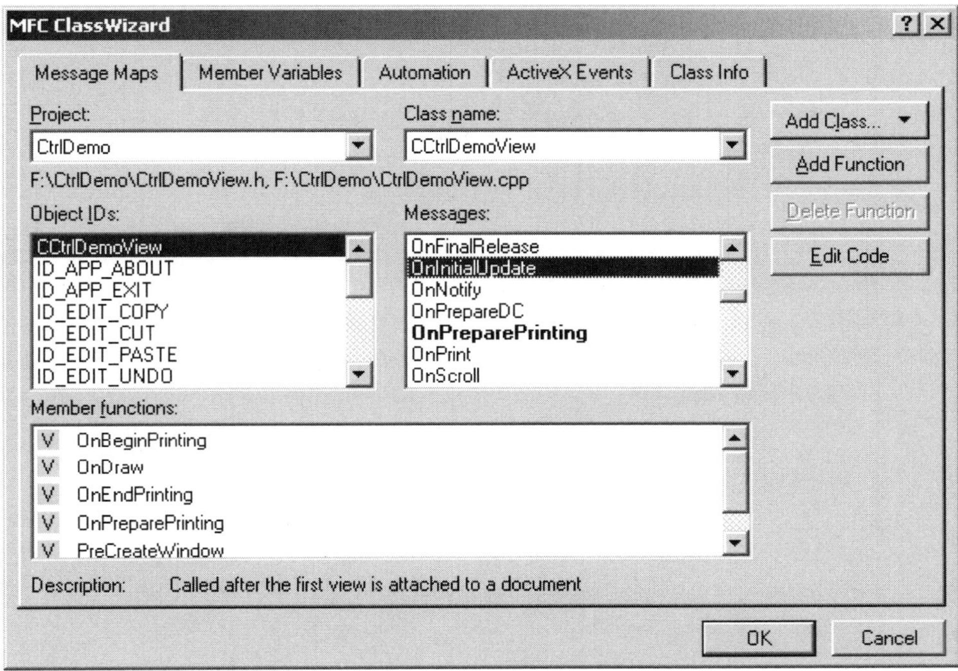

FIGURE 10.2 The InitialUpdate message in ClassWizard.

```
                CRect( 10, 10, 100, 30 ),
                this,
                1 );
}
```

"m_pEditBox = new CEdit;" officially constructs a new CEdit object (allocating memory for it). The next function, *Create()*, then "creates" it; that is, produces an edit box with the specified style and display location.

5. Similarly, generate a handler function for the DestroyWindow command message and add the edit box object destruction code for cleaning up:

```
BOOL CCtrlDemoView::DestroyWindow()
{
      // TODO: Add your specialized code here and/or…
      delete m_pEditBox;
      m_pEditBox = NULL;
      return CView::DestroyWindow();
}
```

6. Compile the application and observe the edit box sitting in the program view area.

We've introduced quite a few new ideas here. Let's review them one by one.

By starting an object with a pointer, we don't waste memory. When we need the object, we create it. When we're finished with it, we delete it, releasing the memory it uses. When you instantiate the object you use the "new" C++ keyword.

In creating the edit box we need to provide several pieces of information as required by the CEdit MFC *Create()* function. First, we must specify the style for the edit box. This is a double word (DWORD) value, which can be a composite of several individual specifications. These values have been defined in MFC and can be used directly without us knowing exactly what their actual numeric values are. All we need to know is that to use them, we "OR" them together using the "|" operator. You can reference these style values (WS_CHILD, WS_VISIBLE, etc.) from the MFC online references.

The second parameter the *Create()* function calls for is the rectangular coordinates of the edit box expressed in the form of an MFC *CRect* class object. A CRect object has four parameters: left, top, right, and bottom. The object CRect(110, 10, 200, 30) scribes a rectangle 90 pixels wide (from 110 to 200), 20 pixels high (from 10 to 30), with the upper-left corner at pixel 110 horizontal and pixel 10 vertical measured downward relative to the *parent* window.

The third parameter is a pointer to the parent CWnd object, which, in our example, is the View (of the CView class derived from the CWnd class), and is therefore identified as "this," a C++ keyword meaning the current object.

The last parameter is an integer value ID. In our example, we merely used at random the value 1.

CREATING A STATIC CONTROL

A static control is created similarly.

1. (Using the previous example for reference) Add a private variable of the CStatic* pointer type in the View class: (CStatic) m_pLblLastname.
2. In the *OnInitialUpdate()* function, enter the code shown in bold:

```
void CCtrlDemoView::OnInitialUpdate()
{
     CView::OnInitialUpdate();
```

```
// TODO: Add your specialized code here and/or...
// Edit box label
m_pLblLastname = new CStatic;
m_pLblLastname->Create( "Lastname:",
     WS_CHILD | WS_VISIBLE | SS_LEFT,
     CRect( 10, 10, 190, 30),
     this );
```

3. Similarly, generate a handler function for the DestroyWindow command message and add the edit box object destruction code for cleaning up:

```
BOOL CCtrlDemoView::DestroyWindow()
{
     // TODO: Add your specialized code here and/or...
     delete m_pLblLastname;
     m_pLblLastname = NULL;
```

4. Compile the program and test it.

As you can see, the approaches to creating the two controls are quite alike. Various other controls are listed next. You should attempt to include them in your own coding to experience the programming process.

CREATING A BUTTON CONTROL

The *Create()* function is:

```
BOOL Create( LPCTSTR lpszCaption, DWORD dwStyle, const RECT& rect,
  CWnd* pParentWnd, UINT nID );
```

Example:

```
   m_pButton->Create( "Data Dialog", WS_CHILD | WS_VISIBLE |
 BS_PUSHBUTTON, CRect( 510, 500, 610, 550), this, 20000);
```

CREATING A CHECK BOX CONTROL

The *Create()* function is the same as CButton, except that the style is different.
Example:

```
    m_pCheck Box->Create( "Member", WS_CHILD | WS_VISIBLE |
BS_CHECKBOX, CRect( 110, 100, 200, 130), this, 20004);
```

CREATING A RADIO BUTTON

The *Create()* function is the same as CButton, except that the style is different. Example:

```
    m_pRadio->Create( "Guest", WS_CHILD | WS_VISIBLE |
BS_AUTORADIOBUTTON, CRect( 110, 300, 200, 330), this, 20004);
```

CREATING A COMBO BOX

The *Create()* function for the combo box is:

```
BOOL Create( DWORD dwStyle, const RECT& rect, CWnd* pParentWnd, UINT
  nID );
```

Example:

```
    m_pCombo->Create( WS_CHILD | WS_VISIBLE | WS_VSCROLL |
CBS_DROPDOWNLIST,
    CRect( 210, 110,400, 200), this, 20006);
    m_pCombo->AddString( "Jeb" );
    m_pCombo->AddString( "Jim" );
    m_pCombo->AddString( "Joan" );
    m_pCombo->AddString( "John" );
    m_pCombo->SetCurSel(0);
```

CREATING A LIST CONTROL

The *Create()* function for the list control is:

```
BOOL Create( DWORD dwStyle, const RECT& rect, CWnd* pParentWnd, UINT
  nID );
```

Example:

```
m_pList->Create( WS_CHILD | WS_VISIBLE | LBS_STANDARD | WS_HSCROLL,
CRect( 210, 10, 400, 100), this, 20007);
m_pList->AddString( "Jeb" );
m_pList->AddString( "Jim" );
m_pList->AddString( "Joan" );
m_pList->AddString( "John" );
m_pList->SetCurSel(0);
```

CREATING A PROGRESS BAR

The *Create()* function is:

```
BOOL Create( DWORD dwStyle, const RECT& rect, CWnd* pParentWnd, UINT
  nID );
```

Example:

```
   m_pProg->Create( WS_CHILD | WS_VISIBLE | PBS_SMOOTH, CRect(
350,200,550,220), this, 2008 );
   m_pProg->SetRange(0,100);
```

CREATING A SLIDER BAR

The *Create()* function is:

```
BOOL Create( DWORD dwStyle, const RECT& rect, CWnd* pParentWnd, UINT
  nID );
```

Example:

```
   m_pSlider->Create( WS_CHILD | WS_VISIBLE | TBS_HORZ, CRect(
50,200,300,230), this, 20009 );
   m_pSlider->SetRange( 0, 100 );
```

CREATING A SPIN CONTROL

The *Create()* function is:

```
BOOL Create( DWORD dwStyle, const RECT& rect, CWnd* pParentWnd, UINT
  nID );
```

Example:

```
     m_pSpin->Create( WS_CHILD | WS_VISIBLE | UDS_SETBUDDYINT |
UDS_AUTOBUDDY,
CRect( 450,10,500,40), this, 20009 );
```

It would be fun to implement a "buddy" by borrowing the code from the DialogDemo you worked on before.

Because they are all derived from the CWnd class, Windows controls' *Create()* functions are much the same in form. They all must be provided with a style prescription, which must at a minimum be WS_CHILD. In most cases, WS_VISIBLE also needs to be specified. Then, a control takes on its own styling parameters.

Each control also must have a CRect description so Windows knows where to place it and how large a control to draw.

All the controls are related to parent windows and every one must have its own unique ID.

11 Dialog and Application Development

Although we used a dialog to facilitate our discussion of Windows controls because it provides us with a resource surface to work with, the dialog itself is the backbone of an application. The dialog-based application is the first Windows desktop application framework you get when developing a new application with AppWizard.

As mentioned, there are two types of dialogs—the modal and the modeless dialog. The modal dialog is easy. All you need is the *DoModal()* function to deploy it. The modeless dialog, in contrast, is a bit more complicated. We'll formally study it in the next chapter, when we have gathered a good understanding of the MFC application classes. In the ensuing chapters, we'll do this and finish up with the issues of user interface.

ANATOMY OF A DIALOG APPLICATION

Now that we have had some experience working with a dialog-based application, let's take time out to study its construction.

The "backbone" of the dialog-based application is the Application class. In the **DialogDemo** project it is the CDialogDemoApp class, derived from the CWinApp class, the granddaddy MFC class for applications.

In this Application class there is basically one function: *InitInstance(). InitInstance()*is equivalent in spirit to the *main()* function of a console-based C application (or the submain function in Visual Basic, for that matter). Because Windows manages multiple applications concurrently, each application is just one instance of *something*. This "something" is a code object. In our case, it is the first program code being executed.

The first function called in the *InitInstance()* function is the *AfxEnableControlContainer()* function. It enables the application to work with ActiveX controls, which you will learn later.

Next, one of the following functions is called: *Enable3dControls()* or *Enable3dControlsStatic()*. As to which is called, it depends on the _AFXDLL setting. If it is set, *Enable3dControls()* is called that causes the CTL3D32.DLL code library to be loaded at runtime. Otherwise, the library functions will be linked and become a part of the compiled program.

This switch is set when you make the choice in Figure 11.1, and it shows up in the Project settings (Figures 11.2 through 11.4).

After these fundamental environmental issues have been dealt with, the application deploys the main dialog:

```
CDialogDemoDlg dlg;
m_pMainWnd = &dlg;
int nResponse = dlg.DoModal();
```

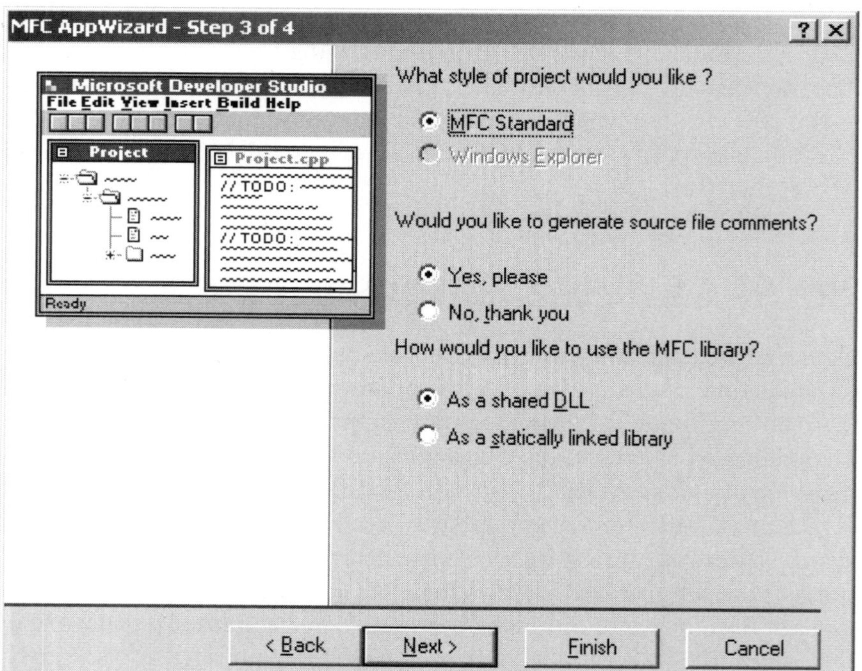

FIGURE 11.1 AppWizard Step 3, electing to share DLL.

FIGURE 11.2 The Project->Settings command.

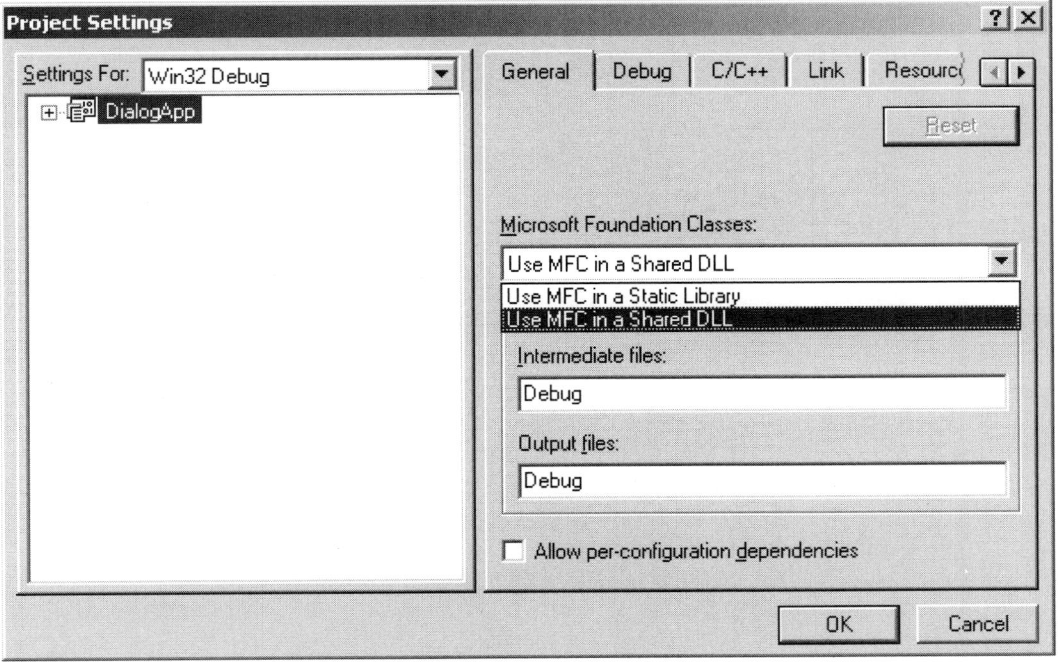

FIGURE 11.3 Project settings: DLL sharing.

Here the Application class provides a member variable **m_pMainWnd** to track the dialog so that whenever you like, you can use it to do something with.

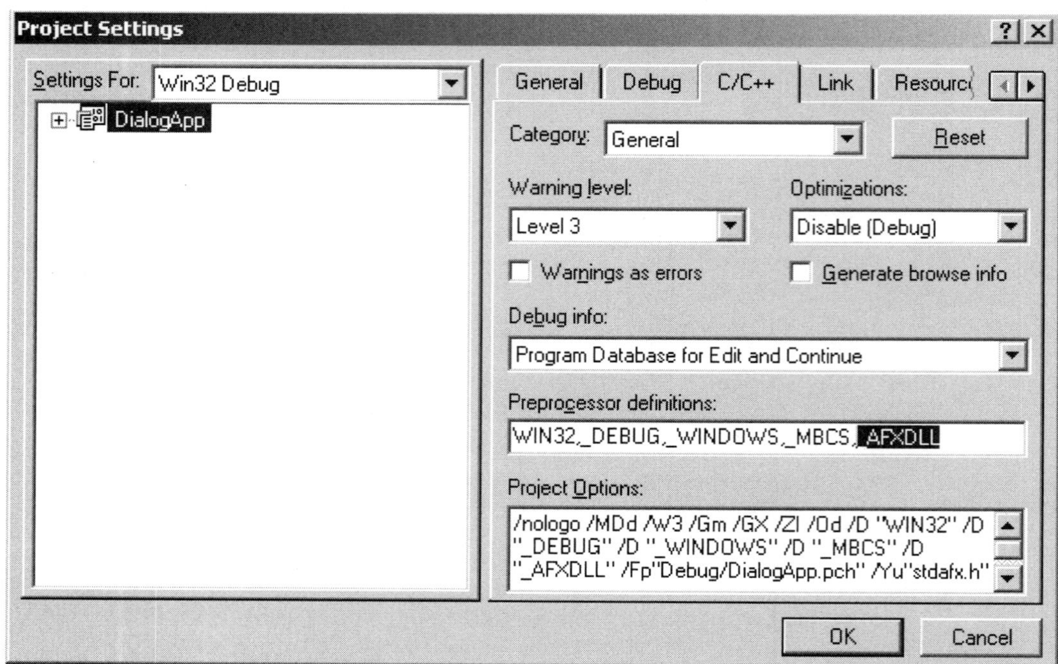

FIGURE 11.4 The _AFXDLL setting.

When the logic returns after the user dispenses with the dialog, the framework even prepares you to handle the aftermath events:

```
if (nResponse == IDOK)
{
     // TODO: Place code here to handle when the dialog is
     //  dismissed with OK
}
else if (nResponse == IDCANCEL)
{
     // TODO: Place code here to handle when the dialog is
     //  dismissed with Cancel
}
```

As you can see, the logic sequence is quite simple. It is something that as a programmer you could have written yourself. However, the automatically generated code does make life more comfortable.

THE MODELESS DIALOG

Before we bring our introductory study of Window GUI to a close, let us revisit the dialog box, which was introduced at the very beginning of this part of the book.

The dialog window we have learned stays on the screen once it has been deployed, and prevents a user from interacting with other parts of the program display, even though they may be visible, until the dialog window is closed. This type of dialog is known as a modal dialog, and in MFC is displayed with the *DoModal()* function.

A dialog window that stays on the screen but does not deter a user from working with other visual elements is called a *modeless* dialog. We will now look at this type of dialog and gain an insight into how it works.

In the following project we will design an application that will display two child dialog windows without having to close each in turn; that is, each dialog can remain open on the screen until you close it. The application will use the SDI framework so that we can create menu commands to control the deployments of the child dialogs. At the same time, it also will accord us the opportunity to complete work on menus that has been left unfinished, thus accomplishing two missions at the same time.

1. Create a new MFC SDI application and name it **ModelessDlg**.
2. Insert a new dialog and assign it the ID of IDD_DIALOG_CHILD1.
3. Insert another dialog and ID it IDD_DIALOG_CHILD2. (You can even copy IDD_DIALOG_CHILD1 and paste it.)
4. Create classes for the two new child dialogs and name the classes CDlgChild1 and CDlgChild2, respectively.
5. Add a private pointer variable of the CDlgChild1 class to the CMainFrame class and name it **m_pDlgChild1** (Figure 11.5). Make sure that you add the "#include "DlgChild1.h"" statement to the MainFrm.h file.

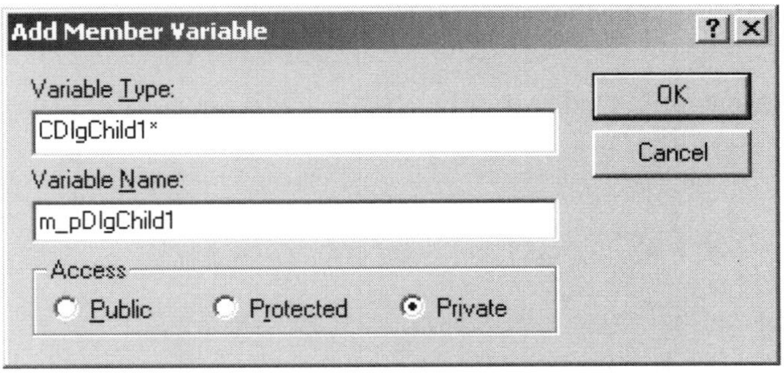

FIGURE 11.5 Adding a dialog pointer variable.

6. Similarly, add a second private pointer variable named **m_pDlgChild2** of the CDlgChild2 class.
7. Provide proper #include directives in the MainFrm.h file:

```
#include "DlgChild1.h"
#include "DlgChild2.h"
```

8. Initialize these two variables to NULL somewhere in the CMainFrame class' *OnCreate()* function:

```
int CMainFrame::OnCreate(LPCREATESTRUCT lpCreateStruct)
{
     m_pDlgChild1 = NULL;
     m_pDlgChild2 = NULL;
     if (CFrameWnd::OnCreate(lpCreateStruct) == -1)
          return -1;
```

These pointer variables will be used to create the child dialogs.

Now, we'll create two commands to launch the child dialogs.

9. Add two commands to the View menu command group after a separator as shown in Figure 11.6. They will be automatically assigned the IDs of ID_VIEW_CHILD1 and ID_VIEW_CHILD2.

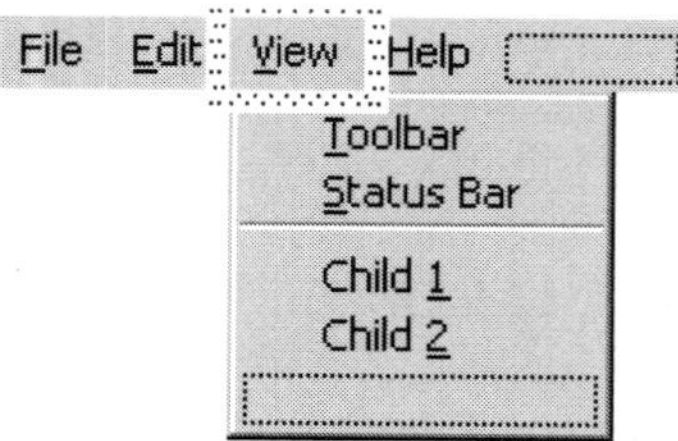

FIGURE 11.6 Adding New "Child" commands to the menu.

10. Add a handler function for the ID_VIEW_CHILD1 command message:

```
void CMainFrame::OnViewChild1()
{
     // TODO: Add your command handler code here
     m_pDlgChild1 = new CDlgChild1;
     m_pDlgChild1->Create( IDD_DIALOG_CHILD1, this );
     m_pDlgChild1->ShowWindow( SW_SHOW );
}
```

11. Similarly, add a function to launch the CDlgChild2 dialog, using its own ID.
12. Compile the program and test it. Launch each dialog only once, close each, and then exit the program because we have not finished our work just yet.

As you can see, modeless dialogs stay on the screen but do not obstruct you from moving on to other parts of the program.

The logic of creating modeless dialogs is simple. You instantiate the object ("m_pDlgChild1 = new CDlgChild1;"), create it by supplying it with the necessary prescriptions ("Create(IDD_DIALOG_CHILD1, this)"), and then make it visible ("ShowWindow(SW_SHOW)").

The reason our program is incomplete is because whereas the *OnViewChild()* functions create the dialogs, the dialog closing mechanisms (OK and Cancel buttons) do not destroy the dialog and release their memory subscriptions. This allows the same commands to be exercised repeatedly, each time creating a new dialog; therefore, eating up computer memories, but never returning them to the system. Moreover, every time a same new dialog is created, the dialog pointer points to the new object and abandons the previous ones, leaving them behind as orphans and inaccessible. What we need whenever we work with modeless dialogs is a dialog management plan in which you can create only one dialog of a kind at a time, and each time a dialog is closed, its memory is returned to the system.

As it turns out, there are several ways to accomplish these goals, with relative degrees of implementation difficulty. One way is to create each child dialog only once, simply hide it when it is "closed," and destroy it only when the program exits. Let's see how this scheme is carried out.

13. Modify the *OnViewChild1()* function as follows:

```
void CMainFrame::OnViewChild1()
{
    // TODO: Add your command handler code here
    if ( m_pDlgChild1 == NULL )
    {
        m_pDlgChild1 = new CDlgChild1;
        m_pDlgChild1->Create( IDD_DIALOG_CHILD1, this );
    }
    m_pDlgChild1->ShowWindow( SW_SHOW );
}
```

First, the pointer is tested for NULL. It would be NULL if it has not yet pointed to anything. In such a case, the child dialog is created and made visible. Otherwise, as long as the child dialog exists (therefore its pointer is not NULL), it is simply made visible.

14. Modify the *OnOK()* function in the child dialog as follows:

```
void CDlgChild1::OnOK()
{
      // TODO: Add extra validation here
      ShowWindow( SW_HIDE );
}
```

All this does is, when the user clicks OK, the program merely makes the dialog invisible. In fact, you can remove the Cancel button if you like, or you should apply the same OK button logic to it as well.

15. Use ClassWizard to add a handler function to the CMainFrame class' WM_CLOSE message (at which time any child dialog that exists would still be alive):

```
void CMainFrame::OnClose()
{
      // TODO: Add your message handler code here...
      if ( m_pDlgChild1 != NULL )
      {
            m_pDlgChild1->ShowWindow( SW_HIDE );
            m_pDlgChild1->DestroyWindow();
            delete m_pDlgChild1;
      }
      CFrameWnd::OnClose();
}
```

16. Apply the same treatment for the second child dialog.
17. Compile and test the program.

Deactivating Menu Commands

The program now works properly. However, it is not quite as sophisticated as we would like it to be. For one, when a child dialog is up, technically the command to display it should be deactivated until the dialog has become invisible. This can be remedied, but it will take some coordination between the main frame and the dialogs.

Up to now the dialog has been doing its own thing (hide and show) while the main frame uses its existence to control their appearances. If the menu commands are to gray out when a dialog is already up, the main frame needs to know the dialog's current status, and only the dialog can communicate this information. Therefore, the dialog must know where the main frame is so that it can work with it. We'll now see how this can be accomplished.

The trick, as it turns out, lies in the main frame passing its identity on to the dialog when the latter is created.

1. First, make the following modification to the DlgChild1.h file:

```
class CMainFrame;
class CDlgChild1 : public CDialog
{
// Construction
public:
     CDlgChild1(CWnd* pParent = NULL);
     CDlgChild1(CMainFrame* pParent = NULL);
```

We are changing the dialog class' constructor to inherit a pointer from the CMainFrame class instead of the default CWnd class. Because the CDlgChild class has no knowledge of the CMainFrame class, the preceding "class CMainFrame;" *forward declaration* tells the compiler that it is defined down the line.

2. Modify the CDlgChild1.cpp file as follows:

```
CDlgChild1::CDlgChild1(CWnd* pParent /*=NULL*/)
     : CDialog(CDlgChild1::IDD, pParent)
{
     //{{AFX_DATA_INIT(CDlgChild1)
          // NOTE: the ClassWizard will add member…
     //}}AFX_DATA_INIT
}
CDlgChild1::CDlgChild1(CMainFrame* pFrame)
{
}
```

This is called *overloading* the constructor. That means we can construct the dialog box in one of two ways.

3. Next, add a pointer variable to the child dialog class to hold the memory address of the CMainFrame class that creates it:

```
     DECLARE_MESSAGE_MAP()
private:
     CMainFrame* m_pFrame;
```

4. Modify the new dialog constructor to preserve the mainframe pointer when the dialog is constructed:

```
CDlgChild1::CDlgChild1(CMainFrame* pFrame)
{
     m_pFrame = pFrame;
}
```

At this point, the dialog knows where to pass information on to the mainframe.

For the mainframe, it needs a variable to track the dialog's visibility status.

5. Add a Boolean variable to the CMainFrame class:

```
// Implementation
public:
     BOOL m_bChild1Visible;
     virtual ~CMainFrame();
```

6. Initialize it to FALSE in the CMainFrame class' *OnCreate()* function; that is, make the Child1 dialog initially invisible:

```
int CMainFrame::OnCreate(LPCREATESTRUCT lpCreateStruct)
{
     m_bChild1Visible = FALSE:
```

7. Modify the *OnViewChild1()* function to use the new child dialog constructor, and set this variable to TRUE:

```
void CMainFrame::OnViewChild1()
{
     // TODO: Add your command handler code here
     if ( m_pDlgChild1 == NULL )
     {
          m_pDlgChild1 = new CDlgChild1( this );
          m_pDlgChild1->Create( IDD_DIALOG_CHILD1 );
     }
     m_pDlgChild1->ShowWindow( SW_SHOW );
     m_bChild1Visible = TRUE:
}
```

8. Modify the *OnOK()* function in the dialog class to set this variable to FALSE:

```
void CDlgChild1::OnOK()
{
```

```
        // TODO: Add extra validation here
        // CDialog::OnOK();
        // m_pFrame->DeleteChild1();
        m_pFrame->m_bChild1Visible = FALSE;
        ShowWindow( SW_HIDE );
}
```

Now we'll use the visibility variable to control the menu command's activeness state.

9. Bring up ClassWizard for the UPDATE_COMMAND_UI message for the ID_VIEW_CHILD1 command ID (Figure 11.7).

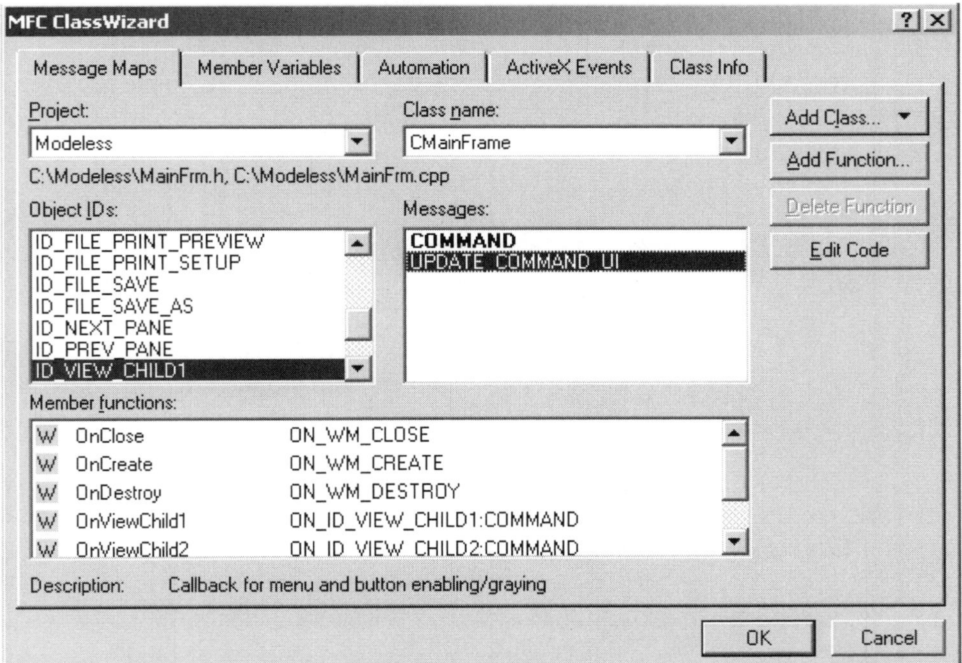

FIGURE 11.7 The UPDATE_COMMAND_UI message in ClassWizard.

10. Add a processing function for it as follows:

```
void CMainFrame::OnUpdateViewChild1(CCmdUI* pCmdUI)
{
        // TODO: Add your command update UI handler code…
        if ( m_bChild1Visible )
```

```
            pCmdUI->Enable( FALSE );
        else
            pCmdUI->Enable( TRUE );
}
```

In this function that is invoked when the menu item is about to go active, the m_bChild1Visible value is used to determine the state of the command. If bChild1Visible indicates that the Child1 dialog is visible—that is, it is up—it grays out the command. Otherwise, it enables the command.

11. Compile the program and test it.

Controlling the Modeless Dialog Programmatically

A modeless dialog is often used to create a screen presence such as a general instruction, and stays on the screen for the duration of an entire program sequence or even the application itself. In such a case, you'll need to control the modeless dialog entirely from the application without user intervention. We'll demonstrate such an implementation by deploying a general information modeless dialog for the Modeless application. In this exercise, we'll create a general info dialog, deploy it at the beginning of the application, sustain it through and bar the user from closing it, and then close it just before the application terminates.

ON THE CD

1. In the **ModelessDlg** project, insert a new dialog with the ID of IDD_DIALOG_INFO, and remove all buttons from it, including the system menu, so that the only way for the user to close the dialog is with [Alt-F4].
2. Create a class for the new dialog named CDlgGeneralInfo.
3. Add a member function to the application's View class:

```
#include "DlgGeneralInfo.h"
...
private:
     CDlgGeneralInfo* m_pDlgInfo;
```

4. Override the *OnInitialUpdate()* function in the View class (or in the MainFrame class if you prefer) and create the dialog there:

```
void CModelessView::OnInitialUpdate()
{
     CView::OnInitialUpdate();
```

```
    // TODO: Add your specialized code here…
    m_pDlgInfo = new  CDlgGeneralInfo( this );
    m_pDlgInfo->Create( IDD_DIALOG_INFO );
    m_pDlgInfo->ShowWindow( SW_SHOW );
}
```

5. Close the dialog in the View class's overridden *DestroyWindow()* function:

```
BOOL CModelessView::DestroyWindow()
{
    // TODO: Add your specialized code here…
    m_pDlgInfo->EndDialog( 1 );
    return CView::DestroyWindow();
}
```

CDialog's *EndDialog()* member function closes the dialog with an integer parameter. In fact, when the *DoModal()* function closes a modal dialog, it calls this same *EndDialog()* function and returns the integer value, informing the caller how the dialog is closed. IDOK and IDCANCEL are two such values. Here we used an arbitrary value because we are not really using the value for decision-making.

6. Finally, generate a message handler function for the ON_CLOSE message in CDlgGeneralInfo and add the following code there:

```
void CDlgGeneralInfo::OnClose()
{
    // TODO: Add your message handler code here…
    return;
    CDialog::OnClose();
}
```

The return statement bypasses the *OnClose()* function so the dialog isn't closed, even though the user might have pressed [Alt-F4].

Try this program and see the modeless dialog stay up.

Clearly, modeless dialogs are more complicated to implement than modal dialogs. It requires a lot more vigilance on the part of the programmer to ensure that they behave properly.

While a modal dialog is deployed with a single *DoModal()* command, you create a modeless dialog with *Create()* and destroy it with *DestroyWindow()*. In between, you must enact a sound dialog-management policy.

THE USER INTERFACE

If you have been using the **DialogDemo** project to try out the basic Windows 95 controls, you'd have ended up with a DlgData dialog that looks something like Figure 11.8.

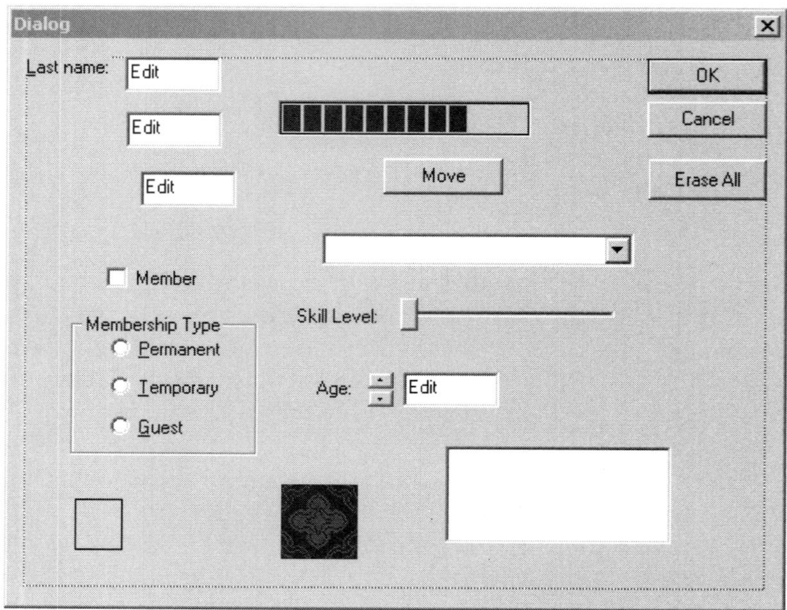

FIGURE 11.8 The Control Trial Program dialog.

This mumble-jumble is simply unacceptable as a professional piece of work.

For a user interface to be considered of professional quality, it must be good looking, and easy and logical to use. When broken down, there are three things that you need to do: align and group the controls, arrange them in a reasonable tab order, and provide quick keys for fast command access and object focus.

Component Layout

Working with the VC++ IDE it is easy to lay out the objects. The procedure is as follows:

1. Hold down the [Ctrl] key and click on the objects you want included in the layout effort to select them (Figure 11.9).

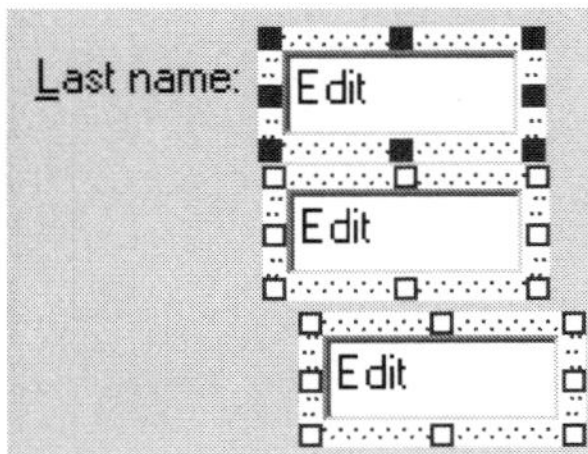

FIGURE 11.9 Selecting objects.

The last one you select will have heavy handles and will be the "anchor," defining the anchor point of the alignment.

2. Choose the Layout command and the appropriate subcommand to align the objects (Figure 11.10).

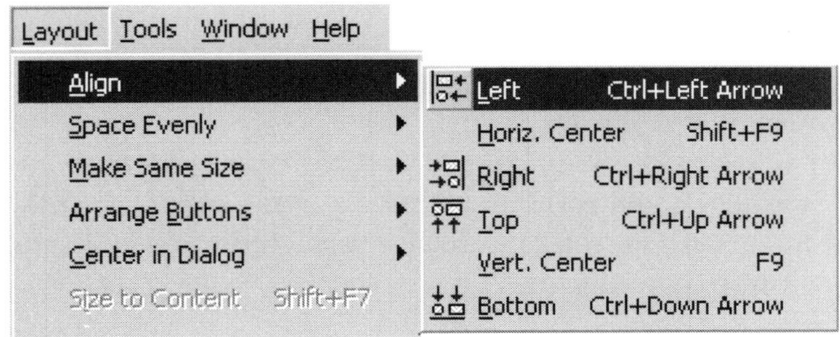

FIGURE 11.10 Aligning objects.

3. Save the new layout by saving the project.

Quick Keys

The easiest way to provide quick keys is to underscore the letter that is intended to be a quick key. For example, express the label "Lastname" with the code "&Lastname."

However, you should make sure that there are no duplicate quick keys in the same control area. You do this by using the Check Mnemonics command from the context menu (Figure 11.11).

If there are duplicates, they will be reported (Figure 11.12).

Ask for the conflicting items to be selected so that you can track them down and fix them.

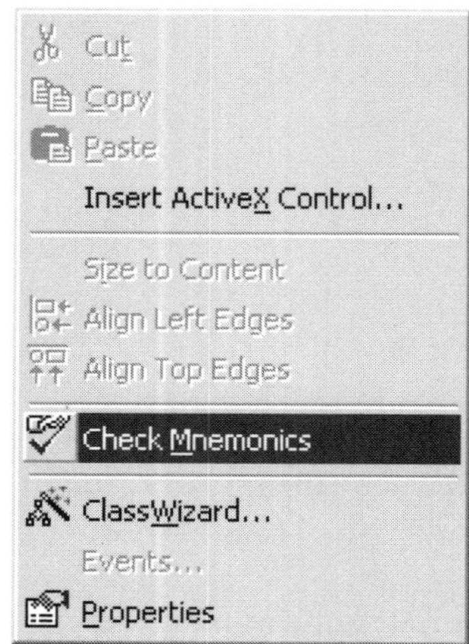

FIGURE 11.11 The Check Mnemonics command.

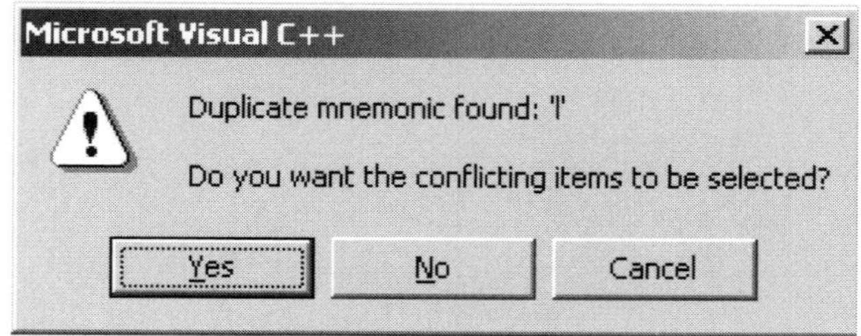

FIGURE 11.12 Conflicting mnemonics.

For the objects that don't come with labels, such as the edit box or the combo box, how does one provide quick keys? As it is, the object's identification is governed by the label (static control) that precedes it in the tab order. Thus, pressing the quick key in the label in front of an edit box will set the focus on the edit box rather than the label.

Tab Order

Setting tab order is also easy in VC++. Choose the Layout->Tab Order command and the tab stops of the object will be revealed, as shown in Figure 11.13.

Clicking on the objects one by one (including those that are not meant to be tab stops, such as labels and groups) in the intended tab order will reset the order. If you miss an object when clicking the mouse, just do it from scratch again.

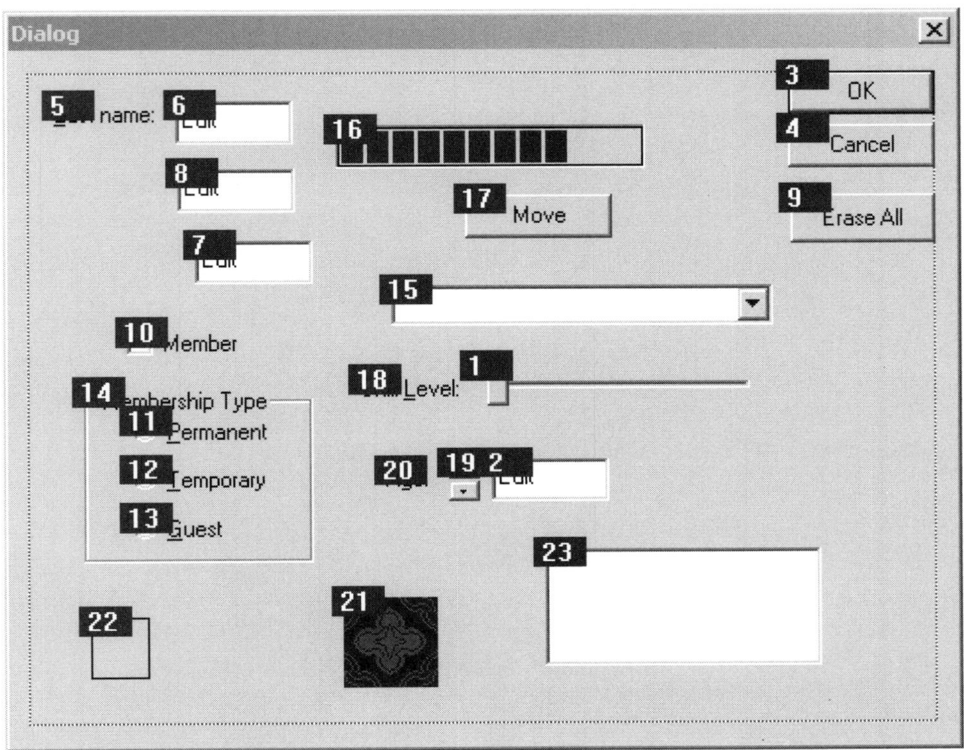

FIGURE 11.13 Tab orders.

PART

III VC++ Projects

In VC++, a work session is called a *project*. Unlike a traditional C or C++ application, a VC++ project entails much more than just the requisite header (.h) and source code (.cpp) files. As you saw in the examples that we performed, a VC++ project has extra components such as resources, and the development/compiler environment has tools such as AppWizard and ClassWizard to help us increase productivity and organize our work. In this part of the book, we'll explore the VC++ projects and their development environment, with an eye to harnessing as much as possible the treasures that will enable us to do our work quickly, efficiently, and with as few unnecessary errors as possible.

12 Working with the IDE

First things first, let's get to know our integrated development environment in some depth by exploring the key facilities that it furnishes.

THE MFC CLASS LIBRARY REFERENCES

VC++ comes with an extensive reference package, and knowing how to exploit its power can greatly enhance our learning of the language and MFC. So far, you have experienced IntelliSense, which is a form of onscreen help. However, the MSDN library is where the real goodies are. Let us use an example to illustrate its use.

1. From the VC++ IDE, choose the Help->Contents command, or execute the MSDN Library icon on the Windows desktop.

The MSDN Library application is launched.

2. Maneuver to Class Library Reference as shown in Figure 12.1, making sure that Active Subset is set to "Visual C++ Documentation."

You should see the entire MFC listed.

3. Select the CDialog tree branch and expand it (Figure 12.2).

You should see all the CDialog member functions listed.

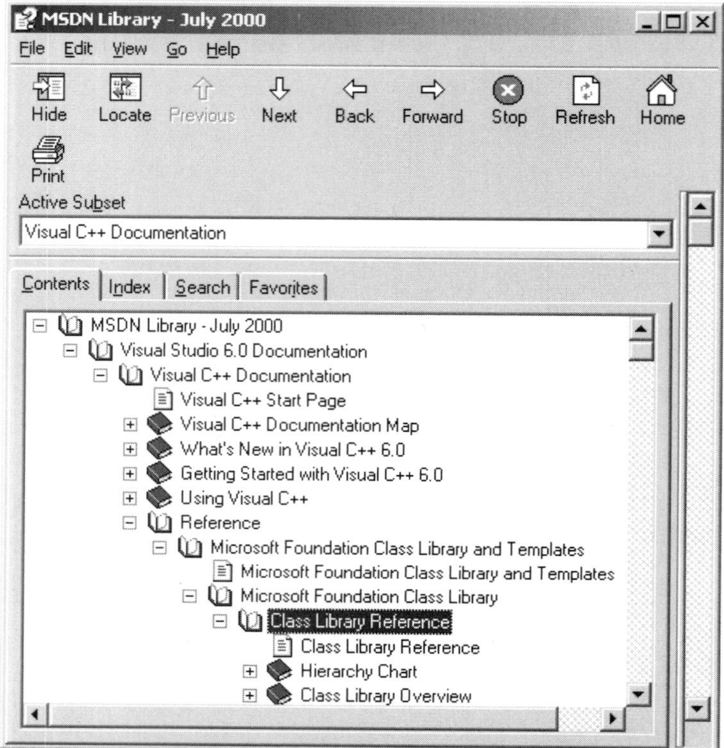

FIGURE 12.1 MSDN Library online reference.

4. Select CDialog::DoModal.

You can now read up on the *DoModal()* function. It tells you that it is a virtual function, and that it returns an integer. If you move down a bit further on the page you'll see an example showing how the function is used, and how the function's return value can be put to good use.

5. If you select the CDialog class tree node, you'll get to see its lineage (Figure 12.3).

Onscreen help shows us that the CDialog class is derived from the CWnd class. Therefore, from now on when we want to know what class functions CDialog has, we can read up on the CDialog references *and* the CWnd references. For example, the CWnd references show a *GetWindowText()* function. Although the CDialog

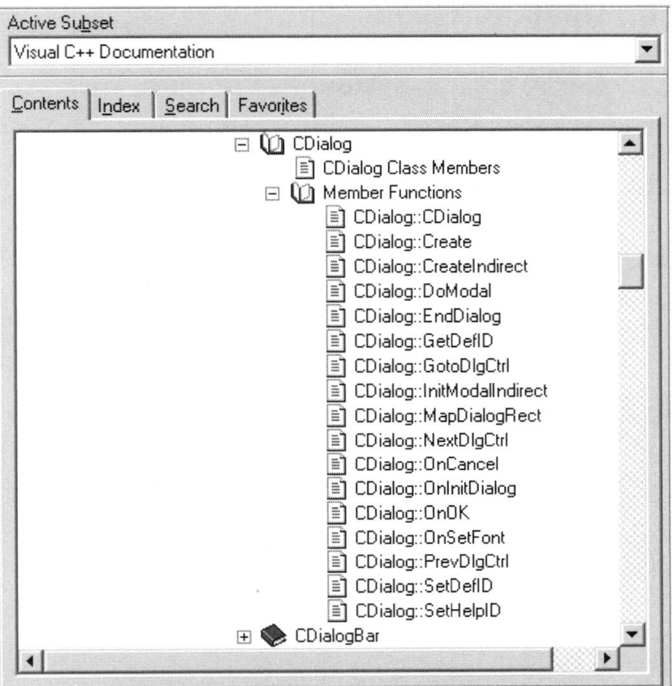

FIGURE 12.2 CDialog class references.

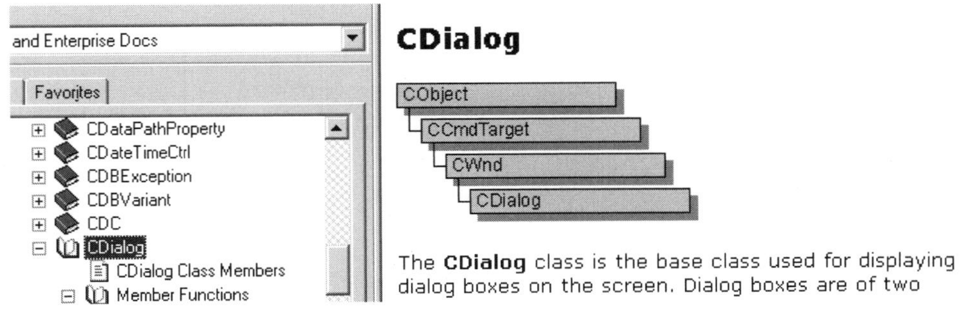

FIGURE 12.3 MFC lineage.

references don't show it, we know we can use it because CDialog is derived from CWnd.

CONTEXT-SENSITIVE HELP

Not only is the VC++ MSDN onscreen help extensive and well structured in its coverage, you can access a search target from context as well. Take the *SetWindowText()* and *GetWindowText()* functions we have learned as example.

1. In **DialogDemo**, place the cursor on the *SetWindowText()* function and press [F1].

MSDN takes you immediately to the possible support points (Figure 12.4).

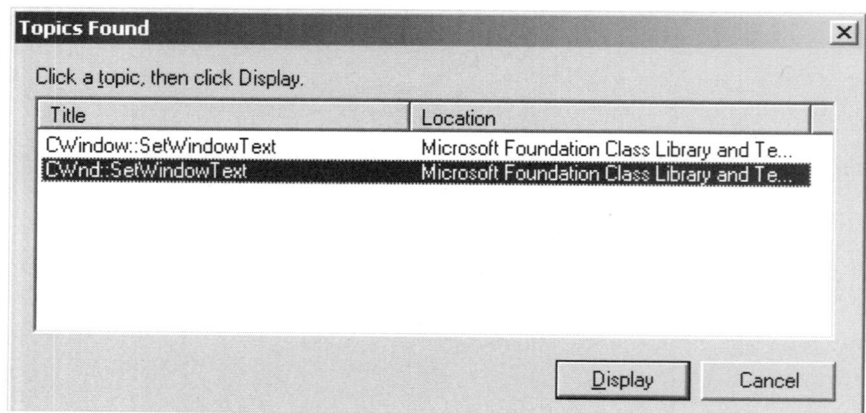

FIGURE 12.4 Selecting an onscreen reference topic.

2. Click Display.

You are at the *SetWindowText()* references.

Using context-sensitive help for learning, especially when tracing example programs, can take you a long way toward understanding MFC.

Taking Advantage of the IDE

Chapter 10 clearly demonstrated how much more involved—not harder, just more work—it is to implement Windows GUI through coding as compared to using the IDE facilities. Unfortunately, having to code is unavoidable. After all, that's what programming is all about. Fortunately, there is a way to cull the best points from both approaches that will help us code controls with less stress.

The most taxing work in coding controls occurs in determining the geometries of the controls and maintaining a set of unique IDs, both tasks done well by the

IDE. Therefore, when we create controls through coding, we should let the IDE do the overhead work for us. Again, we will see how this is done through an example.

Continuing with the last example project **CtrlDemo**, let's say we want to add a command button to the View class, which does not have a visual surface for us to draw on. First, develop the button on such a surface elsewhere.

1. Open the IDD_ABOUTBOX resource and enlarge it to approximate the View window.
2. Use the toolbox to visually install a command button on it, and assign it the ID of IDC_BUTTON_MESSAGE (Figure 12.5).

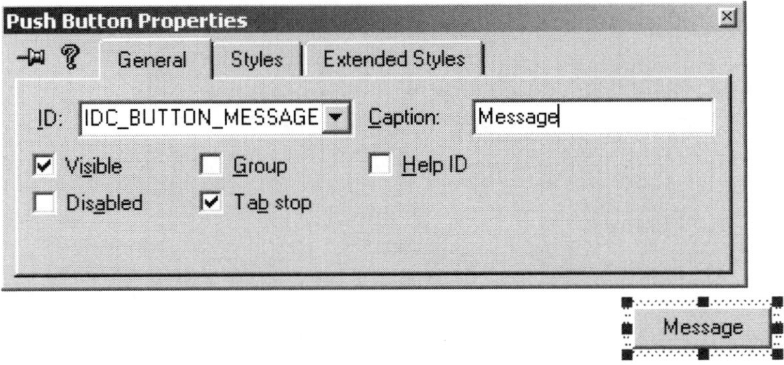

FIGURE 12.5 Assigning a button ID.

3. In ClassWizard, add a handler function for the button's BN_CLICK command message:

```
void CAboutDlg::OnButtonMessage()
{
	// TODO: Add your control notification handler…
	MessageBox( "It works!", "Button", MB_OK );
}
```

You can compile the program now and test the code to ensure that it indeed works. Now let's understand what we have done.

4. Open the Resource.h file.

You should see the definition of the IDC_BUTTON_MESSAGE ID. Its value is 1000, generated by the IDE:

```
#define IDR_MAINFRAME                    128
#define IDR_CTRLDETYPE                   129
#define IDC_BUTTON_MESSAGE               1000
// Next default values for new objects
//
#ifdef APSTUDIO_INVOKED
#ifndef APSTUDIO_READONLY_SYMBOLS
```

5. If you prefer, you can use the "Find In File" facility to identify where this ID is used (see Figure 12.6).

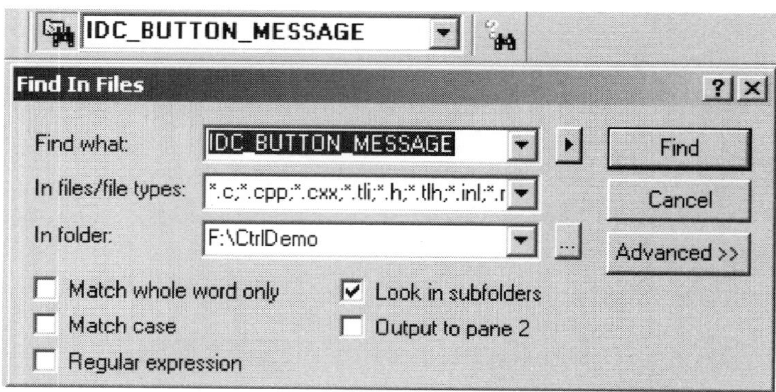

FIGURE 12.6 The Find in Files dialog.

Next, we turn to see the code generated.

6. Use the "Find In File" facility to determine where the function name "On-ButtonMessage" occurs.
7. You should see that it appears at three different locations throughout the project: It is in the function body itself, in the class message map declaration section, and in the message map.

Now that IDE has done its surrogate work, we will transplant the button elements to where we want them to be.

8. First, if you have not done so in the last exercise, create the button in the View class' *OnInitialUpdate()* function as follows, using the geometry provided by the surrogate button:

```
    m_pButton = new CButton;
    m_pButton->Create( "Message", WS_CHILD | WS_VISIBLE |
BS_PUSHBUTTON, CRect(400,250,480,280), this, IDC_BUTTON_MESSAGE );
```

9. Second, move the command code to the corresponding locations in the View class. (You can actually copy the code to the new locations, and comment out the originals.)

In CCtrlDemoView.h:

```
// Generated message map functions
protected:
    //{{AFX_MSG(CCtrlDemoView)
        // NOTE - the ClassWizard will add and…
        //    DO NOT EDIT what you see in these…
    afx_msg void OnButtonMessage();
    //}}AFX_MSG
    DECLARE_MESSAGE_MAP()
```

In CCtrlDemoView.cpp:

```
/////////////////////////////////////////////////////////////////////////
//////// CCtrlDemoView
IMPLEMENT_DYNCREATE(CCtrlDemoView, CView)
BEGIN_MESSAGE_MAP(CCtrlDemoView, CView)
    //{{AFX_MSG_MAP(CCtrlDemoView)
        // NOTE - the ClassWizard will add and…
        //    DO NOT EDIT what you see in these…
    ON_BN_CLICKED(IDC_BUTTON_MESSAGE, OnButtonMessage)
    //}}AFX_MSG_MAP
    // Standard printing commands
    ON_COMMAND(ID_FILE_PRINT, CView::OnFilePrint)
    ON_COMMAND(ID_FILE_PRINT_DIRECT, CView::OnFilePrint)
    ON_COMMAND(ID_FILE_PRINT_PREVIEW, CView::OnFilePrintPreview)
END_MESSAGE_MAP()
and,
void CCtrlDemoView::OnButtonMessage()
{
    // TODO: Add your control notification handler code here
    MessageBox( "It works!", "Button", MB_OK );
}
```

10. Finally, compile the program to verify that the command in the View works, then delete the button in the About dialog, and return the About dialog to its original size.

RECYCLING CODE

What we just did is nothing new for seasoned programmers, and recycling code does not stop within the boundaries of a single application or project. What is nice is that the Visual C++ IDE actually provides means for us to borrow code from ourselves.

Inserting a Project in a Workspace

Let's say while working on the CtrlDemo project, we realize that we can use some of the code developed in the DialogDemo project.

1. Open the CtrlDemo project.
2. In ClassView, select the main class tree node and choose the Project-> Insert Project into Workspace command (Figure 12.7).

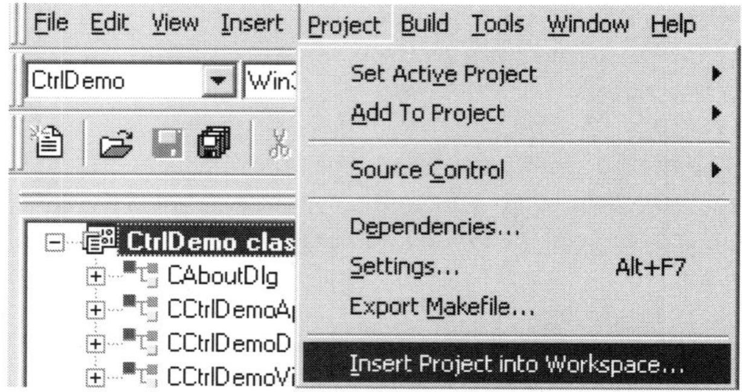

FIGURE 12.7 The Insert Project into Workspace command.

3. Select DialogDemo in the "Insert Project into Workspace" window (Figure 12.8).

Now you have two projects in the same workspace, with one of them being the active project. That means you can compile and test it.

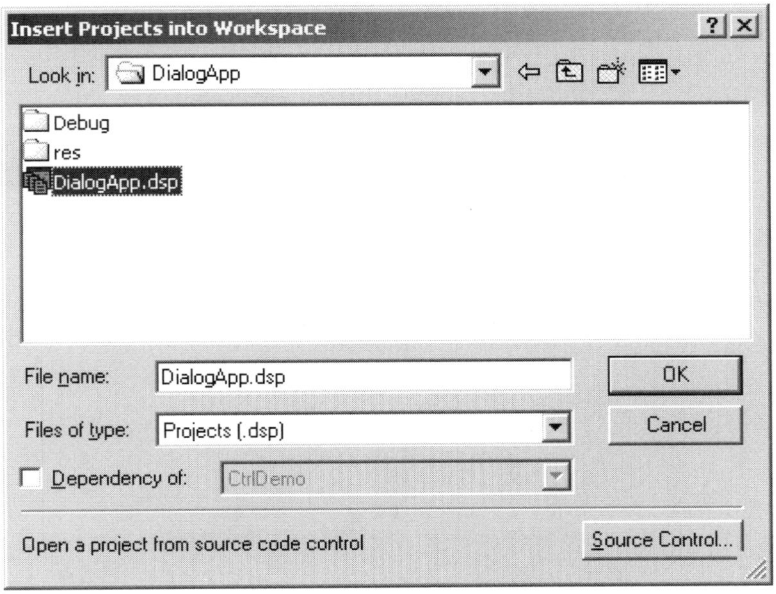

FIGURE 12.8 Inserting a project into the current workspace.

To activate a project, in ClassView, select the project's main class tree node, bring up the context menu, and then choose the Set as Active Project command (Figure 12.9).

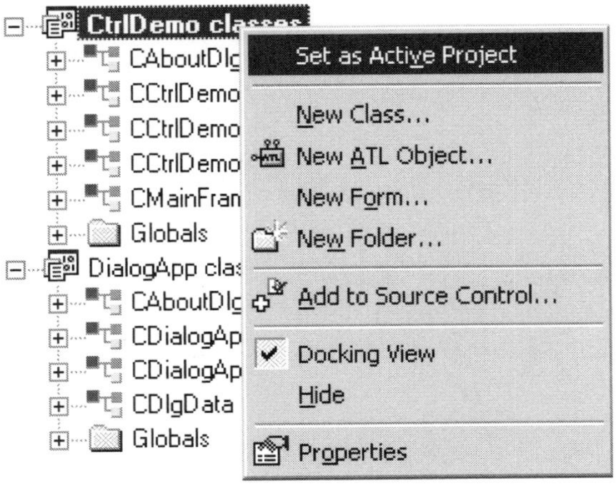

FIGURE 12.9 The Set as Active Project command.

Once you have a project inserted in a workspace, whether it is active or not, you can work with it as any normal project. You can open its resource, select a resource, copy it, and paste it into another project, for instance. This way, you don't have to recreate work that you have already done—just recycle it.

Removing a Project

To remove an inactive project from the workspace, select its main class tree node in ClassView and press [Delete].

13 Error Handling

Before we continue with our study of VC++ and MFC, there is one important topic to discuss so we don't have to deal with it explicitly in the rest of the book, thus simplifying our forthcoming work. The topic is error handling. In this section, we'll explore the various schemes that we can employ to minimize the chances of error occurring in our applications.[1]

FUNCTION RETURN VALUE

Unlike virtually all the computer languages before it, C has error handling built in to the syntax. This is because outside of the basic data types, structures, and logic controls, an entire C program pretty much consists of functions. A main C program module, *main()*, itself is a function, and practically everything in it are functions.

By design, a function has a *type*. Other than *void*, all other types return values. This value is a form of error handling mechanism because it informs us about the status of the function.

Take the CDialog class's *OnInitDialog()* function for example. If it returns a TRUE or nonzero value, it means that Windows might set the focus to the first control on the dialog. Otherwise, you have to set the focus yourself. This return value allows the rest of the program to coordinate with the function.

The CDialog class's *DoModal()* function is another such example. The returned integer tells us how the dialog is closed.

[1] You can almost say that all applications are likely to have errors, or bugs in them, because they are the products of the human mind, and the human mind is known to be frail. Therefore, we can at best reduce errors from happening; we cannot truly guarantee that they can be eradicated.

Because of this built-in advantage, in using functions we should involve return values proactively, which will help to avoid much otherwise unnecessary guesswork, thus reducing the chance of error. In short, get into the habit of writing code in the form of:

```
if ( function() == return-value )
{
}
else
{
}
```

This practice can preclude many potential errors from becoming real ones.

EXCEPTION HANDLING

There are, however, situations in which explicit operational statuses are hard to pin down, or that the causal permutations are so numerous that return values alone cannot do a good job of identifying the error. In such cases, a "catch-all" mechanism akin to the Basic language's "ON ERROR GOTO" may prove more desirable. Well, VC++ has such an error exception-handling device too, the *try-throw-and-catch* construct.

In a try-throw-and-catch code you enclose a suspect code patch in a *try* block and *throw* an *exception* (much like Basic's ON ERROR GOTO), and provide the reaction to the thrown error in a *catch* code block. Take a look at the following sample code:

```
int main(int argc, char* argv[])
{
	int	i = 1;
	char*	errorMsg = "Division by zero.\n";
	try
	{
		if ( i == 0 )
			throw errorMsg;
		else
		{
			int	iResult;
			iResult = 10 / i;
			cout << iResult << '\n';
		}
	}
	catch ( char* msg )
```

```
        {
              cout << msg;
        }
        return 0;
}
```

This is a little console program that has but one function—*main()*. The program has but one purpose—divide a number by another. However, if unmonitored, a division by zero would spell disaster. Therefore, a mechanism is constructed to *catch* the occasion when a division by 0 occurs and *throw an exception* for it.

The suspect portion of the code—that is, where the error can occur—is placed inside a *try* block. In the *try* block we test the divisor for 0 value. Should it be the case, we throw an exception by *handing off* a string message:

```
if ( i == 0 )
      throw errorMsg;
```

The string message is *caught* by the code inside the *catch* block, which, in this example, outputs it and the code moves sequentially forward ending the program. If the divisor is legitimate, nothing will be thrown, and the catch code block is skipped and never invoked.

Of course, any programmer would have noticed that this entire example could have been handled with a simple *if* structure, but that's not the point. This example illustrates the form of the *try-throw-catch* mechanism, and it can be made very complicated to handle very complicated error conditions. For example, consider the following:

```
CFatalError*     pFe;
pFe = new CFatalError;
try
{
      int     I = ui.GetIput();
}
catch ( CFatalError* fe )
{
      fe->DisplayMsg();
}
return 0;
```

Here you can't see anything being thrown, and what is passed to *catch* isn't a string but some object based on a class named CFatalError. This code sample illustrates that first, you can pass anything, including an object of a class of your own definition; and second, throwing of an exception can happen in coding that is called anywhere within the scope of the *try* block but it doesn't have to be directly in the *try* block.

In our example in the *try* block, a member function named *GetInput()* from an object named ui is invoked. It is in this function that an exception is thrown, therefore we cannot see it in the sample code. However, because the event occurs within the domain of the *try* block, it is caught in the caller routine, demonstrating that a *try* and a *catch* don't have to be next to each other. This makes the mechanism much like that of the Basic ON ERROR GOTO. It works because the functions' addresses are placed on the stack, and a *catch* merely looks for the latest stack address to pick up on the program flow. However, the passing of parameters makes the mechanism work just like a function.

In summary, when you want to capture a type of possible error occurrences, it is appropriate to develop a class to handle the errors, sort of like a "general corporate policy." These can be individual class member methods. With this class declared, when you suspect errors, simply instantiate the error handling class, enclose the suspect code in a *try* block, and throw an exception passing the error-handling class object. The class object then takes care of the rest.

DEBUGGING

Unfortunately, as much as you try, errors will occur. The VC++ IDE has ample facilities to help you in tracking down errors.

In the development environment, when an application "bombs," usually the system isn't frozen. This is because the application is really executed in a virtual operating system, and the program is under the supervision of the Debugger, which monitors the states of each event that takes place, and can stop the program and inform you of the location where the error occurred. Using this information, you then can trace down the flaw in the program logic. (Unfortunately, the Debugger cannot tell you what you did wrong.)

One thing, though: to debug a program you must be in the Debug mode (Figure 13.1), which generates code maps that will help the Debugger track the program progress. You will compile in the Release mode only when you're ready to distribute the finished program—hopefully, with the bugs removed.

FIGURE 13.1 Compile mode selection.

Tracking Down Errors

When you execute a program in the IDE under Debug mode and an unrecoverable error occurs as shown in Figure 13.2, click Cancel to debug.

FIGURE 13.2 Application Error warning message.

First, an "Unhandled exception" message box appears (Figure 13.3), informing you of the code location where the error occurred. For most of us this doesn't help much, as we aren't savvy enough to read such esoteric cryptography involving hexadecimal expressions of code block offset. Therefore, click OK, which will bring you to the source code where the error occurred. Often this is embedded in some deep level inside the MFC class library because we failed to correctly provide certain parameters required. Because we're ignorant of the inner workings of the MFC low-level functions, the information presented generally doesn't make that much sense to us. However, the IDE does tell us how we got there, starting with our own code. If you look at the Context drop-down box in Figure 13.4, you'll see the nested calls that invariably originated from some code that we have written.

FIGURE 13.3 Unhandled error.

Select the source code (which has a telltale name that differs from the MFC names) of our program and you'll see precisely where the error occurred.

To stop the debugging, choose the IDE's Debug->Stop Debugging command (Figure 13.5).

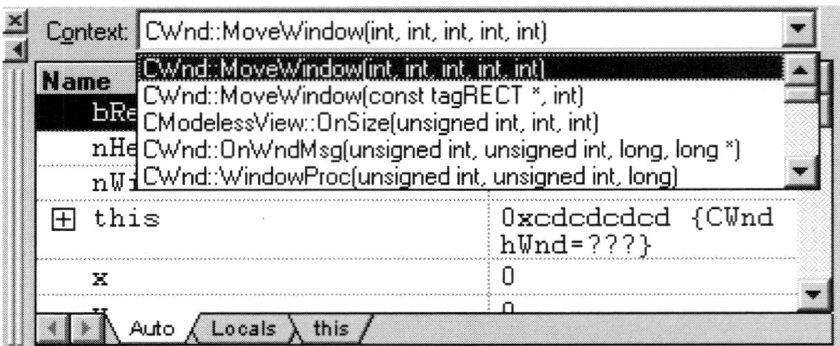

FIGURE 13.4 Error Context listing.

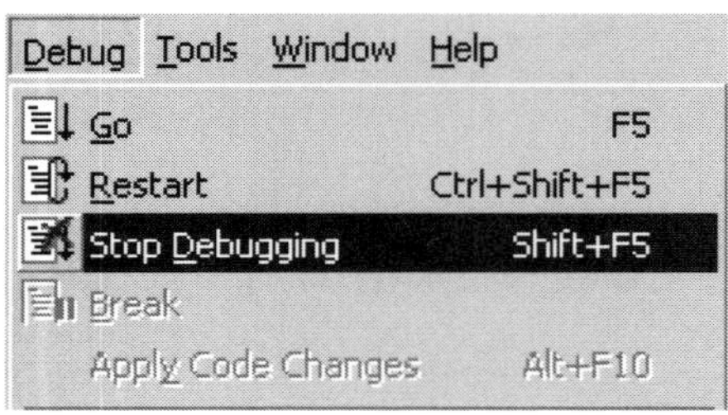

FIGURE 13.5 Stop Debugging.

SETTING BREAK POINTS

Now that you have a good idea where the error source is, you seek information on why it happened. A good way to get this information is to stop the program execution in midstream and observe key values that you have definite ideas about. To do this, you set appropriate *breakpoints* in the program source code.

To set a breakpoint, place the mouse pointer on the suspect code and bring up the context menu, from which you choose Insert/Remove Breakpoint, or click the toolbar icon that resembles a hand. This command is a toggle, which means it also removes the breakpoint if it exists.

After you have set the breakpoints, which may be several because you want to see things at different places as the program execution proceeds, you choose the Build->Start Debug->Go command or press [F5] (Figure 13.6).

The program will stop at the first breakpoint for you to do whatever you have to (Figure 13.7). One of the things that you can do is inspect the key variable values involved in the code at the time of the breakpoint (Figure 13.8).

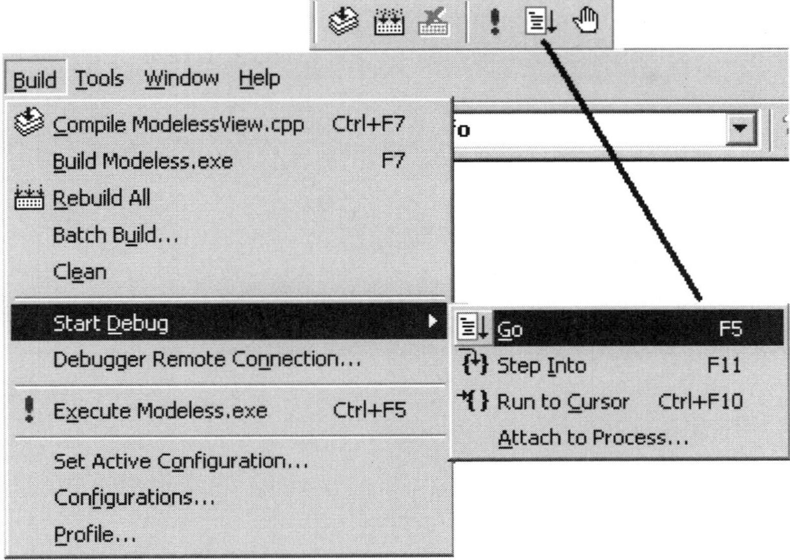

FIGURE 13.6 The Start Debug command.

```
void CModelessView::OnSize(UINT nType, int cx, int cy)
{
    CView::OnSize(nType, cx, cy);

    // TODO: Add your message handler code here
    m_pBtn->MoveWindow( CRect( 0, 0, 5, 5 ) );
}
```

FIGURE 13.7 Breakpoint.

Variables

Context: CModelessView::OnSize(unsigned int, int, int)

Name	Value
cx	0
cy	0
⊞ m_pBtn	0xcdcdcdcd {CButton hWnd=???}
nType	0

Auto / Locals / this

FIGURE 13.8 Breakpoint value inspection.

If this display is insufficient to do the job of identifying the error culprit, you can enter any variable name that you want to study in the Watch window (Figure 13.9).

If the breakpoint is set at the call of a function, you can trace into the function with the Debug->Step Into command (or press [F11]).

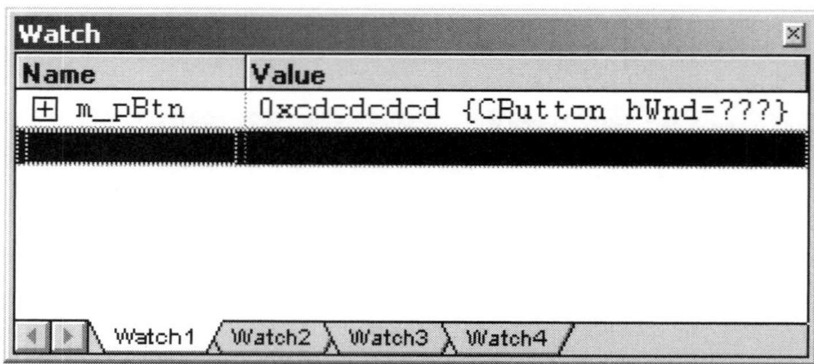

FIGURE 13.9 Setting Watch.

To exit the function, choose Debug->Step Out (or press [Shift-F11]).

To follow the program logic by moving from statement to statement, choose Debug->Step Over (or press [F10]).

Finally, you can stop the debugging session with the Stop Debugging command, or press [F5] to proceed toward the next breakpoint. If there is no ensuing breakpoint, the program just executes until it is terminated.

Explore the Debug menu command. Most of the commands you need are in there and they are easy to understand.

To remove all the breakpoints, choose Edit->Breakpoints and then remove them.

Many MFC functions have built-in *throw* operations. You need to be aware that they do, and when you use these functions, attempt to provide error recovery for them. To streamline our learning, in this book no *throw* discussion will be included in the code illustrations even if the MFC function has it. However, you should not mistake this omission to mean that the classes and functions have no *throw* capabilities, or that error trapping is unimportant. Its omission is merely a matter of the author attempting to simplify the topical discussions.

14 Project Maintenance

As you have experienced, using the IDE—especially AppWizard and ClassWizard—to develop applications is a snap. However, for every advantage there is associated with it a price. In this high-speed adventure we're undertaking, it is easy for one to slip because of an oversight. As a result, what could have been a major achievement can actually turn out bust, and all must be redone anew. This type of undesirable (although foreseeable) outcome can range from a not-quite-right project name to bad class names, wrong classes, unneeded classes and objects, and snarled program code that is so bad that you simply want to do it all over from scratch. The truth is, this type of rework effort does happen in real life. In this chapter, we'll learn how to salvage damaged projects and turn what is bad back into good.

REMOVING CLASSES AND OBJECTS

Removing classes and objects in VC++ isn't as simple as just deleting code entries and files. This is because VC++ uses many auxiliary files to help manage a project. If you look into the folders or disk directory of a typical project, you'll see that they contain more than just .h and .cpp files. The entire VC++ file system must be maintained as a whole, or VC++ will not be able to keep up with the many services that it provides, and in the worst case, mess up your project. Therefore, when making changes to a VC++ project, you must follow certain rules and procedures and be prudent in your actions.

Removing an Object Variable

To remove an object—a variable that is generated by ClassWizard—you should not just edit it out using the text editor. You should go through ClassWizard to remove it, and follow the same procedure as when you first created the object. For instance, you used ClassWizard to create a CString variable for an edit box. To remove the CString variable, you:

1. Select the object (edit box).
2. Bring up ClassWizard.
3. Select the Member Variables tab folder.
4. Click the Delete Variable button.
5. Close ClassWizard.

The reason you must do this is because when you created the variable, ClassWizard also added pertinent data exchange entries for you. Had you removed the variable by deleting it from the header file, the data exchange code would still be in the project, and unnecessary errors would result, costing you extra effort to weed them out.

Removing a Member Variable

When you remove a member variable, remember to delete its declaration statement from the header file, and every usage of it through the project as well. To determine its occurrence, use the search facility (Figure 14.1).

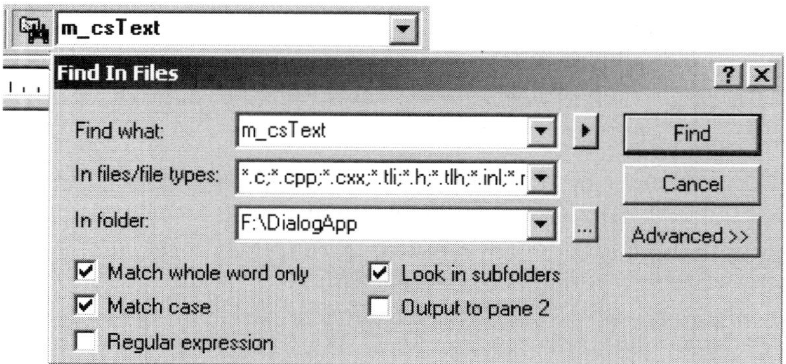

FIGURE 14.1 Find In Files.

Also, if a variable's class requires a special #include reference, take it out too.

Removing a Member Function

Removing a member function depends on what type of function it is. If it is a function you inserted with the Add Member Function command, there are only two places where code needs to be removed: in the .h file and the .cpp file, plus all its callouts.

If the function to remove is a command message handler or a virtual function override, you need to remove it with ClassWizard.

In ClassWizard, you select the function to remove and click the Delete Function button. A message prompts you to remove the actual function body yourself (Figure 14.2). What this means is that the function will be deleted from the message map, but you must remove the function in the .cpp file yourself.

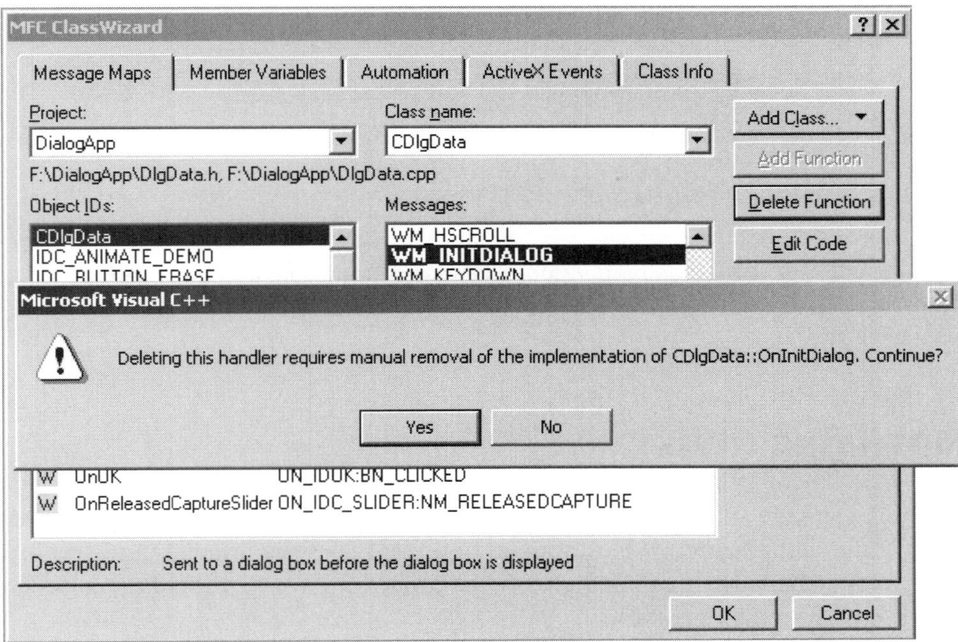

FIGURE 14.2 Deleting a message handler function.

Removing Classes

If you need to remove a class because your application no longer needs it, or because you messed it up and need to redo it, you will have to remove the physical files for the class (which is why you should always dedicate a set of files to each class).

In FileView, select the appropriate class .h and .cpp files from the Header Files and Source Files groups, respectively, and press the [Delete] key to remove them from the IDE. The class will disappear from ClassView. Then, you must delete those files from the hard drive. However, ClassWizard still has knowledge of the class, and will stop you from recreating it if that is indeed your next action.

To purge the class from ClassWizard, you need to delete the project's physical .clw file, which holds class information for ClassWizard in an internal database. Therefore, you must close the project and delete the .clw file from disk.

After the physical files have been deleted, open the project workspace again. Try to access ClassWizard and you'll encounter the message as shown in Figure 14.3. Simply click Yes to rebuild the file from the project source files. You'll be asked to select the files to include from the existing files. Click Add All to restore all the classes (which is why you should delete the unwanted physical files first), and you can proceed to creating new classes again.

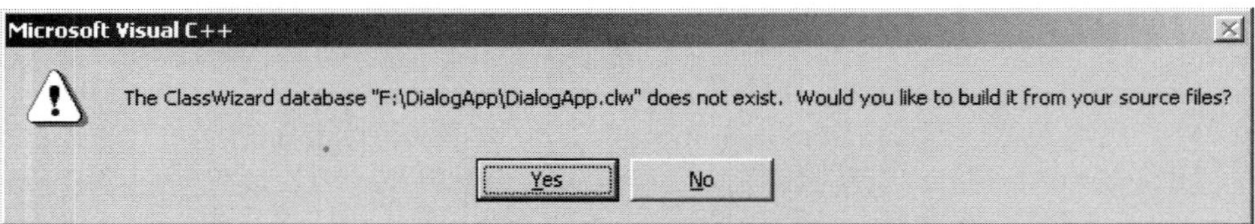

FIGURE 14.3 Prompt to include ClassWizard candidate files.

MODIFYING ITEMS

If an item such as a variable or a class name needs to be altered, make sure that you use global search to flush out all occurrences of the original that is to be changed and change them all. Otherwise, the procedure is straightforward and there is little harm in the operation.

If the change involves the filename of a class, the process is a little more complicated. This is because this filename is used in #include statements. To accomplish this, you need to employ the techniques explained previously to remove the file, change its name, then add it back to the project, and also change the filename in the #include statements.

If the change is in the class name, you need to do all of the above, and also incorporate the class removal procedure to update the ClassWizard database. If you follow the procedures faithfully and methodically, no harm should befall your project.

RECYCLING WORK

Success in programming is measured by how efficiently an application is developed and how robust it is. That is why recycling work is highly encouraged in professional software development. Why, programmers consider the invention of the subroutine—or function, or reusable code—the greatest coup in computer software technique evolution, don't they? VC++ contributes its share in promoting this approach to programming.

Borrowing Resources

If you have developed visual objects in previous projects or know of existing object resources in other applications, you can copy them into your current project, thus saving significant development time.

Borrowing from a Project

If the resources exist in a previous project, you can open those resources and transfer them to your current project. You do so by first opening the existing resource (.rc) file with the File->Open command. The existing resources will show up in a ResourceView. Select the resources that you want to use, and copy and paste them into your present project. Then, close the lending resource file.

Borrowing from an Executable[1]

If the resources that you want to borrow exist in an executable, such as Windows' Notepad.exe program, that was developed from a VC++ equivalent environment, use File->Open to open the executable as a resource as illustrated in Figure 14.4. The resources will show up as resources but without the mnemonic IDs (because the application has already been compiled) as in Figure 14.5. You can copy the resources into your project and then assign it proper IDs. When you're finished, close the executable file.

Borrowing Classes

If a class exists in a previous VC++ project and you can use it, copy the class's header and source files into your present project's file directory or folder, and then switch to FileView. Select the Header Files tree branch and bring up the context menu, in which you choose the Add Files to Folder command. Select the header file from the file folder in the usual Windows manner. Then, do the same for the source file, and the class is added to your present project.

[1] This procedure is dysfunctional if VC++ is running in Windows operating systems earlier than NT, such as Windows 95 or 98.

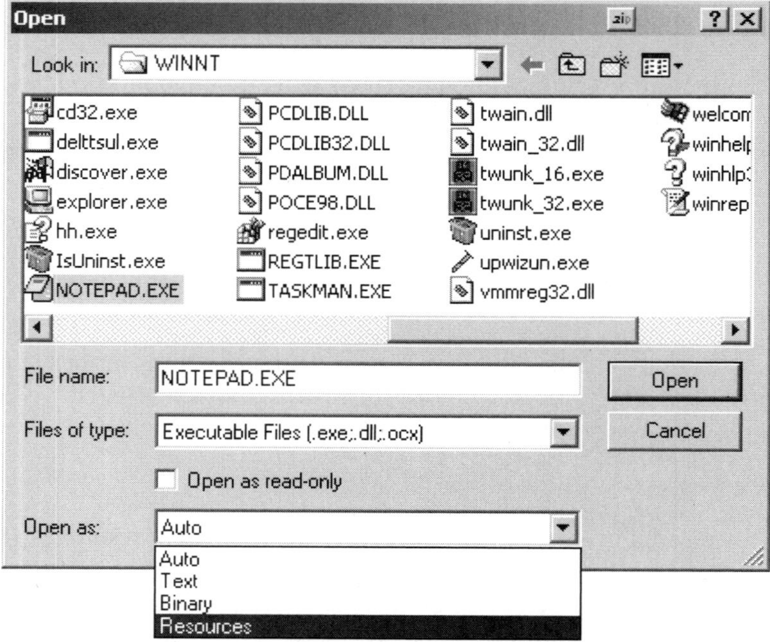

FIGURE 14.4 Opening an external file as a resource.

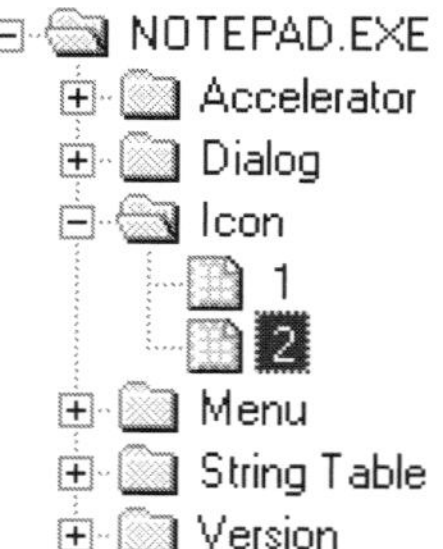

FIGURE 14.5 Generic resource IDs.

Recycling Code

In fact, the "borrowing" technique can be used to recycle virtually anything. To reuse functions or code snippets from another project, just use the File->Open command to open the file containing the target items and use Copy and Paste to transfer them. VC++ even includes a Recent Files command to facilitate the operation.

REJUVENATING A PROJECT

At the end of the day, you might feel that the project is in such a sad state that it needs to be redone. You can accomplish this at two levels.

First, you can clean up the secondary files and regenerate them. These include all the compilation database and temporary files.

You have learned that the .clw file can be regenerated.

The .aps file, used to hold object definition data to help VC++ load the project quickly, can be deleted and regenerated.

The .dsw file is also dispensable. After you have deleted it, you simply open the workspace with the project file. When you save the workspace the .dsw file will be regenerated.

The .opt, workspace option file is automatically generated by VC++, so you can delete it without danger.

The .plg building log html file is also expendable. It contains the application build log entries.

The .ncb, or No Compile Browser, file contains information used by ClassView, WizardBar, and Component Gallery. It is also regenerated if deleted.

In short, all the preceding files and the entire Debug and Release subfolders can be deleted. In fact, if you want to "clean up" your project, delete them all and rebuild the entire project to restore them.

Sometimes, things have gone so wrong that no matter what you try, the "renovated" application doesn't work right. You know something bad exists somewhere inside one of the project files, but you don't know what it is. It might be better to abandon the project and start a new one. However, don't write off the old header and source files so fast, because text files seldom are corrupted to the point of being totally unusable. Simply regenerate a new application framework, replace the newly generated code files (.h and .cpp) with the old ones, and then build the application. Chances are, whatever hidden problem there is will be gone. If an error persists, consider logic flaws as the offenders.

PART IV

The Document/View Paradigm

Let us now turn our attention to the other type of application frameworks offered by AppWizard besides the dialog-based application that has a dialog box as its main window with a resource-friendly surface on which we can easily populate control objects. The second type of application framework, ostensibly more complex than the dialog model, consists of a window frame that houses a data viewing area or areas drawing on data managed by a separate class. Both the SDI and MDI models belong to this type of Windows desktop applications. The main differences between them are that the SDI model has one viewing window, while the MDI model offers multiple viewing windows. While smaller applications, such as system utility programs, employ the dialog model, most complex commercial applications are of the latter type for its superior data and view management facilities. In this part of the book, we'll study the implementations of the SDI and MDI application frameworks.

15 SDI Application Basics

The second type of application we generated using AppWizard was an SDI application. We will now take a look under the hood and see what makes this application framework tick. So, open the **SDIApp** project again and let's begin our investigation.

The main class for the **SDIApp** project again is a CWinApp derived class. In this case, it is the CSDIAppApp class. Once more, the *InitInstance()* function begins with the usual setup: *AfxEnableControlContainer()*, *Enable3dControls()*, and *Enable3dControlsStatic()*. Then comes the following function call:

```
SetRegistryKey(_T("Local AppWizard-Generated Applications"));
```

The *SetRegistryKey()* function creates a key for the application in Windows' registry, allowing us to use the Windows registry for system-level data transaction. You'll learn about this in the third part of this book.

The next function call, *LoadStdProfileSettings()*, initializes the application's basic setup, such as how many past opened documents to maintain under the File command, which you determined in Step 4 of the AppWizard setup process (Figure 15.1).

Next comes the crux of the SDI framework.

```
CSingleDocTemplate* pDocTemplate;
pDocTemplate = new CSingleDocTemplate(
     IDR_MAINFRAME,
     RUNTIME_CLASS(CSDIAppDoc),
     RUNTIME_CLASS(CMainFrame),
     RUNTIME_CLASS(CSDIAppView));
AddDocTemplate(pDocTemplate);
```

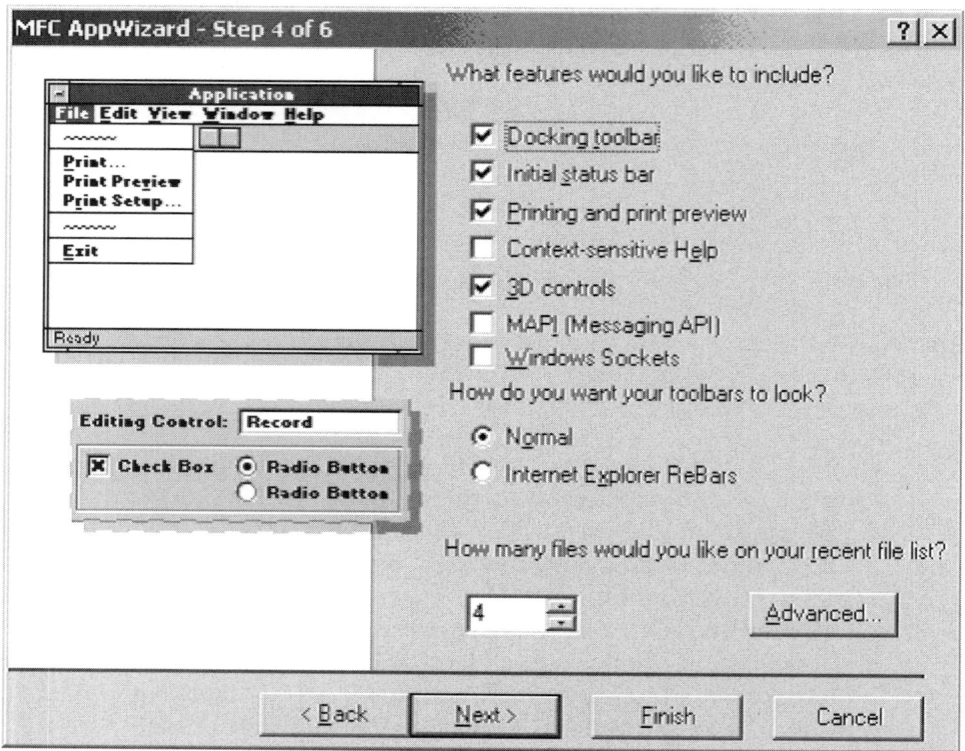

FIGURE 15.1 AppWizard Step 4, Recent Files setting.

A complex framework such as the SDI consists of more than one basic class, each responsible for one set of activities and functional responsibilities, yet well coordinated with each other. The coordinating class is the template class CSingleDocTemplate. In the SDIApp project, the class instantiation is done through the **pDocTemplate** pointer. Without getting too academic about things, the template object simply "binds" the three component class objects together. These three objects are:

- A *Mainframe* class object, which serves as the visible frame of the application on which the menus, toolbars, status bars, and so on, are hung. In **SDIApp**, it is the CMainFrame class.
- A *Document* class object that is responsible for maintaining the data consumed by the application and any persistence issues (that is, saving and retrieving data). In SDIApp, it is the CSDIAppDoc class.

- A *View* class object that is responsible for any display activities. In **SDIApp**, it is the CSDIAppView class.

The three classes are delegated specific roles. While the Document class is responsible for managing the data manipulated by the application, it does so behind the scenes (invisibly) and virtually has no part in the data's presentation on the screen. The View class, on the other hand, is responsible for all the display layout activities, working on a display canvas as large as the computer's memory can handle and is not limited to the size of the monitor screen. What you actually see, though, is through the screen window, which is controlled by the Frame class (Figure 15.2).

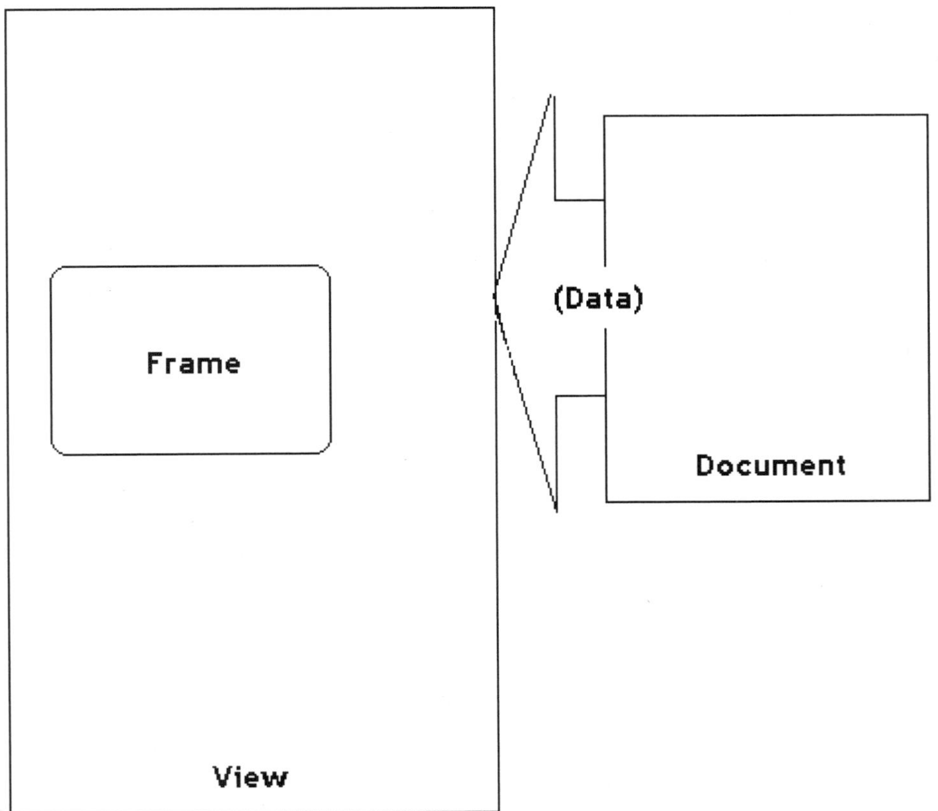

FIGURE 15.2 The Frame/Document/View paradigm.

In short, once the template has been registered, the three classes can work with each other, and you have an SDI application, with the **m_MainWnd** member variable of the CWinApp class defined, identifying the main application window.

After this, any parameters supplied are processed:

```
CCommandLineInfo cmdInfo;
ParseCommandLine(cmdInfo);
if (!ProcessShellCommand(cmdInfo))
     return FALSE;
```

(We'll study command-line parameters later.)

At this time, the application window is deployed (*ShowWindow()*) and Windows is forced to paint it (*UpdateWindow()*):

```
m_pMainWnd->ShowWindow(SW_SHOW);
m_pMainWnd->UpdateWindow();
```

The next step for us is to look at the three component classes in turn.

THE CMAINFRAME CLASS

If you look at the class definition of the CMainFrame class in the header file, derived from the basic CFrameWnd (frame window) class, you will see the following:

```
protected:  // control bar embedded members
     CStatusBar  m_wndStatusBar;
     CToolBar    m_wndToolBar;
```

These are the creations of the status bar and the toolbar.

OnCreate()

Look into the *OnCreate()* function in the Frame class's .cpp file and you'll see the toolbar and status bar constructed using the resources defined (IDR_MAINFRAME) with all the styles specified in the constructors:

```
m_wndToolBar.CreateEx(this, TBSTYLE_FLAT, WS_CHILD | WS_VISIBLE |
CBRS_TOP | CBRS_GRIPPER | CBRS_TOOLTIPS | CBRS_FLYBY |
CBRS_SIZE_DYNAMIC) || !m_wndToolBar.LoadToolBar(IDR_MAINFRAME)
m_wndStatusBar.Create(this) ||
!m_wndStatusBar.SetIndicators(indicators,
sizeof(indicators)/sizeof(UINT))
```

By looking up the references on the CStatusBar and CToolBar classes, you'll get a complete picture on all the styles, and you will be able to modify the code to assume the specific styles you want.

The docking of the toolbar is controlled by:

```
m_wndToolBar.EnableDocking(CBRS_ALIGN_ANY);
EnableDocking(CBRS_ALIGN_ANY);
DockControlBar(&m_wndToolBar);
```

Commenting these three function calls will result in a permanently bonded toolbar that the user cannot detach from the mainframe.

THE CDOCUMENT CLASS

The member function of interest in the CDocument class—in the case of **SDIApp**, the CSDIAppDoc class, is the *Serialize()* function. This function contains the preset code to support data persistence—saving and restoring data to and from disk:

```
void CSDIAppDoc::Serialize(CArchive& ar)
{
	if (ar.IsStoring())
	{
		// TODO: add storing code here
	}
	else
	{
		// TODO: add loading code here
	}
}
```

Soon you'll learn that the class does all this automatically. You merely identify the data to be transacted.

This brings us to the inevitable question: Why have a class nominated as the official handler of data? The answer actually entails an appreciation of the View class. It is true that you can define and hold data anywhere you like. After all, classes are merely code. Just because some classes cause visual effects doesn't make them tangible "things." However, as you'll soon learn, because there can be multiple renditions of views on the same data, it is more efficient programmatically to have one class handle the data in order to support multiple data consumer classes. For example, in the MDI framework you can have many child windows supporting different views. With data handled by the Document class, a function such as *UpdateAllViews()* that updates all the views at the same time becomes feasible.

Otherwise, the programmer would have to manage the many data sets scattered among different views and classes.

THE CVIEW CLASS

The CView class is generally the workhorse of the triumvirate of the SDI classes, because it is responsible for all display operations plus printing.

The Document-to-View Relationship

In the CSDIAppView class, you'll find a function named *GetDocument()*, which returns a pointer to the CSDIAppDoc object. This functions sets up the View class so that it can access members in the CDocument class. That's how data can be kept in the CDocument class and used in the CView class.

For example, suppose we define a public variable in the CSDIAppDoc class:

```
CString     m_csTitle;
```

In the *OnNewDocument()* function of the CSDIAppDoc class, we assign value to it:

```
BOOL CSDIAppDoc::OnNewDocument()
{
      if (!CDocument::OnNewDocument())
            return FALSE;
      // TODO: add reinitialization code here
      // (SDI documents will reuse this document)
      m_csTitle = "Report I";
      return TRUE;
}
```

We then can access this data from the View class with:

```
GetDocument()->m_csTile;
```

The Mainframe-to-View Relationship

Similarly, there is a relationship between the View and the Mainframe. For example, to access members of the Mainframe class, you attain its location with the *GetParentFrame()* function. For example, from the View class you can reach the status bar with (assuming that it has been moved away from being "protect"):

```
GetParentFrame()->m_wndStatusBar;
```

The View-to-Mainframe Relationship

To reach the View from the Mainframe, you use the *GetActiveView()* function. It returns a CView pointer. The function is called *GetActiveView()* because, as you'll learn later, there can be other views that are inactive.

The Mainframe-to-Document Relationship

In a CDocument class, you can get to the Mainframe with the *AfxGetMainWnd()* function, which returns a CWnd pointer.

The View-to-Document Relationship

To reach from the CDocument class into the current View object, you will first go to the Mainframe and then from there, reach the View:

```
AfxGetMainWnd()->GetActiveView()->…;
```

The Relationship to the Application

Ultimately, every component class has a relationship with the Application class, and all can reach it through the theApp variable, which is defined close to the top of the Application class. In the SDIApp.cpp file, you should find:

```
CSDIAppApp theApp;
```

To have this variable accessed from another .cpp file such as SDIAppView.cpp, all you need to do is to add the following code shown in bold to the top of the file:

```
#ifdef _DEBUG
#define new DEBUG_NEW
#undef THIS_FILE
static char THIS_FILE[] = __FILE__;
#endif
extern     CSDIAppApp theApp;
```

16 The SDI Application Model

In virtually all applications involving a View, it is used for displaying purposes. You can draw the display images, or you can write the display images. They all rely on their respective functions. We will begin by looking at how drawing in a View is done.

DEVICE CONTEXT

Associated with a CView class is the CDC class, or *Device Context*, which CView manages. When you generate an SDI application, the device context is inherently constructed for us, which is why the *OnDraw()* function has an incoming parameter of "CDC* pDC" a pointer to the device context.

The best way to understand the device context is to visualize it as a painting canvas of virtually infinite dimensions. You can draw pictures on it or display text. It makes no difference to a Windows application because, unlike in the DOS days, everything is done in graphics anyway. From a programmatic standpoint, what you do—therefore what MFC functions you use—is dictated by the painting mode you select (graphics or text). Once the painting mode has been determined, you select the proper painting tools that pertain to the display mode, and off you go using those tools and the drawing functions to produce the visual effects, all the while conforming to the drawing medium's geometry.

Mapping Mode

The painting mode, called *mapping mode*, selects the coordinate system to use and the graphical units of measurement. It is set using the CDC class's *SetMapMode()* function, which has the form of:

```
virtual int SetMapMode( int nMapMode );
```

The parameter nMapMode can be one of the entries listed in Table 16.1. The default mode is MM_TEXT (Figure 16.1).

TABLE 16.1 Mapping Modes

Mode	***Description***
MM_HIENGLISH	x is to the right; y is up. A logical unit represents 0.001 inch.
MM_HIMETRIC	x is to the right; y is up. A logical unit represents 0.01 millimeter.
MM_ISOTROPIC	A unit is defined by the developer, with the x and y axes having equal scales. You use the *SetWindowExt()* and *SetViewportExt()* member functions to specify the units and the axes' orientation.
MM_LOENGLISH	x is to the right; y is up. A logical unit represents 0.01 inch.
MM_LOMETRIC	x is to the right; y is up. A logical unit represents 0.1 millimeter.
MM_TEXT	x is to the right; y is down. A logical unit represents 1 device pixel.
MM_TWIPS	x is to the right; y is up. A logical unit represents 1/20 of a point. (A point is 1/72 inch. A twip is 1/1440 inch.)

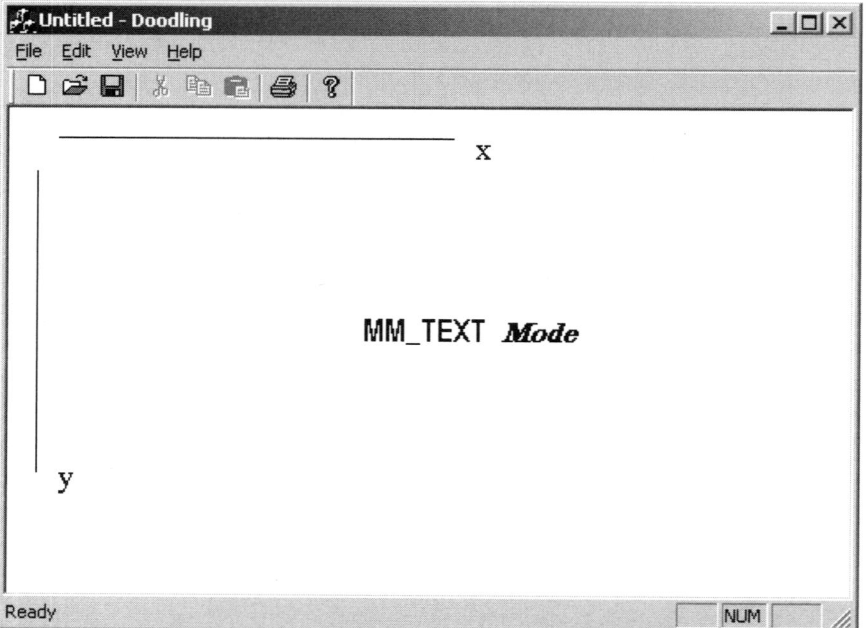

FIGURE 16.1 The MM_TEXT mode coordinates.

Painting Tools

The drawing tools in place dictate the drawing. There are two major drawing tools: the *pen* and the *brush*. The pen controls how a line appears, while the brush dictates how pictures are filled.

The Pen

The drawing pen is epitomized by a CPen object. To deploy a CPen object, use the following procedure:

1. Create a new CPen object.
2. Activate the CPen object and preserve the default one used by the system at the same time.
3. Complete your drawing.
4. Restore the preserved system CPen object.

The reason for this sequence of events is because the system is already using a CPen object. Remember that Windows itself is a graphical application, too. Because the system has a default CPen object, you don't have to create a separate one if the default settings are acceptable for use.

The basic form of a CPen object is:

```
CPen(int nPenStyle, int nWidth, COLORREF crColor);
```

where nPenStyle is one of the entries listed in Table 16.2.

TABLE 16.2 CPen Styles

Pen Style	***Description***
PS_SOLID	Creates a solid pen.
PS_DASH	Creates a dashed pen. Valid only when the pen width is 1 or less, in device units.
PS_DOT	Creates a dotted pen. Valid only when the pen width is 1 or less, in device units.
PS_DASHDOT	Creates a pen with alternating dashes and dots. Valid only when the pen width is 1 or less, in device units.

(Continues)

TABLE 16.2 CPen Styles (*Continued*)

Pen Style	*Description*
PS_DASHDOTDOT	Creates a pen with alternating dashes and double dots. Valid only when the pen width is 1 or less, in device units.
PS_NULL	Creates a null pen.
PS_INSIDEFRAME	Creates a pen that draws a line inside the frame of closed shapes produced by the Windows GDI output functions that specify a bounding rectangle (for example, the **Ellipse**, **Rectangle**, **RoundRect**, **Pie**, and **Chord** member functions). When this style is used with Windows GDI output functions that do not specify a bounding rectangle (for example, the **LineTo** member function), the drawing area of the pen is not limited by a frame.

If you use the following CPen construction form, you can have additional styles that you can look up from the MFC references.

```
CPen( int nPenStyle, int nWidth, const LOGBRUSH* pLogBrush, int
  nStyleCount = 0, const DWORD* lpStyle = NULL );
```

The Brush

To fill in pictures, you specify a brush derived from the CBrush class. The construction of a CBrush object can be one of the following:

```
CBrush( COLORREF crColor );
CBrush( int nIndex, COLORREF crColor );
CBrush( CBitmap* pBitmap );
```

where *nIndex* specifies one of the hatch patterns described in Table 16.3.

The third form suggests that you can use a bitmap picture to fill pictures.

COLORREF

In constructing the drawing tools, you often need to specify the drawing, or foreground color. This is specified by a value conforming to the COLORREF data type.

TABLE 16.3 CBrush Styles

Hatch nIndex	*Description*
HS_BDIAGONAL	Downward hatch (left to right) at 45 degrees
HS_CROSS	Horizontal and vertical crosshatch
HS_DIAGCROSS	Crosshatch at 45 degrees
HS_FDIAGONAL	Upward hatch (left to right) at 45 degrees
HS_HORIZONTAL	Horizontal hatch
HS_VERTICAL	Vertical hatch

For the developers, it is easier to specify color using the RGB macro, which computes the COLORREF value for us if we supply the intensity values of the color's red, green, and blue components. For example, we can specify white as RGB(255,255,255), or black with RGB(0,0,0). 0 and 255 are the extreme values of the color intensities.

A DRAWING APPLICATION

Now we will put these drawing elements to work.

1. Generate a new SDI application named **Doodling**, accepting all the defaults. Compile it and make sure that it works.
2. In the View class's *OnDraw()* function, add the following code:

```
void CDoodlingView::OnDraw(CDC* pDC)
{
     CDoodlingDoc* pDoc = GetDocument();
     ASSERT_VALID(pDoc);
     // TODO: add draw code for native data here
     pDC->SetMapMode( MM_TEXT );
     CPen      pen;
     pen.CreatePen(PS_SOLID, 10, RGB( 0, 255, 255 ));
     CPen*      pCurPen = pDC->SelectObject( &pen );
     pDC->MoveTo( 100, 100 );
     pDC->LineTo( 500, 400 );
     pDC->SelectObject( pCurPen );
     CBrush     brush;
```

```
brush.CreateSolidBrush( RGB( 255, 0, 0 ) );
CBrush*     pCurBrush = pDC->SelectObject(&brush);
pDC->FillRect( CRect( 500, 100, 700, 300 ), &brush );
pDC->SelectObject( &pCurBrush );
```

3. Compile the program and test it.

You should see a line drawn slanting down the application's main window and a red rectangle.

All drawings take place in the View class's *OnDraw()* function. In **Doodling**, first we set up the map mode with "pDC->SetMapMode(MM_TEXT);" (which is not really necessary in this case because it is the default mode). Next, a solid pen is created (PS_SOLID) with a sky-blue drawing color (RGB(0,255,255)). The pen is selected with "CPen* pCurPen = pDC->SelectObject(&pen);" which at the same time preserved the current pen used by the system. At the end of the drawing, the old pen is restored: "pDC->SelectObject(pCurPen);."

The operations with the brush mirror this scheme and the coding is just as straightforward.

DRAWING PICTURES

The actual drawing is done by the CDC class's drawing functions, and there are plenty.

(If you're testing the code in the **Doodling** application, you can erase the trial code from the *OnDraw()* function in turn to leave a clean function for the next try, or you can comment the old code out as you go.)

MoveTo()

MoveTo() positions the drawing "pen nib," or point according to the prevalent x-y coordinate system.

The POINT Structure

The drawing functions that work with x-y coordinates also accept input coordinate parameters in the form of POINT structures. Its form is:

```
typedef struct tagPOINT {
   LONG x;
   LONG y;
} POINT;
```

Therefore, the preceding sample code also can be coded as:

```
POINT     pt;
pt.x = 100;
pt.y = 100;
pDC->MoveTo( pt );
```

CPoint

If you prefer, you can also use the MFC CPoint class, in which case you will be working with an object:

```
CPoint     pt;
pt.x = 100;
pt.y = 100;
pDC->MoveTo( pt );
```

LineTo()

The *LineTo()* function draws a line from the current "point" to the destination point specified by the x-y coordinates as function parameters.

We'll now quickly run down some of the more basic CDC drawing functions.

FillRect()

The *FillRect()* function fills a rectangle with the current brush.

Ellipse()

To draw an ellipse, you use the *Ellipse()* function, which takes on a major axis and a minor axis as input. Example:

```
pDC->Ellipse( 100, 100, 200, 300 );
```

Drawing a Circle

A circle is just an ellipse with equal axes. Therefore, you can draw a circle with:

```
pDC->Ellipse( 100, 100, 400, 400 );
```

Arc()

You draw an arc by first specifying the enveloping rectangle, followed by the starting coordinate point and the ending coordinate point (the latter two not having to be precise points on the arc). For example:

```
pDC->Arc( 100, 100, 200, 200, 120, 120, 180, 180 );
```

The envelop rectangle is: upper-left corner at x=100, y=100; lower-right corner at x=200, y=200; starting from x=120, y=120 and arc toward x=180, y=180.

The *Arc()* function also can work with geometric structures:

```
Arc( LPCRECT lpRect, POINT ptStart, POINT ptEnd );
Arc( CRect lpRect, CPoint ptStart, CPoint ptEnd );
```

THE RECT STRUCTURE

LPCRECT means a long pointer to the RECT structure. The RECT structure is:

```
typedef struct tagRECT {
   LONG left;
   LONG top;
   LONG right;
   LONG bottom;
} RECT;
```

It encapsulates the coordinates of a rectangle.

CRect

CRect is a class, from which you derive a rectangle object. It has class members of *top*, *left*, *bottom*, and *right*, just as the RECT structure. However, it has member functions to set their values, such as *SetRect*(int *x1*, int *y1*, int *x2*, int *y2*).

Therefore,

```
pDC->Arc( 100, 100, 200, 200, 120, 120, 180, 180 );
```

can also be coded as:

```
CRect     rect;
rect.top = 100;
rect.left = 100;
rect.right = 200;
rect.bottom = 200;
CPoint     ptStart;
ptStart.x = 120;
ptStart.y = 120;
CPoint     ptEnd;
ptEnd.x = 180;
ptEnd.y = 180;
pDC->Arc( rect, ptStart, ptEnd );
```

or,

```
CRect     rect( 100, 100, 200, 200);
CPoint     ptStart( 120, 120 );
CPoint     ptEnd( 180, 180 );
pDC->Arc( rect, ptStart, ptEnd );
```

In coding, CRect works the same way as the RECT structure.

1. To see CPen work, enter the following in **Doodling**'s *OnDraw()* function:

```
CPen     pen;
pen.CreatePen( PS_SOLID, 10, RGB( 0, 255, 255 ) );
// Save default pen.
CPen*     pCurPen = pDC->SelectObject( &pen );
CPoint     pt;
pt.x = 100;
pt.y = 100;
pDC->MoveTo( pt );
pDC->LineTo( 500, 400 );
pDC->SelectObject( pCurPen );
```

WRITING TEXT

Outputting text follows a similar procedure as drawing graphical shapes. First, you set the map mode. Next, you create or select a font for the text. Then, you output text using any of the CDC class member functions designed for text output, all the while controlling the display geometry. When all is done, restore the font to the system default.

Using Fonts

Again, whether you specify a font to use or not, the system comes with its own font. However, selecting a font gives you explicit control over your text-displaying operations.

There are several ways to create a font. For example, you can use the CDC class's member function *CreateFont()* to create a font from scratch by specifying every attribute of the new font. However, in most cases most likely you'll be using an existing font, or stock font. The CDC member function to create a stock font is *CreateStockFont()*;

The form of the *CreateStockFont()* function is:

```
CreateStockFont( int iNdx );
```

where iNdx is a value representing the stock font to use. For example, to create a Windows NT/2000 device-dependent font you will use:

```
CreateStockFont( DEVICE_DEFAULT_FONT );
```

To create a font based on the system's font (used in menus and controls, etc.), you use:

```
CreateStockFont( SYSTEM_FONT );
```

The values of the font styles can be referenced from the *GetStockObject()* function under "Visual C++, Platform SDK, and enterprise Docs" in the MSDN Library.

Displaying Text

Once you have determined the font to use, you can output text with two basic CDC member functions: *TextOut()* and *DrawText()*.

TextOut()

1. In **Doodling**, try the following code in the View's *OnDraw()* function:

```
void CDoodlingView::OnDraw(CDC* pDC)
{
     CDoodlingDoc* pDoc = GetDocument();
     ASSERT_VALID(pDoc);
     // TODO: add draw code for native data here
     CFont     font;
     font.CreateStockObject( DEVICE_DEFAULT_FONT );
     CFont* def_font = pDC->SelectObject(&font);
     pDC->TextOut(5, 5, "Hello", 5);
     pDC->SelectObject(def_font);
     font.DeleteObject();
     font.CreateStockObject( ANSI_FIXED_FONT );
     def_font = pDC->SelectObject(&font);
     pDC->TextOut(5, 25, "Hello", 5);
     pDC->SelectObject(def_font);
}
```

In this example, first a stock font object is created based on the system's device-dependent font and selected into play, preserving the existing font object. Then the text "Hello" is output to the screen at coordinate position x=5 and y=5.

The form of the *TextOut()* function is:

```
BOOL TextOut( int x, int y, const CString& str );
```

x and *y* are the starting coordinate point of the output (predicated to the current map mode), and *str* is the text string to output. *TextOut()* displays the text string as a straight line.

Subsequently, another font is created and a second line is output, showing the differences between the two fonts.

DrawText()

Granted, the *TextOut()* function, able to display text in a single line, can prove limiting for general text output. A better function to use is the *DrawText()* function.

The *DrawText()* function has the form of:

```
int DrawText( const CString& str, LPRECT lpRect, UINT nFormat );
```

where *str* is the text string to output, *lpRect* is the rectangular area in which the text is to be displayed, and *nFormat* selects one of the output formats to use.

Try the following code sample in **Doodling**'s View class *OnDraw()* function:

```
void CDoodlingView::OnDraw(CDC* pDC)
{
     CDoodlingDoc* pDoc = GetDocument();
     ASSERT_VALID(pDoc);
     // TODO: add draw code for native data here
     CFont  font;
     font.CreateStockObject( DEVICE_DEFAULT_FONT );
     CFont* def_font = pDC->SelectObject(&font);
     CString     csText = "Congratulations.  You have been selected to
attend an exciting presentation to be held in one of the major hotels
in Las Vegas.  A prize of value $150 has also been held in reserve for
you should you decide to attend.  In fact, if you respond quickly and
call the following 800 number before the deadline printed at the upper
right hand corner of this letter, a second prize of value $100 will be
awarded to you in addition to the price stated above.";
     pDC->DrawText( csText, CRect( 5, 5, 500, 500 ), DT_WORDBREAK );
     pDC->SelectObject(def_font);
     font.DeleteObject();
}
```

In this example, a long text string is displayed in a rectangular area in the application's child window ascribed to by the CRect object using the DEVICE_DEFAULT_FONT format that causes CDC to parse the text string according to word-break opportunities.

GetClientRect()

The size of the CRect object was chosen arbitrarily for demonstration purposes. There was no scientific basis to its dimensions other than that the developer felt that it was probably big enough to envelop the text. Indeed, the output would look something like Figure 16.2.

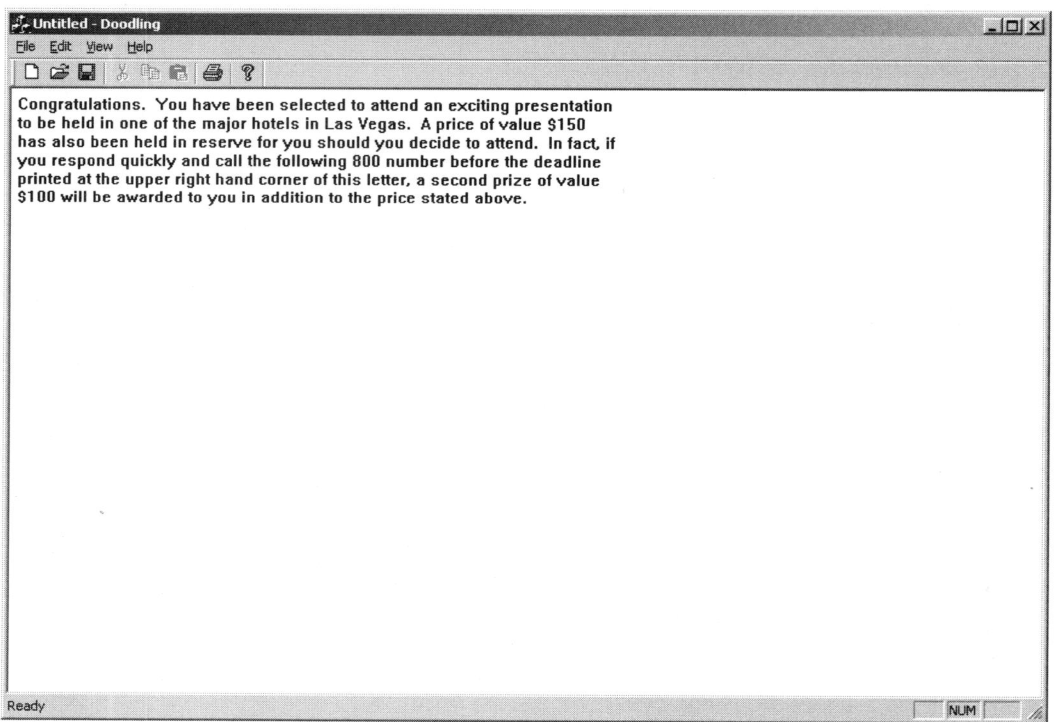

FIGURE 16.2 Text partially filling the View window.

Actually, a better rectangle would have been the application's window itself, and you can get its coordinates with the *GetClientRect()* CWnd member function.

Modify the sample **Doodling** code to:

```
CFont     font;
font.CreateStockObject( DEVICE_DEFAULT_FONT );
CFont* def_font = pDC->SelectObject(&font);
...
CRect     rect;
GetClientRect( rect );
pDC->DrawText( csText, rect, DT_WORDBREAK );
pDC->SelectObject(def_font);
font.DeleteObject();
```

You will see that the text fills the application window nicely (Figure 16.3).

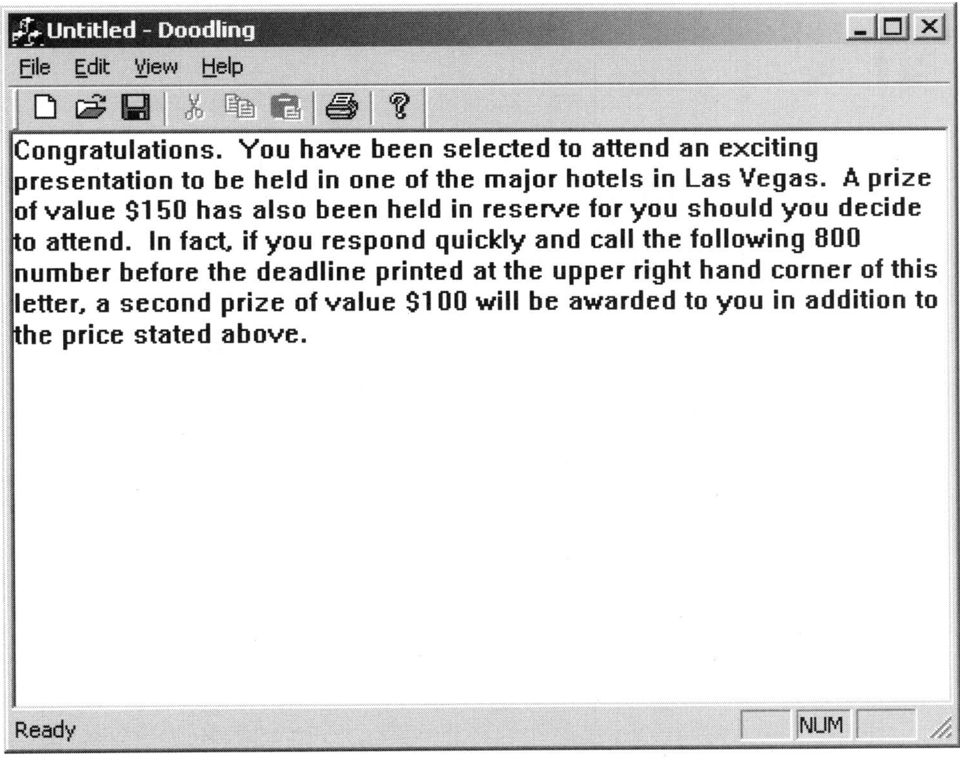

FIGURE 16.3 Text fitting the View window.

Unfortunately in this case, whereas the rectangle fits the application's client area, it takes up the entire window. How do we go about sizing it for the next text paragraph?

The way to deal with the *DrawText()* rectangle is to have the function size it for us, and at the same time adopt a text writing area management procedure so we can move from one paragraph to the next.

First, recognize that a text paragraph will not necessarily fill up the entire client window area. However, the client window's rectangular dimensions do provide us the real values of the left and the right edges. Starting from the top of the client window, we compute the exact rectangular area that is needed for one text paragraph, and then we determine where the bottom of the rectangle is and use it as the top of the next paragraph. Let's see how this scheme works by adding one more long text paragraph to our **Doodling** application:

```
     CString     csText = "Congratulations.  You have been selected to
attend an exciting presentation to be held in one of the major hotels
in Las Vegas.  A prize of value $150 has also been held in reserve for
you should you decide to attend.  In fact, if you respond quickly and
call the following 800 number before the deadline printed at the upper
right hand corner of this letter, a second prize of value $100 will be
awarded to you in addition to the price stated above.";
     CRect     clRect, txtRect;
     GetClientRect( clRect );
     txtRect = clRect;
     pDC->DrawText( csText, txtRect, DT_WORDBREAK | DT_CALCRECT );
     pDC->DrawText( csText, txtRect, DT_WORDBREAK );
     txtRect.top = txtRect.bottom;
     txtRect.bottom = clRect.bottom;
     csText = "In the unfortunate event that you cannot make it to
visit with us on the date of invitation, you may call the 800 number to
schedule a special appointment with us.  Our property consultants will
be happy to conduct a special tour for you alone.";
     pDC->DrawText( csText, txtRect, DT_WORDBREAK | DT_CALCRECT );
     pDC->DrawText( csText, txtRect, DT_WORDBREAK );
```

In this example, we first prepare two CRect objects, both mapped to the application's client area at the beginning. One will be used to guide the text output, while the other preserves the window's geometry. As the working rectangle is used, the dimensions from the original client window are used to help determine the next writing area.

The special form of the *DrawText()* function using the "DT_WORDBREAK | DT_CALCRECT" format does not produce any display output. Instead, it computes the writing area for us. Once the writing area has been determined, a follow-up *DrawText()* displays the text.

DrawText() Formats

The *DrawText()* function comes with many useful formats. Table 16.4 lists the more often used ones.

TABLE 16.4 *DrawText()* Formats

DT_CENTER	Centers text horizontally.
DT_EXPANDTABS	Expands tab characters. The default number of characters per tab is eight.
DT_LEFT	Aligns text flush left.
DT_NOCLIP	Draws without clipping, making the drawing faster than without this specification.
DT_NOPREFIX	Turns off processing of prefix characters. Normally, the ampersand (&) means underscore the following character, while two ampersands (&&) means to print one ampersand.
DT_RIGHT	Aligns text flush right.

INVALIDATE() AND UPDATEWINDOW()

The *OnDraw()* function is the CView class's main screen painting function. It is triggered every time the screen needs to be redrawn, such as when you change the application window's size, or when the view is uncovered from obscurity. It responds to Windows' WM_PAINT message.

However, when programming actions do not result in *OnDraw()* being called, the screen will not update itself automatically. In such situations, you use CWnd class's *Invalidate()* member function to fire off the WM_PAINT message and place it in Windows' message queue, causing the client area to be redrawn when the next *UpdateWindow()* call comes up, which actually updates the client area.

Because Windows processes messages from the queue on a first-come-first-serve basis, if there are lots of messages waiting to be handled, it may take time for a message to reach its turn. Indeed, if Windows cannot clear all the messages in the turnaround time allotted, it may drop some of the lower-priority messages, of which WM_PAINT is one. In those cases you might want to issue the *UpdateWindow()* call yourself in the program to force the issue.

To see how this all works, we'll build a **Doodling** application that will have the user add one text paragraph at a time.

1. In **Doodling**, add a new dialog with the ID of IDD_DIALOG_PARA and use it to generate a new class named CDlgPara.
2. In the CDlgPara dialog, provide an edit control with the ID of IDC_EDIT_PARA for user input as shown in Figure 16.4.

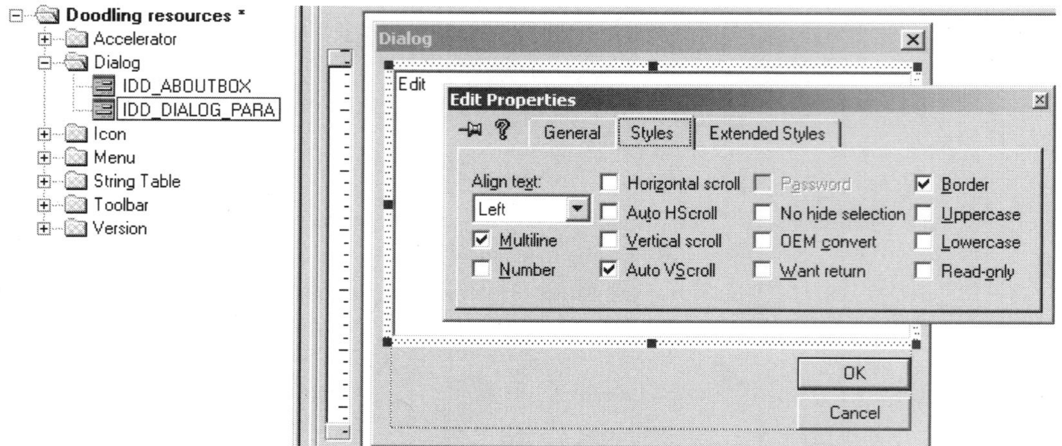

FIGURE 16.4 A multiline vertical-scroll edit box.

Note that the edit box properties are set to "Multiline" and "Auto VScroll," but no horizontal scroll. This way the text will wrap around.

3. Add a CString member variable **m_csPara** for the edit box.
4. Add a handler function for the WM_INITDIALOG message for the new dialog to enable data exchange upload:

```
BOOL CDlgPara::OnInitDialog()
{
      CDialog::OnInitDialog();

      // TODO: Add extra initialization here
      UpdateData( FALSE );
      return TRUE;
}
```

5. Add a message handler function for the OK button's BN_CLICKED event to download data exchange:

```
void CDlgPara::OnOK()
{
     // TODO: Add extra validation here
     UpdateData( TRUE );
     CDialog::OnOK();
}
```

6. Add a New Paragraph command to the menu (Figure 16.5).

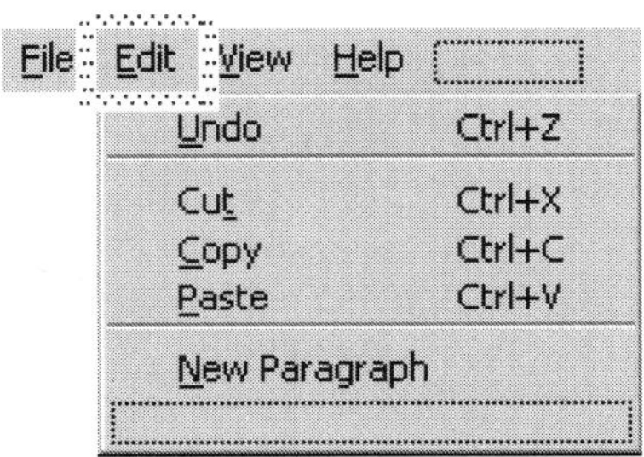

FIGURE 16.5 Sample New Paragraph command.

7. Generate a handler function for the New Paragraph command in the View class:

```
void CDoodlingView::OnEditNewParagraph()
{
     // TODO: Add your command handler code here
}
```

8. In the View class add a private Document pointer variable **m_pDoc**:

```
private:
     CDoodlingDoc* m_pDoc;
```

9. Add a statement in the View class's for *OnInitialUpdate()* function to point the **m_pDoc** variable at the Document object:

```
void CDoodlingView::OnInitialUpdate()
{
     CView::OnInitialUpdate();

     // TODO: Add your specialized code here and/or…
     m_pDoc = GetDocument();
}
```

10. Add a CString variable and an int variable to the Document class:

```
class CDoodlingDoc : public CDocument
{
...
// Implementation
public:
	int m_iPara;
	CString m_csPara[ 10 ];
```

This CString array **m_csPara**[] will store the paragraph text entered by the user (up to 10 paragraphs for this simple design). **m_iPara** will track the array elements.

11. Initialize m_iPara in the *OnNewDocument()* function:

```
BOOL CDoodlingDoc::OnNewDocument()
{
	if (!CDocument::OnNewDocument())
		return FALSE;
	// TODO: add reinitialization code here
	// (SDI documents will reuse this document)
	m_iPara = 0;
	return TRUE;
}
```

12. Add the following code to the View's *OnEditParagaph()* function:

```
#include "DlgPara.h"
void CDoodlingView::OnEditNewParagraph()
{
	// TODO: Add your command handler code here
	CDlgPara	dlg( this );
	if ( dlg.DoModal() == IDOK )
	{
		m_pDoc->m_csPara[ m_pDoc->m_iPara ] = dlg.m_csPara;
		m_pDoc->m_iPara++;
		Invalidate( FALSE );
		UpdateWindow();
	}
}
```

13. Compile the program and test it. Use the Edit->New Paragraph command to enter new paragraph text passages (but not more than 10 paragraphs) and see them progressively displayed.

Let's understand how it all works.

On purpose, we set up an example whereby the application's client area must be redrawn repeatedly, knowing that the *OnDraw()* function is executed automatically only when Windows mandates that it should. Also, we wanted to create a situation whereby different screens must be redrawn every time. The way we did it was to generalize the drawing procedures so that the same logic would apply to different display data sets. All the while we also wanted to demonstrate how to work with data maintained in the Document object.

For simplicity, a CString array was set up in the Document object. An integer variable was defined to track the array's elements. In the View object, a private variable m_pDoc was set up to point to the Document object so that we didn't have to use the *GetDocument()* function repeatedly. The text display logic, as it turned out, was just a generalization of what we have been experimenting with all along, cycling through the text elements held in the Document object.

Because the data updating operations were executed in a separate function, the *OnDraw()* function had no reason to take action and update the screen automatically just because new data had come into being. Therefore, when new data items were incorporated into the data array, the *Invalidate()* function must be called to force a Windows repaint action, which in turn activated the *OnDraw()* function. Then, the *UpdatedWindow()* function was called to cause the screen update to take place immediately.

In general, screen-drawing actions, be they graphical or textual, belong to the domain of the CDC class, an object that is internally maintained by the CView class in the Document/View application framework.

For graphics, you first define and select a drawing pen or brush using the CPen and CBrush classes, respectively. For text, you first create and select a font with the CFont class. Next, you set the output map mode with the *SetMapMode()* function, and use the appropriate CDC member drawing functions to produce the output in the CView class's *OnDraw()* function.

If the output area must be refreshed or redone, you call the CWnd's *Invalidate()* function and force an immediate update if necessary with the *UpdateWindow()* function.

17 Printing and Print Preview

ON THE CD

With the View/Document application framework or paradigm, printing and print previewing are built in. In our **Doodling** program, you will find that the File->Print commands are already in place. From the CView class's command message map, you can see that these commands are built-in members of the CView class:

```
BEGIN_MESSAGE_MAP(CDoodlingView, CView)
      //{{AFX_MSG_MAP(CDoodlingView)
      ON_COMMAND(ID_EDIT_NEWPARAGRAPH, OnEditNewParagraph)
      //}}AFX_MSG_MAP
      // Standard printing commands
      ON_COMMAND(ID_FILE_PRINT, CView::OnFilePrint)
      ON_COMMAND(ID_FILE_PRINT_DIRECT, CView::OnFilePrint)
      ON_COMMAND(ID_FILE_PRINT_PREVIEW, CView::OnFilePrintPreview)
END_MESSAGE_MAP()
```

To use these commands, all the user needs to do is invoke them.

However, if you try **Doodling**'s Print Preview command now, you'll find the output less than satisfactory (Figure 17.1). This is because we are using the same outputting code in the *OnDraw()* function for two distinctly different devices: the screen and the printer.

The right way to handle printing (and print previewing) is to provide separate logic directives apart from those prepared for the screen. For this, the CDC class provides us with a function to discriminate between the two: the *IsPrinting()* function. For example, you can use the following code to call out the printing actions:

```
void CDoodlingView::OnDraw(CDC* pDC)
{
```

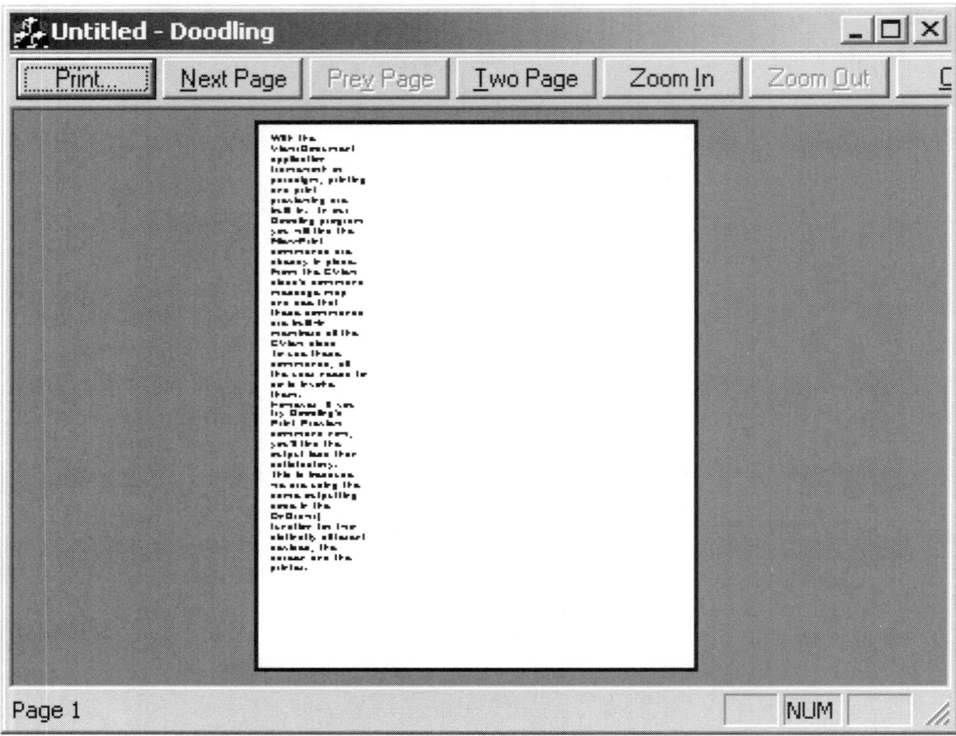

FIGURE 17.1 Print Preview.

```
        if ( pDC->IsPrinting() )
        {
             DoPrinting( pDC );
             return;
        }
   }
```

Of course, the writing of the *DoPrinting()* function now becomes the game.

Setting Up for Printing

To properly handle printing, we need to know the print device (the printer) and capture its attributes, notably the page size, the print margins, and then coordinate them with the printing objects (pen, brush, font, and so on).

ON THE CD

1. Add the following member variables to **Doodling**'s View class, which should be clear by their names:

```
private:
  int    x, y;
  int    m_iCharWidth;
  int    m_iLineHeight;
  int    m_iPageHeight;
  int    m_iPageWidth;
```

Here, int x and int y will be used to mark the x and y coordinates. Although these variables do not conform to our naming convention, they are clearly understood in context.

2. Initialize these variables in the View's *OnInitialUpdate()* function:

```
void CDoodlingView::OnInitialUpdate()
{
     CView::OnInitialUpdate();
     ...

     x = 0;
     y = 0;
     m_iPageHeight = 0;
     m_iLineHeight = 0;
     m_iCharWidth = 0;
     m_iLineHeight = 0;
}
```

When *OnDraw()* prints, it prints the entire document, regardless of how many pages there are. In this process it invokes the services of several functions, each responsible for its share of print activities. The action is depicted in Figure 17.2.

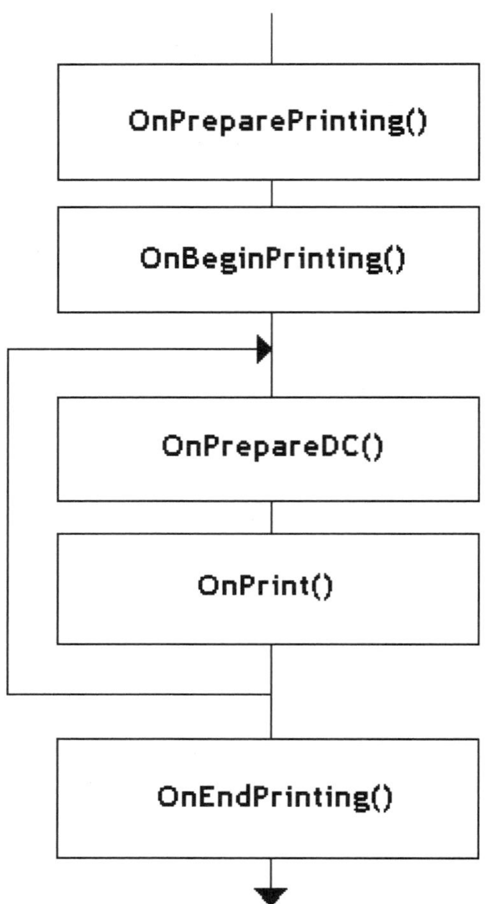

FIGURE 17.2 The Print Flow diagram.

ONPREPAREPRINTING()

The first function called is *OnPreparePrinting()*. You can use this function to perform all your document printing's print device setup work if you want, such as select the CPen object and font, although it is not mandatory.

ONBEGINPRINTING()

You use this function to do initial work involving the device context.

ON THE CD

In **Doodling**, add definition code to the View class's *OnBeginPrinting()* function, making sure that you un-comment its parameters that were originally commented out:

```
void CDoodlingView::OnBeginPrinting(CDC* pDC, CPrintInfo* pInfo)
{
     // TODO: add extra initialization before printing
     m_iPageHeight = pDC->GetDeviceCaps( VERTRES );
     m_iPageWidth = pDC->GetDeviceCaps( HORZRES );
     TEXTMETRIC     tm;
     pDC->GetTextMetrics( &tm );
     m_iLineHeight = tm.tmHeight;
     m_iCharWidth = tm.tmAveCharWidth;
     // Set maximum pages.
     pInfo->SetMaxPage( 1 );
}
```

The CDC class's *GetDeviceCaps()* function returns information about the output device. The VERTRES integer parameter asks for the vertical resolution in millimeters, while the HORZRES parameter values asks for the horizontal resolution in millimeters.

For the printing characters, first we construct a TEXTMETRICS structure, and use CDC's *GetTextMetrics()* member function to fill it. Once the structure is filled, we can access it to obtain the character height value with the **tmHeight** structure member, and the average character width with the **tmAveCharWidth** structure member.

The *OnBeginPrinting()* function can also be optionally passed the CPrintInfo object which, obviously, avails the print information. One of its member function is *SetMaxPage()*, which sets the maximum print page count. This piece of data will be used during print previewing to control the number of pages that you can preview. In this exercise, it is set to 1 arbitrarily.

ONPREPAREDC()

For each page, if you need to reinitialize the device context you'll do it here.

ONPRINT()

This is where the actual printing activities take place.

Generate the *OnPrint()* function and add the following code to it:

```
void CDoodlingView::OnPrint(CDC* pDC, CPrintInfo* pInfo)
{
   // TODO: Add your specialized code here and/or...
   y = 0;
   CRect txtRect;
   int   iPara = 0;
   for ( iPara = 0; iPara < GetDocument()->m_iPara; iPara++ )
   {
          CString     csText = GetDocument()->m_csPara[ iPara ];
          txtRect.SetRect( x, y, m_iPageWidth, y + m_iLineHeight );
          pDC->DrawText( csText, txtRect, DT_WORDBREAK | DT_CALCRECT );
          pDC->DrawText( csText, txtRect, DT_WORDBREAK | DT_NOCLIP );
          y = y + txtRect.bottom;
     }
     CView::OnPrint(pDC, pInfo);
}
```

As you can see, the printing logic parallels that of the output to the screen we discussed earlier. The only salient points expounded here are first, the printer device attributes are used, and second, the y coordinate is set to 0 (zero) every time we print.

We also introduce the new CRect function of *SetRect()*, which sets the members of a CRect object by providing the *left*, *top*, *right*, and *bottom* values.

ONENDPRINTING()

If you have defined any font to use in the *OnBeginPrinting()* function, you clean up the objects here.

Try the preceding sample code and see how the printout looks.

18 Working with Views

From the few examples that we went through, you should have gotten an impression that CView is a very powerful class in which to work because of the rich set of member functions that come with it. Indeed, the View is such an important paradigm in the MFC family of classes that it has spawned a number of variations intended for specific uses under special circumstances. We will now look at some of these classes quickly and explore their possibilities.

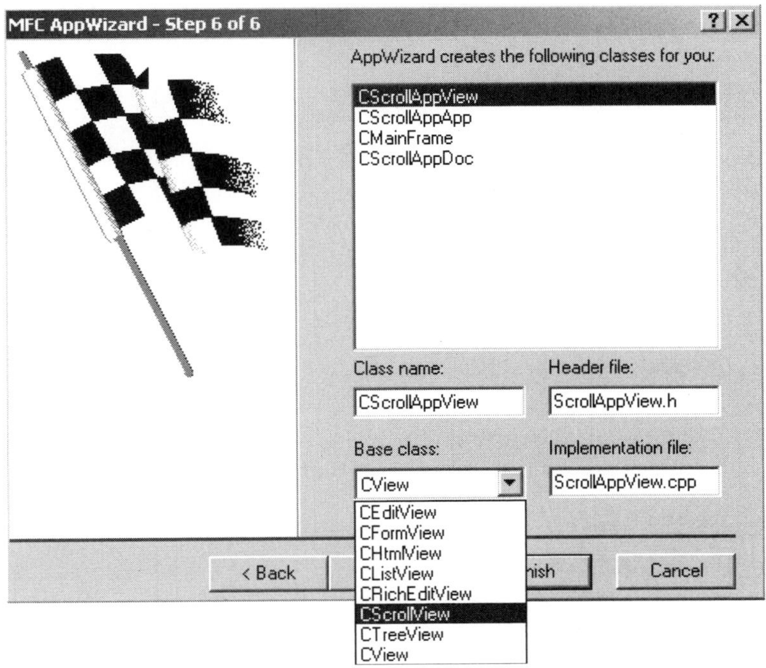

FIGURE 18.1 Selecting the CscrollView.

CSCROLLVIEW

One of the shortcomings of our **Doodling** example is that with a stationary window area we cannot see data displayed beyond its boundaries. The CScrollView class is designed specifically to help us view display data by allowing the window to scroll. The following illustration shows how it works.

ON THE CD

1. Quickly use AppWizard to generate an SDI MFC Windows application named **ScrollApp**. Select the CScrollView class in Step 6 (Figure 18.1).
2. In the View class's *OnDraw()* function, add the following code to produce 500 text lines.

```
void CScrollAppView::OnDraw(CDC* pDC)
{
	CScrollAppDoc* pDoc = GetDocument();
	ASSERT_VALID(pDoc);
	// TODO: add draw code for native data here
	pDC->SetMapMode( MM_TEXT );
	CString     csText;
	for ( int i = 0; i < 500; i++ )
	{
		csText.Format( "%4d", i );
		pDC->TextOut( 5, i * 20, csText );
	}
}
```

3. Compile the program and examine the result to confirm that you can only see the initial set of text lines.
4. Now, add the following code to size the client window's scroll area.

```
void CScrollAppView::OnDraw(CDC* pDC)
{
...
	for ( int i = 0; i < 500; i++ )
	{
		csText.Format( "%4d", i );
		pDC->TextOut( 5, i * 20, csText );
	}
	CRect     rect;
	GetClientRect( rect );
	CSize     size;
	size.cx = rect.right;
```

```
        size.cy = 10000;
        SetScrollSizes( MM_TEXT, size );
}
```

5. Try the finished and compiled program again.

What we have done here is create a CRect rectangular object by first assuming the client window's dimensions. Then, we create a CSize object that has a cx and a cy member to represent a size and pass the client rectangle's dimensions to it. For the display area's length, we compute the overall length of the display and use it to set the lower dimension of the CSize object, and then use the *SetScrollSizes()* member function to set the scroll size. As you can see, the scroll bar(s) are added for us automatically.

The *SetScrollSizes()* function takes four parameters. The first is the integer map mode that we discussed before. The second is the required CSize representing the total scroll area. After that, you can optionally supply a horizontal scroll increment amount and a vertical one; otherwise, default sizes are provided.

As you can see, the basic operations of a CScrollView class are straightforward.

CFORMVIEW

Another useful CView derivative is the CFormView. The CFormView class uses a dialog resource to produce a View that works just like a dialog as in a dialog-based application with which you're already familiar. On a CFormView object, you can directly place control objects such as static controls and edit boxes.

You'll be working with it soon in Chapter 19.

CCTRLVIEW

The CCtrlView supports the Windows 95 plus common controls such as the list control and the tree control. It will be discussed when those controls are introduced in Chapter 27.

CEditView

One of the Windows 95 Windows common controls is the edit control. When it is combined with the CView, you get the CEditView. CEditView is derived from CCtrlView and works just like the edit control but in a View paradigm.

CListView

As the CEditView is derived from CCtrlView, the CListView class provides a list control's operations in a View setting. You'll learn the list control in Chapter 27.

CTreeView

As the CListView is derived from CCtrlView, the CTreeView incorporates the tree control's functionalities in a View. The tree control is also discussed in Chapter 27.

CRICHEDITVIEW

The CRichEditView, derived from CCtrlView, makes a View work like the rich edit control that processes rich text data as a word processor does.

CRECORDVIEW

The CRecordView class combines ODBC database data connections and controls in a CFormView so that the controls are "data aware," simplifying database front-end work for you.

You'll experience the CRecordView class when databases are discussed in Chapter 24.

CDAORECORDVIEW

As does the CRecordView class, the CDaoRecordView works with database data. In this case, it works with the Microsoft Jet Engine designed to work with the Access database and other Microsoft data structures such as Excel. Once you learn to work with ODBC data via the CRecordset class, you'll pretty much know how to work with CDaoRecordset and therefore CDaoRecordView.

19 The MDI Application, Split Windows, and Multiple Views

Should an application demand user interfacing that must go beyond what single-viewed frameworks such as the dialog window and SDI models allow, there are other more sophisticated and measurably more intricate frameworks to turn to.

First, the MDI framework provides us with multiple views of the same data set, or if so designed, diverse data sets and views all in one application. If necessary, a view window can be split to permit the concurrent viewing of different parts of a view. In this part of the book, we'll look at these window styles in turn.

THE MDI APPLICATION MODEL

As the SDI model, the MDI model has a main frame, views, and a document. The only added complexity is the multiple frame windows, called *child frames* or child windows, which can fit inside the main frame. The basic purpose of this framework is to allow the data managed by the Document object to be viewed through multiple frame openings. To observe this effect, perform the following experiment:

ON THE CD

1. In the **MDIApp** application, add a public CString member variable to the Document class:

```
// Implementation
public:
    CString m_csText;
```

2. In the Document class's *OnNewDocument()* function, initialize the variable:

```
BOOL CMDIAppDoc::OnNewDocument()
{
    ...
     m_csText = "Once ";
     return TRUE;
}
```

3. In the View class, add the text output code in the *OnDraw()* function:

```
void CMDIAppView::OnDraw(CDC* pDC)
{
    ...
     // TODO: add draw code for native data here
     pDC->TextOut( 5, 5, GetDocument()->m_csText );
}
```

4. Compile the program and test it to make sure that the text is displayed.
5. Bring up the IDR_MDIAPPTYPE menu resource and add an Edit->New Text command. Generate a command handler function in the View class and add the following code:

```
void CMDIAppView::OnEditNewtext()
{
     // TODO: Add your command handler code here
     GetDocument()->m_csText = GetDocument()->m_csText + "upon a time";
     Invalidate();
}
```

This extra bit of code adds more data to the CString variable in the Document object and forces the View to redraw itself.

6. Compile the program and test it. Invoke the Edit->New Text command and observe the View being refreshed with the new data. Then, terminate the program and try again. This time, open a new child window with the Window->New Window command, and then choose the Edit->New Text command and observe the results.

You should see that the new child window has the new data but not the old. This is because the View class's *Invalidate()* function only redraws the current view.

7. Change the *Invalidate()* function in *OnEditNewtext()* to the following and test the program again.

```
void CMDIAppView::OnEditAddtext()
{
     // TODO: Add your command handler code here
     GetDocument()->m_csText = GetDocument()->m_csText + "upon a time";
     GetDocument()->UpdateAllViews( NULL );
}
```

You should see all the child windows updated.

The Document class's *UpdateAllViews()* function is used to update the multiple views in an MDI application. If the first parameter is NULL, all the views are updated. If the first parameter is the sender view, such as *UpdateAllViews(this)*, all the views but the focused view will be updated. The function also can have two more parameters that are used to convey information on the view update and can be used to impart nuances to the update. When unspecified, default 0 and NULL values will be supplied and those parameters will not be used.

The Main Frame and the Child Frame

The outer frame in an MDI application is derived from the CMDIFrameWnd class, which is derived from the CFrameWnd class, which is also the base class for CMDIChildWnd, the class behind the child window. For the code in the CMDIChildWnd class to reach the outer mainframe, use the *GetParent()* member function to obtain a pointer to it so that you can write code from the child frame class such as:

```
((CMainFrame*)GetParent())->m_wndToolBar;
```

The CMDIFrameWnd has its own member functions to help navigate the child windows. For example, you use the "void MDIActivate(CWnd* pWndActivate)" function to set the focus to a different child window as if the user has clicked on it, provided, of course, that you have the pointer to that window. This implies that as the program opens new child windows, it must keep track of the new windows' pointers.

As you can see, programming with the MDI framework can get awfully messy in a hurry, and requires many of the topics that we have not yet covered to manage its operations, especially if you try to divert from its basic behavior and do something out of the ordinary, such as attempting to use the child windows as individual subprograms to do different things and not just be content to use them to display different aspects of the same data.

In the forthcoming chapters, we'll introduce many of the topics that you'll need to comfortably work with MDI applications.

WORKING WITH SPLIT WINDOWS

Just like Views, the frame window also offers its variations. The most often used style after the default plain frame is almost without question the split window, and it is easy to generate with the IDE.

1. Use AppWizard to generate an MFC SDI Windows application named **SplitWindow** with a special detour in Step 4.
2. In Step 4, click Advanced to bring up the Advanced Options dialog (Figure 19.1).

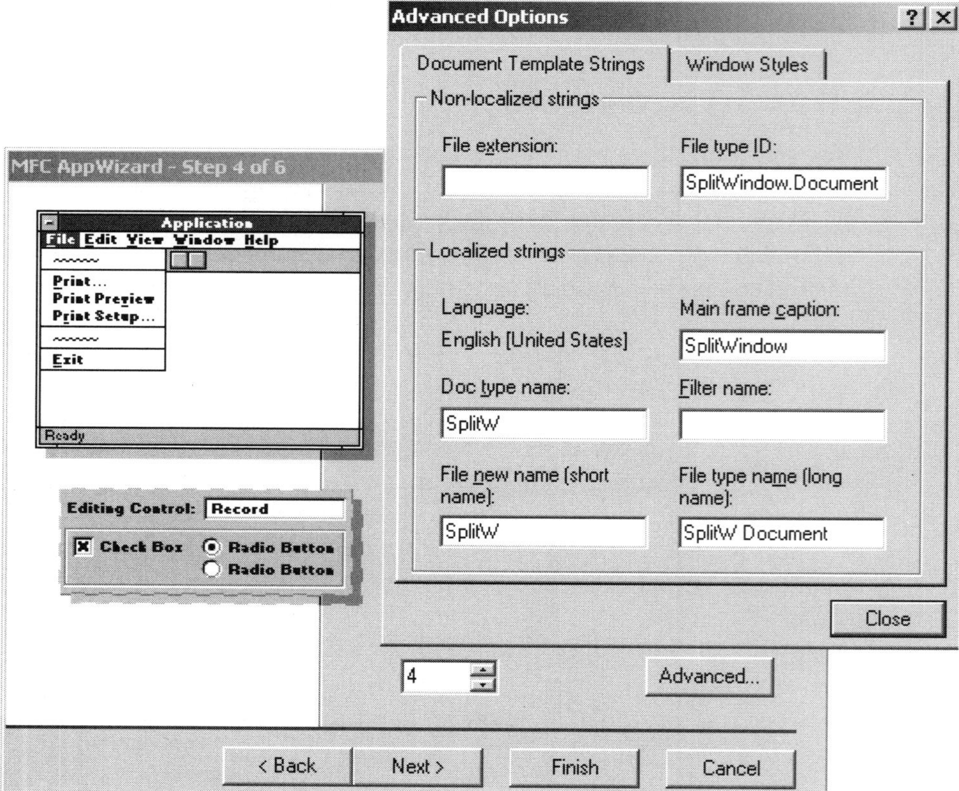

FIGURE 19.1 Advanced Window option.

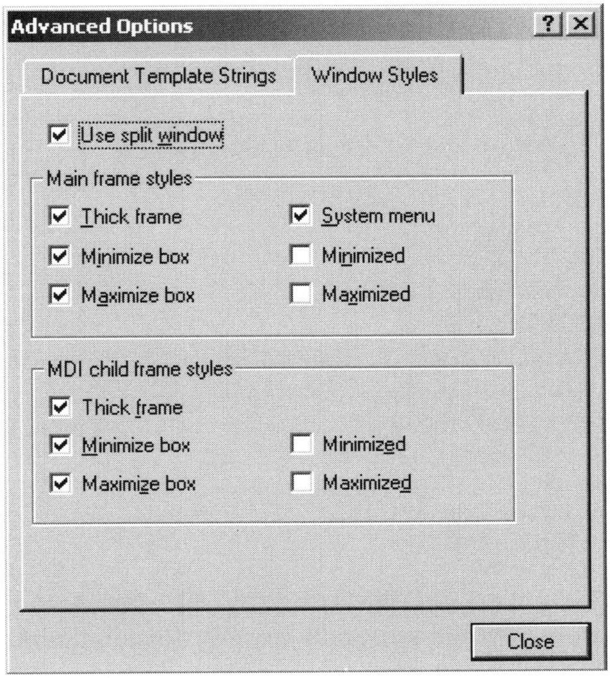

FIGURE 19.2 Using split window.

3. Select the "Use split window" option (Figure 19.2) and complete the application generation process. Compile the application and test it.

You should see split window selector pads provided as in Figure 19.3.

4. Drag on these pads to split the application's client window, and then double-click them to close the split windows.

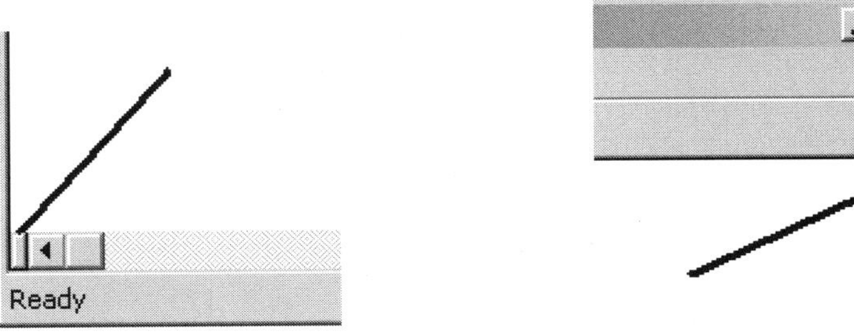

FIGURE 19.3 Split window selector pads.

CSplitterWnd

ON THE CD

In SplitWindow's MainFrm.h header file, you should see an entry of a protected object:

```
// Attributes
protected:
     CSplitterWnd m_wndSplitter;
```

The **m_wndSplitter** object, based on the MFC CSplitterWnd class, is responsible for the actions of the split windows.

In CMainFrm, you'll find the object's creation:

```
BOOL CMainFrame::OnCreateClient(LPCREATESTRUCT /*lpcs*/,
     CCreateContext* pContext)
{
     return m_wndSplitter.Create(this, 2, 2,
   CSize(10, 10), pContext);
}
```

The first parameter in the CSplitterWnd's *Create()* function is the parent CWnd pointer. In this case, it is the mainframe.

The next parameter is the maximum number of rows, not to exceed 2 (but at least 1).

The third parameter is the maximum number of columns, also not to exceed 2, and at least 1.

The fourth parameter specifies the minimum split window size expressed as a CSize object, providing the x and y dimensions. This means that when the split window's size moves below this size, the split window will collapse.

The fifth parameter is a pointer to a CCreateContext object, which, in most cases, is passed on by the parent frame class, which internally maintains one.

Following these are two more parameters that have default values. The sixth is the DWORD window style, which defaults to WS_CHILD | WS_VISIBLE |WS_HSCROLL | WS_VSCROLL | SPLS_DYNAMIC_SPLIT.

The seventh parameter is the unsigned integer child window ID, which defaults to AFX_IDW_PANE_FIRST.

To get a feel for the workings of the splitter windows, try varying the number of windows you can have. For example, try the following:

```
return m_wndSplitter.Create(this, 1, 2,
   CSize(10, 10), pContext);
```

You might also want to increase the CSize values to see how a minimum split window size affects its operations.

The splitter window is used to let a user have different views of the same document data; although, with a little fanciful programming, you can make it present different views as well.

WORKING WITH MULTIPLE VIEWS

Occasionally, you will find a single view or views of the same type insufficient for the purposes of your applications or restrictive for what you need to achieve. In such a case, you can provide alternate views and switch between them. The approach to accomplishing this is actually quite straightforward.

In the following demonstration, we will create two views of different types for an SDI application.

1. Swiftly deploy a vanilla SDI application using all the defaults, with the view being of the CView type. Indeed, you can use the old exercise **SDIApp** for our purposes here if you like.
2. Insert a new dialog resource, giving it the ID of IDD_DIALOG_DATA.

We intend to create an added view for data entry; a form view that allows us to populate it with controls.

3. Use the new dialog's properties to set it to have the "Child" style and no border (Figure 19.4).

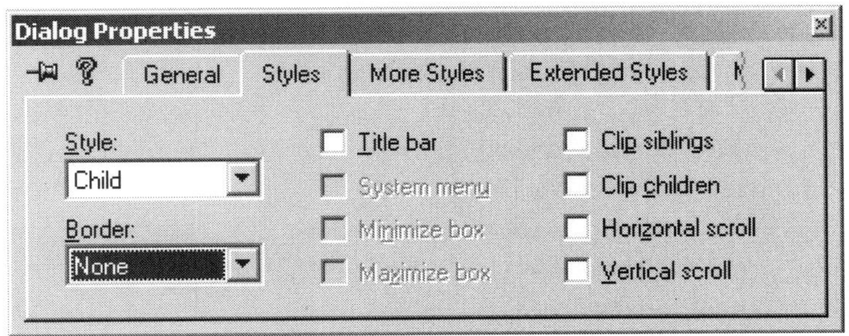

FIGURE 19.4 Child dialog style with no border.

4. Remove all the buttons (OK and Cancel).

A view that will eventually be set in a window frame needs no buttons.

5. Create a new class named CDataView for IDD_DIALOG_DATA derived from CFormView.
6. Open the DataView.h file and move the constructor from:

```
class CDataView : public CFormView
{
protected:
     CDataView();            // protected constructor…
     DECLARE_DYNCREATE(CDataView)
```

to:

```
class CDataView : public CFormView
{
public:
     CDataView();            // protected constructor…
protected:
     DECLARE_DYNCREATE(CDataView)
```

This change will allow the constructor to be called externally, as the program needs to create the view explicitly later.

7. Add two private member variables to the CMainFrame class:

```
private:
     CView* m_pDataView;
     CView* m_pTextView;
```

Each pointer variable will be used to point at a view.

8. Override the *ActivateFrame()* function for the CMainFrame class, and enter the view creation code in it:

```
void CMainFrame::ActivateFrame(int nCmdShow)
{
     // TODO: Add your specialized code here and/or..
     // Set up views
     m_pTextView = GetActiveView();
     m_pDataView = (CView*) new CDataView;
     CCreateContext     ct;
     ct.m_pCurrentDoc = m_pTextView->GetDocument();
```

```
    m_pDataView->Create( NULL, NULL, 0L, CFrameWnd::rectDefault, this,
  IDD_DIALOG_DATA, &ct );
    m_pDataView->OnInitialUpdate();
    CFrameWnd::ActivateFrame(nCmdShow);
}
```

The logic here is simple. When the mainframe is about to be activated, by which time the default view is already constructed, we point the variable **m_pTextView** to the active view of the CView class. Then we request a new pointer for the View object of the CDataView class, but cast it to (CView*) to suit the requirements of the pointer. When this is done, we create a CDataView object and point the pointer to it. Once the View object is successfully created, we initialize it.

Because we implemented code for a new object, we remember to clean it up.

9. Add the *OnDestroy()* message handler for CMainFrame and install code to delete the CDataView object:

```
void CMainFrame::OnDestroy()
{
    CFrameWnd::OnDestroy();

    // TODO: Add your message handler code here
    delete m_pDataView;
    m_pDataView = NULL;
}
```

Now that the view construction code is in place, we implement commands to switch them.

10. Add two new commands to the menu (Figure 19.5).

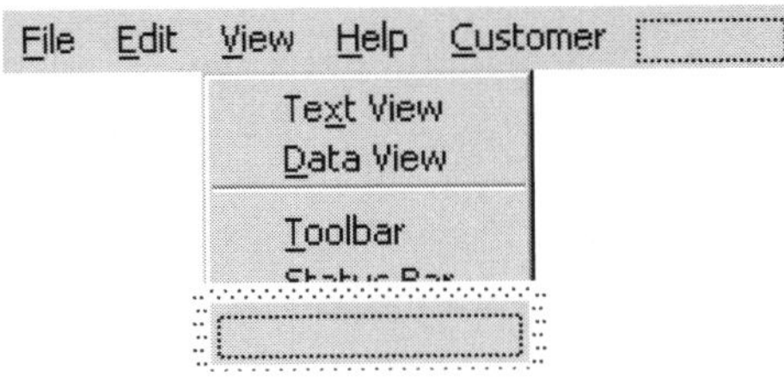

FIGURE 19.5 View Selection commands.

11. Use ClassWizard to create command message handlers in CMainFrame for the two new commands View->Text View and View->Data View, respectively, and enter view switching code in the two functions:

```
void CMainFrame::OnViewTextView()
{
      // TODO: Add your command handler code here
      SetActiveView( m_pTextView );
      m_pDataView->ShowWindow( SW_HIDE );
      m_pTextView->ShowWindow( SW_SHOW );
      m_pTextView->SetDlgCtrlID( AFX_IDW_PANE_FIRST );
      RecalcLayout();
}
void CMainFrame::OnViewDataView()
{
      // TODO: Add your command handler code here
      SetActiveView( m_pDataView );
      m_pTextView->ShowWindow( SW_HIDE );
      m_pDataView->ShowWindow( SW_SHOW );
      m_pDataView->SetDlgCtrlID( AFX_IDW_PANE_FIRST );
      RecalcLayout();
}
```

12. Make sure you have the proper #include directive for the CDataView class in the source code:

```
#include "DataView.h"
```

13. Compile the program and test it.

When switching to another view, first we set the active view to the target view (*SetActiveView()*). Then we hide the old view (*ShowWindow(SW_HIDE)*) and show the new view (*ShowWindow(SW_SHOW)*). Once that is done, we set the control ID for the view as required, and then recompute the window layout.

14. As practice, try placing some controls in the CDataView dialog and see how things pan out. Then try to manage the data in the document and transfer between the views.
15. Close the project.

PART

V Working with MFC Data Classes

With the application framework under our wings, we turn our attention to data. After all, data are the fodder of our applications. Data processing is the real reason for developing applications in the first place. However, the data we are going to be looking at aren't the same old numeric and character data that we studied in C or C++. Rather, we will be looking at the special MFC entries that have been developed specifically to handle institutional data. While doing so, we'll also learn the various ways with which you can organize and access such data.

In this part of the book, we introduce four groups of classes that are meant to deal with data.

- The CString class is used to facilitate work with text data.
- Date and time classes are used when date and time expressions are required.
- Collections extend the basic constructs of arrays and incorporate such heretofore-deemed "advanced" concepts as linked lists.
- I/O-file classes simplify our life in dealing with disk data transactions.

20 CString

For a while now we have been working with a class named CString, and as mentioned, it is MFC's approach to encapsulating the functions and operations of text data that makes working with alphanumeric data as easy in C++ as it is in other high-level languages such as VB and without the cryptic nature of string data inherent in the C language. For example, instead of having to first subscribe to available computer memory and then meticulously placing component strings in it to achieve the effects of concatenation, with CString you can join strings together by simply "adding" them, as in:

```
CString     csName = csFirstName  + " "  + csLastName;
```

A CString object is created by simply instantiating it. For example:

```
CString     csName;
```

You can also assign data to it at the time that the object is created, as exemplified in our first example.

Because by definition a CString object's name is its pointer, a CString object can be used anywhere a traditional C type variable is called for. For example, where a LPCTSTR data type is specified, a CString object can be used, or at least you can use the (LPCTSTR) operator to return its pointer (type casting it), such as:

```
(LPCTSTR) csName
```

In fact, a CString object behaves so much like a regular string that you can even express it as an array of characters. Thus, if csName = "John", csName[0] is the character 'J'.

Because a CString object works exactly as a string data in most other languages, we often simply call it a string variable.

We will now look at some of CString's most popular member functions.

GetLength()

The *GetLength()* member function returns the length (number of characters) of a CString object as an integer.

```
CString     csName = "Alexander";
int      iLen;
iLen = csName.GetLength();
```

Format()

The *Format()* function creates a CString object based on value(s) according to a format string prescription. The form of the *Format()* function is:

```
void Format( LPCTSTR lpszFormat, ... );
```

For example, to make a string of five characters based on an integer:

```
CString     csAcctNum;
csAcctNum.Format( "%5d", iAcctNum );
```

The format string is exactly the same as that used in the C language's *printf()* function, and can be looked up from your online references under "printf."

GetAt()

The *GetAt()* function returns the character at a specified location in a CString object:

```
TCHAR GetAt( int nIndex ) const;
```

Example:

```
CString     csName = "Alexander";
if ( csName.GetAt( 0 ) == 'A' )
     MessageBox( "The name is from the A section.", "", MB_OK );
```

IsEmpty()

You use the Boolean *IsEmpty()* function to determine if a CString object has no character in it. The following example calls a developer-designed *EnterName()* function if no name has been entered:

```
CString     csText = "";
if ( csName.IsEmpty() )
     EnterName();
```

Left() and Right()

The *Left()* function forms a new CString object by taking a number of characters from the left side of an original CString object. For example, to get the initial of a name:

```
CString     csName = "Alexander";
CString     csInitial;
csInitial = csName.Left( 1 );
```

The *Right()* function takes the characters from the right.

Mid()

The *Mid()* function forms a CString object out of a number of specified characters beginning with a specified character position. Example:

```
CString     csKey = "abcdefg";
CString     csCode = csKey.Mid( 3, 2 );
```

csCode is now "de";

MakeLower() and MakeUpper()

The *MakeLower()* function converts the characters in a CString object into lowercase. For example, assuming that a *GetID()* function has been developed by a developer to obtain a string from the user:

```
CString     csID;
csID = GetID();
if ( csID.MakeLower() == "guest" )
     ...
```

The *MakeUpper()* functions converts the characters to uppercase.

TrimLeft() and TrimRight()

These functions shorten a CString object by removing characters from the left or right. If no trim characters are specified, the functions remove white spaces, tab characters ('\t'), newline characters ('\n'), and other non-alphanumeric characters. Example:

```
CString     csName = "      John";
csName.TrimLeft();
```

csName is now "John".

If a matching string is provided, such as csCode.TrimLeft("/***"), those characters will be trimmed.

To VB programmers: do the *Left()*, *Mid()*, *Right()*, *TrimLeft()*, and *TrimRight()* functions look familiar?

LoadString()

Finally, we come to *LoadString()*. If you recall, when we took the IDE tour at the beginning of the book we discussed all the resource departments, including dialogs, menus, toolbars, and icons, but not String Table. Now, we're ready for it.

The string table is where VC++ developers organize the strings used in an application. The idea is, if you define strings as resources and load them into the application programmatically, first, it is easier to track them down and work with them because they're organized as versus embedding them through the program code. If you're a seasoned developer, you'll remember the trouble tracking down message strings in a program. Second, by defining strings as resources, you can easily change resource sets and change strings, such as in developing applications for different languages. The CString function to load a string resource into a CString object is the *LoadString()* functions.

ON THE CD

As an experiment, go in the **SDIApp** sample program and open the string resource.

1. Choose the New String command from the context menu (Figure 20.1).
2. Enter a new string, assign it a proper ID as shown in Figure 20.2, and close the dialog.
3. In the View class, override the *OnInitialUpdate()* virtual function and add the message code:

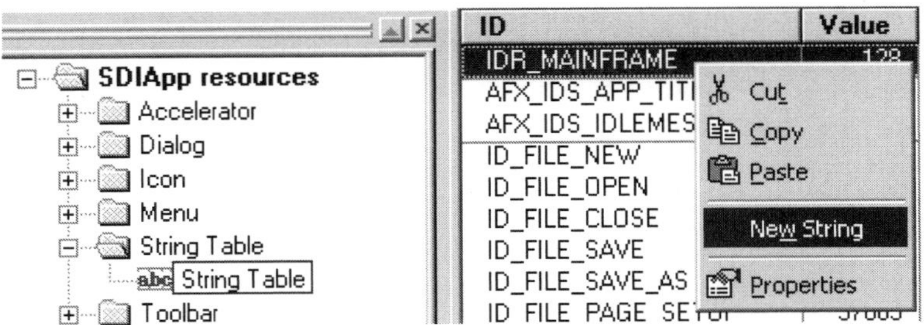

FIGURE 20.1 New String resource.

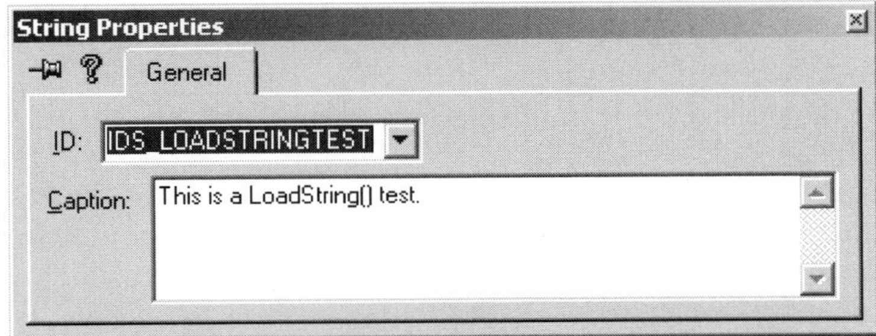

FIGURE 20.2 Adding a New String resource.

```
void CSDIAppView::OnInitialUpdate()
{
    CView::OnInitialUpdate();

    // TODO: Add your specialized code here and/or…
    CString     csMsg;
    csMsg.LoadString( IDS_LOADSTRINGTEST );
    MessageBox( csMsg, "Test", MB_OK );
}
```

4. Compile and test the program.

Where possible, in VC++ programming you're encouraged to use CString for text data. It is a lot more user-friendly than the C language counterparts. CString works very much like other high-level language string data types, and if you have a background in such languages, you should find CString a joy to work with.

Check out other useful CString functions from the language references such as *Find()*, *Insert()*, *Delete()*, *Replace()* and many others.

21 Date and Time

Another type of data developers regularly run across is chronological data: date and time. MFC has several entries devoted to its handling.

In many other languages, date and time are often treated as characters. Such representations are limited in capabilities because character data lack the sense of magnitude, which is inherent with date and time type data. For example, it will be hard-pressed for character data to express the notion that one date is later than another, or to compute the time span between two moments. For this, the MFC date and time classes were created.

CTIME

The CTime class encapsulates *date and time* values in one single construct. You instantiate a CTime object with:

```
CTime      ctDateTime;
```

The value of the CTime object is given by any one of the many member functions provided.

Current Time

To assign the current date and time value based on the computer's system clock, you use the *GetCurrentTime()* function, as in:

```
ctDateTime = CTime::GetCurrentTime();
```

Specific Time

To assign a specific date and time value to a CTime object at construction time, you can use one of many forms, with the following being most straightforward:

```
CTime( int nYear, int nMonth, int nDay, int nHour, int nMin, int nSec,
int nDST = -1 );
```

For example:

```
CTime     ctDateTime( 2001, 9, 2, 0, 0, 0, -1 );
```

The last parameter indicates the involvement of Daylight Savings Time. If nDST is set to 0, Standard time is in effect. If nDST is set to a value greater than 0, Daylight Savings Time is in effect. Otherwise, when nDST is set to a value less than 0, which is the default, the convention to use will be based on the computer's system setting.

Reading Time

Once a CTime object has a value, you can read the date/time components using the *GetYear()*, *GetMonth()*, *GetDay()*, *GetHour()*, *GetMinute()*, *GetSecond()*, and *GetDayOfWeek()* member functions, which all return integers. For example:

```
int     iYear = ctDateTime.GetYear();
```

String Conversion

To facilitate user interfacing, the *Format()* member function can be used to create a CString object representing the CTime object's date/time value. The form of the function is:

```
CString Format( LPCTSTR pFormat ) const;
```

where the pFormat string is made up of the format codes in Table 21.1.

Example:

```
CString     csFormat = "%A,%B %d,%Y";
CString     csDateTime = ctDateTime.Format( csFormat );
```

TABLE 21.1 Date/Time Format Code

Format Code	Description
%a	Abbreviated weekday name
%A	Full weekday name
%b	Abbreviated month name
%B	Full month name
%c	Date and time representation appropriate for locale
%d	Day of month as decimal number (01–31)
%D	Total days in this CTime
%H	Hour in 24-hour format (00–23)
%I	Hour in 12-hour format (01–12)
%j	Day of year as decimal number (001–366)
%m	Month as decimal number (01–12)
%M	Minute as decimal number (00–59)
%p	Current locale's A.M./P.M. indicator for 12-hour clock
%S	Second as decimal number (00–59)
%U	Week of year as decimal number, with Sunday as first day of week (00–53)
%w	Weekday as decimal number (0–6; Sunday is 0)
%W	Week of year as decimal number, with Monday as first day of week (00–53)
%x	Date representation for current locale
%X	Time representation for current locale
%y	Year without century, as decimal number (00–99)
%Y	Year with century, as decimal number
%z, %Z	Time-zone name or abbreviation; no characters if time zone is unknown
%%	Percent sign

The Month Calendar Control

To assist in the handling of date/time data in a Windows graphical display environment, MFC provides a visual object that represents the CMonthCalCtrl class. Here we'll illustrate its use by an example.

In this example, we have two time values, one for today's date and time, and one for a value selected by the user.

1. Use AppWizard to generate a dialog-based MFC Windows application named **MCDemo**.
2. On the main dialog, add a pair of static controls and edit boxes as shown in Figure 21.1. Also, change the Cancel button to a Get Date button. Set the edit boxes to be non-tab stops.

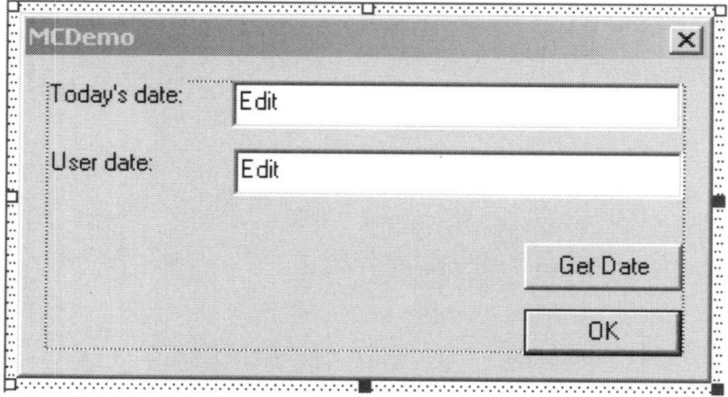

FIGURE 21.1 MCDemo main dialog.

3. Create two CString objects for the two edit boxes:

```
// Dialog Data
     //{{AFX_DATA(CMCDemoDlg)
     enum { IDD = IDD_MCDEMO_DIALOG };
     CString     m_csToday;
     CString     m_csUserDate;
     //}}AFX_DATA
```

4. Add CTime objects for the CMCDemoApp class to hold the current date/time value:

```
class CMCDemoDlg : public CDialog
{
private:
     CTime m_ctToday;
```

These objects will hold today's date and the date specified by the user.

5. Initialize the **m_ctToday** object in the *OnInitDialog()* function:

```
BOOL CMCDemoDlg::OnInitDialog()
{
...
     m_ctToday = CTime::GetCurrentTime();
     m_csToday = m_ctToday.Format( "%A, %B %d, %Y  %H:%m:%S" );
     UpdateData( FALSE );
     return TRUE;  // return TRUE  unless you set the focus to a
control
}
```

This will insert the current date and time in the first edit box as a text. Next, we ask the user to select a date.

6. Add a dialog resource, properly ID it, and populate it with the Month Calendar Control (Figure 21.2).

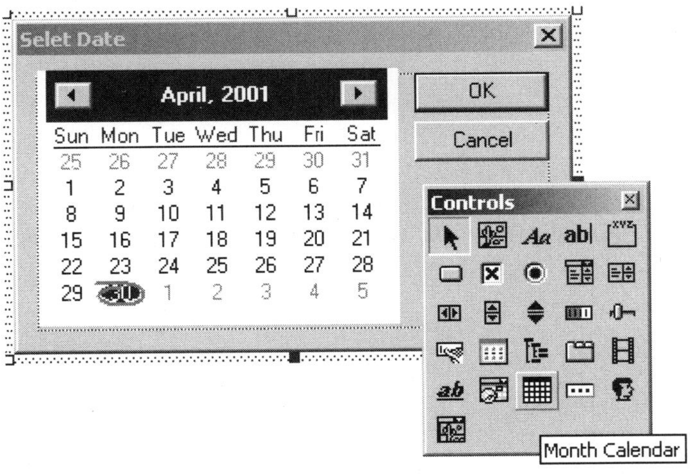

FIGURE 21.2 The Month Calendar control.

7. Create a class for the new dialog named **CDlgDateTime** and add a member variable for the Month Calendar control named **m_mcDateTime**:

```
CMonthCalCtrl     m_mcDateTime;
```

8. Add a public CTime object to hold the user-selected time:

```
class CDlgDateTime : public CDialog
{
// Construction
public:
     CTime m_ctUserDate;
     CDlgDateTime(CWnd* pParent = NULL);
```

9. For the CDlgDateTime class, add a handler function for the OK button's BN_CLICKED message:

```
void CDlgDateTime::OnOK()
{
     // TODO: Add extra validation here
     UpdateData( TRUE );
     m_mcDateTime.GetCurSel( m_ctUserDate );
     CDialog::OnOK();
}
```

This will place the selected date/time in the CTime object **m_ctUserDate.**

10. Generate a BN_CLICKED message handler for the "Get Date" button in the main dialog:

```
void CMCDemoDlg::OnGetDate()
{
     // TODO: Add your control notification handler code here
     CDlgDateTime     dlg( this );
     if ( dlg.DoModal() == IDOK )
     {
          m_csUserDate = dlg.m_ctUserDate.Format( "%A, %B %d, %Y
%H:%m:%S" );
          UpdateData( FALSE );
     }
}
```

11. Compile and try this example. Then, on your own, check out the properties of the Month Calendar control.

The Date Time Picker

If screen real estate is at a premium, you may opt to use the Date Time Picker (Figure 21.3).

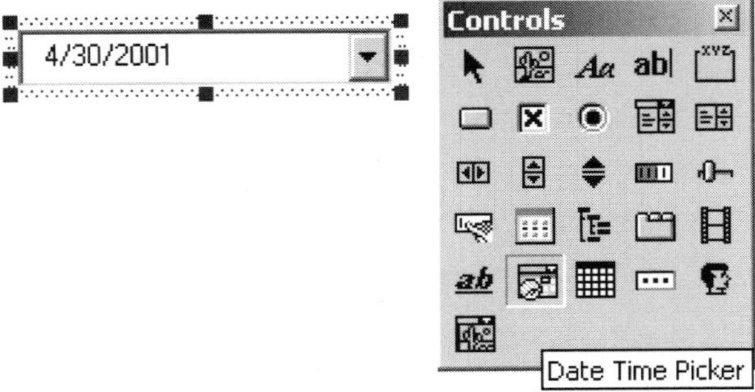

FIGURE 21.3 The Date Time Picker.

The Date Time Picker control is based on the CDateTimeCtrl class, and its operations are similar to that of the Month calendar control. In fact, if you deselect the Date Time Picker's "Use spin control" property, it drops down a Month calendar control. The working of the Date Time Picker is exemplified in the following code:

```
CDateTimeCtrl      m_dtUserDate;
CTime      ctDate;
m_dtUserDate.GetTime( ctDate );
CString     csDate = ctDate.Format( "%A %m %d %Y" );
```

COLEDATETIME

Another time class that warrants mentioning is the COleDateTime. COleDateTime is designed for work in OLE automation, and often surfaces in time data definitions, such as you might come across later when we talk about DAO database operations, the date/time field used in Access data tables.

COleDateTime works more or less like CTime; therefore, special discourse on it is unnecessary.

22 Collections

For best program development and maintenance results, data should be organized. There are many ways to organize data, and ultimately they must be preserved on disk as well. Although you can attempt to organize data by identifying them with systemized individual variable names and deal with them in one centralized coding location, you cannot truly claim that is working with data *groups*. For data to be organized, they must possess some degree of uniformity in their maintenance in memory, characteristics in identification, and efficient processing, such as the application of a loop to run through them.

In VC++ and MFC, there are several ways you can approach dealing with massive amounts of data. The choice is pretty much predicated on the type of data with which we are dealing, and the trade-off between ease of programming and code optimization. Together, the classes that have been developed to achieve these ends are known as *collection classes*, and in the following chapters we will look at a number of them and gain insight into their general use.

ARRAYS

The most fundamental data grouping we know is undoubtedly the array, as in:

```
int     iCode[ 100 ];
```

However, the traditional array suffers from a number of shortcomings. Anyone who has programmed knows that the traditional array doesn't support data groups of unpredictable sizes well, which has to do with the way arrays are normally handled.

Computer memory must be allocated before an array can take on data. This contiguous memory allocation requirement fixes the size of the array. In the Basic language, this problem was circumvented with the adoption of a technique known as *dynamic redimensioning*. All it means is that when you know you need more memory space, the language relocates the data for you and buys more storage space at the cost of memory management overhead.

MFC offers a number of arrays for our consumption beyond those defined in C and C++, and in general they provide exceptional capabilities that ease their use, overcoming much of the clumsiness that comes with the traditional array types.

CArray

The CArray class is actually a template, because it allows you to adopt the usage for any objects. The form of the CArray class is:

```
CArray < class TYPE, class ARG_TYPE > arrayName;
```

Here, "class TYPE" identifies the class of the objects that will be held in the array. "class ARG_TYPE" is the object type that will be used to access the array data; that is, how you would specify the parameter argument for a member function in accessing the data.

For example, to create a CArray object to store a group of CRect data, you would issue the following declaration:

```
CArray <CRect, CRect&> aryRect;
```

In this case, an array named aryRect is declared (but without memory allocation) to hold CRect objects. However, when we work with the objects, such as adding objects to the array, we will be using the object's address for reference (CRect&).

To add an object—that is, data, to the array—you use the CArray *Add()* member function, such as:

```
aryRect.Add( ctrlRect );
```

where ctrlRect is the pointer of a CRect object.

Once you have data in an array you can retrieve it with the CArray *GetAt()* member function, such as:

```
CRect     rect = aryRect.GetAt( 4 );
```

or

```
CRect     rect = aryRect[ 4 ];
```

to obtain the fifth element in the array (the first element being element 0).

Likewise, to define the data at a particular position, you use the *SetAt()* function, such as

```
aryRect.SetAt( 4, ctrlRect );
```

or

```
aryRect[ 4 ] = ctrlRect;
```

All the while in our discussion it appears that the CArray class does not require our explicitly allocating memory for its use. This is true. As you add data to an array, the class handles all the memory requirements for us, including reallocating data if necessary behind the scenes automatically. However, this does not mean that it is the best way to work with a CArray object. In fact, we can help the class work more efficiently if we do subscribe memory for it at the onset.

The way to do that is to estimate the amount of memory—that is, the number of elements that the array will most likely have—and use the *SetSize()* member function to *initialize* the array. Therefore, to set aside enough memory for 100 CRect objects to start with, and grow by 10 more CRect objects should that be needed, issue the following statement right after you set up the array:

```
aryRect.SetSize( 100, 10 );
```

At some point after the array has grown you might want to call the *FreeExtra()* function, which (spends some CPU time and) cleans up any previously allocated but no longer used memory.

You can also use it to shrink an array. First, you reset the array size (*SetSize()*) to the lower threshold that you really need, and then you use *FreeExtra()* to release the data beyond the threshold (but keeping the existing data within the threshold).

To run through the array as in conventional array usages with a loop, you need to know the number of elements in the array. This you can obtain using the *GetSize()* function.

In contrast, the *GetUpperBound()* function returns the size of the array as set by *SetSize()*.

To insert an element, use the *InsertAt*(int nIndex, ARG_TYPE newElement, int nCount = 1) function, which inserts a new element *newElement* at the *nIndex* position for as many insertions as indicated by *nCount* (default 1).

To remove an element, use the *RemoveAt*(int nIndex, int nCount = 1) function to remove the element at the *nIndex* position.

CArray also comes with other useful member functions. The *Append()* function allows you to add the elements of another array of the same type to the present one. The *Copy()* function copies the elements of a second array into the first one.

CObArray

Another class of generalized arrays is CObArray, which stores CObject type elements. It works by and large like CArray, except that it isn't a template and you instantiate an object in the normal fashion, such as:

```
CObArray      rectArray;
```

It also has corresponding processing functions.

CByteArray

The CByteArray is an array class dedicated to the storing of byte-size data.

CDWordArray

The CDWordArray is used to handle double-word 32-bit data. It works just like CArray and CObArray.

CLongBinary

The CLongBinary class, patterned after CObArray, is used strictly to store large binary data objects, such as those BLOB data from databases. It should be of interest to those developers who work with databases such as Oracle.

CStringArray

CStringArray, by implication of its name, works with CString objects, and for most students of programming, string data manipulation is relatively easy to understand. Therefore, let's use it to illustrate the workings of MFC object arrays.

Let's bring back the **Doodling** application.

One of the handicaps engendered in this application is the management of CString data. For simplicity of demonstration we used a simple array **m_csPara[10]** to hold the user-entered data. For the application to work, the user must be smart enough to know not to put in more than 10 text paragraphs. Using the CStringArray class to manage the data array can relieve this restriction.

First, we need to comment out the code that used the old array **m_csPara** and its index counter **m_iPara**. Next, we need to define a new CStringArray object:

```
class CDoodlingDoc : public CDocument
{
// Implementation
public:
     CStringArray m_ParaArray;
     // int m_iPara;
     // CString m_csPara[ 10 ];
```

Then, you initialize it:

```
BOOL CDoodlingDoc::OnNewDocument()
{
     if (!CDocument::OnNewDocument())
          return FALSE;
     // TODO: add reinitialization code here
     // (SDI documents will reuse this document)
     // m_iPara = 0;
     m_ParaArray.SetSize( 10, 5 );
     return TRUE;
}
```

Modify the data entry code to:

```
void CDoodlingView::OnEditNewParagraph()
{
     …
     if ( dlg.DoModal() == IDOK )
     {
          // m_pDoc->m_csPara[ m_pDoc->m_iPara ] = dlg.m_csPara;
          // m_pDoc->m_iPara++;
          m_pDoc->m_ParaArray.Add( dlg.m_csPara );
          Invalidate( FALSE );
          UpdateWindow();
     }
}
```

Finally, modify the *OnDraw()* function to obtain data from the new array:

```
void CDoodlingView::OnDraw(CDC* pDC)
{
     …
     // for ( iPara = 0; iPara < GetDocument()->m_iPara; iPara++ )
     for ( iPara = 0; iPara < m_pDoc->m_ParaArray.GetSize(); iPara++ )
```

```
{
    CString     csText = GetDocument()->m_ParaArray[ iPara ];
    pDC->DrawText( csText, txtRect, DT_WORDBREAK | DT_CALCRECT );
    pDC->DrawText( csText, txtRect, DT_WORDBREAK | DT_NOCLIP );
```

LISTS

Traditionally, the approach to programmatically defeat the hindrance of the array's size restriction is to abandon the use of the dimensioned array altogether. In its place, we use the linked list.

If you're unfamiliar with the concept of the linked list, visualize a chain link in which each link is hooked to the next. At the beginning of a linked list we have a pointer. Each time an element is added to the list, a new pointer is created to point to the next one. This way, only enough memory is bought for the new element and no "dimensioning" of an array is needed.

CList

The prototype of the MFC linked list is CList, a template that patterns its behavior after that of CArray. For example, this is how you declare a CList of CString objects:

```
CList     <CString, CString&>     myList;
```

Again, the first parameter determines that the list elements will be CString objects, and the second element indicates that member function calls will be passing CString object references. Its workings are presented with CObList.

CObList

The linked list class in MFC is CObList, and it behaves like the CObArray class. You create a CObList object as you normally would with most other classes by instantiating it:

```
CObList     lstObject( 100 );
```

where 100 mandates that 100 memory blocks will be reserved for the list immediately upon creation.

Once you have instantiated a CObList object, you add new elements to it with the *AddTail()* or *AddHead()* member function. *AddTail()* adds the new element to the end of the list, while *AddHead()* does it at the opposite end. Both functions return a POSITION value, which marks the current position in the list. For example:

```
POSITION     posMember = lstMember.AddTail( obNewMember );
```

Once you have added elements to the list, you can work with it by inserting new elements, removing elements, overwrite an element, and so forth. In any case, you almost always begin by knowing if the list has anything in it, and by identifying its extremities.

The *IsEmpty()* CObList member function returns a Boolean value, such as:

```
if ( !lstMember.IsEmpty() )
{
     // Do something if the list isn't empty.
}
```

Once you have decided that the list has contents, you obtain the list head position with:

```
POSITION     posMember = lstMember.GetHeadPosition():
```

or the tail position with:

```
POSITION     posMember = lstMember.GetTailPosition():
```

With the position in the list marked, you extract data from it with the *GetAt()* function, such as:

```
CObject*     obMember = lstMember.GetAt( posMember );
```

To traverse the list, you can employ a loop to run through all the elements. The *GetCount()* function will return an integer reporting to you the element count in the list. Once the count is known, you can get each element and move the list position tracker down not with the *GetAt()* function, but with the *GetNext(* POSITION& rPosition*)* or *GetPrev(* POSITION& rPosition *)* function, which gets the data and moves the position pointer for you, depending on the traveling direction.

Another facility that the CObList has that CObArray doesn't is the capability to position the list index or position through search.

First, with a list you can move the position tracker with the *FindIndex(int iIndex)* function, which will mark the "iIndexth" list data element with the position pointer.

The *Find(CObject* searchValue, POSITION startAfter = NULL)* function, on the other hand, lets you specify a CObject pointer and find where it is in the list. If it isn't there, the returned position is null. For example:

```
POSITION     posTarget;
posTarget = lstMember.Find( obMember );
if ( posTarget != NULL )
     RemoveAt( posTarget );
```

You use the *InsertAfter*(POSITION position, CObject* newElement) or *InsertBefore*(POSITION position, CObject* newElement) function to insert new elements.

You use the *RemoveAt*(POSITION position) function to remove the element pointed to by the position pointer.

You use the *RemoveHead()* function to remove the element at the list head, *RemoveTail()* function to remove the element at the list tail, or *RemoveAll()* function to clear out the list.

CStringList

A variation of CObList is CStringList, which is designed specifically to work with CString objects, and is therefore ideal for use in our **Doodling** application.

To apply CStringList in **Doodling** taking the place of the CStringArray object, first comment out the **m_ParaArray** code. Then add:

```
class CDoodlingDoc : public CDocument
{
     ...
// Implementation
public:
     CStringList m_lstPara;
```

Next, modify the data entry code:

```
void CDoodlingView::OnEditNewParagraph()
{
     ...
     if ( dlg.DoModal() == IDOK )
     {
          // m_pDoc->m_ParaArray.Add( dlg.m_csPara );
          m_pDoc->m_lstPara.AddTail( dlg.m_csPara );
          Invalidate( FALSE );
          UpdateWindow();
     }
}
```

Then update the *OnDraw()* function:

```
void CDoodlingView::OnDraw(CDC* pDC)
{
     …
     // for ( iPara = 0; iPara < m_pDoc->m_ParaArray.GetSize(); iPara++
)
     POSITION     pos = m_pDoc->m_lstPara.GetHeadPosition();
     for ( iPara = 0; iPara < m_pDoc->m_lstPara.GetCount(); iPara++ )
     {
          CString     csText = m_pDoc->m_lstPara.GetNext( pos );;
          pDC->DrawText( csText, txtRect, DT_WORDBREAK | DT_CALCRECT );
          pDC->DrawText( csText, txtRect, DT_WORDBREAK | DT_NOCLIP );
```

23 Data I/O

Eventually, the data processed by an application will have to be preserved or saved to disk. The same data also need to be read back and reprocessed. MFC has a slew of classes and procedures designed to help us achieve these ends. In this chapter, we will explore these options.

SERIALIZING

We must now address a topic that has been delayed for quite some time: why data should be maintained in the Document object. To assist our discussions, please refer to the **Doodling** application.

In the Document class you should see a virtual function named *Serialize()*:

```
void CDoodlingDoc::Serialize(CArchive& ar)
{
     if (ar.IsStoring())
     {
          // TODO: add storing code here
     }
     else
     {
          // TODO: add loading code here
     }
}
```

As you can see, the *Serialize()* function is passed a parameter of the CArchive type. The CArchive class enables what we call I/O persistence. In simple terms, it means the function will carry out the saving and restoring of data to and from the disk for us automatically, as long as we provide information on what data are involved and what file to transact with.

In the CArchive class the *IsStoring()* member function determines whether the I/O persistence action involved is storing or retrieving data. When you invoke the application's File->Save command, the *IsStoring()* function returns a true value. When you attempt to open a file with the File->Open command, the function returns a false value. In either case, the *Serialize()* function is triggered, and the appropriate program code is activated.

Serialization works because of a couple of initiatives that are built in to the application framework. First, in the Document class you have the following macro:

```
class CDoodlingDoc : public CDocument
{
protected: // create from serialization only
     CDoodlingDoc();
     DECLARE_DYNCREATE(CDoodlingDoc)
```

The DECLARE_DYNCREATE macro enables objects that are derived from CObject or its derived classes to be created dynamically at runtime, a necessary condition for serialization to work. This declaration is implemented in the .cpp file by:

```
///////////////////////////////////////////////////////////////////////////
//////
// CDoodlingDoc
IMPLEMENT_DYNCREATE(CDoodlingDoc, CDocument)
```

Whereas the Document class is thus enabled to service serialization, the CArchive class is the actual implementer of the serialization process, and its coding is extremely simple.

To see serialization work, add the following code to the **Doodling** program. The code isn't elegant, but it illustrates the serialization principle:

```
void CDoodlingDoc::Serialize(CArchive& ar)
{
     int      iPara;
     if (ar.IsStoring())
     {
          // TODO: add storing code here
          ar << m_lstPara.GetCount();
          POSITION     pos = m_lstPara.GetHeadPosition();
          for ( iPara = 0; iPara < m_lstPara.GetCount(); iPara++ )
```

```
            {
                ar << m_lstPara.GetNext( pos );;
            }
        }
        else
        {
            // TODO: add loading code here
            m_lstPara.RemoveAll();
            CString     csText;
            ar >> iPara;
            for ( int i = 0; i < iPara; i++ )
            {
                ar >> csText;
                m_lstPara.AddTail( csText );
            }
            UpdateAllViews( NULL );
        }
}
```

First, let us look at the data saving operation (*IsStoring()* being true).

As you can see, we intend to run through the gamut of the data preserved in the Document object. However, anticipating that we'll need to know the number of data items to retrieve later on, we first save that information. Once that is done, the count is used to drive a loop that runs through the linked list.

As for data retrieval, the data count is first read and stored in an integer variable. This integer is then used to control a loop that collects all the stored text data and adds them to the linked list that is cleared out first with the *RemoveAll()* function, just in case we have existing data in the system. After all the data have been retrieved, the Views are forced to update themselves with the *UpdateAllViews()* function.

To test our serialization scheme, first add data to the system as you did before. When you have a number of text paragraphs to play with, choose the File-> Save command to bring up the dialog box. In this dialog box, enter a filename of your choice, such as "TestPara." Then, quit the application. Execute the application again and enter a couple of text paragraphs. Then, choose the File->Open command and choose the filename you just used in saving the data. This time you should see the data restored.

When serialization saves data, it uses its own data format. Essentially, binary data are saved in native binary code form, text data are saved as ASCII text, CPoint data are saved as CPoint data, and CRect data are saved as CRect data. The only requirement for serialization to work is for you to match up what you write out with what you read.

Although this data format is straightforward and self-contained, it isn't the universal format used by most commercial programs, such as the rich text format and others. To work with specific, known data formats, you would have to devise your own file saving and retrieval logic to do exactly that, and serialization might not work for you in those situations. In the next section, we explore reading and writing to conventional files.

FILE I/O

If you insist on handling file I/O yourself, you can construct your program logic based on the MFC CFile class. It directly provides unbuffered, binary disk input/output services so you can have complete control over any file read/write processes.

The CFile class also engenders two other file classes: CStdioFile (which stands for std-I/O, not studio) and CMemFile. CStdioFile provides functions for stream files, while CMemFile simulates a CFile disk file in memory (therefore, it is not a true permanent file but works much faster than one).

Because the CStdioFile class is quite simple and uncomplicated in operations, we'll study it first.

CStdioFile

The simplest file I/O operations are those of sequential file I/O. In MFC, sequential file data processing is encapsulated in the CStdioFile class. The operations of a CStdioFile object are almost mechanical. You create a file object, open the file, perform the I/O operations, and close the file. We'll show how it works with a small example.

Reading Text

1. Use AppWizard to generate an MFC SDI Windows application named **ReadTextApp**, accepting all the defaults.
2. Add a member variable to the View class to point to the Document object:

```
private:
    CReadTextAppDoc* m_pDoc;
```

3. Instantiate a CStringList object in the Document class to hold a series of text paragraphs:

```
public:
     CStringList m_lstText;
```

4. Implement *OnDraw()* logic to display the list text as we did in Doodling:

```
void CReadTextAppView::OnDraw(CDC* pDC)
{
     CReadTextAppDoc* pDoc = GetDocument();
     ASSERT_VALID(pDoc);
     // TODO: add draw code for native data here
     CString     csText;
     CRect     clRect, txtRect;
     GetClientRect( clRect );
     txtRect = clRect;
     POSITION     pos = m_pDoc->m_lstText.GetHeadPosition();
     while ( pos  )
     {
          csText = m_pDoc->m_lstText.GetNext( pos );;
          pDC->DrawText( csText, txtRect, DT_WORDBREAK | DT_CALCRECT );
          pDC->DrawText( csText, txtRect, DT_WORDBREAK | DT_NOCLIP );
          txtRect.top = txtRect.bottom;
          if ( txtRect.bottom < clRect.bottom )
               txtRect.bottom = clRect.bottom;
          else
               txtRect.bottom = txtRect.bottom + 1000;
     }
}
```

5. In the Document class, add a public function to read the text from a text file:

```
void CReadTextAppDoc::GetData()
{
     CStdioFile     txtFile( "F:\\Sample.txt", CFile::modeRead |
CFile::typeText );
     CString     csText;
     while ( txtFile.ReadString( csText ) )
          m_lstText.AddTail( csText );
}
```

6. Override the *OnInitialUpdate()* virtual function in the View class to read the file data:

```
void CReadTextAppView::OnInitialUpdate()
{
     CView::OnInitialUpdate();

     // TODO: Add your specialized code here and/or…
     m_pDoc = GetDocument();
     m_pDoc->GetData();
}
```

7. Use Notepad to create a file named Sample.txt and save it to disk. Then, test the program.

The crux of the program, of course, is the *GetData()* function. In this function, a CStdioFile object is instantiated for a sample text file named Sample.txt saved on, say, drive F ("F:\\Sample.txt"). When the CStdioFile object is instantiated the file is opened in the read-only mode as a text file: "CFile::modeRead | CFile::typeText." The text paragraphs from this file are read one by one in a while loop until no more text exists: "while (txtFile.ReadString(csText))." As the text paragraphs are read, they are added to the string list: "m_lstText.AddTail(csText)." When the CStdioFile object goes out of scope at the end of the *GetData()* function, it is closed.

The form of the CStdioFile construction is:

```
CStdioFile(LPCTSTR lpsz FileName, UINT nOpenFlags);
```

The first parameter provides the filename, and the second parameter specifies the file-opening mode, which can be one of the entries listed in Table 23.1.

TABLE 23.1 File Open Modes

nOpenFlag	*Description*
CFile::modeCreate	Directs the constructor to create a new file. If the file already exists, it is truncated to 0 length.
CFile::modeNoTruncate	Combine this value with **modeCreate**. If the file being created already exists, it is not truncated to 0 length. Thus, the file is guaranteed to open, either as a newly created file or as an existing file. This might be useful, for example, when opening a settings file that may or may not already exist. This option applies to **CStdioFile** as well.
CFile::modeRead	Opens the file for reading only.
CFile::modeReadWrite	Opens the file for reading and writing.

TABLE 23.1 File Open Modes *(Continued)*

nOpenFlag	*Description*
CFile::modeWrite	Opens the file for writing only.
CFile::modeNoInherit	Prevents the file from being inherited by child processes.
CFile::shareDenyNone	Opens the file without denying other processes read or write access to the file. **Create** fails if the file has been opened in compatibility mode by any other process.
CFile::shareDenyRead	Opens the file and denies other processes read access to the file. **Create** fails if the file has been opened in compatibility mode or for read access by any other process.
CFile::shareDenyWrite	Opens the file and denies other processes write access to the file. **Create** fails if the file has been opened in compatibility mode or for write access by any other process.
CFile::shareExclusive	Opens the file with exclusive mode, denying other processes both read and write access to the file. Construction fails if the file has been opened in any other mode for read or write access, even by the current process.
CFile::shareCompat	This flag is not available in 32-bit MFC. This flag maps to **CFile::shareExclusive** when used in **CFile::Open**.
CFile::typeText	Sets text mode with special processing for carriage return–linefeed pairs (used in derived classes only).
CFile::typeBinary	Sets binary mode (used in derived classes only).

As you can see, the values are all inherited from the CFile class.

Note that when a CStdioFile file object is a sequential text file as in our example program, when you read a text paragraph, a byte pair (0x0A, 0x0D, line-feed and carriage return) is translated to a single 0x0A byte.

Writing Text

In writing to a file, you would instantiate the CStdioFile object with the `modeCreate` and `modeWrite` flag:

```
    CStdioFile     txtFile( "F:\\Sample.txt", CFile::modeCreate |
CFile::modeWrite | CFile::typeText );
```

You then write data with the *WriteString()* function, as in:

```
txtFile.WriteString( csText );
```

When you write data, the terminating null character ('\0') is not written to the file, and the newline character (0x0A) is converted to the byte pair (0x0D, 0x0A) for you.

Also, if the text data are represented by a CString object as in our program, any '/n' character present would be removed. If you use LPTSTR, the '/n' character is preserved.

CFile

CFile is the base class for MFC file classes, and you can use it to perform virtually any type of operation on a disk file. The following example demonstrates its working.

In the following example, we'll attempt to copy a file, thereby showing both CFile's read and write operations. (Note that we're not trying to reinvent the file copying operation here. Microsoft's platform SDK already has a *CopyFile()* function and a *CopyFileEx()* function designed for that purpose.)

ON THE CD

1. Generate an MFC dialog-based Windows application named **FileCopyApp**.
2. Use the Cancel button to create a Copy File button.
3. Generate a handler function for the Copy File button's BN_CLICKED message:

```
void CFileCopyAppDlg::OnCopy()
{
     // TODO: Add your control notification handler…
     CFile     fromFile;
     CFile     toFile;
     fromFile.Open( "C:\\WINNT\\explorer.exe", CFile::modeRead );
     toFile.Open( "myexplorer.exe", CFile::modeCreate |
 CFile::modeWrite );
     char      buffer[ 256 ];
     DWORD     dwTotal = 0;
     DWORD     dwLength = fromFile.GetLength();
     while ( dwTotal < dwLength )
     {
          fromFile.Read( buffer, 256 );
          toFile.Write( buffer, 256 );
          dwTotal = dwTotal + 256;
          fromFile.Seek( (LONG) dwTotal, CFile::begin );
          toFile.Seek( (LONG) dwTotal, CFile::begin );
```

```
        }
        toFile.Close();
        fromFile.Close();
        MessageBox( "File copied.", "", MB_OK );
    }
```

In this function, the core of our application, two CFile objects are created: fromFile and toFile. fromFile is the file being copied, and is opened with the "CFile::modeRead" open flag. For this exercise I used Windows Explore.exe program for experimentation. You can choose your own.

toFile, the file copy, is opened in the "CFile::modeCreate | CFile::modeWrite" mode. Therefore, the file for write operations also will be created if it doesn't exist. I named it without an absolute file path so that it will be written to the local directory.

At the beginning, the length of the source file is determined (dwLength = fromFile.GetLength();). An accumulator dwTotal is initialized to 0, but will keep track of the number of bytes traversed in the files. A buffer of arbitrary size is set up to receive the data bytes read, and the operation begins. For as long as there are bytes to traverse, more data bytes are read and written with the file position trackers updated as the operation goes on (toFile.Seek((LONG) dwTotal, CFile::begin);). When all the data have been thus copied, the files are closed.

CFile has many useful member functions, and they are easy to understand. You might want to become familiar with them so that you can put them to good use.

CMemFile

CMemFile, another derived class from CFile, simulates CFile's operations in memory. In other words, it works like a CFile (using its member functions for read, write, etc.), but a CMemFile object does not create a disk file and remains in memory. You use a CMemFile object primarily for speed of operations.

To use a CMemFile, simply create it and begin using it. There is no file to open. For example:

```
CMemFile     fileTemp;
fileTemp.SeekToEnd();
```

When you have finished working with the data, usually you then copy the data from the CMemFile object to a real disk file for safekeeping.

PART

VI Database Processing

In this part of the book we will explore MFC's toolsets for database processing. One point should be made clear from the outset: we are not learning databases in this book. Indeed, it is assumed that you are already versed in database operations involving standard database repertoire such as Oracle 8, MS SQL 7.0, Access, and so on. Here, we are merely learning to develop applications in VC++ and MFC to process database data.

The illustrations used in the following exercises are based on a simple Access database. This does not mean Access is always the best choice. It is just that an Access database is easy to distribute, and that it is needed to illustrate the CDaoDatabase class. With ODBC, it works just like Oracle or MS SQL. As a matter of fact, those of you who are partial to your own database models should feel free to replicate the data provided in your own platform and hook them up to ODBC to try the examples.

THE SAMPLE DATABASE

ON THE CD

The sample Access database named **books.mdb**, is a simple relational database involving three tables: a table name **tblBook** for book titles, a table named **tblPublisher** for book publishers, and a table name **tblAuthor** for book authors. The tables are related, but no relationship is maintained in the database, allowing us to learn to work table relationship in our code. The database also has only a few records, giving us ample opportunities for data entry tryouts.

The tables are, in original Access presentation forms, illustrated in Figures VI.1, VI.2, and VI.3.

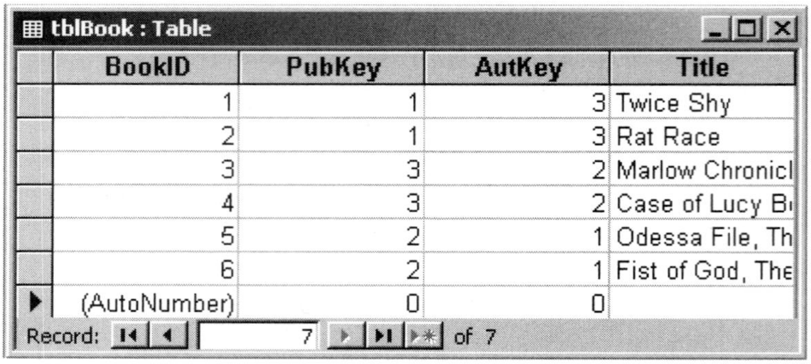

tblBook : Table

BookID	PubKey	AutKey	Title
1	1	3	Twice Shy
2	1	3	Rat Race
3	3	2	Marlow Chronicl
4	3	2	Case of Lucy B
5	2	1	Odessa File, Th
6	2	1	Fist of God, The
(AutoNumber)	0	0	

Record: 7 of 7

FIGURE VI.1 The tblBook table.

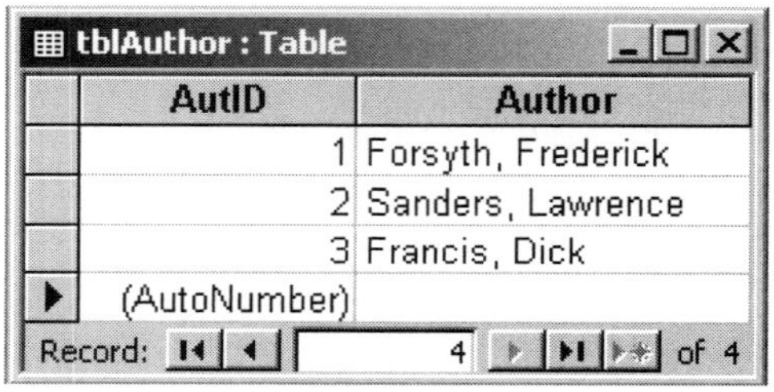

tblAuthor : Table

AutID	Author
1	Forsyth, Frederick
2	Sanders, Lawrence
3	Francis, Dick
(AutoNumber)	

Record: 4 of 4

FIGURE VI.2 The tblAuthor table.

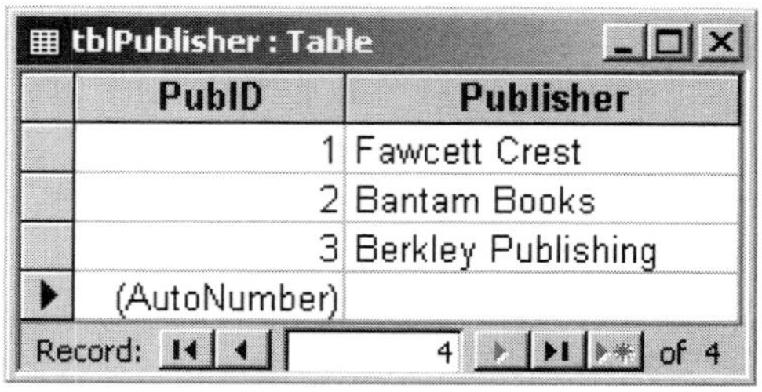

tblPublisher : Table

PubID	Publisher
1	Fawcett Crest
2	Bantam Books
3	Berkley Publishing
(AutoNumber)	

Record: 4 of 4

FIGURE VI.3 The tblPublisher table.

Setting Up the ODBC Data Source

To perform the exercises, you'll need to set up an ODBC data source for the sample database. Follow these steps if you're unfamiliar with the procedure. The sample database is in the root directory of the C drive for simplicity of expression. You can put yours anywhere you wish.

1. From Windows' Control Panel Administrative Tools, execute Data Source (ODBC).

2. From the System DSN tab, click Add (Figure VI.4).

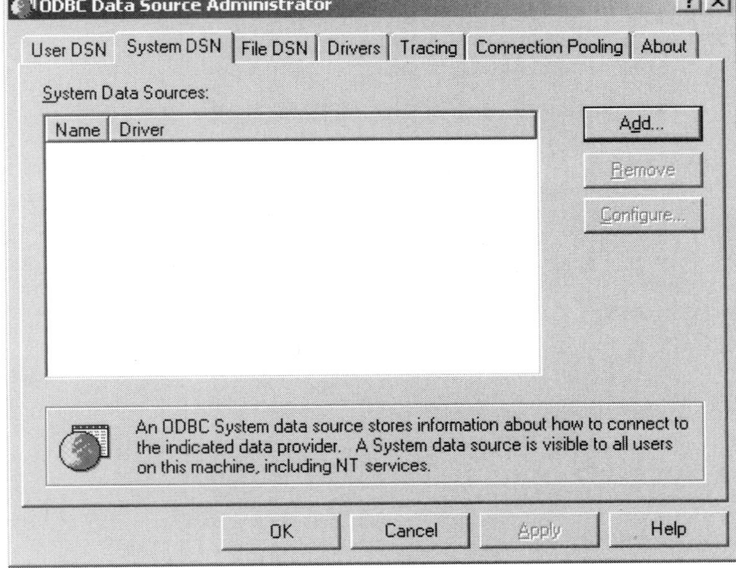

FIGURE VI.4 Adding a system data source.

3. Select Access Driver, and then click Finish (Figure VI.5).

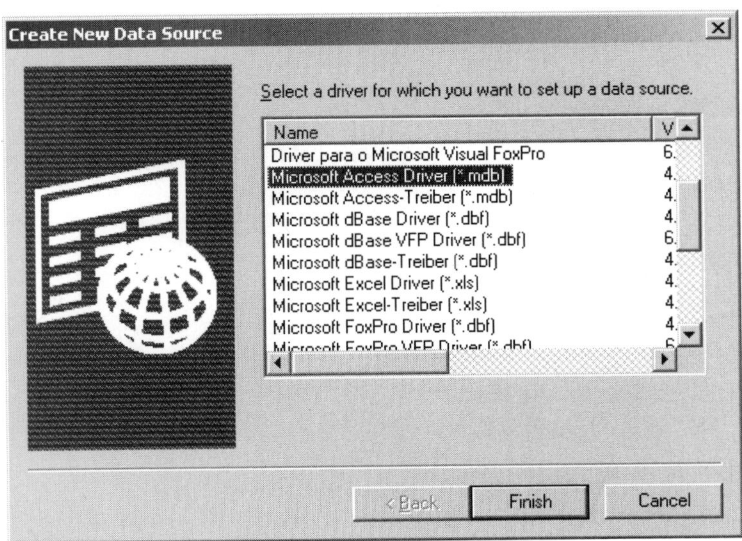

FIGURE VI.5 Data sources.

4. In the setup dialog, enter the data source name **Books**, and then click Select (Figure VI.6).

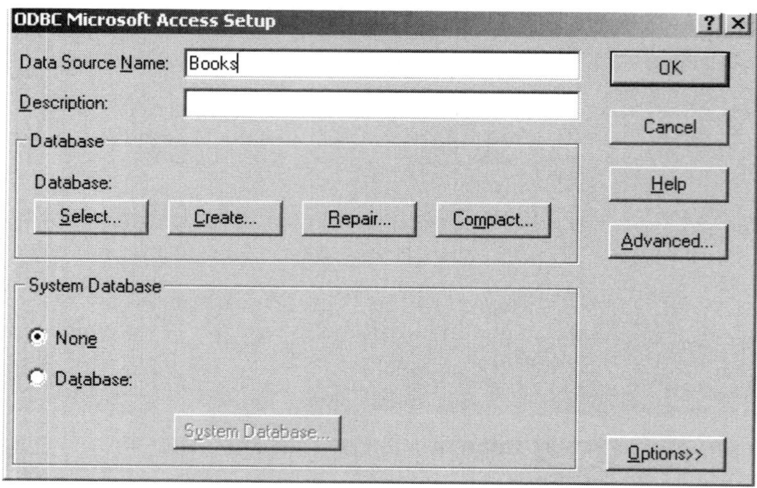

FIGURE VI.6 Access ODBC Setup

5. Select the Access database, and click OK all the way out (Figure VI.7).

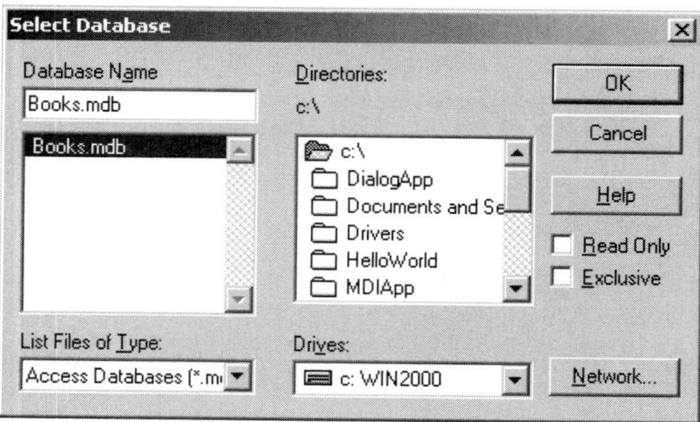

FIGURE VI.7 Selecting ODBC database.

The ODBC data source is defined.

24 An AppWizard ODBC Database Application

The first demonstration shows you how you can use AppWizard to develop an application with database support with virtually no coding.

1. From AppWizard, start a new MFC AppWizard (exe) project and name it **WizDB**.
2. Select the Single document model.
3. Select "Database view with file support" and click the Data Source button (Figure 24.1).

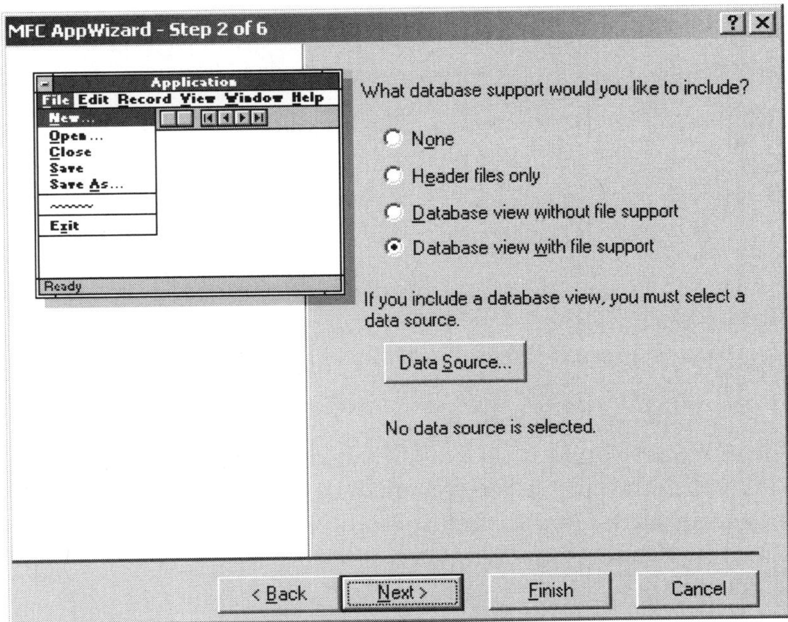

FIGURE 24.1 Application generation with database support.

4. Select the Books ODBC data source, select the dynaset option, and click OK (Figure 24.2).

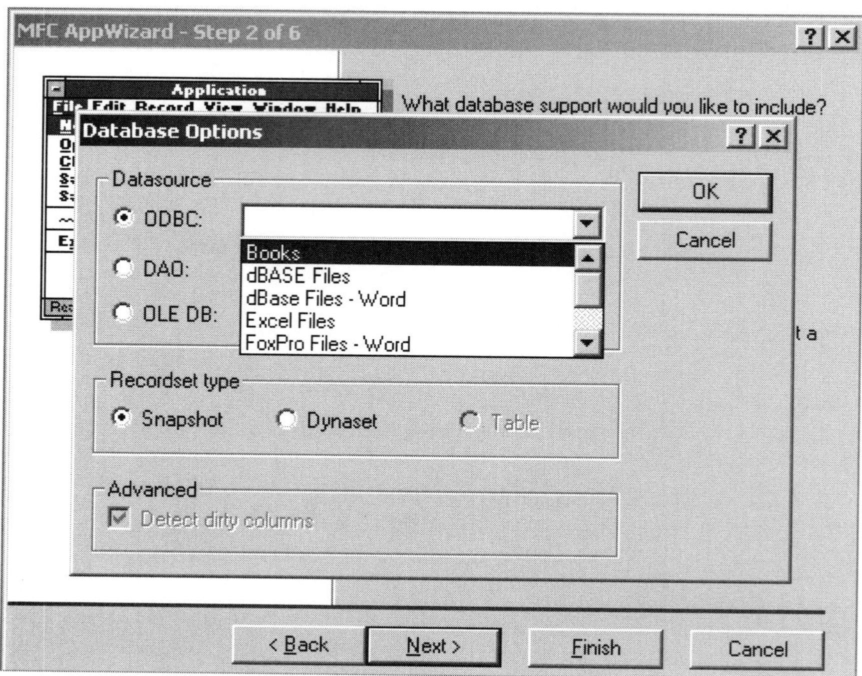

FIGURE 24.2 AppWizard database connection specification.

The *dynaset* record type allows you to update the data. A *snapshot* is an instantaneous image of the data at the time the database is opened. Use dynaset if you intend to provide data update capabilities (add new records, modify existing data, and so on) to your program. If you just want to read the data, such as for printing a report, open the data set as a snapshot.

5. Select the **tblBooks** table and OK out (Figure 24.3).
6. Accept all the defaults for the remainder of the steps (noting that the View class chosen by AppWizard is the CRecordView class), compile the database application, and then execute it.

You have an instant application with database support, except, of course, with no actual data processing.

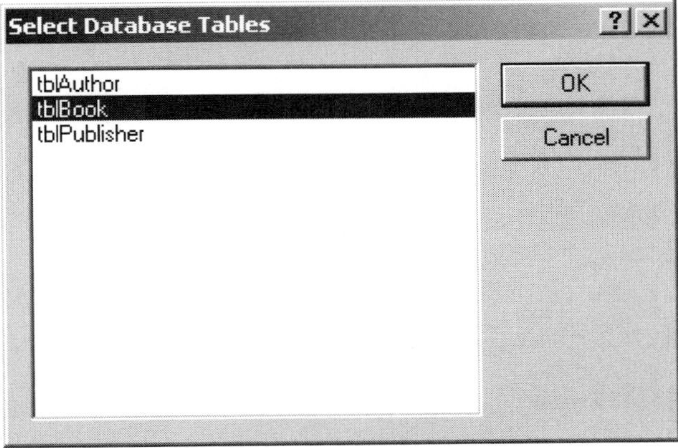

FIGURE 24.3 AppWizard data table selection.

7. Look at the menu in Figure 24.4.

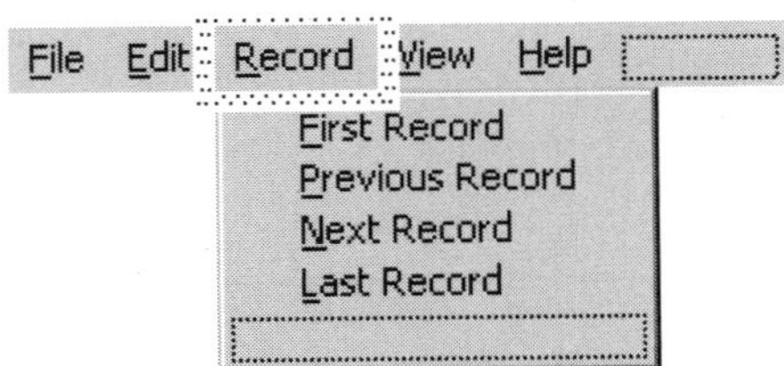

FIGURE 24.4 Record Navigation commands.

You can see that the record navigation entries are already in.

8. Look at the toolbar in Figure 24.5.

FIGURE 24.5 WizDB Record Navigation toolbar buttons.

It is ready to go, too.

9. Look at the ClassView tree in Figure 24.6.

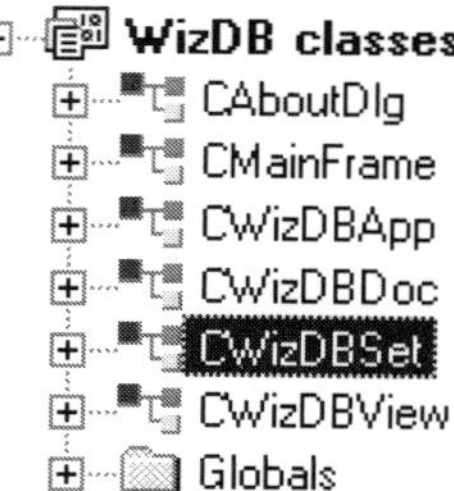

FIGURE 24.6 WizDB classes.

Here it is shown that AppWizard has generated a class named CWizDBSet. This is the class containing the necessary database support code for our program. Open the CWizDBSt class files and quickly study the code generated. You should see member variables set up for the data fields, and functions for returning the database DSN and connecting to the database.

The details of the workings of the database mechanisms will not be discussed here. We will examine them closely when we explicitly set up the database operations in a subsequent demonstration.

DISPLAYING DATA

First, let us install controls to display the database data.

1. Open the IDD_WIZDB_FORM resource, remove the "TODO: Place form controls on this dialog" static control, and add controls as shown (using IDC_EDIT_TITLE for the edit box ID) in Figure 24.7.

FIGURE 24.7 Data field display.

2. Use ClassWizard to create a CString variable for the edit box, but choose the database variables instead of creating one of your own (Figure 24.8).

This way, the edit box is directly "bonded" to the database variable, making it "data aware."

3. Compile the program and execute it.

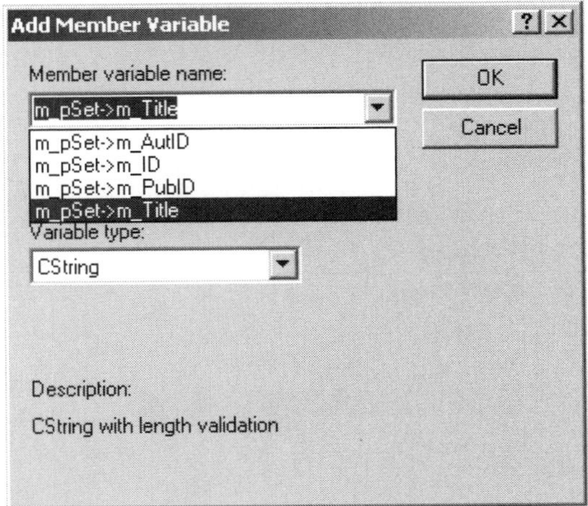

FIGURE 24.8 Connecting variable to field data.

You should see the first book title displayed, proving that the program is connected to the database, and all the database opening and closing operations have been implemented for you implicitly in the CRecordView class.

At this point, we should remark on the approach to handling database data as exemplified in the preceding demonstration program.

With CRecordView, AppWizard has "bonded" the data table fields directly to the program data variables, making the variables "data aware." It is an attractive way of programming for many developers because what you do with the variables (via the onscreen controls) is directly reflected in the database, eliminating many otherwise taxing programming steps. Unfortunately, this also makes the database data vulnerable. A misstep on the part of the developer can inflict great damage to the precious database data. Many experts advise against such an approach to database data processing.

The correct way, according to the pundits, is to isolate the activities. Do all the data modification work in variables without ties to the database, and then commit the data update only when it is safe. In the forthcoming examples, we'll show how this is accomplished.

NAVIGATING DATA RECORDS

Now let's deal with the issue of data navigation. Again, we demonstrate with the **WizDB** application.

1. Use ClassWizard to create a Windows message handler function for the menu command "Last Record" in the CWizDBView class (Figure 24.9).

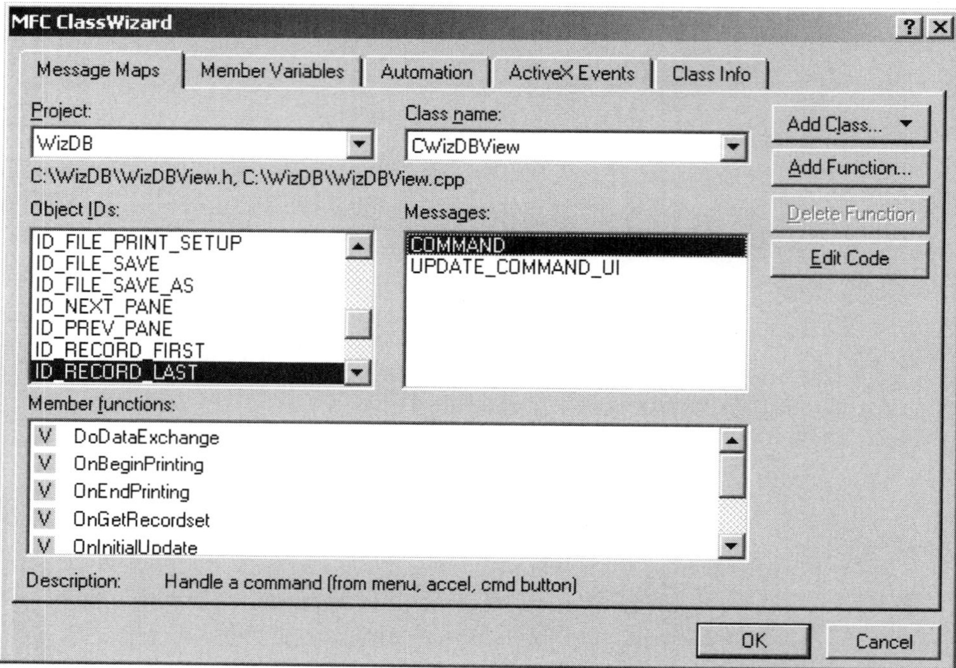

FIGURE 24.9 Record Navigation command message

2. Implement the code in bold:

```
void CWizDBView::OnRecordLast()
{
	// TODO: Add your command handler code here
	m_pSet->MoveLast();
	UpdateData( FALSE );
}
```

3. Compile the program and test the Last Record command.

Complete the remaining three navigation commands using the functions in Table 24.1.

TABLE 24.1 Record Navigation Commands

Command	*MFC Function*
First Record	MoveFirst()
Last Record	MoveLast()
Previous Record	MovePrev()
Next Record	MoveNext()

DATA UPDATING

To support data updating, we need two more commands as shown in Figure 24.10.

Once you have added the two new commands to the menu (and toolbar, if you like), we will implement the coding for them.

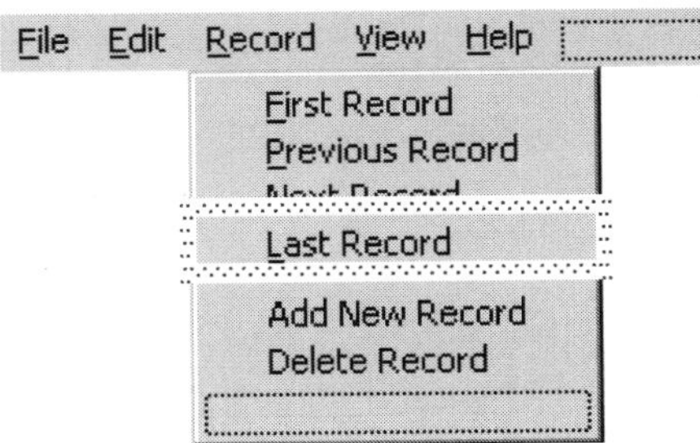

FIGURE 24.10 Record Add and Delete commands.

Adding New Records

For adding data records, enter the following code:

```
void CWizDBView::OnRecordAddNew()
{
    // TODO: Add your command handler code here
    m_pSet->AddNew();
    UpdateData( FALSE );
}
```

OnMove()

We now face an operational dilemma. How does the program know that data entry is finished so that we can proceed to update the data?

You can add a button or command to have the user signal the program explicitly that it is time to update the database, but then the program would feel amateurish.

Actually, there is a signal that indicates data entry is finished when the user moves away from the data record by going to the next, the previous, the first, or the last record. Therefore, one place to implement the data updating logic is in the CRecordView class's *OnMove()* function.

1. Bring up ClassWizard and locate the OnMove message in the CWizDB-View class (Figure 24.11).

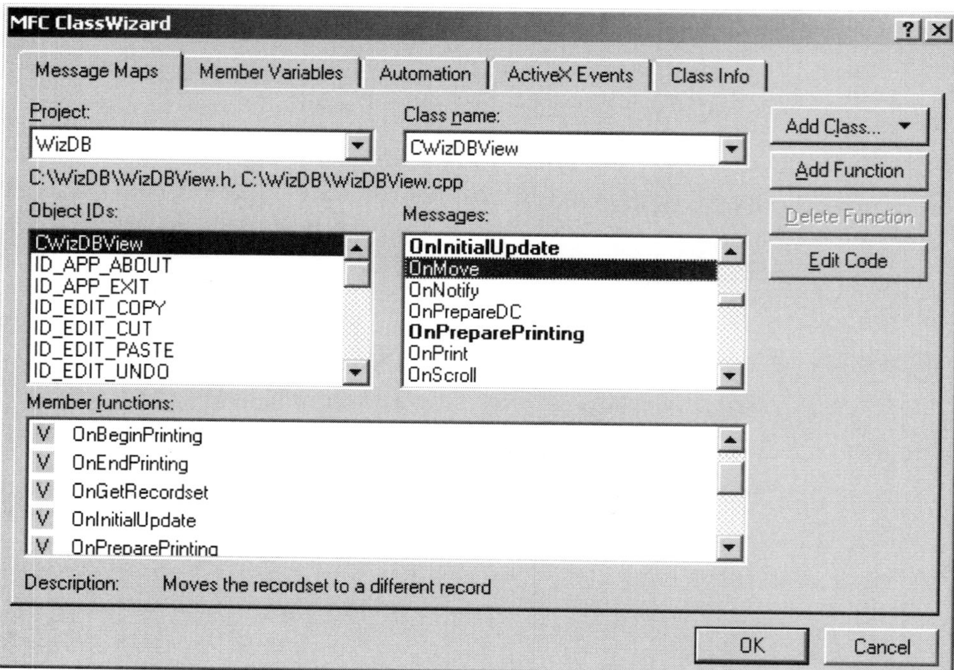

FIGURE 24.11 The *OnMove()* virtual function.

2. Create a handler function for it (overriding the class's *OnMove()* function), and then enter the following code:

```
BOOL CWizDBView::OnMove(UINT nIDMoveCommand)
{
    // TODO: Add your specialized code here and/or…
```

```
        UpdateData( TRUE );      // Get data from edit box.
        // Update database if record is unlocked.
        if ( m_pSet->CanUpdate() )
             m_pSet->Update();
        // In any case, re-query the database
        m_pSet->Requery();
        UpdateData( FALSE );      // Install data in edit box.
        return TRUE;
        // return CRecordView::OnMove(nIDMoveCommand);
}
```

When the user moves away from the current record, the data from the controls are downloaded into their variables. The program then checks to see if the database record is updatable (*m_pSet->CanUpdate()*). If it is, meaning that no other user is using the data record at the same time, the data record is updated.

Subsequently, the data are refreshed from the database (*m_pSet->Requery()*) and used to reload the controls.

This illustration is rudimentary in its implementation, but it points out several follow-up thoughts. First, in designing database-driven applications you should always be aware that you are not doing it for one dedicated user. Multiple users can be accessing the same database at the same time, especially when you're designing code for network or Internet use. Therefore, you should always check the data record's accessibility (*CanUpdate()*) before you commit any new data.

Such is the case, our illustration falls short of handling the situation when the data record cannot be updated. Instead of just abandoning the data, the program should provide a fallback function to handle the situation. One thing you can do is prompt the user for action. Perhaps you can offer the user a second chance and wait for the data record to become free.

Deleting Records

For deleting a data record, we must make sure that once the data are deleted, we move on to the next record and display it. If we shoot past the records because the record deleted happened to be the last record in the data table, the program should simply move to the current last record. If the record deleted was the only record in the table, we should show an empty record on the screen and disallow any editing work to be done on the "none data." The following code snippet illustrates how this is implemented.

```
void CWizDBView::OnRecordDelete()
{
     // TODO: Add your command handler code here
```

```
        m_pSet->Delete();
        m_pSet->MoveNext();
        if ( m_pSet->IsEOF() )
            m_pSet->MoveLast();
        if ( m_pSet->IsBOF() )
            m_pSet->SetFieldNull( NULL );
        UpdateData( FALSE );
}
```

Protecting the Data

As pointed out previously, assigning the edit box to exchange data directly with a database record field invites data error. In the next example, you'll learn to separate the two issues.

In our current example code, we are also committing another sin: we are leaving the data open to abuse by allowing the edit box to be editable at all times. If you feel strongly about it, you can set the edit box to read-only mode. This way, when navigating data the user cannot accidentally maim the data. However, then you will have to "open up" the data for editing and adding new records. For example, you will have to modify the add record logic by first creating a CWizDBView class member variable for the edit control so that you can set its read mode:

```
CEdit     m_edtTitle;
```

Then you modify the *OnRecordAddNew()* function:

```
void CWizDBView::OnRecordAddNew()
{
        // TODO: Add your command handler code here
        m_edtTitle.SetReadOnly( FALSE );      // Allow edit
        m_pSet->AddNew();
        UpdateData( FALSE );
}
```

Of course, you would have to set read-only back (*SetReadOnly(TRUE)*) in *OnMove()* so that the data cannot be edited by mistake again.

Update()

We are not yet through with our example. We have an issue with the *OnMove()* override function that we still have to take care of.

As it stands, the function tries to update the database even if we are not modifying data, and this is incorrect. The reason is that the *Update()* function only works when the *AddNew()* or *Edit()* function is called, and should not be called when not preceded by either. We need to set a flag to determine if data updating needs to be performed.

First, we would create a Boolean variable as a View class member to indicate if data have changed:

```
BOOL     bAltered;
```

We can initialize the variable to FALSE in the View class's *OnInitialUpdate()* function:

```
bAltered = FALSE;
```

In the *OnRecordAddNew()* function, the flag will be set to TRUE, and the data update operation in *OnMove()* will be exercised only if the flag says so:

```
BOOL CWizDBView::OnMove(UINT nIDMoveCommand)
{
     // TODO: Add your specialized code here and/or…
     UpdateData( TRUE );      // Get data from edit box.
     if ( bAltered )
     {
  // Update database if record is unlocked.
      if ( m_pSet->CanUpdate() )
           m_pSet->Update();
      // In any case, re-query the database
      m_pSet->Requery();
      UpdateData( FALSE );      // Install data in edit box.
      return TRUE;
     }
     else
          return CRecordView::OnMove(nIDMoveCommand);
}
```

Try to implement this and observe the result.

25 An ODBC Data Table Processor

We will now attempt to replicate the operations introduced in the WizDB project by explicitly implementing the database classes ourselves. When AppWizard generated the database-aware application using the CRecordView class for the main display, the database connection activities are tugged away under the surface, making it difficult for us to do anything that diverts from the built-in model. By basing the display view on the CFormView class (Figure 25.1) and populating it with controls ourselves, while at the same time handling

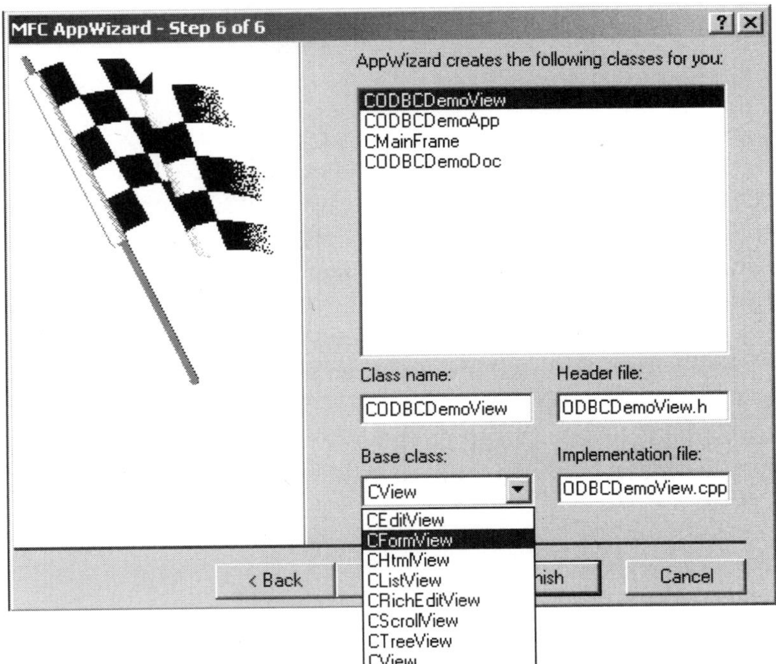

FIGURE 25.1 Application with SformView.

our own database connection with the proper data record set classes, we are free to handle all data-related actions our own way.

ON THE CD

1. Start a new SDI application named **ODBCDemo** with CFormView as the prototype of the View class (Step 6, Figure 25.1) with no built-in database support.

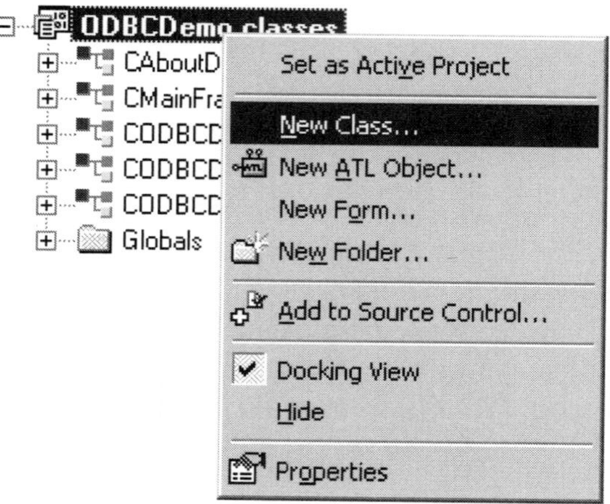

FIGURE 25.2 Generating a new class.

2. Select the "ODBCDemo classes" tree node in ClassView (Figure 25.2), and use the New Class command in the context menu to add a new class named **CSetTitle** derived from the CRecordset (not CRecordView) class (Figure 25.3). For the database connection, select ODBC Books as in the WizDB project, and select **tblBook** as the database table for access (Figure 25.4), using the dynaset record type.

The preceding procedure shows how we implement a class to support the operations of data processing for a data table.

If you were to compile the program now, you'd be in trouble. This is because to use the CRecordset class, you need to include the **afxdb.h** header file.

3. Open the **stdafx.h** file and add the statement shown in bold:

```
#ifndef _AFX_NO_AFXCMN_SUPPORT
#include <afxcmn.h>                // MFC support…
#include <afxdb.h>
#endif // _AFX_NO_AFXCMN_SUPPORT
```

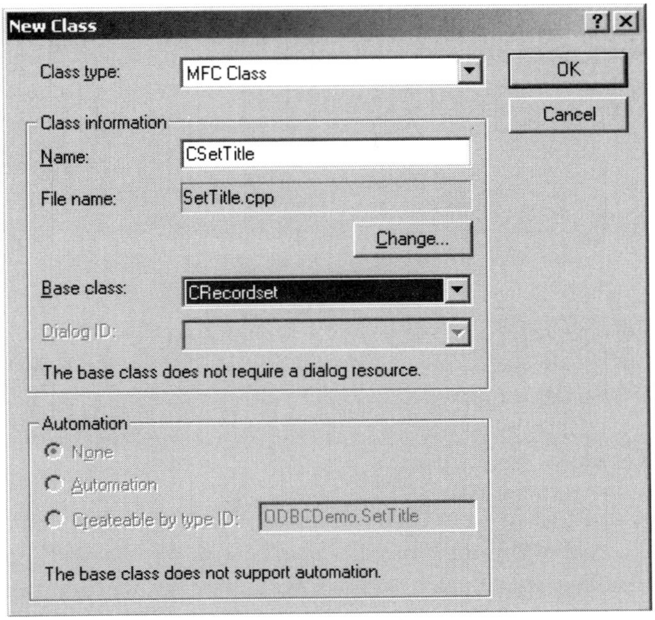

FIGURE 25.3 Defining a new CRecordset class.

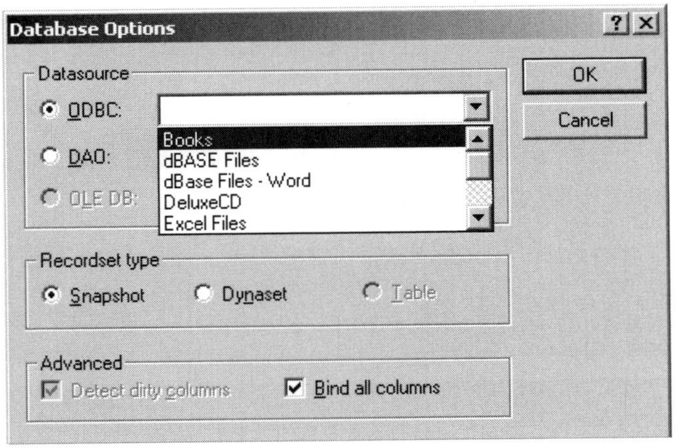

FIGURE 25.4 Defining a CRecordset class data connection.

DATA ABSTRACTION

We'll now sidetrack from MFC a bit and take time to discuss a small subject that has to do with basic database design.

If you look at the field variable definitions in CSetTitle, you'll find that they are public, and therefore open to direct manipulation:

```
class CSetTitle : public CRecordset
{
public:
     CSetTitle(CDatabase* pDatabase = NULL);
     DECLARE_DYNAMIC(CSetTitle)
// Field/Param Data
     //{{AFX_FIELD(CSetTitle, CRecordset)
     long      m_BookID;
     long      m_PubKey;
     long      m_AutKey;
     CString      m_Title;
     //}}AFX_FIELD
```

This is in direct contrast to what OOP people espouse, that data should be insulated from direct access and manipulation. This is why, for example, in Java we have entity beans enacted specifically to work with data so a program's general processing logic does not. Likewise in spirit, we can achieve the same in C++ by making the CSetTitle class member data variables private and creating separate, dedicated helper functions to assume the roles of data access, thereby providing a layer of data abstraction. Later you'll see this approach clearly employed when we discuss component development such as DLL and ActiveX objects, and learn other techniques to further "objectize" data elements.

4. In SetTitle.h move the block of code shown in bold and add the "private:" designation as shown here:

```
class CSetTitle : public CRecordset
{
public:
     CSetTitle(CDatabase* pDatabase = NULL);
     DECLARE_DYNAMIC(CSetTitle)
// Overrides
     // ClassWizard generated virtual function overrides
     //{{AFX_VIRTUAL(CSetTitle)
     public:
     virtual CString GetDefaultConnect();     // Default connection
string
     virtual CString GetDefaultSQL();     // Default SQL for Recordset
     virtual void DoFieldExchange(CFieldExchange* pFX);  // RFX support
     //}}AFX_VIRTUAL
```

```
// Implementation
#ifdef _DEBUG
     virtual void AssertValid() const;
     virtual void Dump(CDumpContext& dc) const;
#endif
private:
// Field/Param Data
     //{{AFX_FIELD(CSetTitle, CRecordset)
     long      m_ID;
     long      m_PubID;
     long      m_AutID;
     CString     m_Title;
     //}}AFX_FIELD
};
```

5. Next, add a public member function *GetTitle()* for the CSetTitle class:

```
CString CSetTitle::GetTitle()
{
     return m_Title;
}
```

This function will be used to obtain book titles from the data table.

6. Similarly, add a function to set the book title:

```
void CSetTitle::SetTitle( CString title )
{
     m_Title = title;
}
```

These public helper functions will be the main transaction mechanisms between the application's processing logic and the data sources. No coding will directly work with the data variables themselves.

OPENING AND CLOSING THE DATABASE

Next, we will address the policies of data connection "opening" and "closing."

There are essentially two ways to manage data connections: you either establish them at the onset of the application and sever them during program exit, or you maintain the connections only while you need them. The choice is pretty much determined by how often the connections are needed, and how the program will share data use with other users. If the data connections are needed throughout the application and nobody else is using the database at the same time, you might want to keep them open so that you don't have to worry about them when coding the details of the program. You can assume that the data connections are there and focus on the processing logic at hand. We will use this approach in this exercise.

1. Use "Add Member Variable" to add a private variable named **m_setTitle** of the CSetTitle type in CODBCDemoView (Figure 25.5).

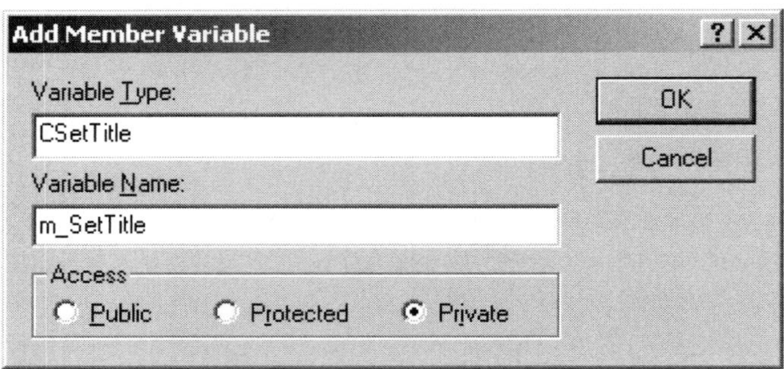

FIGURE 25.5 Adding a Recordset variable.

2. Add the code shown in bold in CODBCDemoView's *OnInitialUpdate()* function:

```
void CODBCDemoView::OnInitialUpdate()
{
      CFormView::OnInitialUpdate();
      GetParentFrame()->RecalcLayout();
      ResizeParentToFit();
      m_setBook.Open();
      m_setBook.MoveFirst();
}
```

3. Use "Add Window Message Handle" to create a handler function for the WM_CLOSE message (Figure 25.6) for CODBCDemoView:

```
void CODBCDemoView::OnClose()
{
      // TODO: Add your message handler code here,,,
      m_setBook.Close();
      CFormView::OnClose();
}
```

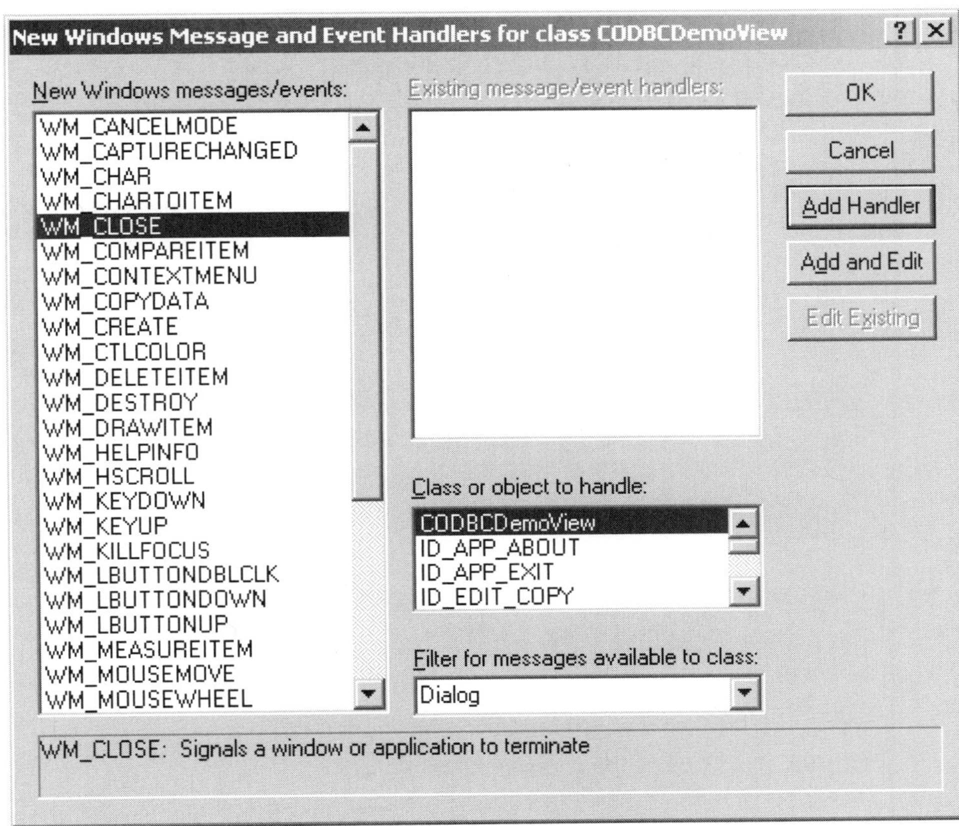

FIGURE 25.6 The WM_CLOSE Windows message.

Now we can process data.

DISPLAYING DATA

First, we'll take care of displaying data.

1. Add a static control and an edit box to the application's main form view (Figure 25.7).

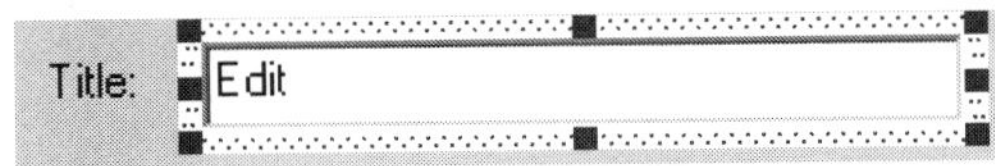

FIGURE 25.7 The Title field display.

2. Use ClassWizard to create a member variable named **m_csTitle** of the CString type for the edit box resource.
3. Add a private function of the void type to CODBCDemoView to display the book title (Figure 25.8), and enter the following code:

```
void CODBCDemoView::ShowBookTitle()
{
     m_csTitle = m_setBook.GetTitle();
     UpdateData( FALSE );
}
```

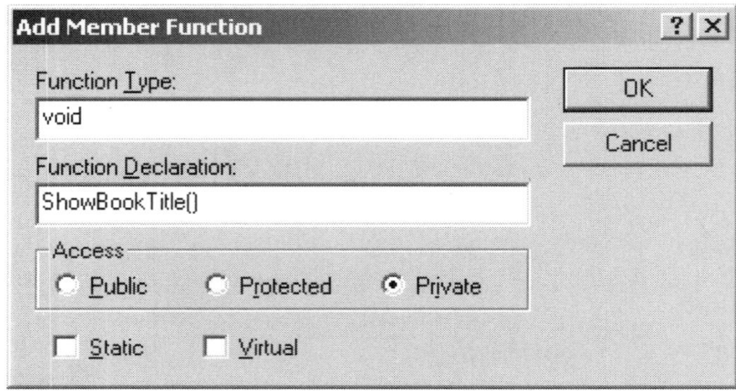

FIGURE 25.8 Adding the *ShowBookTitle()* function.

4. Finally, call the ShowBookTitle() function from *OnInitialUpdate()* to display the data:

```
m_setBook.Open();
m_setBook.MoveFirst();
ShowBookTitle();
```

ADDING A NEW RECORD

Compared to the WizDB project, adding a data record here is a bit more complicated. For one, we don't have the luxury of the *OnMove()* function to work with in a CFormView as with CRecordView. Therefore, we cannot rely on it to signal data updating. In fact, we will have to rely on the navigation commands being evoked to initiate our own data updating action.

1. In the View menu command category, add the "First Record," "Previous Record," "Next Record," and "Last Record" commands as in Figure 25.9.

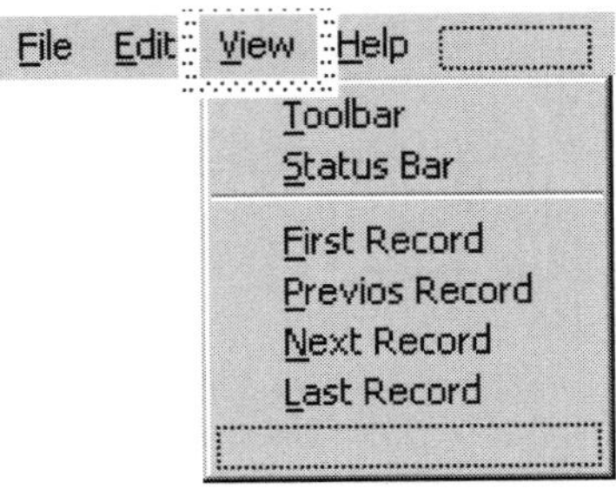

FIGURE 25.9 ODBCDemo Navigation commands.

2. Create message handler functions for the commands.
3. Add a new "Record" command category to the menu, and then add the "New," "Edit," and "Delete" commands as in Figure 25.10.

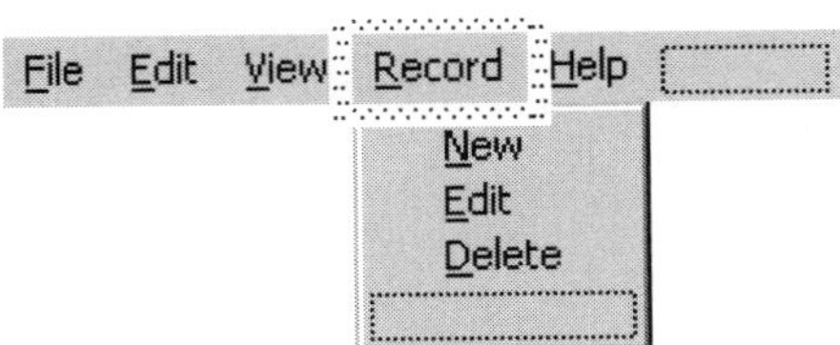

FIGURE 25.10 ODBCDemo Record Manipulation commands.

4. Create message handler functions for the commands.
5. Add a private, Boolean CODBCDemoView member variable named **m_bAltered** to control the data update operations just as we did in WizDB, and initialize it in the *OnInitialUpdate()* function:

```
m_bAltered = FALSE;
```

6. For the Record->New command, create a handler function named *OnRecordNew()*:

```
void CODBCDemoView::OnRecordNew()
{
     // TODO: Add your command handler code here
```

```
        m_setBook.AddNew();
        m_bAltered = TRUE;
        m_csTitle = "";
        UpdateData( FALSE );
}
```

This command merely "sets things up" by placing an empty string in the **m_csTitle** variable and displays it in the edit box. When the user moves to a different record or quits the program, the data will be updated.

NAVIGATING THE RECORDS

The next item on the agenda is record navigation, and we will use the *OnViewNext()* function to illustrate the data update operations.

1. Implement the *OnViewNext()* message handler function for the View-> Next Record command as follows:

```
void CODBCDemoView::OnViewNext()
{
        // TODO: Add your command handler code here
        UpdateRecord();
        m_setTitle.MoveNext();
        ShowBookTitle();
}
```

Here we call on another helper function *UpdateRecord()* that has yet to be coded. This function will be used in all the navigation operations and the *OnClose()* function of CODBCDemoView as well.

2. Add the private *UpdateRecord()* function of the void type in ODBCDemoView:

```
void CODBCDemoView::UpdateRecord()
{
        UpdateData( TRUE );      //Edit box to m_csTitle
        m_setTitle.SetTitle( m_csTitle );
        if ( m_bAltered )
        {
                if (m_setTitle.CanUpdate() )
```

```
            m_setTitle.Update();
        }
        m_bAltered = FALSE;
}
```

3. Implement the *OnFirstRecord()*, *OnPreviousRecord()*, and *OnLastRecord()* functions on your own.
4. Attempt to code the record editing and deleting functions on your own, using WizDB as a model, and then compile and test the finished program.

26 An ODBC Database Application

Data table processing is essential to database processing. The techniques are directly employed to add new data to the system, data editing, data lookup, and other auxiliary database processing operations.

The next step after data table processing is database processing.

In a relational database, meaningful data often are culled from multiple tables governed by a relational criterion (or, in application parlance, *business rules*). Take the Books database for example. A book's complete description involves its title from the tblBook table, the author from the tblAuthor table, and the publisher from the tblPublisher table. The governing relationship is called a *filter* or database *view*. When expressed in programming terms, a business rule often translates into an SQL statement.

In this chapter, we will illustrate the processing of databases by building an application that will show the Books information in total. However, we'll also take a slight turn from the materials presented in the last chapter.

The CRecordView combines the navigation and presentation of data with the CView class. This often masks the underlying operations of the database—it makes life too easy, sort of like driving with automatic transmission, you don't feel the gruffness of the pavement. In the following example, we'll derive our own database classes to work with the CFormView class instead.

1. Start a new SDI application named **Books** with CFormView as the prototype of the View class with no built-in database support, just as we did in the ODBCDemo project. (In fact, you can just continue from the ODBCDemo project if you like.)
2. Select the "Books classes" tree node in ClassView, and use the New Class command in the context menu to add a new class named **CSetTitle** derived

from CRecordset. For the database connection, select ODBC Books, and then select tblBook as the database table for access, using the dynaset record type.

3. In similar fashion, create classes for the data tables tblAuthor and tblPublisher named CSetAuthor and CSetPublisher, respectively, based on the CRecordset class. The resultant classes should appear in ClassView.
4. Render the classes' data private as in the last example ODBCDemo, and provide appropriate *Set* and *Get* helper functions for their access.
5. Add "#include **afxdb.h**" in the StdAfx.h header file.

A set of meaningful book data involves three data tables: tblBook, tblAuthor, and tblPublisher, not individually, but as coordinated "view" records. This "logical" record is obtained through a "query" relating the records from the three separate tables. To obtain such a composite record, we use an SQL statement.

IMPLEMENTING A QUERY

We will now create a CRecordset class that will give us the equivalent of an SQL selection or query that will get us all the pertinent book data.

1. Create a new class named **CSetBook** in the usual manner, based on the CRecordset class and connected to the database via ODBC. This time, however, set the data access mode to be "Snapshot."

We use a snapshot in this case because for query data, we read from but do not write to the database.

2. When it comes to selecting the database table, select all three tables as shown in Figure 26.1.

What you get is a "SQL" statement that looks like this:

```
CString CSetBook::GetDefaultSQL()
{
     return _T("[ tblAuthor], [ tblBook],[ tblPublisher]");
}
```

Note also that all the data fields are returned in the class:

```
CSetBook::CSetBook(CDatabase* pdb)
     : CRecordset(pdb)
```

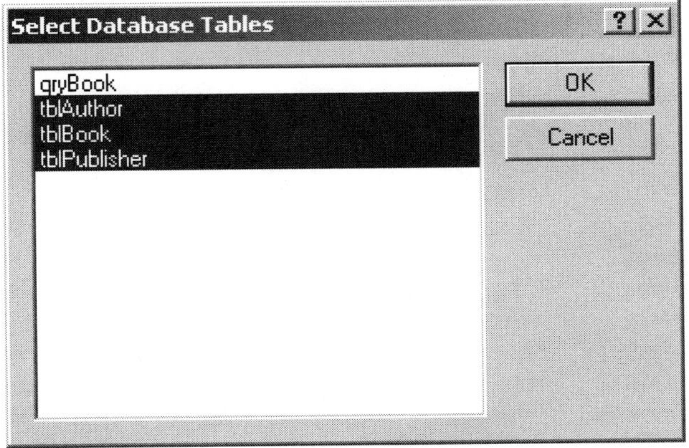

FIGURE 26.1 Selecting tables for data record set.

```
{
    //{{AFX_FIELD_INIT(CSetBook)
    m_AutID = 0;
    m_Author = _T("");
    m_BookID = 0;
    m_PubKey = 0;
    m_AutKey = 0;
    m_Title = _T("");
    m_PubID = 0;
    m_Publisher = _T("");
    m_nFields = 8;
    //}}AFX_FIELD_INIT
    m_nDefaultType = snapshot;
}
```

With the CSetBook class we can then set a proper filter, open the data connection, and read the data.

In this example, we'll also do something different from before. Instead of opening the data connections right from the beginning, we will only instantiate them when we need them. Therefore, we will only create pointer member variables to these data classes.

3. Add pointer member variables to the CBookView class:

```
private:
    CSetBook* m_pSetBook;
    CSetTitle* m_pSetTitle;
```

```
CSetAuthor* m_pSetAuthor;
CSetPublisher* m_pSetPublisher;
```

Now that the data classes and variables have been set up, we will concern ourselves with how we can best present the data in a useful way.

WORKING WITH A GRID

For tabular data, which is what a list of the book information will look like, a good way to display them is through a grid in which the data can be placed in columns and rows. Microsoft provides us with such a grid called the FlexGrid.

To use the FlexGrid, which is a visual control, we need to first install it.

1. Choose the Project->Add To Project->Components and Controls command (Figure 26.2).

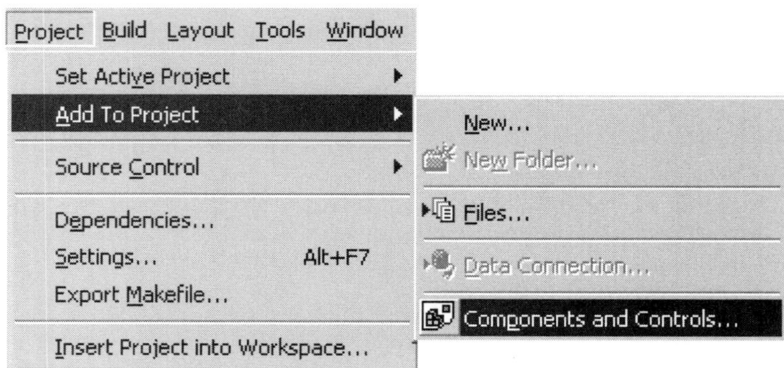

FIGURE 26.2 Adding a component or control to a project.

The Components and Controls Gallery dialog appears (Figure 26.3).

2. Select "Registered ActiveX Controls" and click Insert (or just double-click on the selection).

The available controls are compiled from the system and presented (Figure 26.4).

3. Select "Microsoft FlexGrid Control, version 6.0" and click insert.

You'll be asked to confirm the action as in Figure 26.5.

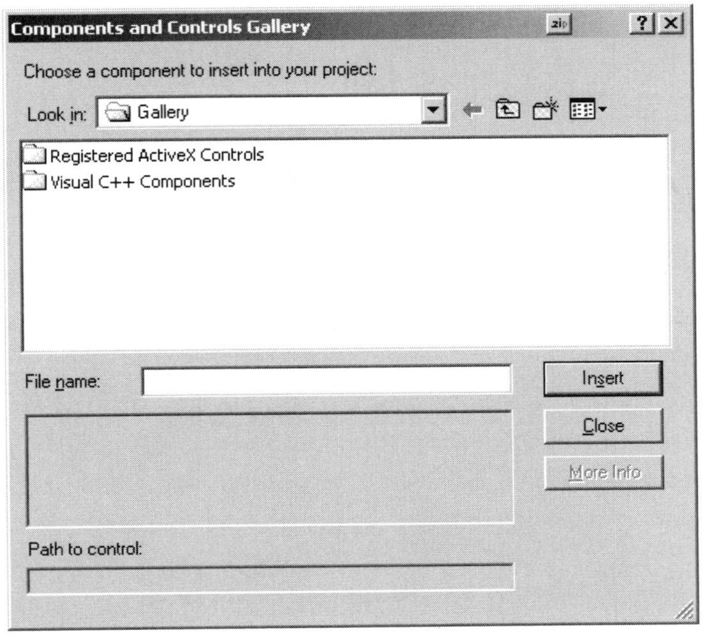

FIGURE 26.3 The Components and Controls Gallery dialog.

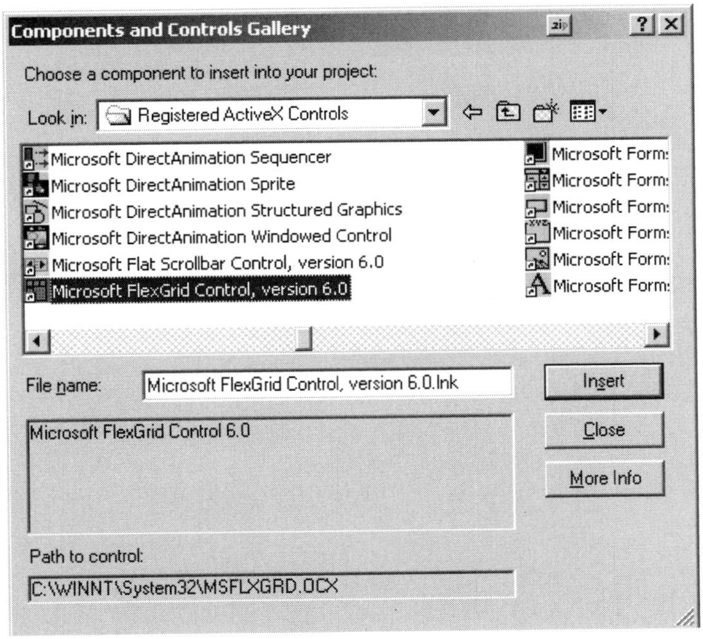

FIGURE 26.4 Components and Controls Gallery.

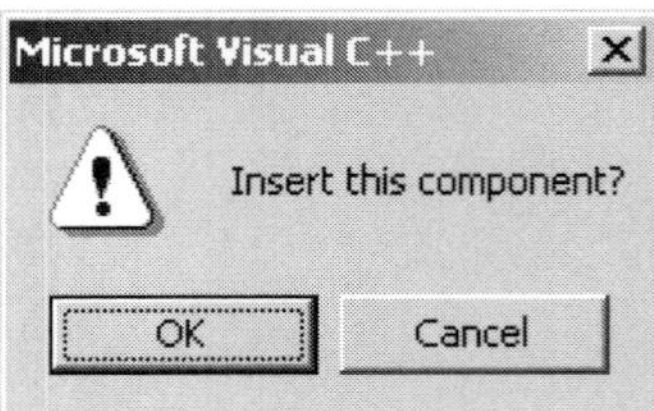

FIGURE 26.5 Component insertion prompt.

4. Click OK to insert the ActiveX control in the project.

You'll be presented with the new classes (and code files) that will be added to the project (Figure 26.6).

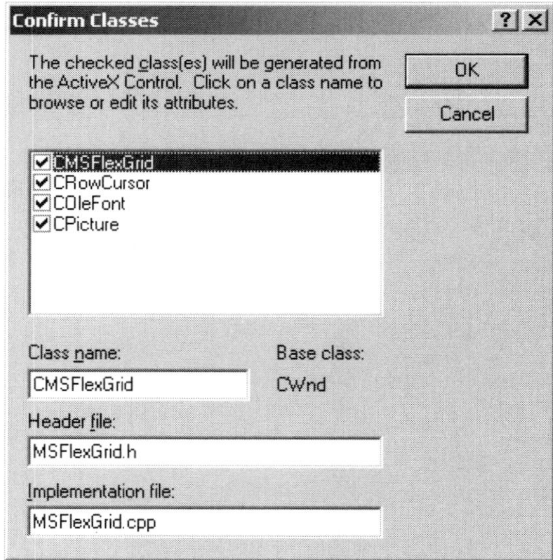

FIGURE 26.6 Classes confirmation.

5. Click OK and then close the Components and Controls Gallery dialog.

A new tool now appears in the toolbox (Figure 26.7).

6. Use the new tool for the FlexGrid and install it on the application's Form view (Figure 26.8).

FIGURE 26.7 New grid control in the toolbox.

FIGURE 26.8 A FlexGrid.

7. Bring up the new grid resource's properties and set them as follows: 2 rows and 9 columns (Figure 26.9).
8. Use ClassWizard to add a member variable for the grid:

CBookView.h:

```
//{{AFX_INCLUDES()
#include "msflexgrid.h"
//}}AFX_INCLUDES
```

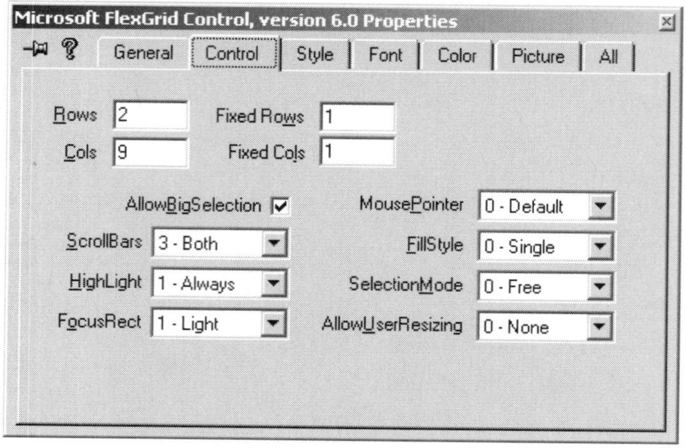

FIGURE 26.9 FlexGrid control properties.

```
#if …
…
class CBooksView : public CFormView
{
protected: // create from serialization only
      CBooksView();
      DECLARE_DYNCREATE(CBooksView)
public:
      //{{AFX_DATA(CBooksView)
      enum { IDD = IDD_BOOKS_FORM };
      CMSFlexGrid      m_grdBooks;
      //}}AFX_DATA
```

Note how the appropriate include file has been added to the top of the CBookView.h file for us.

With this control variable **m_grdBooks**, we can now initialize the grid and put database data in it.

The workings of the FlexGrid are actually quite straightforward, although the resultant coding often appears complicated. This is because you need to attend to every grid element involved.

First, we need to set up the correct number of grid rows to accommodate the number of records we have in the data record set. Second, we need to set up the column headers for the data fields. Third, we need to set the column widths for the best display. Finally, we load the data in the grid cells.

Determining Grid Row Count

To determine the number of rows the grid should have is a matter of knowing how many data records there are in the data record set. This you can obtain using the CRecordset class' *GetRecordCount()* member function. Unfortunately, MFC does not guarantee that the record count will be correct until the records themselves have been traversed. As a result, the code to ascertain the record count is as follows:

```
m_pSetBook->MoveFirst();
while ( !m_pSetBook->IsEOF() )
{
     m_pSetBook->MoveNext();
}
m_pSetBook->MoveFirst();
// Set row count for records plus header.
iRows = m_pSetBook->GetRecordCount() + 1;
```

We begin at the top of the record set ("m_pSetBook->MoveFirst();"). Then, we move through each record ("m_pSetBook->MoveNext();") until the end of the file is reached ("while (!m_pSetBook->IsEOF())"). Next, we obtain the record count and increment the record count by 1 to accommodate the grid header row. The grid is then set up with:

```
m_grdBooks.SetRows( iRows );
```

Note the form of the member function: *SetRows()*, with a plural for "Row." This is important because there is a function *SetRow()* too.

Setting Up Grid Column Headers

Next, we set up the column headers. The scheme is also simple: you focus on each grid cell and set its text contents. For example, the following would set the cell at the top row (row 0), first column to "BookID:"

```
m_grdBooks.SetRow( 0 );
m_grdBooks.SetCol( 1 );
m_grdBooks.SetText( "BookID" );
```

Setting Grid Column Width

To set the column width you use the grid member function *SetColWidth(long lCol, long lWidth)*, where *lCol* is the target column and *lWidth* is its width. (Just to let you know, the width is often best decided by direct observation as opposed to by any rigid scientific means.) A sample is listed here:

```
m_grdBooks.SetColWidth( 0, 500 );
m_grdBooks.SetColWidth( 2, 3000 );
m_grdBooks.SetColWidth( 6, 2500 );
m_grdBooks.SetColWidth( 8, 2000 );
```

Setting Grid Cell Data

Once you're finished with the overhead setup activities you can begin loading the data. The mechanism is the same as that used to set up the headers, except that we'll be using live data from the record set. For example:

```
m_grdBooks.SetCol( 2 );
m_grdBooks.SetText( m_pSetBook->m_Title );
```

However, because cell data are text, any number that is to be placed in a cell must first be converted to a string, as in:

```
CString     csNum;
m_grdBooks.SetRow( row );
m_grdBooks.SetCol( 1 );
csNum.Format( "%3d", m_pSetBook->m_BookID );
m_grdBooks.SetText( csNum );
```

Recall that the CString *Format()* function constructs a string out of a value based on a format specification string. In our example, the value to be used is "m_pSet-Book->m_BookID." The format specification is "%3d", which means "3 digits."

FILTERING

Now, theoretically, our scheme is complete except for one thing.

If we were to connect the three tables with the CRecordset class *Open()* function using the default CSetBook class SQL specification as is, we'd be getting every permutation of the data records between the tables. What we need is a SQL "WHERE" type clause to filter the table, such as "WHERE AutKey = AutID AND PubKey = PubID."

The CRecordset class comes with a member CString variable **m_strFilter** designed specifically for setting filters. Therefore, the record set opening logic will look like this:

```
m_pSetBook->m_strFilter = "AutKey = AutID AND PubKey = PubID";
m_pSetBook->Open();
```

Putting everything together, we have the logic to prepare the display grid, and it should be implemented in the CBookView class' *OnInitialUpdate()* function. However, because the coding will be lengthy, we'll set up a separate helper function to do the job, and then invoke the helper function from *CBookView::OnInitialUpdate()*.

The complete helper function is now presented. Go through the code carefully. It includes safeguards against empty data sets.

1. In the CBookView class, create a helper function named *LoadBookGrid()* to load data into the grid:

```
void CBooksView::LoadBookGrid()
{
     m_pSetBook = new CSetBook;
     m_pSetBook->m_strFilter = "AutKey = AutID AND PubKey = PubID";
     m_pSetBook->Open();
     // Cycle through records to force count.
     int     iRows;
     if ( m_pSetBook->IsBOF() || m_pSetBook->IsEOF() )
          iRows = 1;
     else
     {
          m_pSetBook->MoveFirst();
          while ( !m_pSetBook->IsEOF() )
          {
               m_pSetBook->MoveNext();
          }
          m_pSetBook->MoveFirst();
          // Set row count to accommodate records plus header.
          iRows = m_pSetBook->GetRecordCount() + 1;
     }
     m_grdBooks.Clear();
     m_grdBooks.SetRows( iRows );
     // Install headers
     m_grdBooks.SetRow( 0 );
     m_grdBooks.SetCol( 1 );
     m_grdBooks.SetText( "BookID" );
     m_grdBooks.SetCol( 2 );
     m_grdBooks.SetText( "Title" );
     m_grdBooks.SetCol( 3 );
     m_grdBooks.SetText( "AutKey" );
```

```
m_grdBooks.SetCol( 4 );
m_grdBooks.SetText( "PubKey" );
m_grdBooks.SetCol( 5 );
m_grdBooks.SetText( "AutID" );
m_grdBooks.SetCol( 6 );
m_grdBooks.SetText( "Author" );
m_grdBooks.SetCol( 7 );
m_grdBooks.SetText( "PubID" );
m_grdBooks.SetCol( 8 );
m_grdBooks.SetText( "Publisher" );
// Set column widths
m_grdBooks.SetColWidth( 1, 0 );
m_grdBooks.SetColWidth( 3, 0 );
m_grdBooks.SetColWidth( 4, 0 );
m_grdBooks.SetColWidth( 5, 0 );
m_grdBooks.SetColWidth( 7, 0 );
m_grdBooks.SetColWidth( 0, 500 );
m_grdBooks.SetColWidth( 2, 3000 );
m_grdBooks.SetColWidth( 6, 2500 );
m_grdBooks.SetColWidth( 8, 2000 );
// Load data
if ( iRows > 1 )
{
      CString     csNum;
      for ( int row = 1; row < iRows; row++ )
      {
            m_grdBooks.SetRow( row );
            m_grdBooks.SetCol( 1 );
            csNum.Format( "%3d", m_pSetBook->m_BookID );
            m_grdBooks.SetText( csNum );
            m_grdBooks.SetCol( 2 );
            m_grdBooks.SetText( m_pSetBook->m_Title );
            m_grdBooks.SetCol( 3 );
            csNum.Format( "%3d", m_pSetBook->m_AutKey );
            m_grdBooks.SetText( csNum );
            m_grdBooks.SetCol( 4 );
            csNum.Format( "%3d", m_pSetBook->m_PubKey );
            m_grdBooks.SetText( csNum );
            m_grdBooks.SetCol( 5 );
            csNum.Format( "%3d", m_pSetBook->m_AutID );
            m_grdBooks.SetText( csNum );
            m_grdBooks.SetCol( 6 );
            m_grdBooks.SetText( m_pSetBook->m_Author );
```

```
                m_grdBooks.SetCol( 7 );
                csNum.Format( "%3d", m_pSetBook->m_PubID );
                m_grdBooks.SetText( csNum );
                m_grdBooks.SetCol( 8 );
                m_grdBooks.SetText( m_pSetBook->m_Publisher );
                m_pSetBook->MoveNext();
            }
        }
        if ( iRows > 1 )
            m_grdBooks.SetRow( 1 );
        else
            m_grdBooks.SetRow( 0 );
        m_grdBooks.SetCol( 0 );
        m_pSetBook->Close();
        delete m_pSetBook;
    }
```

2. Call the *LoadBookGrid()* function in CBookView's *OnInitialUpdate()* function:

```
void CBooksView::OnInitialUpdate()
{
    CFormView::OnInitialUpdate();
    GetParentFrame()->RecalcLayout();
    ResizeParentToFit();
    LoadBookGrid();
}
```

3. Temporarily comment out the column width setting section, and compile and test the program. You should see a display like that shown in Figure 26.10.

The reason for exposing the data key values this way is that a default grid will let us see everything, thus allowing us to inspect the raw data for errors. Once we have decided that the coding logic is correct, we can then activate the column width setting code to produce the final result, adjusting the column widths visually until the optimal display is achieved.

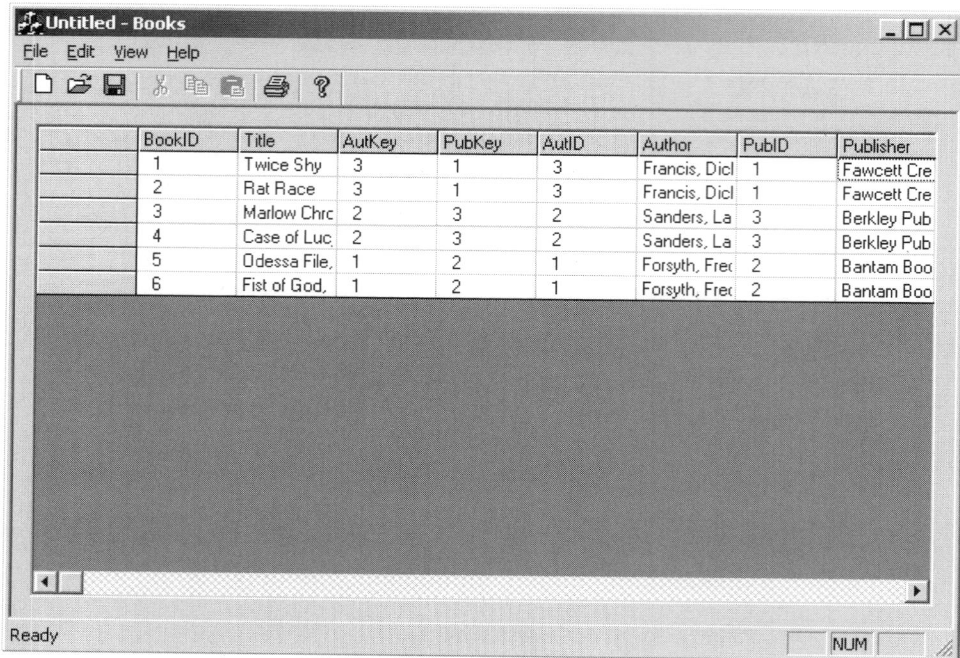

FIGURE 26.10 FlexGrid displaying data.

DATA MAINTENANCE

With the data in view we now turn our attention to data maintenance; namely, editing existing data, adding new data, and deleting data.

Actually, we've gone over these topics in previous sections. Nevertheless, because of the grid-oriented data view, some interesting data manipulation options now present themselves. For example, data record selection is now based on grid focus rather than record navigation.

When a user decides to do something with the existing data, he or she can first select the data record onscreen and then invoke the appropriate command to process the selected data. Let's illustrate this with an example.

Deleting a Grid Record

To delete a data record, the user will select it from the grid and choose the Record Deletion command. In response, the program must figure out which record has been selected by reading the grid's BookID field data under scrutiny, and then track it down in the actual data file. Once there, the file record is deleted, and the grid is refreshed to show that the record is gone.

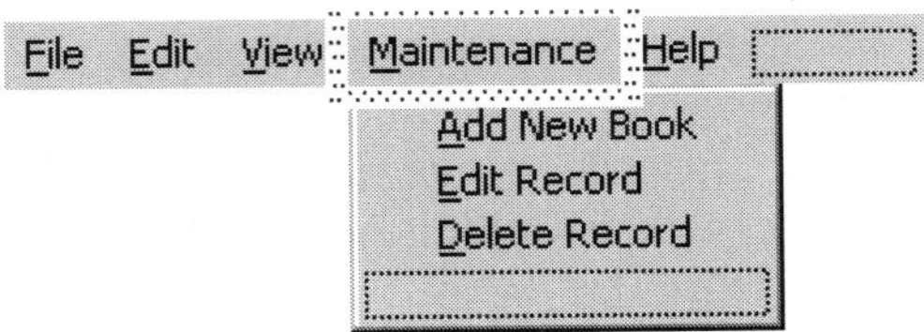

FIGURE 26.11 Data Maintenance commands.

1. Continuing with the Books project, add the commands to the menu as in Figure 26.11.

2. Add a processing function for the Delete Record command:

```
void CBooksView::OnDeleteRecord()
{
    // TODO: Add your command handler code here

}
```

To obtain the book ID of the record selected, you can use the grid's *GetText()* function. Once you know the book ID, you use it to set a filter for the CSetTitle record set to return a single data record, the record to be deleted. You then delete the record, close the CSetTitle records set, and rebuild the grid to reflect the current record status. The code is:

```
    CString     csBookID;
    m_grdBooks.SetCol( 1 );
    csBookID = m_grdBooks.GetText();
    m_pSetTitle = new CSetTitle;
    m_pSetTitle->m_strFilter = "BookID = " + csBookID;
    m_pSetTitle->Open();
    m_pSetTitle->MoveFirst();
    m_pSetTitle->Delete();
    m_pSetTitle->Close();
    delete m_pSetTitle;
    LoadBookGrid();
```

Editing Data

FlexGrid does not permit *in situ* (in place) data editing (although other commercially available grids do), but it isn't unreasonable to pop up a dialog specifically designed for data record editing use. In fact, if the same dialog is popped up without pre-populated data, it can be used for adding new records as well.

In data editing, we populate the dialog's data editing controls with the data from the currently selected row cells. After editing, the data from the dialog controls will be used to update the grid row. Then the same data will be used to update the data in the data tables.

In updating the data in the database, we are only concerned with the tblBook data. This is because we cannot change the lookup data—tblAuthor and tblPublisher—when editing book data. Those data must be edited in maintenance provisions of their own.[1]

1. Insert a new dialog and use it to generate a new CDialog-derived class named **CDlgEdit**.
2. Add static, edit, and combo box control to the dialog as shown in Figure 26.12 (making sure, of course, that the combo boxes are not set to the "Sort" order).

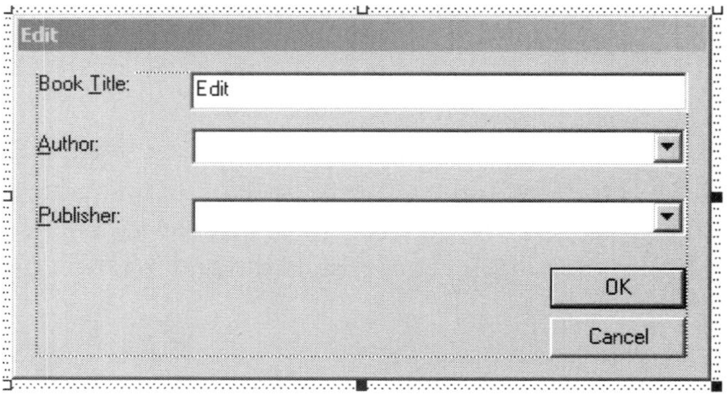

FIGURE 26.12 Data record editing form.

3. Add a processing function for the menu command for data editing:

[1] In a commercially viable version of the program, you might want to permit the user to edit all data freehand in the grid. After the editing, the program can look up the edited data in their respective data tables to check if they exist. If the edited Author and Publisher do not exist in their tables, the program can assume that those data are to be added to the system. You may want to turn this scenario into a coding exercise for yourself.

```
void CBooksView::OnEditRecord()
{
     // TODO: Add your command handler code here

}
```

Coding for data editing can be involved. First, we need to instantiate a data-editing dialog and populate its data controls:

```
CDlgEdit     dlg( this );
m_grdBooks.SetCol( 2 );
dlg.m_csTitle = m_grdBooks.GetText();
m_grdBooks.SetCol( 6 );
dlg.m_csAuthor =  m_grdBooks.GetText();
m_grdBooks.SetCol( 8 );
dlg.m_csPublisher =  m_grdBooks.GetText();
```

Here we pluck the data to be edited from the grid cells and place them in their respective editing controls. For example, for the book title in column 2, we set the grid focus to column 2, and then use the *GetText()* function to get the text in it.

Next, we launch the Edit dialog and let the user edit the data. If the user closes the dialog with the OK button, we'll process the editing by updating the record data in the tblBook table.

Immediately afterward, we refresh the grid's display data:

```
// Update data in grid.
m_grdBooks.SetCol( 2 );
m_grdBooks.SetText( dlg.m_csTitle );
m_grdBooks.SetCol( 6 );
m_grdBooks.SetText( dlg.m_csAuthor );
m_grdBooks.SetCol( 8 );
m_grdBooks.SetText( dlg.m_csPublisher );
```

We must recognize that a book record from tblBook contains not just the book title, but the author and publisher records' foreign key as well. To obtain the edited Author and Publisher data, we must use the text data to look up the keys in their data tables, and then update the keys in the tblBook record. The coding for the extraction of the Author key is:

```
CString     csNum;
// Update Author
m_pSetAuthor = new CSetAuthor;
long     lAutID;
```

```
m_pSetAuthor->m_strFilter = "Author = '" + dlg.m_csAuthor + "'";
m_pSetAuthor->Open();
m_pSetAuthor->MoveFirst();
lAutID = m_pSetAuthor->GetAuthorID();
csNum.Format( "%3d", lAutID );
m_grdBooks.SetCol( 5 );
m_grdBooks.SetText( csNum );
m_pSetAuthor->Close();
delete m_pSetAuthor;
```

Once more we instantiate the data connection only when we need to use it. We then open the table with the appropriate filter (SQL statement) to get a single return record, and extract the key from the return record to update the existing data.

The Publisher key and book title are updated in the same way.

Putting it all together, the coding in *OnEditRecord()* looks like this:

```
void CBooksView::OnEditRecord()
{
     // TODO: Add your command handler code here
     CDlgEdit     dlg( this );
     m_grdBooks.SetCol( 2 );
     dlg.m_csTitle = m_grdBooks.GetText();
     m_grdBooks.SetCol( 6 );
     dlg.m_csAuthor =  m_grdBooks.GetText();
     m_grdBooks.SetCol( 8 );
     dlg.m_csPublisher =  m_grdBooks.GetText();
     if ( dlg.DoModal() == IDOK )
     {
          // Update data in grid.
          m_grdBooks.SetCol( 2 );
          m_grdBooks.SetText( dlg.m_csTitle );
          m_grdBooks.SetCol( 6 );
          m_grdBooks.SetText( dlg.m_csAuthor );
          m_grdBooks.SetCol( 8 );
          m_grdBooks.SetText( dlg.m_csPublisher );
          CString     csNum;
          // Update Author
          m_pSetAuthor = new CSetAuthor;
          long     lAutID;
          m_pSetAuthor->m_strFilter = "Author = '" + dlg.m_csAuthor +
"'";
          m_pSetAuthor->Open();
          m_pSetAuthor->MoveFirst();
          lAutID = m_pSetAuthor->GetAuthorID();
```

```
            csNum.Format( "%3d", lAutID );
            m_grdBooks.SetCol( 5 );
            m_grdBooks.SetText( csNum );
            m_pSetAuthor->Close();
            delete m_pSetAuthor;
            // Update Publisher
            m_pSetPublisher = new CSetPublisher;
            long      lPubID;
            m_pSetPublisher->m_strFilter = "Publisher = '" +
    dlg.m_csPublisher + "'";
            m_pSetPublisher->Open();
            m_pSetPublisher->MoveFirst();
            lPubID = m_pSetPublisher->GetPublisherID();
            csNum.Format( "%3d", lPubID );
            m_grdBooks.SetCol( 7 );
            m_grdBooks.SetText( csNum );
            m_pSetPublisher->Close();
            delete m_pSetPublisher;
            // Update Book record.
            m_pSetTitle = new CSetTitle;
            m_grdBooks.SetCol( 1 );
            m_pSetTitle->m_strFilter = "BookID = " +
    m_grdBooks.GetText();
            m_pSetTitle->Open();
            m_pSetTitle->MoveFirst();
            m_pSetTitle->Edit();
            m_pSetTitle->SetTitle( dlg.m_csTitle );
            m_grdBooks.SetCol( 5 );
            m_pSetTitle->SetAuthorID( m_grdBooks.GetText() );
            m_grdBooks.SetCol( 7 );
            m_pSetTitle->SetPublisherID( m_grdBooks.GetText() );
            m_pSetTitle->Update();
            m_pSetTitle->Close();
            delete m_pSetTitle;
        }
}
```

The initialization code for setting up the edit dialog is listed here for your reference.

```
BOOL CDlgEdit::OnInitDialog()
{
     CDialog::OnInitDialog();
```

```
        // TODO: Add extra initialization here

        // Populate Author combo box.
        CSetAuthor*     pSetAuthor;
        pSetAuthor = new CSetAuthor;
        int     iNdx, iSel;
        pSetAuthor->Open();
        pSetAuthor->MoveFirst();
        iNdx = 0;
        while ( !pSetAuthor->IsEOF() )
        {
             m_cboAuthor.AddString( pSetAuthor->GetAuthor() );
             if ( pSetAuthor->GetAuthor() == m_csAuthor )
                  iSel = iNdx;
             pSetAuthor->MoveNext();
             iNdx++;
        }
        m_cboAuthor.SetCurSel( iSel );
        pSetAuthor->Close();
        delete pSetAuthor;
        // Populate Publisher combo box.
        CSetPublisher*     pSetPublisher;
        pSetPublisher = new CSetPublisher;
        pSetPublisher->Open();
        pSetPublisher->MoveFirst();
        iNdx = 0;
        while ( !pSetPublisher->IsEOF() )
        {
             m_cboPublisher.AddString( pSetPublisher->GetPublisher() );
             if ( pSetPublisher->GetPublisher() == m_csPublisher )
                  iSel = iNdx;
             pSetPublisher->MoveNext();
             iNdx++;
        }
        m_cboPublisher.SetCurSel( iSel );
        pSetPublisher->Close();
        delete pSetPublisher;
        return TRUE;  // return TRUE unless you set the focus to a control
                      // EXCEPTION: OCX Property Pages should return FALSE
}
```

The preceding example is a simplistic program design. For example, do we want to immediately delete a record just because the user asks for it? As an exercise, you should try to put in security safeguards such as querying the user for confirmation to delete the record, and checking the data table to see if the deletion failed.

Command Shortcut

Finally, as customary, when working with grids a user tends to try to invoke commands by double-clicking the mouse on them. We can provide this feature as follows:

1. Use ClassWizard to create a message processing function for the grid's double-clicking event (Figure 26.13).

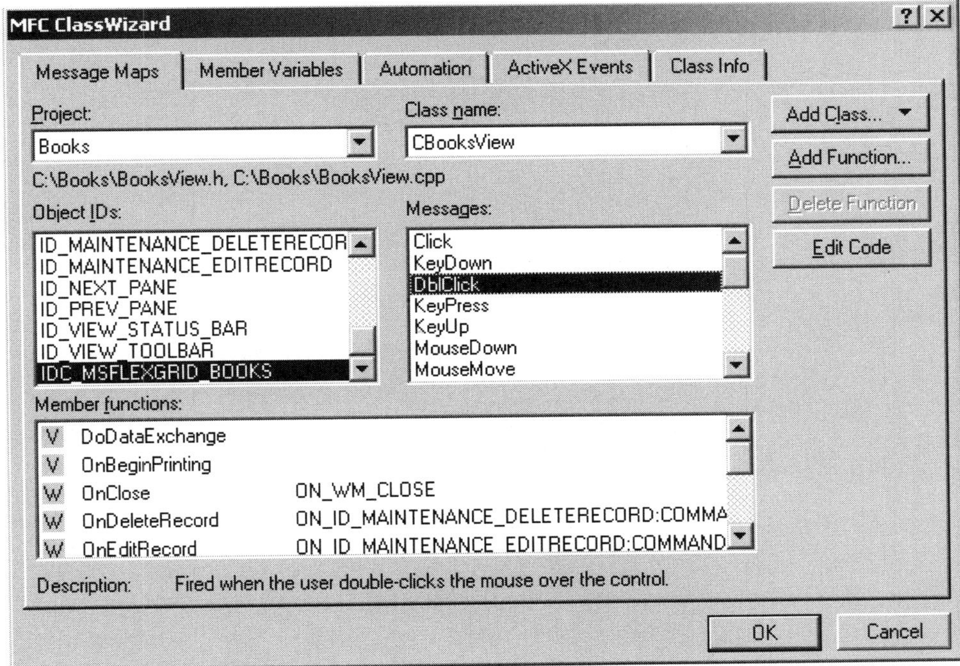

FIGURE 26.13 FlexGrid double-click virtual function.

2. Add the *EditOnRecord ()* function call in the processing function:

```
void CBooksView::OnDblClickMsflexgridBooks()
{
     // TODO: Add your control notification handler code here
     OnEditRecord();
}
```

You can now double-click on a record in the grid to edit it.

27 The List View, Image List, and Tree View

Individual data records are most often presented onscreen using individual controls with one control to a field. This is a most logical arrangement, especially when data editing is involved. With individual controls you have the flexibility of choosing the best candidate for the job. For example, for data entry the edit box is probably the best candidate. On the other hand, for data lookup, you might logically opt for the combo box.

When it comes to full record array displaying, we have demonstrated that the grid works quite well. However, that doesn't imply that the grid is always the best tool for such massive data displays, primarily because it is indiscriminate—it treats all data the same way. Sometimes you would want to be able to display data with a certain amount of contextual structure, and there are instruments for such purposes. In this chapter, we'll explore a couple of alternative forms of data display: the list control (List view) and the tree control (Tree view), even though they aren't specifically designed for database use. Along the way, we'll investigate the CImageList class as well.

THE LIST VIEW CONTROL

The list control displays data as a list, and often with images to enhance the effect. Because of the complexity the list control can attain, and the often-confusing terminology used to describe it, we'll use a hands-on exercise to illustrate the various stages of a list control's development.

To implement a list control (Figure 27.1), select it from the Control toolbox, place it on a display surface, assign it an ID, and create a control variable for it with ClassWizard, such as:

```
CListCtrl      m_List;
```

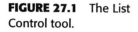

FIGURE 27.1 The List Control tool.

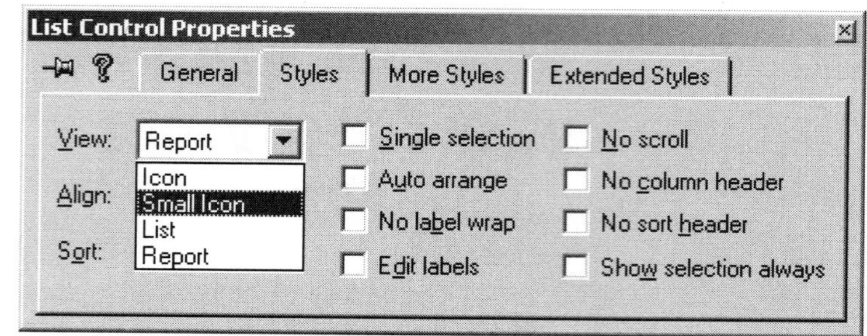

FIGURE 27.2 List Control Properties.

The first thing you do in setting up a list control is decide which style of display you want, as illustrated in Figure 27.2. To simulate a grid, you want to show it as a report.

Once you have instantiated the CListCtrl object you can begin setting it up, such as in the *OnInitDialog()* function of the parent dialog class.

The first thing you do is set up the list columns, such as the following:

```
m_List.InsertColumn( 0, "Publisher", LVCFMT_LEFT, 200 );
m_List.InsertColumn( 1, "Author", LVCFMT_LEFT, 200 );
m_List.InsertColumn( 2, "Book Title", LVCFMT_LEFT, 500 );
```

The *InsertColumn()* function has two forms. The form used here takes on the integer column index as the first parameter, followed by the LPCTSTR column heading, an integer format (LVCFMT_LEFT means left-justified), an integer column width, and an integer *subitem* index, which by default is –1, meaning there isn't any. A subitem is nothing but a column, or field, to the right.

At this time, you already have sufficient information to compile and display the list control to observe the display effect.

To enter data in the left column of the list you use the *InsertItem()* member function, which has four different incarnates. The following illustrates the simplest form used to add text data to a list.

```
m_List.InsertItem( 0, "Publisher 1" );
m_List.InsertItem( 1, "Publisher 2" );
m_List.InsertItem( 2, "Publisher 3" );
```

The first parameter is an integer index; that is, the row or record number, starting with 0. The second parameter is the LPCTSTR data to display. The preceding three function calls will give you three records, filling in the left column only.

For our database example, to display the data from a file, the code would look like this:

```
int     iNdx = 0;
while ( !pSetPublisher->IsEOF() )
{
     m_List.InsertItem( iNdx, pSetPublisher->GetPublisher() );
     pSetPublisher->MoveNext();
     iNdx++;
}
```

To set the data to the columns on the right, the subitems, you use the *SetItemText()* function. For example, to fill the two remaining fields for the first data row (index 0), you use:

```
     m_List.SetItemText( 0, 1, "Chien" );
     m_List.SetItemText( 0, 2, "VC++" );
```

The first integer parameter is the item index; that is, row. The second integer parameter is the subitem index; that is, column or field number counting from the left. The third parameter is the LPCTSTR data for the column.

By using a loop, you can display all the data from a database table in a grid-like structure.

THE CIMAGELIST CLASS

One of the attractions of using a list control is that it can incorporate images in its display. The images used are collected in a list based on the CImageList class, popularly used in constructing toolbars. To add image display to a list control, we need to create a CImageList bitmap object.

In ResourceView, insert a new bitmap resource. Bring up the Properties dialog and set the size of the new bitmap resource to an 80 x 16 strip (Figure 27.3). This will allow five 16-pixel wide color buttons to be prepared.

Color five buttons in the strip for use in the list control.

When the bitmap resource is ready, return to the code, generate a CImageList object, and add the image list construction code before the control list *InsertColumn()* calls as follows:

```
CImageList     m_SmallBitmap;
m_SmallBitmap.Create( IDB_BITMAP_COLORS, 16, 1, CLR_NONE );
m_List.SetImageList( &m_SmallBitmap, LVSIL_SMALL );
```

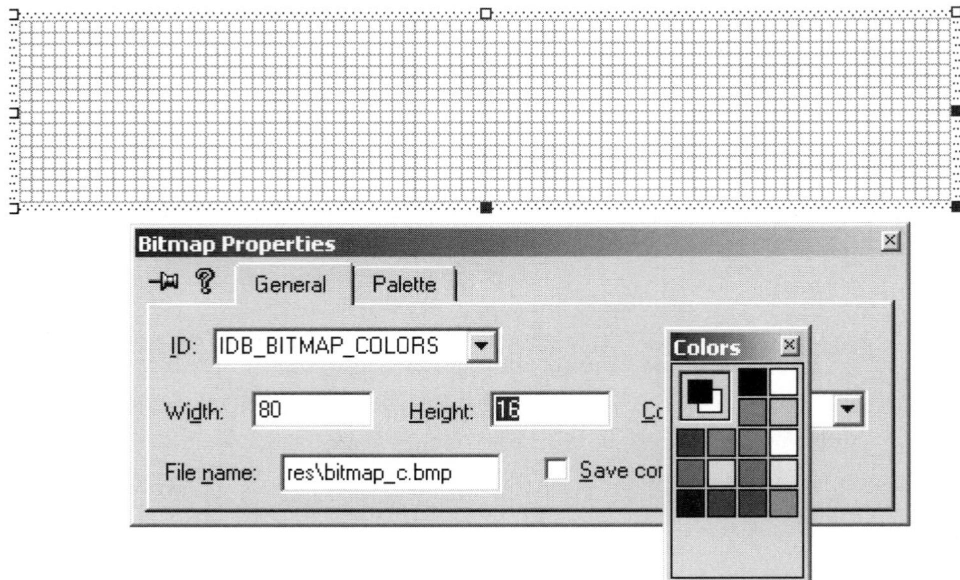

FIGURE 27.3 Creating a bitmap image.

The *Create()* function of the CImageList class creates an image list based on a specified resource ID.

The second parameter informs it of the width in pixels of each equal-sized image, which is, in this example, 16.

The third parameter specifies the growth size for the list (which means you could have constructed the list one bitmap image at a time).

The last parameter specifies a COLORREF *mask*. This mask is the color of the background. In other words, if the background color is red, the red in the image list will be treated as the background, and if the background color changes, that color in the image will change, too.

CLR_NONE means no background color, or transparent.

To specify the image list for use by the list control, you use CListCtrl's *SetImageList()* member function.

The first parameter is the pointer to the image list.

The second parameter is a flag indicating the type of image to set up. LVSIL_SMALL means small image. If you use the LVSIL_NORMAL flag you would be creating large icons for use with the list control's large icon display style. In fact, you should prepare both a large icon image list and a small one, and set them up in the list control at the same time to support switching display styles.

Now we'll incorporate the images in the list control data rows.

Modify the *InsertItem()* functions as follows:

```
m_List.InsertItem( 0, "Charles River", 0 );
```

The third added parameter (0, in this case) is the index of the image to use off the image list, starting with 0. Try different values on your own for effect.

To try the different displays you can set up a series of button commands or menu commands to trigger the CWnd class's *ModifyStyle()* function:

```
m_List.ModifyStyle( LVS_REPORT, LVS_ICON );
```

The first parameter is the style to remove, the second the style to add, and the third (default 0), if specified, the flag to pass on to the *SetWindowPos()* CWnd function for repositioning the window.

The CListCtrl and CImageList classes have armies of member functions to support their many operations. With the afore-presented introduction, you should have little difficulty exploring them on your own.

THE TREE VIEW CONTROL

The tree view control or tree control is similar to the list control in that you can incorporate images in its display. The tree view control, however, displays data in a hierarchical form as in the Explorer.exe program displaying file folders as tree branches.

You install a tree control (Figure 27.4) on a display surface or create it in the usual manner:

```
BOOL Create( DWORD dwStyle, const RECT& rect, CWnd* pParentWnd, UINT
nID );
```

FIGURE 27.4 The Tree Control tool.

Once a tree control resource is in place, you can set its style, such as that shown in Figure 27.5. The "Has lines" style (TVS_HASLINES) must be in for the "Has buttons" style (TVS_HASBUTTONS) and "Lines at root" (TVS_LINESATROOT) to work. To observe the effects of these styles first hand, compile different versions of an example program and test them.

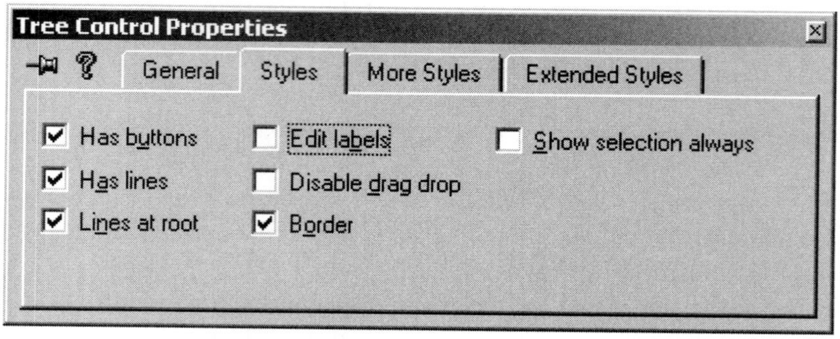

FIGURE 27.5 Tree Control Properties.

When the tree control resource is settled upon, you create a member control variable for it:

```
CTreeCtrl     m_BookTree;
```

With the CTreeCtrl object, you can begin adding data to the "root" positions. A root data node is one that has no parent in the data structure hierarchy, such as the Desktop node in the Explorer.exe program. The following are examples of root data node creations:

```
HTREEITEM     hCharlesRiver = m_BookTree.InsertItem( "Charles River" );
HTREEITEM     hSams = m_BookTree.InsertItem( "Sams" );
HTREEITEM     hQue = m_BookTree.InsertItem( "Que" );
```

InsertItem() comes with four varieties, each returning an HTREEITEM handle of the node inserted. The form of the *InsertItem()* function used in these examples takes three parameters. The first parameter is the LPCTSTR data to be inserted. The second is an HTREEITEM handle to the parent; that is, the tree node under which the data is to be inserted. By default it is TVI_ROOT, which represents a root node. The third parameter is the insertion node position. By default, it is TVI_LAST, meaning behind everybody in that node.

For example, to insert an entry under the hCharlesRiver node, you would call the function as follows:

```
HTREEITEM      hChien = m_BookTree.InsertItem( "Chien", hCharlesRiver );
```

This function call will insert the text data "Chien" under the "Charles River" node.

By repeatedly using the *InsertItem()* function, you build the entire tree display.

A tree structure gives logical meaning to the data display, as opposed to a grid, which infers no inter-data dependency.

Adding Images

For each item in a tree control, you can have two associated images: one for the item's selected state and one for normal display. To accomplish this you need to provide the tree control with an image list containing those two images. The procedure is as follows:

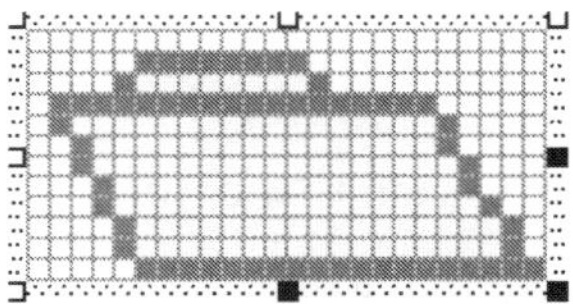

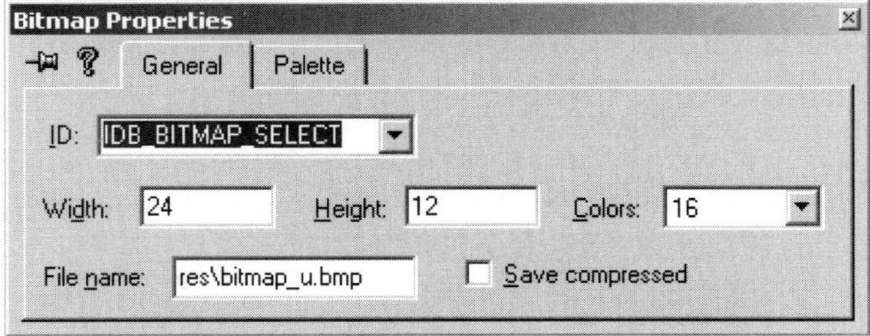

FIGURE 27.6 Bitmap properties.

First, create two bitmap resources, such as in Figure 27.6. Next, generate a CImageList object, such as:

```
CImageList m_ImgSelection;
```

Then you construct the image list as follows:

```
CBitmap     bitmap;
bitmap.LoadBitmap( IDB_BITMAP_SELECT );
m_ImgSelection.Create( IDB_BITMAP_UNSELECT, 24, 1, RGB( 0, 0, 0 ) );
m_Selection.Add( &bitmap, RGB( 0, 0, 0 ) );
```

In this example you create a CBitmap object and use its *LoadBitmap()* function to load the first bitmap using the selected image's resource ID IDB_BITMAP_SELECT. Then, you create the image list based on the deselected image. With the deselect image as the initial image in the image list, you then add the second image from the bitmap containing the select image with the *Add()* function.

With the image list containing the two images to use (which are of the same size), you assign them to the tree control items as follows (and yes, to every single item explicitly):

```
m_BookTree.SetItemImage( hFawcett, 0, 1 );
m_BookTree.SetItemImage( hBantam, 0, 1 );
m_BookTree.SetItemImage( hBerkley, 0, 1 );
m_BookTree.SetItemImage( hForsyth, 0, 1 );
```

The *SetItemImage()* function uses three parameters. The first identifies the tree control item with its HTREEITEM handle. The second is the image list index to use for the normal display state. The third is the image index for the selected state.

With this you have an Explorer.exe style image for each tree control item, as in Figure 27.7.

You now have the basic tools to implement alternate presentation for the Books database data. Attempt to program both list control and tree control displays for the publisher, author, and book titles as exercises.

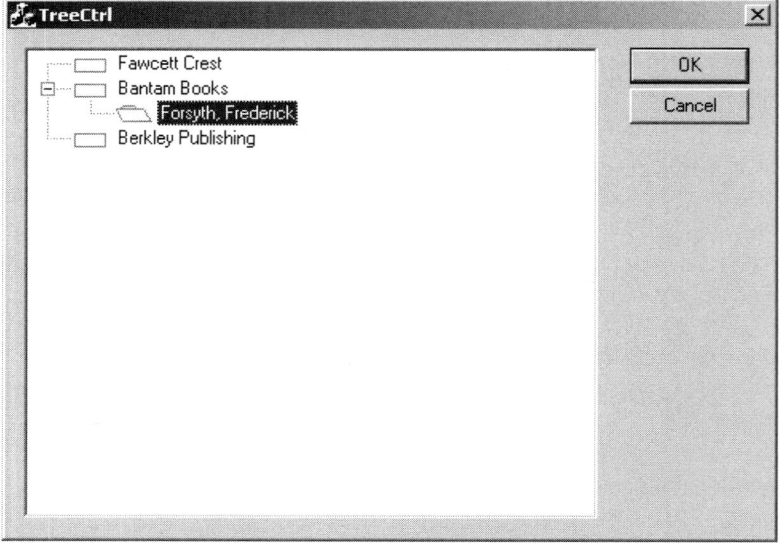

FIGURE 27.7 A tree control display with graphical images.

28 SQL, DAO, OLE DB, and ADO

Database is a vast and complex subject, and MFC includes supports to many database processing approaches, methodologies, mechanisms, conventions, standards, and philosophies. Some of them have been devised to supplant earlier efforts and models, while others are designed to function in specific environments.

SQL, or Structured Query Language, is a term that can be applied to a specific database processing language, or it can refer to the generic language adopted for most modern relational databases. In this book it assumes the latter understanding and specifically infers working through ODBC.

DAO, OLE DB, and ADO are all Microsoft technologies, and are addressed in the sections that are dedicated to them.

The materials contained in this chapter are brief and concise, and are intended for those who must work with these technologies and expect the essences of using these schemes.

SQL PROCESSING (CDATABASE)

In our dealings with the CRecordset class so far, all the actions take place with single data units, such as editing one data record and deleting one data record. In database processing, the advantage is often the capability to deal with massive amounts of data at a time; hence, the attraction of SQL commands. Well, in MFC you can execute SQL statements, too.

As it turns out, the CRecordset class is intimately related to the CDatabase class, and with the CDatabase class, you can issue SQL commands.[1]

[1] SELECT statements, though, are still operated through CRecordset with the proper *Open()* filter and using *MoveNext()* to collect the data.

When you construct a CRecordset object, you have the opportunity to create the associated CDatabase object right there because the official construction of a CRecordset object is:

```
CRecor dset( CDatabase* pDatabase = NULL);
```

By omitting the CDatabase parameter, we are merely setting it to NULL. Using our Books example's classes for illustration, it would have been:

```
CDatabase     db;
CSetTitle     m_setTitle( &db );
```

If, say, we plan to update all the Publishers in the tblBook table currently with the key value of 2 to the publisher with the ID of 7, we would use the following code example:

```
CDatabase     db;
CSetTitle     setTitle( &db );
setTitle.Open();
db.ExecuteSQL( "UPDATE tblBook SET PubID = 7 WHERE PubID = 2" );
```

With CDatabase, you can also perform transactions and rollbacks, and exercise cursor-oriented actions. Check out the CDatabase in the online references. It is quite easy to understand. If you're a SQL person, you'll really appreciate it.

Working with a Database Directly

While the CRecordset class is popularly used to deal with data table record data, there are other MFC members that allow you to do work on the database level. The aforementioned CDatabase is one of them.

CDatabase

In brief, the following are the essential steps to applying the CDatabase class:

1. Instantiate a CDatabase object; for example:

   ```
   CDatabase m_db;
   ```

2. Open the DSN; for example:

```
m_db.Open( "Books", FALSE, FALSE, "ODBC;", FALSE );
```

Or, allow the user to select the DSN by bringing up the data source selection dialog with:

```
m_db.OpenEx( NULL, CDatabase::forceOdbcDialog );
```

From this point on, you can do what you want with the database, using the CDatabase class member functions.

DAO

Whereas the MFC classes and features expanded on previously primarily deal with ODBC database connections, Microsoft's Access users are not necessarily out of luck. The MFC "CDao*" series of classes have been developed specifically to enable the processing of Access data through Microsoft's Jet Engine. The CDaoRecordset, in particular, is the direct counterpart to the ODBC CRecordset class, and you work with it in much the same way. The procedure is explained next.

1. You subclass a CDaoRecordset class by selecting the DAO data option and selecting the Access database directly without going through ODBC (Figure 28.1).

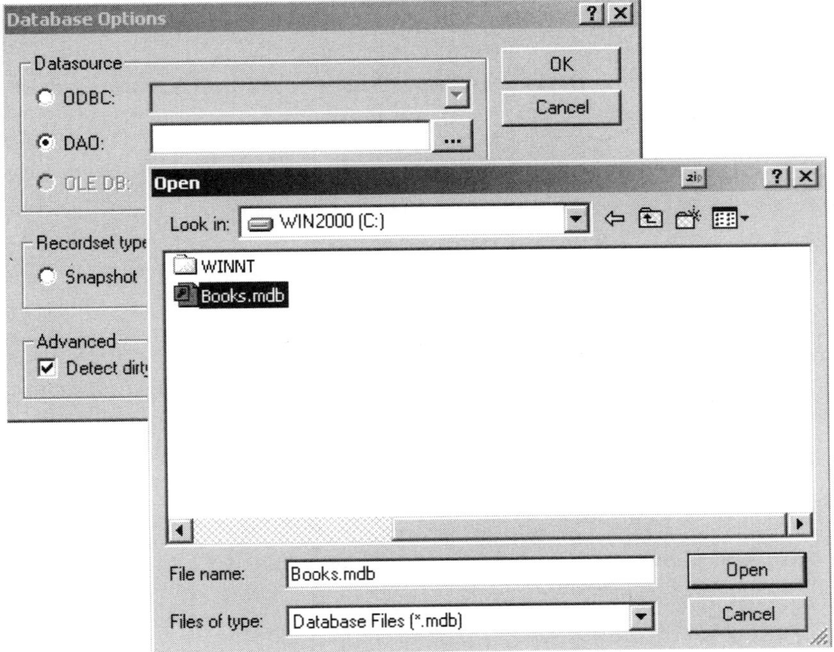

FIGURE 28.1 Making a DAO connection.

2. Add "#include <afxdao.h>" to the StdAfx.h header file just as you added #include <afxdb.h> for the CRecordset class.

Once you have instantiated a CDaoRecordset object, you process data almost exactly like as you did with CRecordset.

Adding a New Record

To add a new record, call the *AddNew()* CDaoRecordset member function to create a new set of data record variables, install the new record data in them, and then call the *Update()* member function to append the new record to the data source. For example, assuming the CSetInvoice class is based on CDaoRecordset:

```
CSetInvoice      m_setInv;
m_setInv.AddNew();
...
if ( m_setInv.CanUpdate() )
   m_setInv.Update();
```

Editing a Record

To edit a record, call the *Edit()* CDaoRecordset member function to place the current record data in the editing buffer. After the record data variables have been edited, call the *Update()* member function to save the new data to the data source. For example, assuming the CSetInvoice class is based on CDaoRecordset:

```
CSetInvoice      m_setInv;
m_setInv.MoveFirst();
m_setInv.Edit();
...
if ( m_setInv.CanUpdate() )
   m_setInv.Update();
```

Deleting a Record

To delete the current record, call the *Delete()* member function, and then move off the record, exactly as you would with CRecordset.

CDaoDatabase

As with CRecordset, you can also relate a CDaoRecordset object to its corresponding CDaoDatabase class object, as:

```
CDaoDatabase     m_dbAcct;
CDaoRecordset    m_setInv( &m_dbAcct );
```

Then you can perform many operations at the database level.

In most regards, CDaoRecordset works just like CRecordset. However, it has many more class member functions. For example, the *Find()* function takes you directly to the target record and makes it current. For example:

```
m_setInv.Find( AFX_DAO_FIRST, "InvNo = 2007" );
```

This command moves the current record pointer to the first record that has an InvNo value of 2007.

In a sense, CDaoRecordset is a richer class than CRecordset, and is often necessary to use in preference over the latter. For example, the database involved in the application might be a genuine Access database and contain data types that aren't supported by ODBC, such as *memo* data. However, you must be aware that the current VC++ version does not recognize the new Access 2000 database format.

OLE DB AND ADO

Finally, for those of you who are into database management, let's look at two more database interface *paradigms*: OLE DB and ADO.

OLE DB

OLE DB is a set of COM interface specifications governing the encapsulation of data in a component environment, a subject outside the scope of this book. However, if you have a background in COM, VC++ 6.0 comes with facilities to quickly produce a framework for an OLE DB server or consumer. The procedure is detailed in the online reference, employing the services of the ATL. Basically, you use AppWizard to generate an ATL COM project, and then insert a Data Access object. The selection of the data source is just point and click, and in just a few keystrokes you have the framework of an executable, dynamic link library, or a COM service. All you do from then on is implement your data access service calls. However, the programming effort is not trivial. If you're a beginner to VC++ and COM, it might take some time before you consider tackling an OLE DB project.

ADO

ADO, or *ActiveX Data Objects*, again a specification, in contrast uses ActiveX technology to provide componentized data access. It already is heavily employed in ASP Web page development to assist in data access, as in the following example that many of you who have worked on ASP recognize.

```
Dim objConnect, objRecordset
Dim strConnect
Set objConnect = Server.CreateObject( "ADODB.Connection" )
objConnect.Open …
```

This is a standard sequence of VB code to open a database connection with ADO in ASP.

Because ADO is merely a standard, it can be implemented in any form you choose, and VC++ comes with controls that are based on ADO ready for use, greatly simplifying database connection. The following example shows how you can use the VC++ IDE to develop a data connection to a database source using ADO.

1. Use AppWizard to generate a bare-bones MFC SDI application.
2. Choose the Project->Add to Project->Components and Controls command to insert the ADO Data Bound Dialog control from the Visual C++ Components folder.
3. In the ADO Data Bound Wizard Step 1 dialog, click Build to build the data connection.
4. Select the "Use data source name" radio button and select the Books data source.
5. Under "Enter the initial catalog to use," select Books and click Test Connection to test the data connection.
6. In Step 2, select the Table radio button, select the tblBook table, and finish the wizardry.
7. When all is well, click OK to insert the ADO dialog component.
8. In your application's menu resource, add a View->Book Data command and generate a command message handler function for it. This function should provide for the following code:

```
#include "RsCgDlg.h"
void CAdodbView::OnViewBookdata()
{
     // TODO: Add your command handler code here
     CRsCgDlg     dlg( this );
     dlg.DoModal();
}
```

9. Compile the program and test viewing the ADO dialog (Figure 28.2).

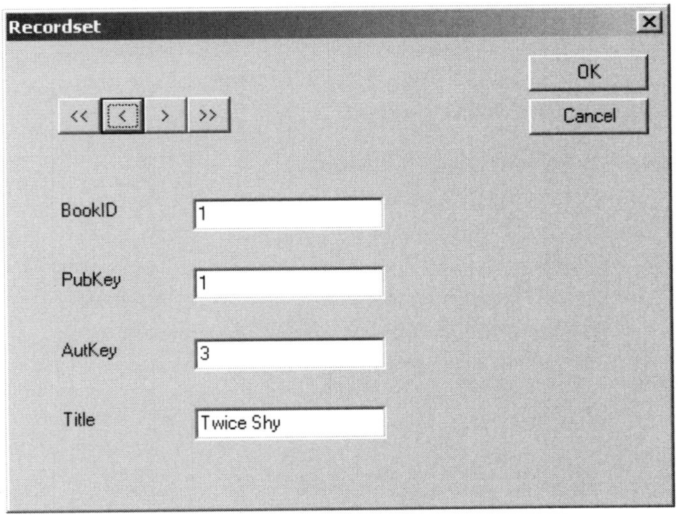

FIGURE 28.2 ADO data navigation.

Data Controls

VC++ also comes with ADO ActiveX controls to help us develop data-aware applications. Development projects using ActiveX controls can reduce development time significantly, as the basic data processing logic already has been worked out for us. The next example shows how easy it is to build a database connected application. In this example, we will display the data from the Books tblBook table in a grid (Figure 28.3), completing the entire program in less than two minutes.

1. Either initiate a new application or continue from the last example and generate a new dialog resource. Create a class for the resource and implement a command or button to deploy it, such as:

```
CDlgClass     dlg( this );
dlg.DoModal();
```

2. Choose the Project->Add to Project->Components and Controls command to insert the Microsoft ADO Data Control 6.0 (SP4)[2] (OLEDB) in the project, this time from the Registered ActiveX Controls folder.

This should add a new entry in the Resource toolbox.

[2] SP4 stands for Service Pack 4 (or later), which should be installed on the PC.

3. Use the ADO Data Control tool to install a control on the new dialog resource (Figure 28.3).

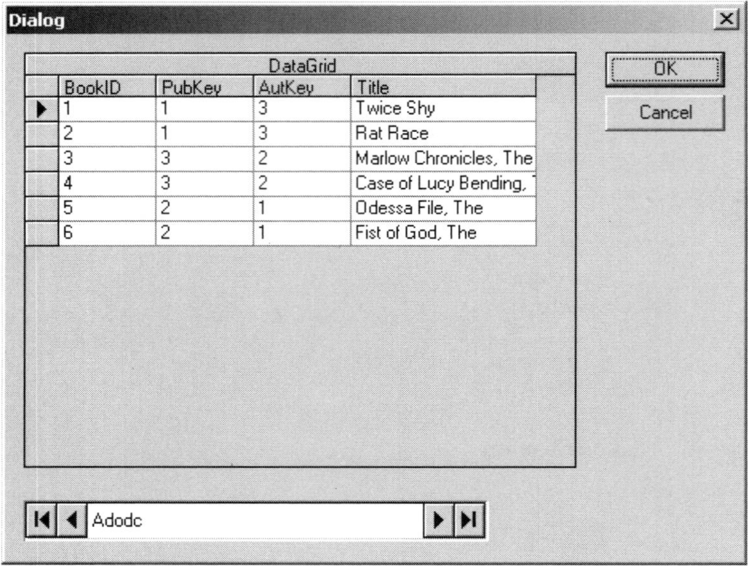

FIGURE 28.3 ADO ActiveX controls.

4. Bring up the control's properties, and in the Control pane click Build to build a connection to the Books database exactly as you did in the previous OLE DB example.
5. In the RecordSource pane, select "2. adCmdTable" in Command Type, then the tblBook table in Table or Stored Procedure Name, and close the properties.
6. Size the control to properly show the navigation buttons if you wish.
7. Return to the Registered ActiveX Controls folder and insert the Microsoft DataGrid Control 6.0 (SP5) (OLEDB) control in the project.
8. Use the new control tool in the Resource toolbox and install a data grid on the new dialog resource. Enlarge it for data display if necessary.
9. Bring up the data grid's properties, and in the All pane select the data control name (such as IDC_ADODC) for DataSource.
10. Close the properties and compile the program for testing.

As you can see, you have a grid connected to live data. Such is the power of using ActiveX controls.

11. Optionally, you can go to the grid's properties and in the Layout pane set the column widths of the key value column to 0 and retry the program. This time, only the book titles show.

The ActiveX controls introduced here are powerful and detailed code components loaded with capabilities. Just inspect the CDataGrid class members in ClassView and you'll get an idea about what you can accomplish with them.

PART VII Component Programming

One of the most powerful approaches to effective and efficient programming is modularization. Modularization can be practiced on the physical level, and it can be on the intellectual level. A developer who can think in logical blocks is generally considered, if not superior or better, at least a more organized technician than one who doesn't. The ultimate manifestation of modular thinking, of course, is OOP, or *object-oriented programming*. In OOP, one thinks in terms of things, or *objects*, as opposed to code lines.

Modularization, when implemented physically, gives rise to program routines, functional libraries, and components. Such code units encourage design reuse and resource conservation. MFC is a prime example.

Code components have many forms. Source code units that can be assembled and compiled include functions and subroutines. Compiled code units that can be linked to main program modules are typified by object files. Generalized code entities that can be loaded and placed dynamically in memory are called *dynamic link libraries*, or DLLs. When standardized specifications are imposed to guarantee that code components will interface with each other, we get COM—*Common Object Model*.

Although it is not the primary interest of this book to dwell on the philosophy of code engineering, VC++ does provide powerful tools to apply the concept. In this part of the book, we'll learn to develop two of the most widely used componentization devices: the DLL and ActiveX controls.

29 Building DLLs

A DLL, or *dynamic link library*, is a collection of code components that exists as an individual file. It contains functions just like those you have been working with, except that they exist apart from the main program. Imagine that you split up a program's source code into different groups and compile the parts separately to produce distinct executable files that are saved on disk. When you execute the program, the various components are loaded into the computer's memory to form an integral code piece. Because the program doesn't necessarily reside in the same memory location every time it is executed, the support library pieces must be "dynamically" linked up with the main program to produce the correct logic flow; hence, its name "dynamic link library."

Fortunately, we don't have to worry about the mechanics of the placement of these program pieces in memory. Windows does that for us automatically, guided by instructions embedded in the DLLs. All we need to concern ourselves with is to organize our program functions properly and code them.

C++ REGULAR DLLS

To demonstrate how easy it is to develop DLLs in the VC++ IDE, we'll create the simplest and fastest (but not necessarily the most useful) DLL in the world. We'll generate a DLL that houses one function, a function to display the message "Hello, World."

ON THE CD

1. Start a new project named **SayHello** in AppWizard as shown in Figure 29.1.

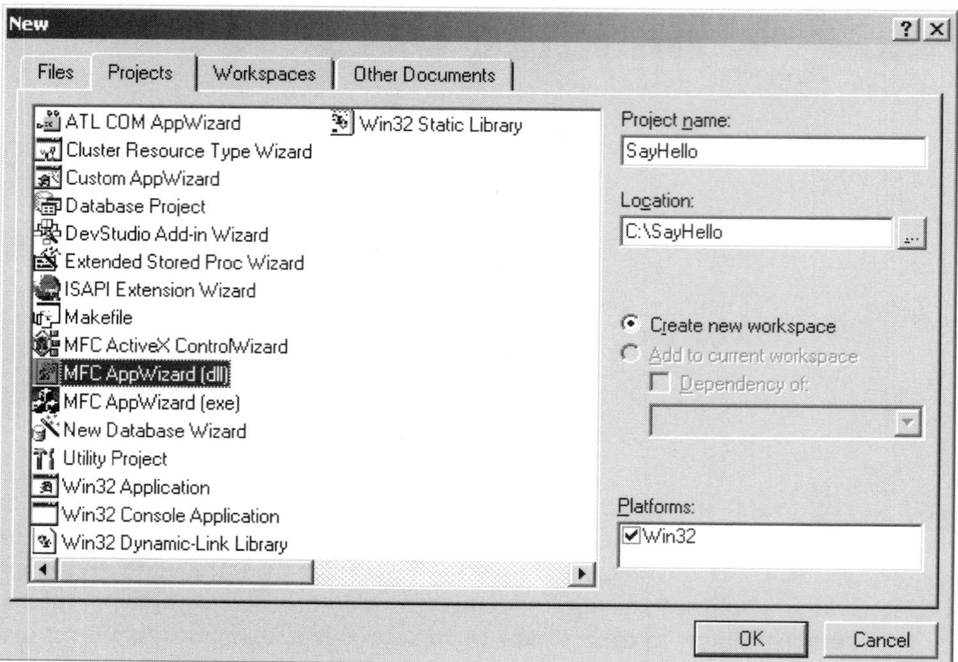

FIGURE 29.1 Starting a DLL project.

2. Select "Regular DLL using shared MFC DLL" in Step 1 (Figure 29.2), and be done with AppWizard.
3. Open the SayHello.cpp source file and you'll see instructions telling you how to implement a DLL function:

```
//          For example:
//
//          extern "C" BOOL PASCAL EXPORT ExportedFunc…
```

Adding a Header File

Because in linking a program with a DLL it needs to use the DLL's header file, we need to produce a header file that can eventually be used by the main program. Although we can use the DLL's built-in header file, it would be nice if the header file were "uncluttered," containing only information about the externally accessible DLL functions.

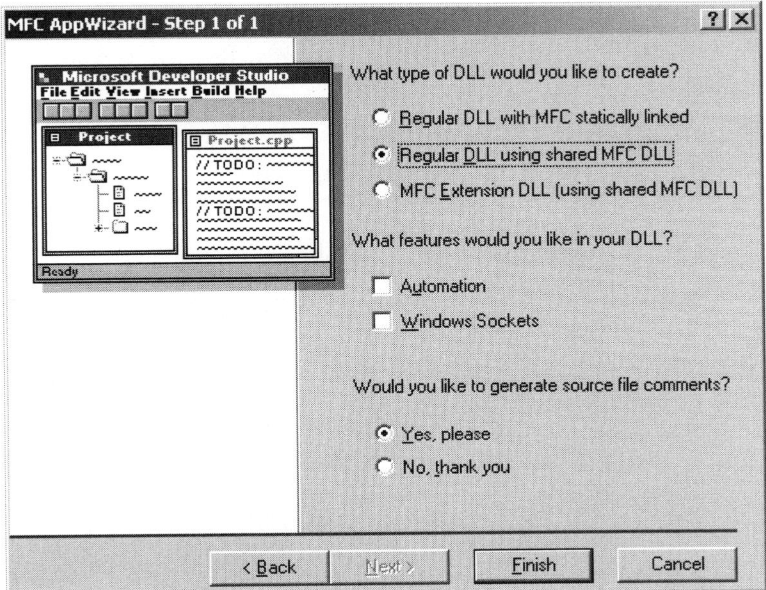

FIGURE 29.2 Selecting the regular DLL model.

1. In FileView, choose the Add Files To Folder command from the context menu (Figure 29.3).

FIGURE 29.3 Adding a file to the project.

For the filename of the header file, use one indicating that it is used by a DLL, as illustrated in Figure 29.4.

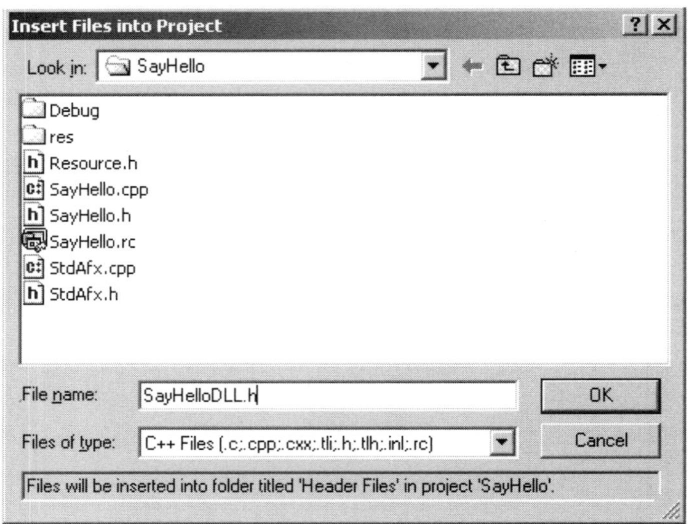

FIGURE 29.4 Selecting a file for insertion into the project.

2. When prompted, indicate that you want to add a reference to the non-existing file.
3. Open the non-existing **SayHelloDLL.h** file and indicate that you want to create it.

A blank file appears.

Writing an Export Function

1. Enter the following header declaration and save the file:

```
extern "C" void PASCAL EXPORT HelloWorld();
```

2. At the end of SayHello.cpp, enter the export function:

```
extern "C" void PASCAL EXPORT HelloWorld()
{
     AfxMessageBox( "Hello, World.", MB_OK );
}
```

AfxMessagebox() is a VC++ software development kit (SDK) non-window dependent function for displaying a message on the screen, much like the CWnd *MessageBox()* function.

3. Open the **SayHello.def** file and add the statement as shown:

```
EXPORTS
    ; Explicit exports can go here
HelloWorld
```

4. Compile the DLL.
5. Save and close the DLL project.

USING A DLL

Now we will write a test program to try out the new DLL.

ON THE CD

1. Start a new dialog-based Windows exe application with AppWizard, and simply accept all the defaults, naming it **TestDLLs**.
2. Borrow the Cancel button generated by AppWizard and rename it **IDC_SAY** with the caption "Say."
3. Use ClassWizard to generate a command message handler function for the button and call the *HelloWorld()* function as follows:

```
void CTestDLLsDlg::OnSay()
{
     // TODO: Add your control notification handler…
     HelloWorld();
}
```

Of course, you need to include the header file that has the *HelloWorld()* function prototype:

```
#include "stdafx.h"
#include "TestDLLs.h"
#include "TestDLLsDlg.h"
#include "SayHelloDLL.h"
```

If you were to compile the program now, you'd be in trouble because VC++ has no idea where the **SayHelloDLL.h** file is. For this, you need to tell VC++ what other include file directory to check.

Project Settings

1. Use the Project->Settings command to bring up the Project Settings dialog window, select the "C/C++" pane, and enter the path of the SayHello project for the Preprocessor category (Figure 29.5).

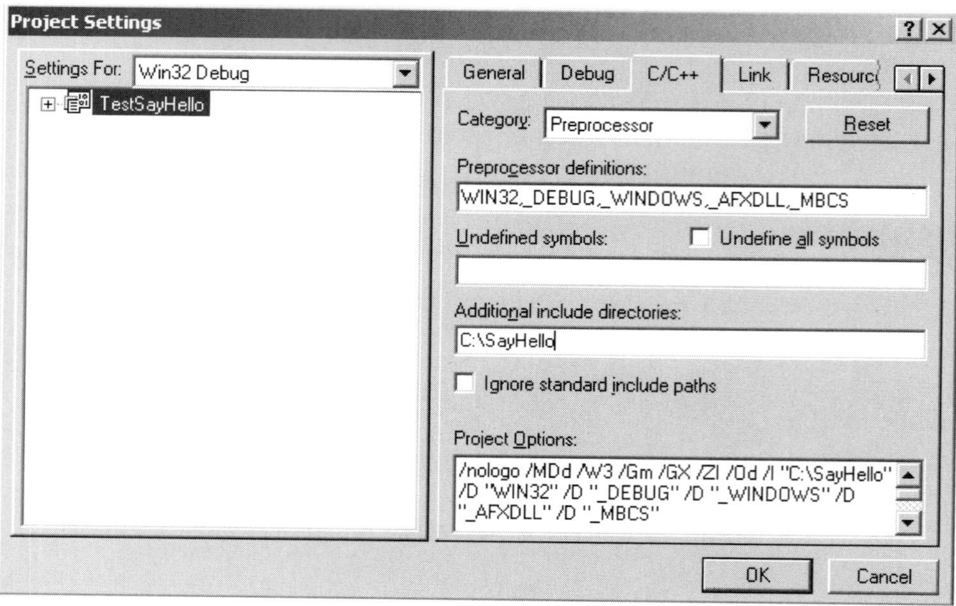

FIGURE 29.5 Preprocessor project settings.

Next, you need to tell VC++ where the library file is.

2. In the Link pane, set the objects/libraries path as shown in Figure 29.6.
3. Compile the application, but do not execute it.
4. Copy the **SayHello.dll** file to the TestDLLs.exe's file directory so that it can be located.
5. Execute the TestDLLs.exe program and test it.

ON THE CD

It is important that you follow the sequence of events described because of the program linking process. The main program module TestDLLs.exe knows where to get the external function and precisely where it is located in memory because of the header file and library file information provided during the program linking

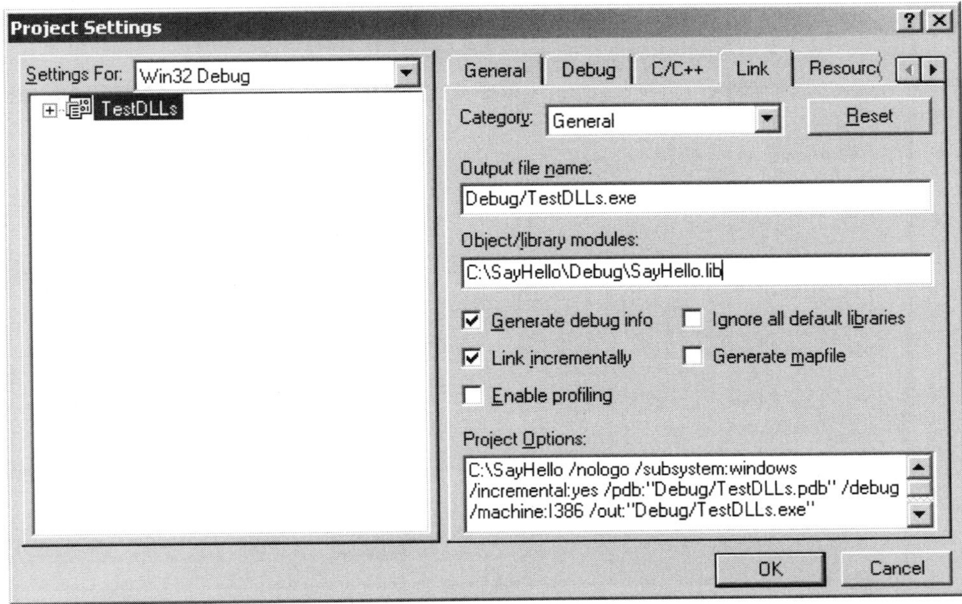

FIGURE 29.6 Link parameters in Project Settings.

process. Once you go back and work on **SayHello** again and recompile it, such information might become outdated. Make sure that every time you modify a DLL project, you recompile the executables that use it.

MFC EXTENSION DLLS

If you intend to create classes in a DLL that will be derived from MFC, you'll need to use an MFC Extension DLL. We'll now see how one is developed. We'll develop a DLL to bring up the About box so that we can use it for any of our applications.

1. From AppWizard, start a new DLL project as in Figure 29.7.
2. Select MFC Extension DLL (Figure 29.8) and complete the AppWizard steps.
3. From ResourceView, insert a new dialog box, give it the ID of IDD_DIALOG_ABOUT, and add a blurb about yourself with a static control.
4. Use ClassWizard to derive a new CDialog-based class named **CDlgAbout** for the new dialog resource.
5. Add a new export function in **AboutDlg.cpp**:

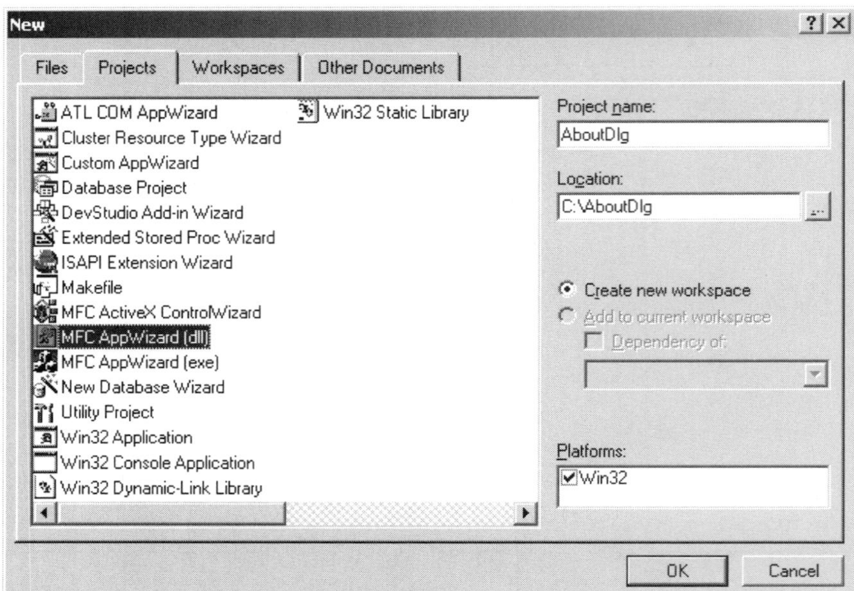

FIGURE 29.7 Starting the AboutDlg DLL.

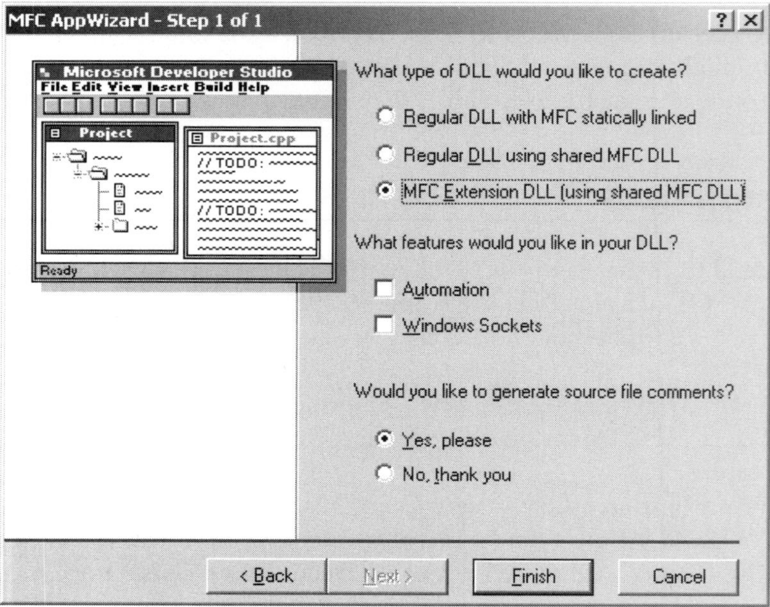

FIGURE 29.8 Selecting the MFC Extension DLL model.

```
extern "C" void PASCAL EXPORT AboutDlg()
{
        CDlgAbout    dlg;
        dlg.DoModal();
}
```

6. Add a new header file named AboutDlgDLL.h and enter the function prototype in it:

```
extern "C" void PASCAL EXPORT AboutDlg();
```

7. Add the appropriate include statements in **AboutDlg.cpp**:

```
#include "stdafx.h"
#include <afxdllx.h>
#include "AboutDlgDLL.h"
#include "DlgAbout.h"
```

8. Add the #include directive in **DlgAbout.h** for the resource header file so that the About dialog ID is referenced:

```
#include "Resource.h"
```

9. Add the **AboutDlg** entry in the AboutDlg.def file.
10. Compile the DLL.
11. Create a test program to launch the About box just as we did in the last demonstration. In fact, if you like, you can use the same **TestDLLs** program and just add one more command button to trigger the modal dialog, calling the *AboutDlg()* DLL function.

(Remember to update the project settings to include the AboutDlg header and library files, separated from the SayHello files by semicolons, and copy the AboutDlg.dll file to the TestDLLs.exe directory.)

CONFLICTING RESOURCES

Now let's have a little fun.

1. Add a dialog box to the **TestDLLs** project and install a static control in it that says something like "Local promotion." Give the new dialog resource an ID of IDD_DIALOG_LOCAL_PROMO.

2. Add a button to the main dialog window to deploy the new dialog.
3. Compile the **TestDLLs** program and test the buttons, making sure that both dialogs—local and from the **AboutDlg** DLL—function, and display different messages in them.
4. Open (File->Open) the **Resource.h** file of the **AboutDlg** DLL project and inspect the value of the IDD_DIALOG_ABOUT resource ID. It should look something like this:

```
#define IDD_DIALOG_ABOUT                    4000
```

5. Open the **Resource.h** file of the **TestDLLs** project and manually edit the IDD_DIALOG_LOCAL_PROMO to assume the same value as that of the **AboutDlg** DLL's dialog resource (such as 4000).
6. Rebuild all (Build->Rebuild All) the files in **TestDLLs** to ensure all the changes and updates are recompiled.
7. Test the two dialog launching buttons. Do you see two different dialog messages?

What we have done is simulate a common problem working with MFC extension DLLs, especially if they involve resources. Because the dialog resource in the DLL happened to have the same value as the local resource, which can happen if you work with large programs with lots of resources, the local resource is used on first encounter. The program never got to see the DLL resource.

In our example, two resource streams are involved: one for the TestDLLs program, and one for the DLL, compiled independently not knowing the existence of the other. When the TestDLL program is executed, the application maintains a pointer to identify the resource stream to use. This pointer first points to the local resource stream at program startup. As long as this pointer continues to point to the local resource stream, the one in the DLL never gets used, unless, of course, the resource ID cannot be found in the local resources. Then, the program will be compelled to look into the DLL.

The solution to the problem is, therefore, quite simple. Just point to the DLL's resource stream when its functions are called, and restore the pointer to its previous value upon exit.

We will see how it is done by an example.

Insulating Resources

To insulate resources from diverse program modules that might result in clashes as we saw previously, adopt the following resource insulation approach:

1. Open the **AboutDlg** DLL project.
2. Modify the *AboutBox()* export function as follows:

```
extern "C" void PASCAL EXPORT AboutDlg()
{
     // Preserve resource handle and
     HINSTANCE     hInstOld = AfxGetResourceHandle();
     // Use local one.
     AfxSetResourceHandle( AboutDlgDLL.hModule );
     CDlgAbout     dlg;
     dlg.DoModal();
     // Restore resource handler.
     AfxSetResourceHandle( hInstOld );
}
```

3. Compile the DLL, re-link it to the TestDLLs project (remembering to copy the new DLL file to the TestDLLs executable directory), and then test it.

In this case, first we identify the current resource handle and hold it in the variable **hInstOld** of the HINSTANCE type. The parameter required by the *AfxSetResourceHandle()* function "AboutDlgDLL" is provided from the top part of the function generated by AppWizard. When the execution of the DLL function is finished, the old value is restored.

30 Building ActiveX Controls

First, it must be noted that with the name "ActiveX" we confront a controversy. This is because the names ActiveX, COM, and COM object (sometimes with OLE and VBX thrown in) have been used to mean different and, at the same time, same things. Officially, COM is not a code product but a set of specifications developed by Microsoft governing the construction of code components that interact with each other. Therefore, there is no such thing as "a COM," as you'll often find in job requisition descriptions. Indeed, few developers truly "know" COM—they mostly know how to develop code objects that comply with COM.

Yet, what are these code objects called? Sometimes programmers called them COM, and sometimes ActiveX, although according to Microsoft technical writings they are not the same. While the VC++ project wizard calls it ActiveX, the creative result, is decidedly a .OCX program file.

In any case, the purpose of the ensuing discussion isn't to condense a subject that in its own right easily commands a book of hundreds of pages, into a few paragraphs, but to show you the procedure to creating such an object.

CREATING AN ACTIVEX COMPONENT

Because of the complex operations that the creation of an ActiveX object entails, we must first describe what we're going to be doing in the following example project.

In the following exposition, we'll develop an ActiveX (.OCX) object that displays a text phrase, sort of like a static control. The result should be a component that you can insert in an application by adding it to a project (yes, with the Project-> Add to Project command). The control will do only one thing, display a text phrase;

therefore, you can pretty much consider it a "do-nothing" control. The steps to constructing an ActiveX control aren't trivial, and we don't want the process to be detracted by application functional details. A "do-nothing" project allows us to focus on the engineering issues.

1. To initiate an ActiveX project, in Visual Studio select the File->New command as usual.
2. In the Project pane, select MFC ActiveX control Wizard, enter the project name **Label**, and click OK to start the wizard.

3. In Step 1 of the wizard, select 1 control for the project (Figure 30.1). Leave everything else as defaults and move to Step 2.

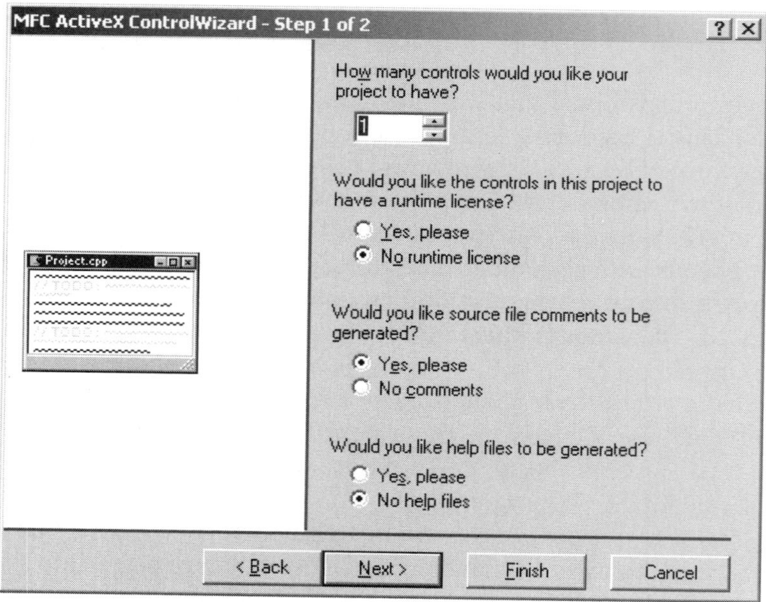

FIGURE 30.1 Initiating an ActiveX control project.

4. In Step 2, if you feel that the control should have a different name, use the Edit Names button to modify it. Leave everything as is, but click Advanced.
5. In the Advanced ActiveX Features dialog, check everything but the first one, Windowless activation.

- *Unclipped device context* ensures that displays in the control won't run over into the container—the application that will be hosting the control.

- *Flicker-free activation* uses a screen drawing method that eliminates flickering.
- *Mouse pointer notification when inactive* causes mouse pointer messages to be generated even when the control is inactive.
- *Optimized drawing code* elects to draw the user interface in an optimized manner if the container provides for such capabilities.
- *Loads properties asynchronously* allows the control and container to proceed with startup activities without having to wait for the control's property data to load and waste time.

6. Click Finish to complete the wizardry.
7. Build the project to produce an .OCX file.

Trying the ActiveX Control

At this time, without a single line of coding, we have a functional .OCX, although what function it serves is a mystery.

1. To try out this new control, choose the Tools->ActiveX Control Test Container command.
2. When the ActiveX Control Test Container dialog appears, choose the Edit->Insert New Control command and select the Label Control.

The control now should be executed, displaying an ellipse (Figure 30.2).

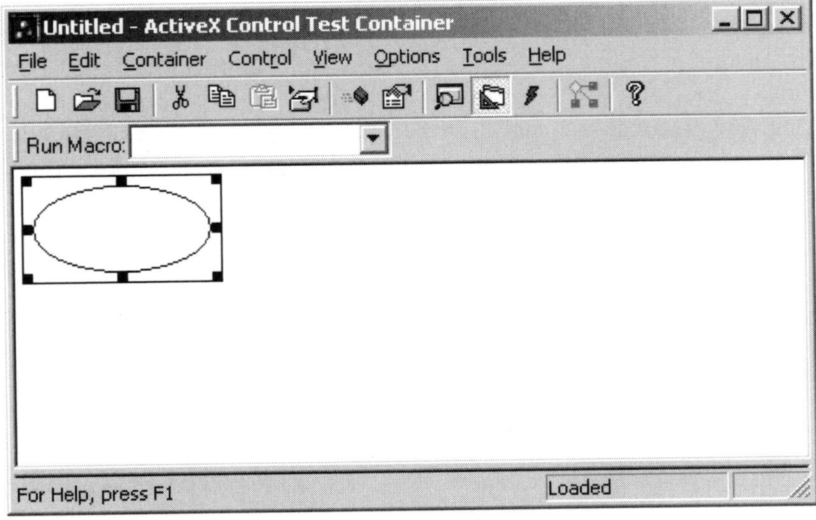

FIGURE 30.2 Testing an ActiveX control.

3. Try to size the control.

The ellipse should hug the control's boundary rectangle.

The OnDraw() Function

1. Close the test application.
2. Go to the *OnDraw()* function of the CLabelCtrl class.

The first two ellipse function calls are responsible for the appearance of the ellipse in the control's user interface window. Again, the *OnDraw()* function is where the visual action takes place.

3. To implement our titling requirement, simply comment out these two functions and add our own:

```
// pdc->FillRect(rcBounds,
CBrush::FromHandle((HBRUSH)GetStockObject(WHITE_BRUSH)));
// pdc->Ellipse(rcBounds);
pdc->TextOut( 0, 0, "Title" );
```

4. Compile the control and use the test application to try it again.

This time you should see the word "title" appear.

Properties

A control that displays an inflexible phrase "Title" is of little practical use. To display any text supplied at any display position, we need variables to give the needed flexibilities, and there are several ways to do this.

One way is to use internally defined variables in exactly the same way as we have learned throughout this book, and provide access functions for the user container to set variable values programmatically. Another way is to define variables that can be directly accessed by the user. Such a variable is called a *property* of the control. Specifically, those properties defined by the developer are called *custom properties.*

Custom Properties

To generalize the text title, we need a property whose value can be set.

1. Bring up ClassWizard and switch to the Automation pane (Figure 30.3).
2. With the CLabelCtrl class selected, click Add Property.
3. Enter the first property as in Figure 30.4.

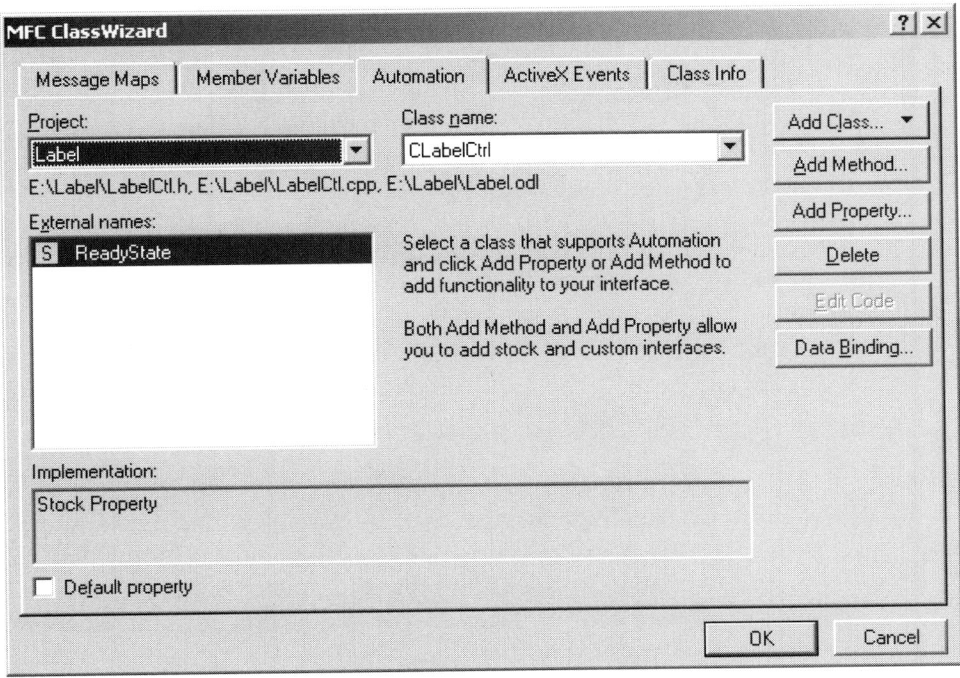

FIGURE 30.3 ActiveX Control ClassWizard Automation pane.

FIGURE 30.4 Defining an ActiveX variable.

In this example, we create a property named **m_csTitle** of the CString type with an "External" name **Title**, the name that will be used by the user.

Note that in Figure 30.4 the Member variable radio button is checked as opposed to the Get/Set methods radio button. This causes the wizard to create a member variable named **m_csTitle** and expose it to the outside world—the user container, under the name of **Title**. In other words, the user will have direct access to the variable, or the variable/property will later show up in the control's property sheet under the "external" name of **Title**. At the same time, a pair of Get and Set functions will be constructed for the user to programmatically access the property as well.

In contrast, if you check the Set/Get methods radio button, the variable will not be directly accessible to the user. All manipulation of the property's value will go through a Get or Set function.

4. Similarly, generate a property of the type short with an external name XPosition and an internal name m_iX, and a corresponding one also of the type short with an external name of YPosition and an internal name of m_iX.
5. In preparation for an option that the control will offer, create a property named externally as **Transparent** and internally as **m_bTransparent** of the Bool type.

Stock Properties

Another type of property you can include in the control is called *stock* property. These properties "come with" the control and include values such as background color and so on. To expose a stock property for user manipulation, simply create a property for it and designate it so.

1. In ClassWizard's Automation pane, click Add Property for the CLabelCtrl class and select an external name from the drop-down list as in Figure 30.5.

The BackColor property is now in the property list.

Ambient Properties

The last type of property you can have is the *ambient* property. While stock properties deal with those innate properties of the control, ambient properties belong to the container that will be using the control. Ambient properties are commonly used to integrate the control into its surrounding. Typically, the control uses the ambient properties to adjust its own.

To get the ambient property, the control uses the *GetAmbientProperty()* function. For example, suppose the control permits the background color to be set, and

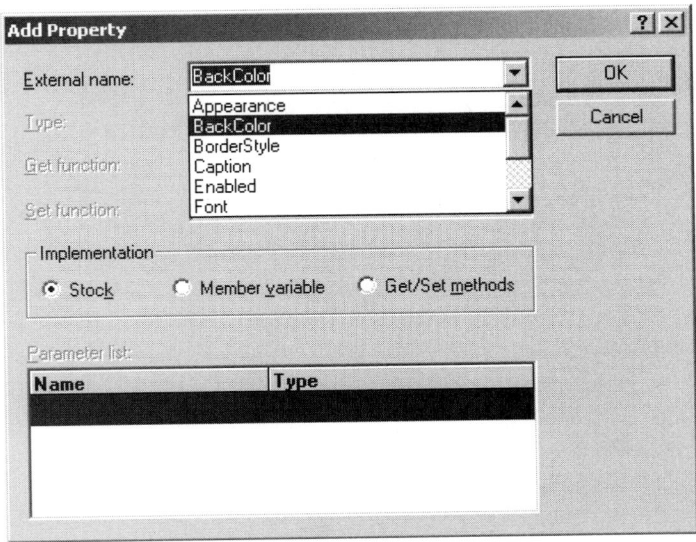

FIGURE 30.5 Adding a stock property.

the variable controlling the background color is m_clrBack, the code in the control's constructor or *OnDraw()* function to set the background color would be:

```
OLE_COLOR     m_clrBack;
GetAmbientProperty( DISPID_AMBIENT_BACKCOLOR, VT_COLOR, &m_clrBack );
SetBackColor( m_clrBack );
```

We will be implementing this in our sample Label control in just a bit.

The PX_ Macros

In order for the property values to be updated and used by the various parts of the program whenever the properties undergo changes, we need to implement a property exchange mechanism, much like the data exchange mechanism we learned between controls and their member variables.

1. Go to the *DoPropExchange()* function in CLabelCtrl and add the following code:

```
void CLabelCtrl::DoPropExchange(CPropExchange* pPX)
{
    ...
    // TODO: Call PX_ functions for each persistent…
```

```
        PX_String( pPX, "Title", m_csTitle, "Title" );
        PX_Short( pPX, "XPosition", m_iX, (short) 0 );
        PX_Short( pPX, "YPosition", m_iY, (short) 0 );
        PX_Bool( pPX, "Transparent", m_bTransparent, TRUE );
}
```

For each property, we provide a PX_ call. In each PX_ call, the first parameter is the property exchange object pointer. The second parameter is the external name. The third is the property variable, and the fourth is a default value for that property.

With these mechanisms in place, the values provided by the user via the control's Properties sheet later will be automatically updated in the properties.

Property Page

With the operational ingredients—the properties—in place, we can now proceed to provide a visual user interface for them: the control's property sheet.

1. In ResourceView, open the IDD_PROPPAGE_LABEL dialog resource and populate it with controls as shown in Figure 30.6, with the x and y edit boxes set to numeric data only.

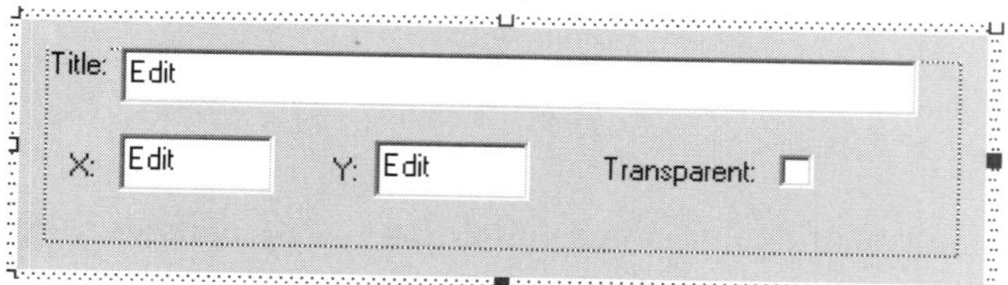

FIGURE 30.6 An ActiveX Control property page.

2. Use ClassWizard to add a member variable for the Title edit box as shown in Figure 30.7.

The last entry **Title** "Optional property name" is the same external name defined in the control for the title string earlier, the name that will be used to identify the Title variable in OLE interfacing. Remember that the variable created here belongs to the CLabelPropPage class. We really need the value to be used in the CLabelCtrl class. How does the value get across to the destination? The answer is the PX_ series of data exchange function that we implemented earlier.

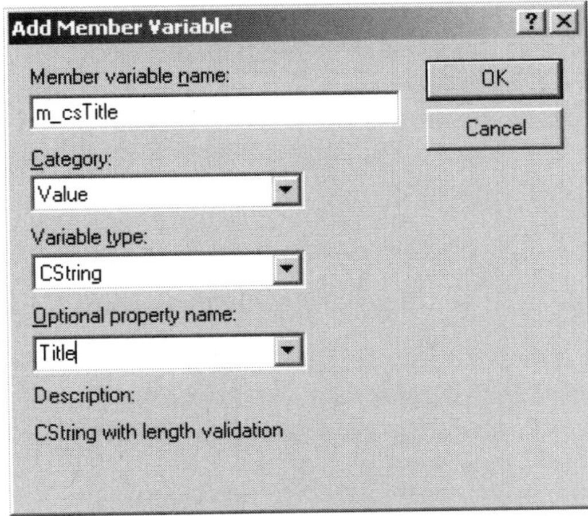

FIGURE 30.7 Defining an optional property.

3. Establish all the Properties page variables as listed in Table 30.1.
4. The Property page class CLabelPropPage has its own data exchange mechanisms, and you should adjust them accordingly at this time:

TABLE 30.1 Property Page Variables

Resource ID	*Variable*	*Type*	*Property Name*
IDC_EDIT_TITLE	m_csTitle	CString	TitleProp
IDC_EDIT_X	m_iX	int	XProp
IDC_EDIT_Y	m_iY	int	YProp
IDC_CHECK_TRANSPARENT	m_bTransparent	Bool	Transparent

```
void CLabelPropPage::DoDataExchange(CDataExchange* pDX)
{
    //{{AFX_DATA_MAP(CTitleControlPropPage)
    DDP_Text(pDX, IDC_EDIT_TITLE, m_csTitle, _T("Title") );
    DDX_Text(pDX, IDC_EDIT_TITLE, m_csTitle);
    DDP_CBIndex(pDX, IDC_EDIT_X, m_iX, _T("XPosition") );
    DDX_CBIndex(pDX, IDC_EDIT_X, m_iX);
    DDP_CBIndex(pDX, IDC_EDIT_Y, m_iY, _T("YPosition") );
```

```
        DDX_CBIndex(pDX, IDC_EDIT_Y, m_iY);
        DDP_Check(pDX, IDC_CHECK_TRANSPARENT, m_bTransparent,
    _T("Transparent") );
        DDX_Check(pDX, IDC_CHECK_TRANSPARENT, m_bTransparent);
        //}}AFX_DATA_MAP
        DDP_PostProcessing(pDX);
}
```

Whereas DDP_Text and DDX_Text are generated by the wizard for text variables, you need to edit the entries for integer values to _CBIndex.

Adding a Stock Property Page

Next, we need to create a property page for the color selection, which is already done by the framework. All we need to do is activate it.

1. Track down the code in CLabelCtrl responsible for managing the property pages, and modify it as follows:

```
BEGIN_PROPPAGEIDS(CTitleControlCtrl, 2)
     PROPPAGEID(CTitleControlPropPage::guid)
     PROPPAGEID(CLSID_CColorPropPage)
END_PROPPAGEIDS(CTitleControlCtrl)
```

The stock color property page has the ID of CLSID_CColorPropPage. Note that the property page count has been upped to 2.

Adding a Second Custom Property Page

If there is the need, you can add more custom property pages. The procedure is as follows:

1. Add a new dialog resource in ResourceView and size it to be that of the first property page. (Therefore, the best way to create this new dialog is to copy it from the original page and remove the controls on it.)
2. Remove the default OK and Cancel buttons if necessary.
3. Style it to Child (Style: Child) with no border (Border: None). Also, select no Titlebar and not Visible and save it (so the settings will take effect).
4. Create a new class based on the COlePropertyPage class for the new property page dialog resource.
5. Adjust the property page control code as you did for the stock property page, such as:

```
BEGIN_PROPPAGEIDS(CLabelCtrl, 3)
     PROPPAGEID(CLabelPropPage::guid)
     PROPPAGEID(CLabelPropPage2::guid)
     PROPPAGEID(CLSID_CColorPropPage)
END_PROPPAGEIDS(CLabelCtrl)
```

6. Don't forget to add an "#include *header.h*" instruction at the top of the CCtrl class file.

Now we need two entries in String table to support the operations of the new property sheet. If you look at the String Table entries you should see two strings dedicated to the first property page: IDS_LABEL_PPG to identify the page, and IDS_LABEL_PPG_CAPTION for the caption on the pane. We need two new strings for the new page as well, such as IDS_LABEL_PPG2 and IDS_LABEL_PPG2_CAPTION.

7. Add the two new String Table entries as described previously, one for the page's identification and one for its caption.
8. Modify the new property page class's *UpdateRegistry()* function to use the new string ID, such as:

```
BOOL CLabelPropPage2::CLabelPropPage2Factory::UpdateRegistry(BOOL
bRegister)
{
     // TODO: Define string resource for page type;…
     if (bRegister)
          return
AfxOleRegisterPropertyPageClass(AfxGetInstanceHandle(),
               m_clsid, IDS_LABEL_PPG2);
     else
          return AfxOleUnregisterClass(m_clsid, NULL);
}
```

9. Modify the constructor to use the new string ID as well:

```
CLabelPropPage2::CLabelPropPage2() :
     COlePropertyPage(IDD, IDS_LABEL_PPG2_CAPTION)
{
     //{{AFX_DATA_INIT(CLabelPropPage2)
     // NOTE: ClassWizard will add member initialization here
     //    DO NOT EDIT what you see in these blocks of generated code !
     //}}AFX_DATA_INIT
}
```

Now you can add controls on the new property page dialog resource to achieve the user interface you have in mind and compile the control. When it is done, test it in the ActiveX Control Test Container and use the Property icon (Figure 30.8) to bring up the property sheet.

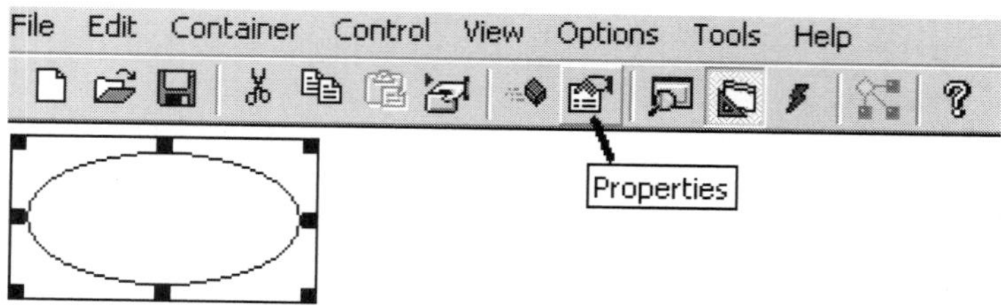

FIGURE 30.8 Test Container Property icon.

Methods

Besides properties, the control also can provide public functions called *methods* for the container user to invoke operations—although properties also come with their Get and Set methods. Therefore, you can think of methods as user functions that are not tied to properties. For the Label Control, we need to provide functions for the users to refresh the display after they have modified property values.

1. To create a method, bring up ClassWizard and switch to the Automation pane.
2. With CLabelCtrl in Class name, click Add Method.
3. Enter **Update** as the External name with a return type **void**, and click OK. Then, exit ClassWizard.
4. Bring up the *Update()* function and enter the following code:

```
void CLabelCtrl::Update()
{
     // TODO: Add your dispatch handler code here
     InvalidateControl();
}
```

The control is simply told to redraw itself with *InvalidateControl()*;

Drawing the Control

Finally, we'll modify the *OnDraw()* function of the control to make use of all the elements:

```
COLORREF     backColor;
if ( m_bTransparent )
{
     OLE_COLOR     backOleColor;
     GetAmbientProperty( DISPID_AMBIENT_BACKCOLOR, VT_COLOR,
&backOleColor );
     backColor = TranslateColor( backOleColor );
}
else
{
     backColor = TranslateColor( GetBackColor() );
}
CBrush     brush;
brush.CreateSolidBrush( backColor );
pdc->FillRect( rcBounds, &brush );
pdc->SetBkColor( backColor );
pdc->TextOut( m_iX, m_iY, m_csTitle );
```

Let's understand what the *OnDraw()* function does.

Before we output the title text string, first we set up two background painting schemes whose activation will be decided by the m_bTransparent variable.

If the m_bTransparent variable is set to be TRUE—that is, the control should be transparent—we'll use the ambient background color from the container. The *GetAmbientProperty()* function will do that for us. The color obtained is of the OLE_COLOR type; therefore, it needs to be converted to COLORREF before it can be use by CDC. The *TranslateColor()* function does the translation.

If the user elects to specify the background color, the *GetBackColor()* function is used to obtain the value, again, in the OLE_COLOR format.

Once the COLORREF color is determined, a brush is defined and used to fill the entire control rectangle with the CDC class's *FillRect()* function.

The title text is then output using the user-defined value at the designated output position with the proper background color.

Using the ActiveX Control

Now we'll see the control in action.

1. Close the Label Control project, use AppWizard to generate a new MFC dialog-based application, and turn to ResourceView.
2. Use the Project->Add to Project->Components and Controls command to bring up the Components and Controls Gallery, and then switch to the

Registered ActiveX Controls folder, in which you'll select Label Control and insert it in the new project.

You should see a new entry in the toolbox with the word "OCX" in it (assuming that you have not changed the default icon) as in Figure 30.9.

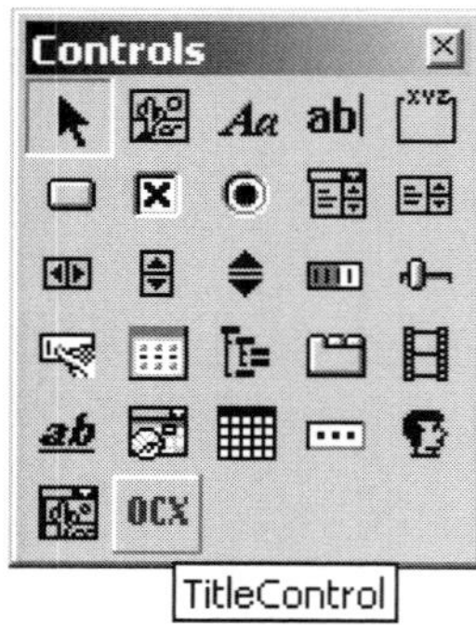

FIGURE 30.9 A system-recognized ActiveX control.

(In a finished project you would discard this stock bitmap image resource with the ID of IDB_TITLECONTROL and furnish your own with the same ID as you learned to do in the first part of this book.)

3. Install a Label Control on the dialog in the usual manner, and instantiate an object for it named **m_Title**.
4. Add a button on the dialog and caption it **Redraw**.
5. For the Redraw button, generate a command message handler function for it and add the following code:

```
void CDlg1::OnButtonRedraw()
{
    // TODO: Add your control notification handler…
    m_Title.SetTitle( "New Title" );
    m_Title.SetTransparent( FALSE );
    m_Title.Update();
}
```

6. Bring up the control's property sheet, set an initial title for it, and select a background color with Transparent set to Yes or checked.
7. Compile the test program and observe the result. Try the Redraw button also.

DLL and ActiveX are two of the most popular and often utilized program componentizing techniques in Windows (and Internet). They differ in form and implementation, but they strive to achieve by and large the same goals: code flexibility, universality, and reusability.

We have touched on but a small fraction of the possibilities that these technologies offer; however, to address them all, many books will need to be written. The coverage in this book was designed to take you through the fundamental and essential aspects of the approaches. With what you learned, you should find yourself prepared to venture deeper into the programming realms of component engineering.

PART

VIII Professional Software Development

With what we have covered up to this point, you already have the basic toolset to design the majority of the Windows-based applications that you're likely to encounter. However, there is a real difference between a journeyman exercise and a professional-quality product that customers are willing to pay money for. I am speaking of that extra edge that distinguishes a programming effort, that pizzazz that makes a user feel that the program is more than run-of-the-mill. Call it bells-and-whistles if you like, but outstanding merchandise must have outstanding features and attractive packaging. In this part of the book, we'll go over some of these "frill" items—that extra 10 percent—and in the process gain more insight into the machination of VC++ and MFC.

Once more, we'll carry out our mission via a demonstration project. This time, we'll develop a form filler program that can print stock forms. It doesn't do much, but then, as the other examples in this book, small and straightforward programs facilitate learning. All we want is a program that helps us teach the subjects. In fact, you can use this exercise as a template for developing future commercial-quality software.

31 A Professional-Quality Application

To show how a professional-quality application is developed, we will construct a form-filling program for a small local newspaper to take subscription orders and produce two business forms: an invoice and a subscription routing slip. The program will look something like that shown in Figure 31.1.

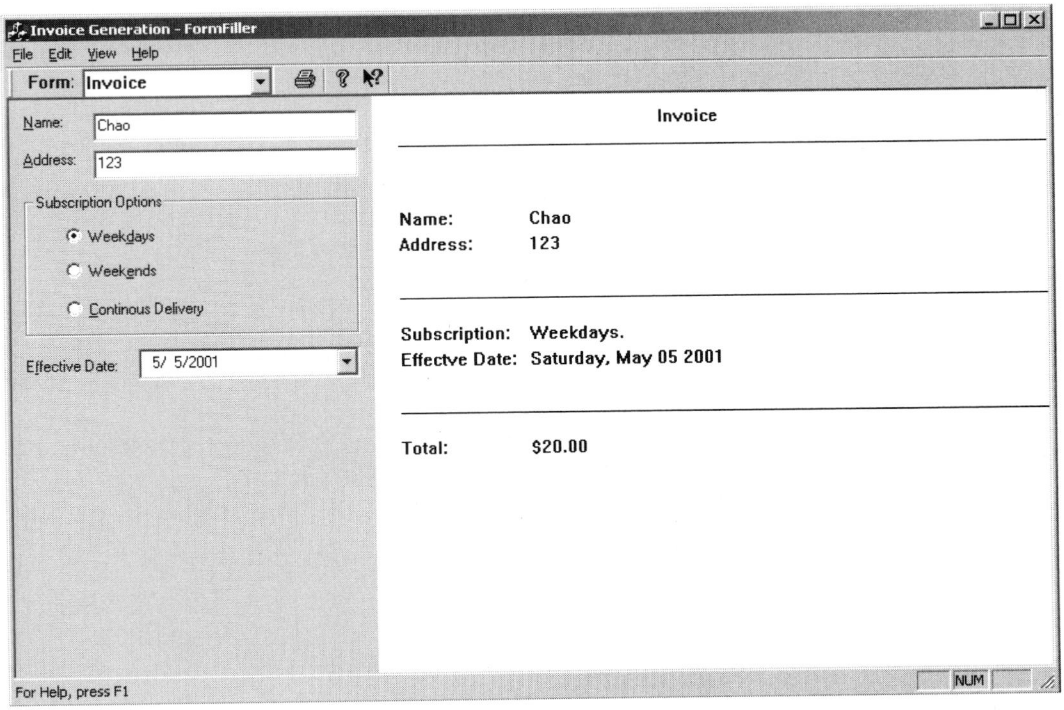

FIGURE 31.1 A form-filling application.

(If you're interested in the description that follows but are not inclined to perform the hands-on exercises, you can open the FormFiller project on the accompanying CD-ROM and follow the code in it.)

1. Generate an SDI MFC Windows application named **FormFiller** with the following special requirements:

Step	**Option**
4	Select Context-sensitive Help
6	Select the CScrollView base class for View

(As we move on in our exercise, feel free to compile the program and test it as it grows.)

CHILD DIALOG

As you can see in Figure 31.1, data entry is supposed to be carried out on the left-hand side of the View window. This portion of the screen is really a dialog with controls. When a dialog serves as a part of a View as opposed to a deployed dialog window of its own, it is known as a *child* form.

1. Insert a new dialog resource, assign it the ID of IDD_DIALOG_ENTRY, and remove all the buttons on it. Set the properties to:

Property	**Specification**
Style	Child
Border	None
Visible	Selected

2. Use ClassWizard to create a new class named CDlgEntry based on the CDialog class and the IDD_DIALOG_ENTRY resource.
3. Add controls to the dialog resource as follows (Figure 31.2):

Edit boxes:

Function	ID	Variable
Name	IDC_EDIT_NAME	CString m_csName
Address	IDC_EDIT_ADDRESS	CString m_csAddress

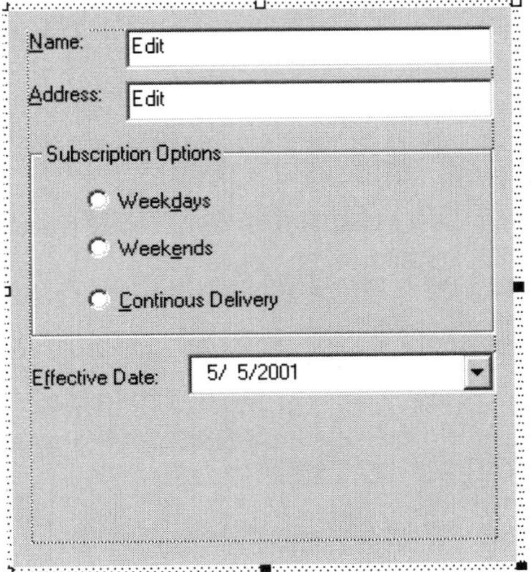

FIGURE 31.2 The data entry child form.

Radio buttons:

Function	ID	Variable	Group
Weekdays	IDC_RADIO_WKDAYS	int m_iDelivery	Yes
Weekends	IDC_RADIO_WKENDS		No
Continuous	IDC_RADIO_ALL		No

Date Time Picker:

ID	Variable
IDC_DATETIMEPICKER	CDateTimeCtrl m_dtEffectiveDate

4. Add a private variable of the CDlgEntry class named **m_wndEntry** to the View class:

```
private:
    CDlgEntry m_wndEntry;
```

5. Because there will be communications between the "parent" View and the "child" dialog, we need a variable in the dialog class to point to the View. Therefore, add a public variable to the child dialog class:

```
class CDlgEntry : public CDialog
{
// Construction
public:
      CView* m_pView;
```

6. In the View class's *OnInitialUpdate()* virtual function, create the child dialog, identify itself, and initialize its data:

```
void CFormFillerView::OnInitialUpdate()
{
      CScrollView::OnInitialUpdate();
      ...
      m_wndEntry.Create( IDD_DIALOG_ENTRY, this );
      m_wndEntry.m_pView = this;
      m_wndEntry.m_csName = "";
      m_wndEntry.m_csAddress = "";
      m_wndEntry.m_iDelivery = WKDYS;
      m_wndEntry.UpdateData( FALSE );
      m_wndEntry.m_ctEffectiveDate.GetCurrentTime();
}
```

DRAWING DIFFERENT VIEW DISPLAYS

A requirement of the program is the capability to accommodate different forms. How can the same and one-and-only *OnDraw()* function serve both purposes? By using a switch.

1. In the View class, add a public integer variable named **m_iForm** to identify the form to be produced.
2. Initialize it in the View's *OnInitialUpdate()* virtual function override:

```
enum { INVOICE = 0, SUBSCRIPTION = 1 };
void CFormFillerView::OnInitialUpdate()
{
      CScrollView::OnInitialUpdate();
      ...
      m_iForm = INVOICE;
```

3. In the *OnDraw()* function, this value is used to switch between two form outputs:

```
void CFormFillerView::OnDraw(CDC* pDC)
{
     CFormFillerDoc* pDoc = GetDocument();
     ...
     // Draw form.
     switch ( m_iForm )
     {
     case INVOICE:
          DrawInvoice( pDC );
          GetDocument()->SetTitle( "Invoice Generation" );
          break;
     default:
          DrawRoutingSlip( pDC );
          GetDocument()->SetTitle( "New Subscription" );
     }
}
```

The *SetTitle()* member function of the Document class sets the title in the title bar; in this case, identifying the form being processed.

The two form drawing functions are Invoice and Subscription Routing Slip.

Invoice

```
void CFormFillerView::DrawInvoice( CDC* pDC )
{
     x = m_iLeftMargin;
     y = m_iTopMargin;
     CString     csTotal;
     CString     csDate;
     pDC->TextOut( x + 200, y, "Invoice" );
     y = y + 30;
     pDC->MoveTo( x, y );
     pDC->LineTo( x + 500, y );
     y = y + 50;
     pDC->TextOut( x, y, "Name:" );
     pDC->TextOut( x + 100, y, m_wndEntry.m_csName );
     y = y + 20;
     pDC->TextOut( x, y, "Address:" );
     pDC->TextOut( x + 100, y, m_wndEntry.m_csAddress );
     y = y + 50;
     pDC->MoveTo( x, y );
     pDC->LineTo( x + 500, y );
     y = y + 20;
     pDC->TextOut( x, y, "Subscription:" );
```

```
        switch ( m_wndEntry.m_iDelivery )
        {
        case WKDYS:
            pDC->TextOut( x + 100, y, "Weekdays." );
            csTotal = "$20.00";
            break;
        case WKENDS:
            pDC->TextOut( x + 100, y, "Weekends." );
            csTotal = "$15.00";
            break;
        default:
            pDC->TextOut( x + 100, y, "Continuous." );
            csTotal = "$30.00";
        }
        y = y + 20;
        pDC->TextOut( x, y, "Effectve Date:" );
        m_wndEntry.m_dtEffectiveDate.GetTime( m_wndEntry.m_ctEffectiveDate
    );
        csDate = m_wndEntry.m_ctEffectiveDate.Format( "%A, %B %d %Y" );
        pDC->TextOut( x + 100, y, csDate );
        y = y + 50;
        pDC->MoveTo( x, y );
        pDC->LineTo( x + 500, y );
        y = y + 20;
        pDC->TextOut( x, y, "Total:" );
        pDC->TextOut( x + 100, y, csTotal );
    }
```

Subscription Routing Slip

```
    void CFormFillerView::DrawRoutingSlip(CDC *pDC)
    {
        x = m_iLeftMargin;
        y = m_iTopMargin;
        CString     csTotal;
        CString     csDate;
        pDC->TextOut( x + 200, y, "New Subscription" );
        y = y + 30;
        pDC->MoveTo( x, y );
        pDC->LineTo( x + 500, y );
        y = y + 50;
        pDC->TextOut( x, y, "Subscriber:" );
```

```
        pDC->TextOut( x + 100, y, m_wndEntry.m_csName );
        y = y + 20;
        pDC->TextOut( x, y, "Address:" );
        pDC->TextOut( x + 100, y, m_wndEntry.m_csAddress );
        y = y + 20;
        pDC->TextOut( x, y, "Subscription:" );
        switch ( m_wndEntry.m_iDelivery )
        {
        case WKDYS:
                pDC->TextOut( x + 100, y, "Weekdays." );
                csTotal = "$20.00";
                break;
        case WKENDS:
                pDC->TextOut( x + 100, y, "Weekends." );
                csTotal = "$15.00";
                break;
        default:
                pDC->TextOut( x + 100, y, "Continuous." );
                csTotal = "$30.00";
        }
        y = y + 20;
        pDC->TextOut( x, y, "Effectve Date:" );
        m_wndEntry.m_dtEffectiveDate.GetTime( m_wndEntry.m_ctEffectiveDate
);
        csDate = m_wndEntry.m_ctEffectiveDate.Format( "%A, %B %d %Y" );
        pDC->TextOut( x + 100, y, csDate );
        y = y + 30;
        pDC->MoveTo( x, y );
        pDC->LineTo( x + 500, y );
        y = y + 20;
        pDC->TextOut( x, y, "Sales:" );
        pDC->TextOut( x + 100, y, m_csSales );
}
```

Here we added two more variables for the View class to help track the drawing locations:

```
private:
        int y;
        int x;
```

As the forms are constructed, the values of x and y can be used to set the properties of the scroll bar.

We add another two View class variables, the private integers **m_iLeftMargin** and **m_iTopMargin**, to help define the x and y drawing axes' limits. It is initialized in the *OnInitialUpdate()* function:

```
m_iLeftMargin = 300;
m_iTopMargin = 10;
```

Finally, we define another View class private CString variable named **m_csSales** to hold the identification of the sales agent taking the subscription order. It is initialized in *OnInitialUpdate()* as well.

The child dialog is identified by **m_wndEntry**; therefore, its members are **m_wndEntry**.*member*. In turn, the member's own member function must be expressed as **m_wndEntry**.*member.function()*. Therefore, the Date Time Picker, a member of **m_wndEntry**, is expressed as **m_wndEntry.m_ctEffectiveDate**, and its member function *Format()* is expressed as:

```
csDate = m_wndEntry.m_ctEffectiveDate.Format( "%A, %B %d %Y" );
```

EVENT-DRIVEN PROGRAMMING

There are several ways to update a form with new data. One way is to provide a button or command for the user to command the form to be updated when all the pertinent data are entered. However, to make the program snazzy, let's update the forms automatically as the data are entered. In other words, as the subscriber's name is entered, we want to display the changes in the form immediately. To do this, we want the program to react to such changes—we need to provide helper functions to be triggered when such events occur.

1. Use ClassWizard to generate a message processing function for the child dialog's IDC_EDIT_NAME's **EN_CHANGE** message:

```
void CDlgEntry::OnChangeEditName()
{
    ...
    // TODO: Add your control notification handler...
    RedrawForm();
|
```

The *RedrawForm()* function is a private helper function that asks for the form to be redrawn:

```
void CDlgEntry::RedrawForm()
{
     UpdateData( TRUE );
     m_pView->Invalidate();
}
```

If you compile and test the program, you should see the form updated as you enter the subscriber's name.

2. Add the following message processing functions, all triggering the same *RedrawForm()* function.

Control	Event	Function
IDC_EDIT_ADDRESS	EN_CHANGE	OnChangeEditAddress()
IDC_RADIO_WKDAYS	BN_CLICKED	OnRadioWkdays()
IDC_RADIO_WKENDS	BN_CLICKED	OnRadioWkends()
IDC_RADIO_ALL	BN_CLICKED	OnRadioAll()
IDC_DATETIMEPICKER	DTN_DATETI MECHANGE	OnDatetimechange Datetimepicker()

WINDOW SIZING

As it is, the child dialog window shows up as a rectangular patch located at the upper-left corner of the View window. This doesn't look good. We need the child dialog to fit snugly on the left of the View and, most important, when the View window is resized, the child dialog must follow suit. To do this, the child dialog must be resized every time the application window size changes.

As it turns out, when a CWnd object—a window—is resized, it generates a WM_SIZE message that triggers the *OnSize()* function. To resize the child dialog to fit the View, we must work with this function. However, there is a catch.

The *OnSize()* function is called by the framework early on during its construction process, before the child dialog is formed. We certainly don't want to do any resizing of the child dialog until it actually exists. Therefore, we must bear this in mind when we develop our window resizing logic to avoid any mishap.

1. Use ClassWizard to generate a processing function for the View class's WM_SIZE message Figure 31.3.
2. Enter the following code:

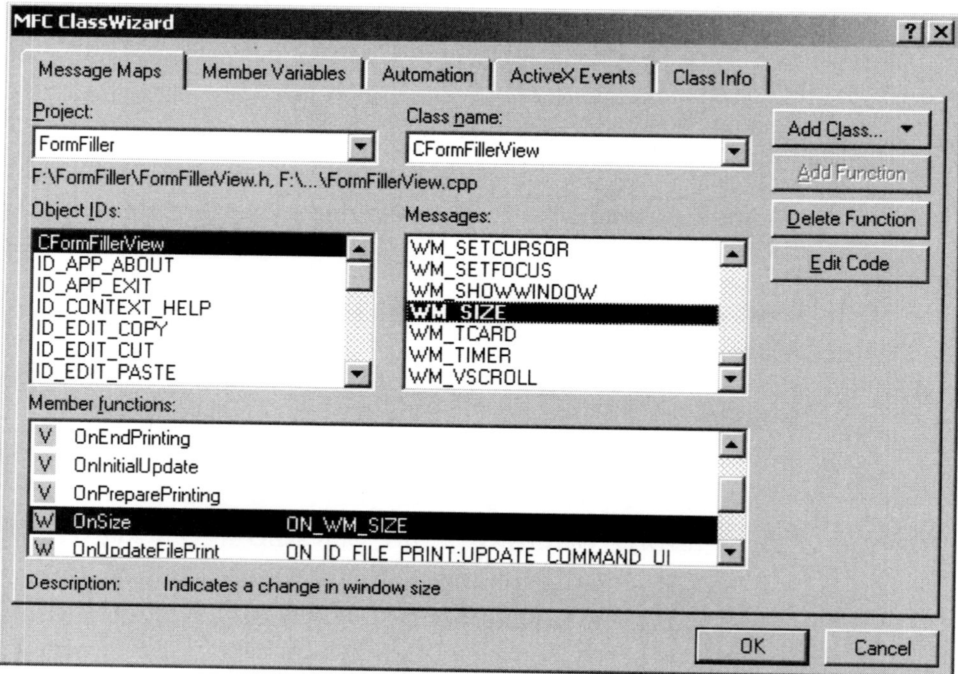

FIGURE 31.3 The WM_SIZE message.

```
void CFormFillerView::OnSize(UINT nType, int cx, int cy)
{
     CScrollView::OnSize(nType, cx, cy);

     // TODO: Add your message handler code here
     CRect     rect;
     GetClientRect( rect );
     rect.right = rect.left + m_iLeftMargin - 20;
     if ( m_wndEntry.GetSafeHwnd() != NULL )
          m_wndEntry.MoveWindow( rect );
}
```

To size the child dialog, we need a rectangle, or CRect object. At first, this object is sized to the client window, the View, using the CWnd *GetClientRect()* member function. However, we don't want to size the child dialog to the entire window; we only want the child dialog to fill the application window partially; specifically the left portion of the window only. Therefore, we set the *right* member of the CRect object to shrink the child dialog window to size.

Once the rectangle size is determined, we use the CWnd *MoveWindow()* function to "move" the child dialog. However, remember that we must do this only when the child dialog exists. Therefore, we safeguard this condition with:

```
if ( m_wndEntry.GetSafeHwnd() )
```

The *GetSafeHwnd()* CWnd member function returns the handle to the CWnd object, of which the child dialog is one. If the object has yet to be constructed when the *OnSize()* function is called, the handle would be NULL. We only move the window when its handle is not NULL.

The UINT *nType* parameter of the *OnSize()* function tells us what sizing event (such as maximizing or minimizing) is taking place, so, if we choose to, we can set different processing logic to handle each event. Here, the value has no operational significance.

The approach we employed to size a window component is regularly used in a variety of situations. For example, controls are often sized and positioned this way. Let's divert for a moment and use a different program to illustrate how that is done. In this second illustration program, we'll make the controls in a dialog application fit nicely under all circumstances.

A Sizable Dialog Application

(You might want to complete the FormFiller project and come back to try this demo later.)

ON THE CD

1. Construct a dialog-based MFC Windows application named **WordPadlet** with controls as shown in Figure 31.4.

The controls in this application are an edit control and a button. We got rid of the Cancel button generated by AppWizard because we don't need it.

2. Set the main dialog's Border style to Resizing, uncheck System Menu, and then set the edit control's properties to Multiline and Auto VScroll with no Auto HScroll.

The dialog Resizing property allows you to resize it at runtime.

If you do resize it, though, you'll find that, as they currently are, the controls don't move with the resizing dialog. To make the controls move with the dialog, you'll need to do the following:

FIGURE 31.4 The WordPadlet application.

3. Use ClassWizard to create control variables for the edit control and the OK button:

```
class CWordPadletDlg : public CDialog
{
...
// Dialog Data
     //{{AFX_DATA(CWordPadletDlg)
     enum { IDD = IDD_WORDPADLET_DIALOG };
     CButton  m_btnOK;
     CEdit    m_edtBox;
     //}}AFX_DATA
```

4. Add a private member function *LayoutControls()* to the CWordPadletDlg class where we'll implement the object layout logic.
5. Enter the following code:

```
void CWordPadletDlg::LayoutControls()
{
     CRect     rectDlg, rectEdit;
```

```
        GetClientRect( rectDlg );
        rectEdit.bottom = rectDlg.bottom - 50;
        rectEdit.top = rectDlg.top + 10;
        rectEdit.left = rectDlg.left + 10;
        rectEdit.right = rectDlg.right - 10;
        // Lay out edit control.
        if ( m_edtBox.GetSafeHwnd() != NULL )
             m_edtBox.MoveWindow( rectEdit );
        // Lay out OK button
        CRect     rectOK;
        if ( m_btnOK.GetSafeHwnd() != NULL )
        {
             m_btnOK.GetClientRect( rectOK );
             rectOK.top = rectDlg.bottom - rectOK.Height() - 10;
             rectOK.bottom = rectDlg.bottom - 10;
             rectOK.left = rectDlg.right - rectOK.Width() - 10;
             rectOK.right = rectDlg.right - 10;
             m_btnOK.MoveWindow( rectOK );
        }
}
```

Now examine what we've done.

First, we obtain information on the geometry of the main dialog with *GetClientRect(rectDlg)*. Then, a CRect object is defined for the edit control, with its dimensions set to appropriate margins from the parent dialog's outer perimeter. The edit control is then resized to those dimensions using the *MoveWindow()* function.

For the OK button, first its dimensions are obtained with "*m_btnOK.GetClientRect(rectOK);*". While the height and width of the button are maintained, its relative positions to the parent dialog are revised. The CRect *Height()* and *Width()* member functions return the object's height and width, respectively.

CUSTOMIZING THE TOOLBAR

Back to the **FormFiller** project.

We'll next install a combo box on the toolbar. Yes, we can do that because a toolbar is a window object, too.

To do this, we need to have a class for the toolbar to work with. Therefore, first we must construct our own toolbar class.

1. In ClassView, create a new MFC-derived CFFToolBar class based on the CToolBarCtrl (because the CToolBar class is not included in the Wizard) class (see Figure 31.5).

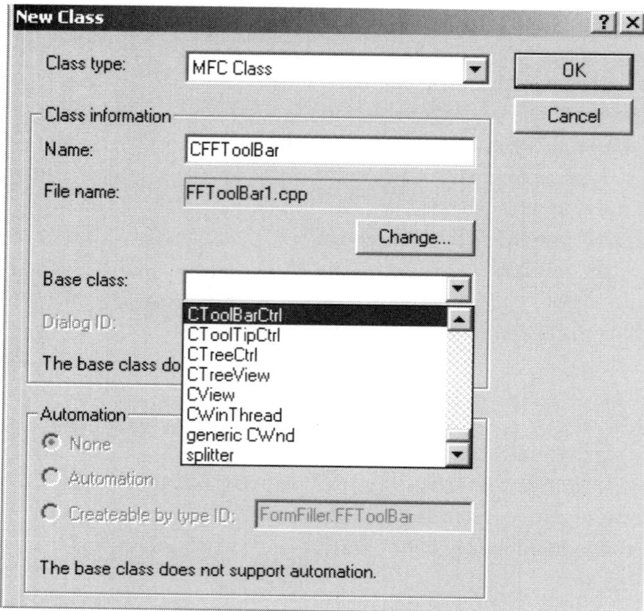

FIGURE 31.5 Deriving a CToolBarCtrl-based class.

2. In FFToolBar.h and FFToolBar.cpp, change all references of CToolBarCtrl to CToolBar, such as "class CFFToolBar : public CToolBar."
3. In MainFrm.h, edit the toolbar declaration to use the CFFToolBar class:

```
#include "FFToolBar.h"
class CMainFrame : public CFrameWnd
{
...
protected:  // control bar embedded members
     CStatusBar  m_wndStatusBar;
     CFFToolBar  m_wndToolBar;
```

Now we have our own toolbar class that we can modify.

If you enjoy coding, you can write the combo box code in the new CFFToolBar class by hand. Many of us cannot remember all that MFC code by heart, the thousands of classes, methods, members, and rules. Let the wizards work for you.

4. On the main dialog, install a new combo box resource and give it the ID of IDC_COMBO_FORM (Figure 31.6).

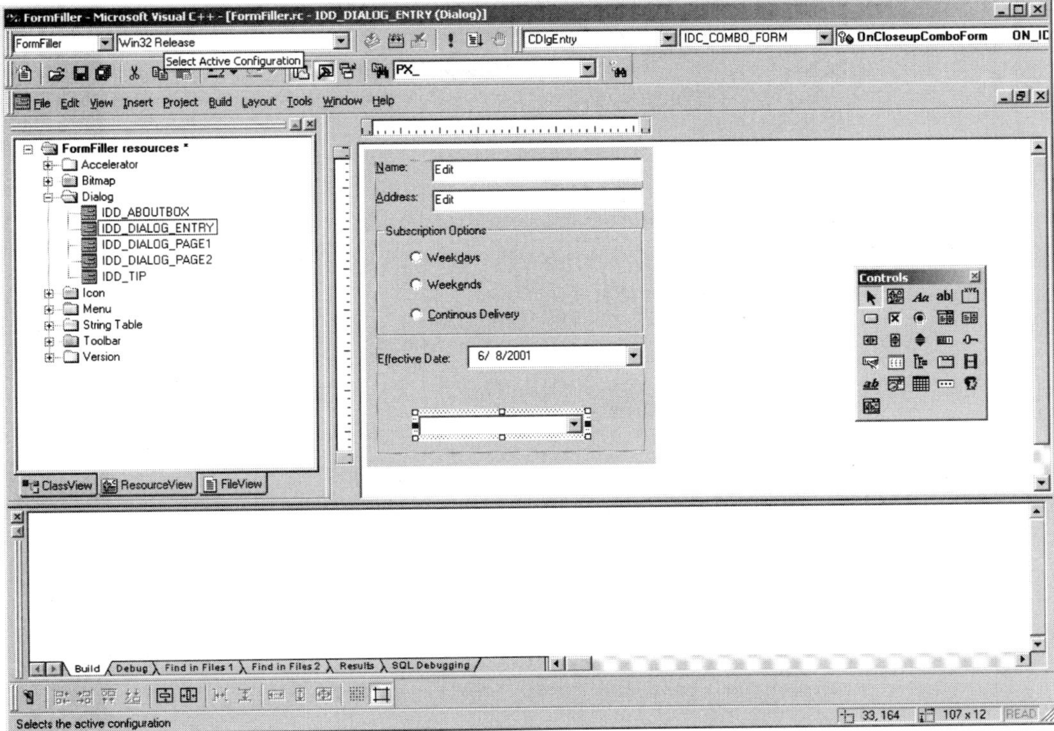

FIGURE 31.6 Installing a surrogate combo box.

5. Use ClassWizard to generate a control variable for it named **m_cboForm**.
6. Next, generate a message handler function for the combo box's CBN_CLOSEUP function:

```
void CDlgEntry::OnCloseupComboForm()
{
     // TODO: Add your control notification handler…
}
```

This function will be processed when the user selects a combo box entry and the drop-down list closes up.

At this time, the wizard has produced:

In DlgEntry.h:

```
class CDlgEntry : public CDialog
{
...
// Dialog Data
	//{{AFX_DATA(CDlgEntry)
	enum { IDD = IDD_DIALOG_ENTRY };
	CComboBox	m_cboForm;
   ...
	//}}AFX_DATA
// Implementation
protected:
	// Generated message map functions
	//{{AFX_MSG(CDlgEntry)
...
	afx_msg void OnCloseupComboForm();
	//}}AFX_MSG
	DECLARE_MESSAGE_MAP()
```

In DlgEntry.cpp:

```
void CDlgEntry::DoDataExchange(CDataExchange* pDX)
{
	CDialog::DoDataExchange(pDX);
	//{{AFX_DATA_MAP(CDlgEntry)
	DDX_Control(pDX, IDC_COMBO_FORM, m_cboForm);
	...
	//}}AFX_DATA_MAP
}
BEGIN_MESSAGE_MAP(CDlgEntry, CDialog)
	//{{AFX_MSG_MAP(CDlgEntry)
	...
	ON_CBN_CLOSEUP(IDC_COMBO_FORM, OnCloseupComboForm)
	//}}AFX_MSG_MAP
END_MESSAGE_MAP()
```

7. The truth is, we want these elements to be in the toolbar files, not in the dialog files. (We're really just using the dialog as a proving ground on which to generate the combo box code.) Therefore, move them to the corresponding locations in the CFFToolBar files.

In FFToolBar.h:

```
class CFFToolBar : public CToolBar
{
// Implementation
public:
	CComboBox m_cboForm;
```

```
    // Generated message map functions
protected:
    //{{AFX_MSG(CFFToolBar)
    afx_msg int OnCreate(LPCREATESTRUCT lpCreateStruct);
    afx_msg void OnCloseupComboForm();
    //}}AFX_MSG
```

In FFToolBar.cpp:

```
BEGIN_MESSAGE_MAP(CFFToolBar, CToolBar)
    //{{AFX_MSG_MAP(CFFToolBar)
    ON_WM_CREATE()
    ON_CBN_CLOSEUP(IDC_COMBO_FORM, OnCloseupComboForm)
    //}}AFX_MSG_MAP
END_MESSAGE_MAP()
void CFFToolBar::OnCloseupComboForm()
{
    // TODO: Add your control notification handler…
}
```

The only remaining action items are to write code to create the combo box and install the response logic to the combo box's drop-down action.

The creation of the combo box follows straight by the book:

```
int CFFToolBar::OnCreate(LPCREATESTRUCT …)
{
    if (CToolBar::OnCreate(lpCreateStruct) == -1)
        return -1;

    // TODO: Add your specialized creation code here
    m_cboForm.Create( WS_CHILD | WS_VISIBLE | CBS_DROPDOWN | CBS_SORT
| WS_VSCROLL | WS_TABSTOP,
        CRect( 52,0,200,100 ), this, IDC_COMBO_FORM );
    m_cboForm.AddString( _T( "Invoice" ) );
    m_cboForm.AddString( _T( "Subscription" ) );
    m_cboForm.SetCurSel( 0 );
    SetWindowText( _T( "Select Form" ) );
    return 0;
}
```

Note that in creating the combo box we used the same ID of the combo box on the CDlgEntry dialog. Well, that's the whole point in using the wizard in the first place: it even generated a unique combo box ID for us.

Once the combo box is created, we add contents to it with *AddString()*. We initialize it to the first list entry with *SetCurSel(0)*, and, with an added touch of forethought, use the *SetWindowTitle()* function to set a proper title for the toolbar. When docked, the toolbar looks like a toolbar. However, when it is undocked, it looks like a window because a toolbar is in fact a CWnd-derived object. As a window, the toolbar can show a title. By providing the toolbar a window title, it won't appear naked.

As for the processing of the combo box selection, the logic is:

```
void CFFToolBar::OnCloseupComboForm()
{
     // TODO: Add your control notification handler…
     CFormFillerView*      pView = (CFormFillerView*) GetParentFrame()-
>GetActiveView();
     pView->m_iForm = m_cboForm.GetCurSel();
     pView->Invalidate();
}
```

First, we use the *GetParentFrame()* function to identify the toolbar's parent frame. Then, from the frame we used the Frame class's *GetActiveView()* function to identify the View object. With the View object identified, we can exercise its public members.

We read the current selection from the combo box and pass it on to the integer variable in the View class responsible for identifying the form to draw. Then, we ask the View's *Invalidate()* function to initiate the form drawing.

As for the sizing and positioning of the combo box, if you really want to, you can go through a formal analysis of the various objects' geometries involved, including the font used and other pertinent factors. For illustration purposes (and for real, too), we are using a bunch of empty buttons, all with the IDC_STATIC ID, to occupy spaces on the toolbar (Figure 31.7).

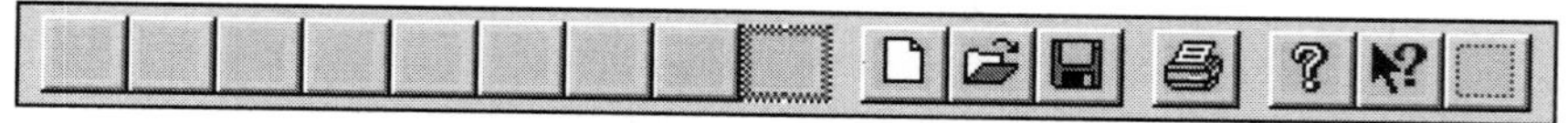

FIGURE 31.7 Spacing the toolbar.

The whole proceeding looks pretty straightforward, doesn't it?

CUSTOMIZING THE STATUS BAR

As with the toolbar, the status bar is also a CWnd-derived object, and therefore can be customized in like manner. For example, you can place a combo box on it, too.

In the following example project, we'll show how you can install a progress bar right on the status bar, a popular design approach adopted by many programmers.

1. Quickly generate an MFC SDI Windows application named **StatusBarDemo**.
2. Use ClassWizard to create a new class named **CDemoStatusBar** based on the MFC CStatusBarCtrl class just as you did with the toolbar.
3. Replace all references to CStatusBarCtrl with CStatusBar in the new class.
4. Edit the declaration of **m_wndStatusBar** from CStatusBar to CDemoStatusBar. (Remember to add an #include directive for the new class.)
5. In the new CDemoStatusBar class, add a public variable:

```
public:
     CProgressCtrl m_pgBar;
```

6. In the IDD_ABOUTBOX resource, install a progress bar control (so we get a free ID).
7. Create the progress bar in the status bar with:

```
int CDemoStatusBar::OnCreate(LPCREATESTRUCT lpCreateStruct)
{
     ...
     // TODO: Add your specialized creation code here
     m_pgBar.Create( WS_CHILD | WS_VISIBLE, CRect( 300, 2, 500, 18 ),
this, IDC_PROGRESS );
     m_pgBar.SetRange( 10, 100 );
     return 0;
}
```

That's it. If you like to see the bar move, you'll have to trigger the *StepIt()* function with some event, or you can test it by adding a command to the menu and have it call the *StepIt()* function, such as:

```
void CMainFrame::OnEditStepit()
{
     // TODO: Add your command handler code here
     m_wndStatusBar.m_pgBar.StepIt();
}
```

THE TIMER

The reason that the status bar is called a status bar is because it is really designed for displaying statuses, and it has its own way of displaying statuses. Let's return to the **FormFiller** project. If you open the MainFrm.cpp file, you'll see the following code close to the top of the file:

```
static UINT indicators[] =
{
     ID_SEPARATOR,             // status line indicator
     ID_INDICATOR_CAPS,
     ID_INDICATOR_NUM,
     ID_INDICATOR_SCRL,
};
```

Now, open the string resource. You'll see the ID_INDICATOR_CAPS and ID_INDICATOR_NUM entries there. What we have is an array of string resource IDs. The framework uses these IDs to create *panes* in the status bar. Therefore, if we want to display another status on the status bar, all we need to do is add a string resource and include it in the indicator array.

As a demonstration, we'll display a running clock in the status bar.

1. In **FormFiller**, add a new string resource ID_INDICATOR_TIME with an initial value of **Saturday, December 29, 2001 12:59:59**.

We chose a long initial string to represent a date/time display, because although you can set them explicitly, when the status bar is first created, the widths of the panes are based on the lengths of their string resources. By using a long initial string, we ensure that we have a long pane to start with.

To provide for a clock, we'll create a timer.

2. In the MainFrame class's creation function, add the following:

```
int CMainFrame::OnCreate(LPCREATESTRUCT lpCreateStruct)
{
     ...
     SetTimer( 1, 1000, NULL );
     return 0;
}
```

The *SetTimer()* function sets a timer based on an ID with a tick setting measured by 1/1000th seconds. A timer is basically a separate program thread.

Therefore, as your application runs, a separate logic runs alongside and keeps track of time.

Because it is the first timer set in the application, we used the ID value 1 to identify it. (If we ever need to have a second timer, it might be IDed 2.)

The second parameter 1000 causes the timer to tick every second.

The third parameter dictates where the tick messages should be sent. NULL means we want them to go to the Windows message queue.

3. Generate a processing function for the ON_DESTROY message and kill the timer object of ID 1 there:

```
void CMainFrame::OnDestroy()
{
     CFrameWnd::OnDestroy();

     // TODO: Add your message handler code here
     KillTimer( 1 );
}
```

4. Finally, generate a processing function for the MainFrame's ON_TIMER function to display the current time:

```
void CMainFrame::OnTimer(UINT nIDEvent)
{
     // TODO: Add your message handler code here…
     CTime      t = CTime::GetCurrentTime();
     CString    csTime;
     csTime = t.Format( "%A, %b %d, %Y  %H:%m:%S" );
     m_wndStatusBar.SetPaneText( 1, csTime );
     CFrameWnd::OnTimer(nIDEvent);
}
```

The status bar class's *SetPaneText()* function displays a text in the pane specified by its index number; that is, its position in the indicator array.

(Note that you might have to artificially move the new string resource value to be ahead of the existing indicator resources in the Resource.h file if the clock pane does not show, and rebuild the entire project.)

The CStatusBar class comes with many helpful functions for use to achieve different operational goals. For example, if there is the need, you can gain control of the status bar panes individually and work with them. You use the *SetPaneInfo()* function to set a pane's style and width, or *SetPaneStyle()* to set its style only.

The CStatusBar class is built around the CStatusBarCtrl class. To gain access to the underlying status bar control, you use the *GetStatusBarCtrl()* function, which returns a pointer to the control. With the pointer, you can then reach the control's internal functions and members, such as the rectangle information and so on. You can look up on these features from the MFC references. They actually make for rather easy but interesting reading.

MENU

The menu provides access to user-activated program functions. However, for an application to be considered robust, the menu must be more than just a holder of commands. It also must be flexible to represent the true states of the program in context, and even implicitly provide guidance to the user so that he or she can correctly operate the program.

Earlier you learned to disable (gray out) a menu command when it is contextually inapplicable. At other times, the menu must alter itself to fit a new program condition. Sometimes you might even want to take out a command completely. For example, in an MDI application, the Window menu's internal command structure changes as child windows are created or removed.

A professionally designed menu system should always be true to the application's context. This means that if the application's operations are dynamic, then the menu system should reflect that.

Take our **FormFiller** application as example. Technically, you're not supposed to permit a form to be printed if key data components such as the subscriber's name are missing. The code to achieve this is:

```
void CFormFillerView::OnUpdateFilePrint(CCmdUI* pCmdUI)
{
     // TODO: Add your command update UI handler code…
     m_wndEntry.UpdateData( TRUE );
     if ( m_wndEntry.m_csAddress.IsEmpty() ||
          m_wndEntry.m_csName.IsEmpty() )
          pCmdUI->Enable( FALSE );
     else
          pCmdUI->Enable( TRUE );
}
```

Here the edit control for the subscriber's name (m_csName) on the data entry child form (m_wndEntry) is examined for contents (*IsEmpty()*). If it is empty, the command is grayed out (*pCmdUI->Enable(FALSE)*).

The same approach can be used to handle the Print Preview command.

If circumstances call for it, you can even selectively deploy menus, and the way to do it is quite simple.

First, you set up the various applicable menu resources. Usually you start with a main menu resource, say, IDR_MAINFRAME, which is a superset of all the commands. From it, you produce variations by replicating IDR_MAINFRAME (selecting the resource ID in ResourceView, [Ctrl-C] it, then [Ctrl-V] to reproduce). Then you edit the offspring menu resources to achieve the menus that will be used in the program, perhaps one has no Edit commands, another has no Print commands, and so on.

The menu switching is then mechanically carried out with the following sequence of function calls in the Frame class:

```
CMenu      menu;
menu.LoadMenu( IDR_SHORTMENU );
SetMenu( &menu );
menu.Detach();
DrawMenuBar();
```

In this little illustration, a CMenu object (named menu) is first instantiated. The menu is then constructed by loading the proper resource (*menu.LoadMenu(IDR_SHORTMENU)*). The parent CWnd class then calls its *SetMenu()* function to set the menu for use, and the menu object then divorces itself from the physical menu and lets the Frame take over its operations (*menu.Detach()*). The menu bar is then redrawn. You simply use this scheme to switch from one menu to the next triggered by whatever appropriate events.

If the design of the application calls for dynamic menu reconstruction, you can manipulate the menu items individually. For example, to remove the File->Print menu command altogether at runtime, you use the following code sequence (from the menu's parent class):

```
CMenu*      pMainMenu = GetMenu();
CMenu*      pFileMenu = pMainMenu->GetSubMenu( 0 );
pFileMenu->RemoveMenu( ID_FILE_PRINT, MF_BYCOMMAND );
```

First, you create a CMenu pointer to point to the existing menu (*GetMenu()*). With this pointer, you then use the *GetSubMenu()* function to point to a submenu; in this case, that which is associated with the main menu command "File," which is indexed 0 because it is the first menu entry. Once you're pointing at the File command menu, you remove (*RemoveMenu()*) its entry; in this case, IDed by ID_FILE_PRINT. The MF_BYCOMMAND parameter indicates that you're identifying the command by its ID. Otherwise, if you were to identify the command by index position, you would use the function form *RemoveMenu(6, MF_BYPOSITION)*, "Print" being the sixth command.

There are many useful CMenu class member functions that you can employ to customize a menu. For example, you can restore a menu command with the *AppendMenu()*, *InsertMenu()*, and *ModifyMenu()* functions. You can give a command a check mark with the *CheckMenuItem()* function. You can make menu commands behave like radio buttons with the *CheckMenuRadioItem()* function. You should check these functions out and use them with prudence to increase the quality of your program's user interfaces.

Adding Menus to Dialogs

Incidentally, just because the dialog-based application framework does not automatically provide command menus, doesn't mean that it cannot have one. In fact, it is rather simple to provide a dialog application with a menu. The following little illustration project demonstrates how this is done.

1. Generate a dialog-based MFC Windows application named **WordPad** in the usual manner.
2. In ResourceView, insert a new menu (Figure 31.8) by clicking New. When the new menu is generated, make sure you assign it a proper ID, such as IDR_MAINMENU.

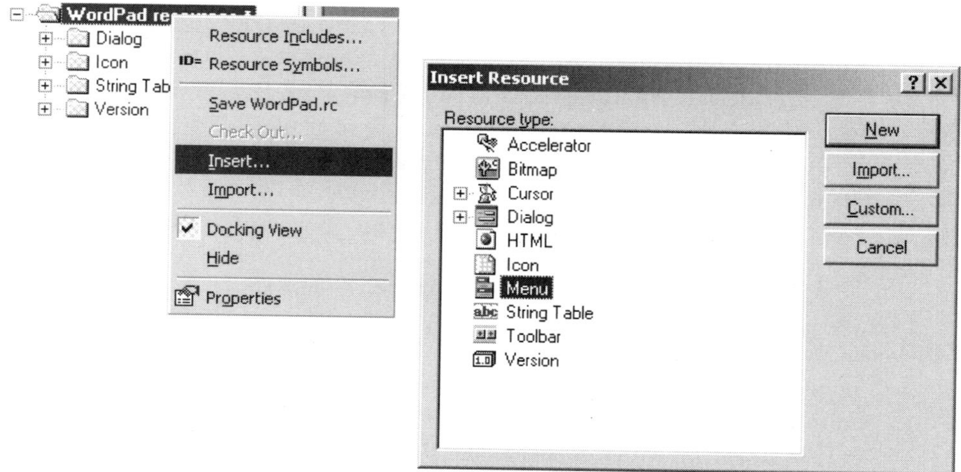

FIGURE 31.8 Inserting a new menu resource.

3. Add commands to the menu in the usual fashion, such as File, File->New, File->Save, and File->Exit.
4. Bring up the main dialog and its properties. Under Menu, select IDR_MAINMENU (Figure 31.9).

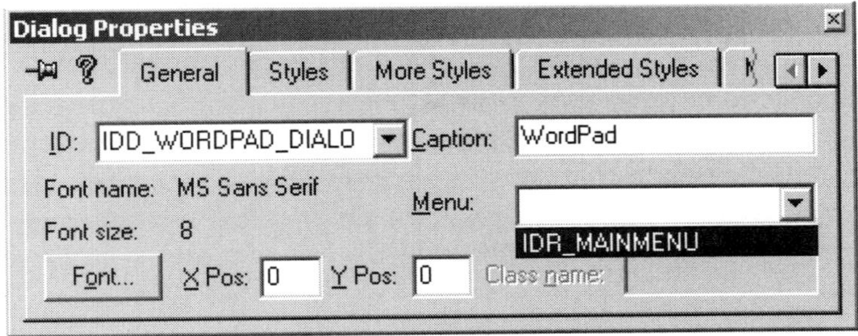

FIGURE 31.9 Assigning a menu to a dialog.

5. Compile the program and test it. You should see a File command in the upper-left corner of the main program dialog.
6. To hook the commands up to their operations, with the menu resource selected bring up ClassWizard.

You'll be asked to decide a class to assign the menu to (Figure 31.10).

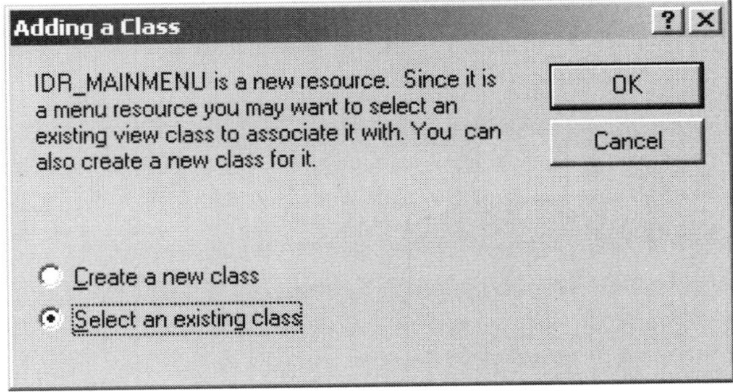

FIGURE 31.10 Associating a resource with an existing class.

7. Select "Select an existing class," select CWordPadDlg, and close ClassWizard.
8. Change the ID for the File->Exit command to IDOK, the same as the OK button, and then compile the program again and test it.

This time, you should be able to exit the program without clicking OK.

9. Now you can remove the OK and the Cancel buttons.

32 Common Dialogs

ON THE CD

Let's return to the **FormFiller** project.

New subscriptions need to be saved. Existing subscriptions might need to be reviewed. For this, we need to provide reasonable data exchange facilities.

Because of the simplicity of the data, you might get by using persistence I/O to quickly preserve the data as a data list. If you want to be sophisticated about it, you can employ a database to service it. Here we'll learn to save the data to individual files.

To perform our own file I/O, we need to override CWinApp's *OnFileOpen()* and *OnFileNew()* functions. We'll start with saving data.

CFileDialog

When the user opens or saves a file, instead of using a predetermined filename and path, we should provide a file dialog box for the user to specify his own filespec[1]. The dialog is based on the CFileDialog class, and is operated on just like a modal dialog. However, upon closure of the dialog, the user's entry can be read.

SAVE AS

1. In FormFiller, generate an *OnFileSaveAs()* function for the File->Save As menu command in the View class:

[1] Note the choice of the term *filespec*, which includes the filename and the file path. A filename would not include the file folder or directory.

```
void CFormFillerView::OnFileSaveAs()
{
    // TODO: Add your command handler code here
    CFileDialog     dlg( FALSE,
        "txt",
        NULL,
        OFN_ENABLESIZING | OFN_FILEMUSTEXIST | OFN_HIDEREADONLY,
        "Subscription Files (*.txt)|*.txt|Documents (*.doc)|*.doc||",
        this );
    dlg.DoModal();
    CString     csFilename = dlg.GetPathName();
}
```

To construct the file dialog, you need to provide a series of parameters as shown in Figure 32.1.

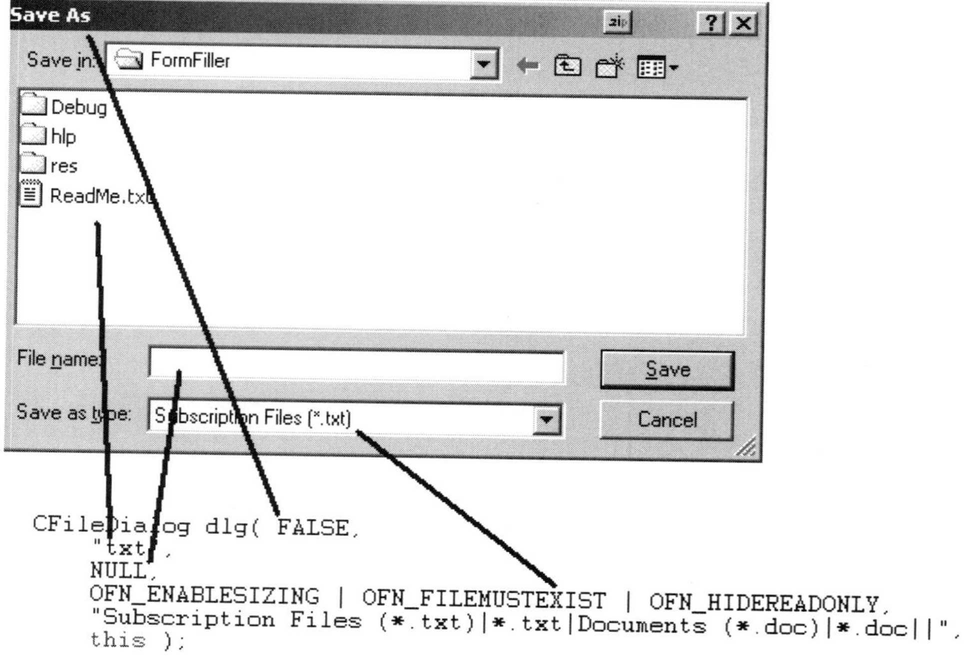

FIGURE 32.1 CFileDialog parameters.

The first parameter specifies whether the dialog will be an "Open" or "Save" dialog. A TRUE value makes it "Open." A FALSE value makes it "Save."

The second parameter specifies the default filename extension. In this example, we are making the saved file a .txt file automatically if unspecified.

The third parameter is the default filename. NULL means we aren't providing one.

The fourth parameter is a series of DWORD flags that prescribe how the dialog should behave. These you can look up from your references.

The next parameter, the most complicated one, allows you to construct a file filter string. This string will be used to populate the Save As type drop-down box.

The entries in the box are separated by the "|" sign, with the string ending in a pair of them. Each entry itself has two components. They are also separated by the "|" sign. The first component is a literal display text of the file type. The second is the filter. For example, in our demo application, the first filter has the display text "Subscription Files (*.txt)." The second component, the filter, is "*.txt."

The last parameter is the pointer to the parent CWnd object.

After the user has closed the dialog, you read the filespec entered with the *GetPathName()* member function. Once you have this data, you can use it to open/create a text file in which to save the subscription data, which you have learned, such as:

```
CStdioFile    f;
f.Open( csFilename, CFile::modeCreate | CFile::modeWrite |
CFile::typeText )
```

SAVE

The reason we did the Save As command first is because Save As indicates that the user wants to save the data in a brand new file. In other words, if the data are from an existing file, the File->Save command merely saves the data back to the original file, and no file dialog should be provided.

To tell the difference, you might want to maintain a current filename CString object that is initialized to empty. If the string is empty, indicating that the data have not been saved, either Save or Save As will bring up the file dialog. If the object already has a string in it, indicating that the data came from an existing file, the data should be saved to the existing file.

According to this line of reasoning, when the File->New command is chosen, indicating that a new form is constructed, this CString filename object should be emptied and so should all the form data.

OPEN

In contrast, for opening files, you use exactly the same scheme as Save As, except that the first parameter for the file dialog construction should be TRUE. Also, depending on the sophistication of your application design, you might allow multiple file selections. You do that by specifying the OFN_ALLOWMULTISELECT flag, as in:

```
        CFileDialog     dlg( TRUE,
            "txt",
            NULL,
            OFN_ENABLESIZING | OFN_FILEMUSTEXIST | OFN_HIDEREADONLY |
OFN_ALLOWMULTISELECT,
            "Subscription Files (*.txt)|*.txt|Documents (*.doc)|*.doc||",
            this );
```

To read the multiple filespec selection returns, you start with the *GetStartPosition()* member function, which initializes a POSITION pointer. The sequence of filespecs are then read with the *GetNextPathName(POSITION& pos)* function. Such an *OnFileOpen()* command processing function would be:

```
POSITION     pos = dlg.GetStartPosition();
CString     csFilename;
while ( pos != NULL )
{
     csFilename = dlg.GetNextPathName( pos );
     lstFile.AddTail( csFilename );
}
```

In this example, to process all the files selected, a CStringList object lstFile is used. As each selected file is obtained, it is added to the list with *AddTail()*. Afterward, the files are opened and processed in turn.

CFileDialog comes with many useful member functions that are easy to understand and that you can put to good use. For example, if you need more refined information on the selected files, you can get the filename with *GetFileName()*, the filename extension with *GetFileEx()*, the filename prefix part without the extension with *GetFileTitle()*, and many others. These helpful functions have eliminated much string parsing activities that otherwise you would have to perform yourself.

The CFileDialog is derived from MFC's CCommonDialog class. From this class, many other useful dialog classes are engendered. We'll now quickly look at them in turn.

CFontDialog

You use the CFontDialog to produce a dialog for font selection. To create a CFontDialog object, you use its constructor, such as:

```
LOGFONT lf;
memset( &lf, 0, sizeof( LOGFONT ) );
CFontDialog dlg( &lf, CF_EFFECTS | CF_SCREENFONTS, NULL, this );
```

Here, LOGFONT is a font descriptive structure. It is required in the CFont-Dialog construction. Therefore, first, such a structure object is declared, and sufficient memory is subscribed for it and initialized to 0 (*memset()* the structure to 0, doing it for as many bytes as a LOGFONT structure requires with *sizeof()*). This structure is then passed to the CFontDialog object constructor, along with the proper DWORD flags (CF_EFFECTS | CF_SCREENFONTS), an optional printer device context pointer (set to NULL here), and the parent CWnd pointer.

To get the font after the user has selected it, you use the *GetCurrentFont()* member function, such as:

```
dlg.DoModal();
dlg.GetCurrentFont( &lf );
```

In our example scenario, we did not bother to initialize the font dialog when it opened; that is, we did not select a font before we deployed the font dialog. As a result, the dialog did not display an initial font. To preset a font going in, you need to initialize the LOGFONT structure before you open the dialog with *DoModal()*. For example:

```
strcpy( lf.lfFaceName, "Arial Narrow" );
CFontDialog dlg( &lf, CF_EFFECTS | CF_SCREENFONTS, NULL, this );
dlg.DoModal();
```

With a little study of the LOGFONT structure, you'll learn to preset the font weight and size as well.

Once you've obtained the information on the font selected, you can set it to use in your application with "m_font.CreateFontIndirect(&lf);", where *m_font* is a View class member CFont object.

CColorDialog

You provide a CColorDialog object—a color section dialog—for the user to select a color. The constructor of a CColorDialog object is:

CColorDialog(COLORREF *clrInit* = 0, DWORD *dwFlags* = 0, CWnd* *pParentWnd* = NULL);

This means that you can deploy a CColorDialog with:

```
CColorDialog    dlg( RGB(255, 255, 255) );
dlg.DoModal();
```

or, if you want to have more say about the dialog specifics, with something like:

```
CColorDialog     dlg( RGB( 255, 255, 255 ), CC_FULLOPEN, this );
```

To obtain the color selected by the user, use the *GetColor()* member function, such as:

```
COLORREF     color = dlg.GetColor();
```

CPageSetupDialog

To afford control over the printed page, you use the CPageSetupDialog. As you should know by now, all you need to do is instantiate an object, initialize it, and use *DoModal()* to launch it. If the user clicks OK, you have a valid set of print page settings, which you can read and use to configure your printed page. A typical sequence would be:

```
CPageSetupDialog     dlg( PSD_DEFAULTMINMARGINS | PSD_MARGINS, this );
if ( dlg.DoModal() == IDOK )
{
}
```

A CPageSetupDialog object requires two parameters to construct: a set of DWORD flags to initialize it, and the parent CWnd pointer, which can be NULL.

As for the flags, there are many of them. You can look them up in the references.

The useful member functions that you can immediately use to configure your printing include *GetDeviceMode()* to retrieve an LPDEVMODE structure that contains the device's information such as paper size and orientation, the *GetMargins()* function to obtain both the margins set and the minimum margins as CRect objects, and the *GetPaperSize()* function to return a CSize object for the paper size.

CPrintDialog

The CPrintDialog, of course, constructs a print dialog. A typical construction of a print dialog is:

```
CPrintDialog     dlg( TRUE,
   PD_ALLPAGES |
   PD_USEDEVMODECOPIES |
   PD_NOPAGENUMS,
   this );
```

Here the first parameter TRUE signifies that the dialog is set up for printer setup use only. If you want to enable actual printing, you set the parameter to FALSE.

The second DWORD parameter lets you customize the dialog settings. For example, PD_ALLPAGES preselects the "All pages" radio button.

The third parameter is the parent CWnd pointer.

Th CPrintDialog class is quite easy to use, and so are its member functions. For example, the *GetCopies()* function returns the number of print copies set by the user as an integer. The *GetFromPage()* and *GetToPage()* functions inform you of the namesake page numbers. The Boolean *PrintAll()* function tells us if the "All pages" radio button has been selected. Likewise, the Boolean *PrintCollate()*, *PrintRange()*, and *PrintSelection()* functions offer similar information on the user's print elections.

Of all these functions, the *GetDefaults()* function is often of particular interest to the application developer. Without deploying the dialog with *DoModal()* at all, the program can use this function immediately after the object is instantiated to obtain default information on the printer. The information is contained in the **m_pd** member variable of the dialog.

CFindReplaceDialog and COleDialog

Before we end our quick tour of common dialog boxes, let's mention two more topics: the CFindReplaceDialog and the COleDialog group of dialog classes.

CFindReplaceDialog is used only when your application deals with text editing, and most of you have encountered this dialog in one commercial application or another. It works pretty much like the other common dialogs discussed previously, so you should be able to learn it on your own. However, the one feature that warrants addressing is that a CFindReplaceDialog dialog is deployed as a modeless dialog without a *DoModal()* function. Once deployed, it stays on the screen. You must dispense of it programmatically. Also, it must be constructed on the heap; therefore, you must "new" it, as in:

```
CFindReplaceDialog*     pDlg = new CFindReplaceDialog();
pDlg->Create( TRUE, "", "", FR_DOWN, this );
```

Although it provides facilities for obtaining information on the text to find and replace and so on, it does *not* perform any text manipulation. You merely use the information extracted to assist in your own text processing.

The COleDialog, on the other hand, is a group of dialogs including COleInsertDialog for inserting a file from the system, COleConvertDialog, COleUpdateDialog, and many others to perform specific OLE-oriented tasks. All these require familiarity with OLE operations. If you're working on OLE-intensive applications, you'll find these classes more than helpful.

33 Application Preferences

When a variable takes on value for the first time, it is called *initialization*. An application has its initializations too. They are called *preferences* or program *options*, which are usually collections of initial values and settings. These settings can be initialized in different ways. Certainly the program can initialize them within its coding, but sometimes you may allow the user to get in on the act of setting initial values too.

How you enable a user to set or change operational values of an application is a matter of design. For instance, you can get by with a simple dialog box. However, with the standards set by today's Windows applications, such a simple approach probably won't do.

Two design styles are now almost accepted norms in application preferences interfacing: the tab control and the wizard.

A tab control (Figure 33.1) is similar to a wizard in that it consists of a number of dialogs grouped together to form a single interface unit, and with all the work that we've done with AppWizard, ClassWizard, and property dialogs that are tab controls and wizards, you are now familiar with both.

The difference between a tab control and a wizard lies in the dependencies between the dialogs within the structures.

A tab control is nothing but a convenient and compact way of grouping a set of dialogs. It offers a user a maximum degree of freedom in navigating the dialogs.

In a tab control dialogs are superimposed on top of each other with only access tabs exposed with which a user can select a dialog, called a *pane*, to work with.

In contrast, a wizard is a number of dialogs arranged for strict sequential navigation. In other words, a user cannot jump between dialogs at will in a wizard. One must progress from one dialog to the next in either the forward or backward direction.

FIGURE 33.1 A tab control

When it comes to tab controls you have two options of approach. You can create a formal tab control, or you can make use of property pages. We will now explore all these mechanisms.

PROPERTY SHEETS AND WIZARDS

Another way to achieve the appearance of a tab control is the property sheet. As it turns out, in VC++ property sheets and wizards are built the same way. Therefore we'll investigate them together.

Property Sheets

A property sheet is a structure that contains child dialogs. As a result, when building property sheets you start with the component dialogs.

1. In the **FormFiller** project insert two new dialogs with specifics and controls on them as follows:

ID	*IDD_DIALOG_PAGE1*	*IDD_DIALOG_PAGE2*
Caption	Sales Rep Info	Subscription Default
Control	Static "Sales Rep:", Edit box	Radio Button "Weekdays"

2. Remove all their buttons and set their properties as follows:

Property	*Setting*
Style	Child
Border	Thin
System Menu	Unchecked
Visible	Checked
Disabled	Checked

3. Create new classes for them, both based on the CPropertyPage class (and make sure that you do not mistakenly select CPropertySheet):

ID	*IDD_DIALOG_PAGE1*	*IDD_DIALOG_PAGE2*
Class	CPage1	CPage2

4. For CPage1, use ClassWizard to add a CString member variable for the edit control named **m_csSalesRep** to be used to hold the default sales rep's name.
5. In ClassView use ClassWizard to define a new MFC derived class named CPreferences based on the CPropertySheet class.
6. For this new class, use the Add Member Variable command to add two public member variables:

```
// Implementation
public:
	CPage2 m_page2;
	CPage1 m_page1;
	virtual ~CPreferences();
```

The property sheet is set up. We will now add the property pages to it.

If you look at the constructor definitions of the CPreference class you'll see two constructors, one using a string resource and the other a code expressed string literal for title. You can use either one to construct the object.

7. Here, for simplicity we'll choose the second one and enter the page construction code there:

```
CPreferences::CPreferences(LPCTSTR pszCaption, CWnd* pParentWnd, …,
iSelectPage)
{
      AddPage( &m_page1 );
      AddPage( &m_page2 );
}
```

You use the CPropertySheet *AddPage()* member function to add a property page. If you prefer, you can also implement this after you have instantiated the property sheet below and then add the pages.

8. To activate the property sheet, add a new command to the View menu for "&Preferences" and generate a command message handler for it in the View class:

```
void CFormFillerView::OnViewPreferences()
{
      // TODO: Add your command handler code here
      CPreferences      prpSheet( "Preferences", this, 0 );
      if ( prpSheet.DoModal() == IDOK )
      {
      }
}
```

You construct a property sheet by specifying the sheet title as a CString object, the parent CWnd pointer, and the initial page to display. In our example we chose to display page 1, indexed 0.

Although not based on any dialog resource, a property sheet is very much a dialog. You deploy it with *DoModal()*.

If you test this program you should see Figure 33.1 when you choose the View-> Preferences command.

Although the purpose of this property sheet is to set the system's preference variables, those features have been left out to make the demonstration simple. There is only one example **m_csSalesRep** variable for illustration purposes. If you're interested, to complete the preference-editing feature, just add member variables to the View class and receive data from the dialogs, such as:

```
m_csDefaultSalesRep = prpSheet.m_page1.m_csSalesRep;
```

Of course, you'd have a default value to begin with, which you would load in the property page's control before you display the property sheet. You may attempt to do this as an exercise.

Property Sheet Buttons

Underneath a property sheet's simple set-up actually is another layer of operational sophistication. First, there are the default buttons, which may not be set up exactly the way you want them. For example, you may choose to offer no Apply or Help button in your design. To remove the Apply button you can include the following code segment just before you use *DoModal()* to launch the property sheet (or in the Property Sheet class's *OnInitDialog()* function):

```
CWnd* pWnd = GetDlgItem( ID_APPLY_NOW );
if (pWnd->GetSafeHwnd() != NULL )
   pWnd->ShowWindow(FALSE);
```

ID_APPLY_NOW is the ID for the Apply button. The ID for the Help button is IDHELP.

While you may choose not to offer onscreen help, the Apply button is there for a reason. It allows the user to sanction the settings in the page currently in focus while continuing to make changes with an option to cancel. The handling of this is implemented in the property page class's *OnApply()* virtual function. You use ClassWizard to generate the function override for the particular page and enter the Apply button implementation code there, such as:

```
BOOL CPage1::OnApply()
{
     // TODO: Add your specialized code here

     return CPropertyPage::OnApply();
}
```

Things that you can do here include copying the edited preference settings on the page into the appropriate variables. Note that initially the Apply button is grayed out, or disabled. This is because before any value has been changed there is nothing to apply. However, the button should be activated when the property sheet data change. This is effected in the property page class's *SetModified(BOOL bState)* function. All you need to do is to set the "modified" state to TRUE when there is something to apply, such as when the edit control's EN_CHANGE message is sent:

```
void CPage1::OnChangeEditSalesRep()
{
     SetModified( TRUE );
}
```

Under different situations, an applied setting change may not be undoable. In such a case you would want the Cancel button to be deactivated. You do this with the *CancelToClose()* function, which turns the Cancel button into a Close button, which, of course, becomes de facto an OK button, returning the IDOK value when the modal property sheet is closed.

Other useful property page functions include the usual ones, such as *OnOK()* and *OnCancel()*, called when the property sheet is closed. The *OnSetActive()* function is called when a page is selected by the user. You can do something useful then, such as initializing the variables. Similarly, when the user leaves a property page, the *OnKillActive()* function is called. You can do some clean-up work there also.

Modeless Property Sheets

If there is the need, you can deploy the property sheet as a modeless dialog too. The procedure is:

```
CPropertySheet*      pPS;
pPS = new CPropertySheet();
CPropertyPage1*      pPP1;
pPP1 = new CPropertyPage1();
CPropertyPage2*      pPP2;
pPP2 = new CPropertyPage2();
pPS->AddPage( pPP1 );
pPS->AddPage( pPP2 );
pPS->Create();
```

The destruction of the property pages should be carried out in the property sheet's PostNcDestroy() virtual function, and the logic is:

```
CPropertyPage*      pPP = GetPage(0);
if ( pPP->GetSafeHWnd() != NULL )
     delete pPP;
CPropertyPage*      pPP = GetPage(1);
if ( pPP->GetSafeHWnd() != NULL )
     delete pPP;
```

Needless to say, you can use a *for* loop to iterate through the pages.

Wizards

A wizard is actually a special version of the property sheet. You build a wizard exactly the same way you do a property sheet, except with a number of setting changes.

In fact, to show how the wizard is closely associated with the property sheet, we'll convert our property sheet example into a wizard (even though it should not be) just so that you'll see how the events progress.

1. First, you turn the property sheet into a wizard with:

```
void CFormFillerView::OnViewPreferences()
{
    // TODO: Add your command handler code here
    CPreferences     prpSheet( "Preferences", this, 0 );
    prpSheet.SetWizardMode();
    if ( prpSheet.DoModal() == IDOK )
    {
    }
}
```

2. For page 1, override the *OnSetActive()* virtual function and enter the button customization code to activate the Next button:

```
BOOL CPage1::OnSetActive()
{
    // TODO: Add your specialized code here and/or...
    CPropertySheet* pPS = (CPropertySheet*) GetParent();
    pPS->SetWizardButtons( PSWIZB_NEXT );
    return CPropertyPage::OnSetActive();
}
```

3. Similarly, for page 2, activate the Back and Finish buttons:

```
BOOL CPage2::OnSetActive()
{
    // TODO: Add your specialized code here and/or...
    CPropertySheet* pPS = (CPropertySheet*) GetParent();
    pPS->SetWizardButtons( PSWIZB_BACK | PSWIZB_FINISH );
    return CPropertyPage::OnSetActive();
}
```

The *SetWizardButton()* function of CPropertySheet, to be called from the pages when they're activated because the pages should assume different button arrangements, takes a DWORD flag parameter which dictates which buttons should be activated. This flag can be an ORed combination of the following: PSWIZB_BACK, PSWIZB_NEXT, PSWIZB_FINISH, and PSWIZB_DISABLEDFINISH. You simply apply them according to the requirements of the pages.

Again, the choice between a property page and a wizard isn't arbitrary. You use a property sheet to organize controls into groups to simplify the user interface and for real estate optimization reasons. The data, or controls, must exhibit clear grouping characteristics.

In contrast, for a wizard, not only should there be a quality of grouping but there also must be a sense of data dependency. For example, what is presented on step 2 of a wizard should be dictated by the responses to those on page 1, just like AppWizard. These controls should not be used just to make the program look "cool."

THE TAB CONTROL

A set of tabs can also be created based on the CTabCtrl control, and the approach to its working is quite different from that of the property sheet, although the end results look pretty much the same.

1. Use AppWizard to generate a new MFC Dialog-based project named TabCtrl.
2. On the dialog resource install a tab control as shown in Figure 33.2.

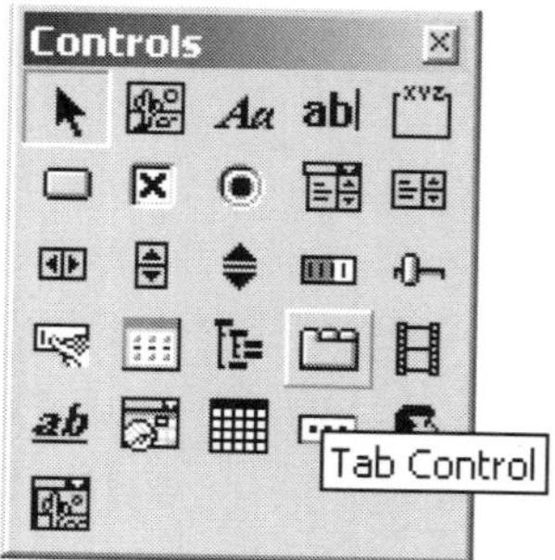

FIGURE 33.2 The Tab control.

3. Add a member object for the tab control:

```
class CTabCtrlDlg : public CDialog
{
        ...
// Dialog Data
     //{{AFX_DATA(CTabCtrlDlg)
     enum { IDD = IDD_TABCTRL_DIALOG };
```

```
    CTabCtrl     m_Tabs;
    //}}AFX_DATA
```

4. In the Dialog class's `OnInitDialog()` function create the tabs as follows:

```
BOOL CTabCtrlDlg::OnInitDialog()
{
    CDialog::OnInitDialog();
    ...
    // TODO: Add extra initialization here
    TC_ITEM     TabCtrlItem;
    TabCtrlItem.mask = TCIF_TEXT;
    TabCtrlItem.pszText = "Sales Representative";
    m_Tabs.InsertItem( 0, &TabCtrlItem );
    TabCtrlItem.pszText = "System Defaults";
    m_Tabs.InsertItem( 1, &TabCtrlItem );
    TabCtrlItem.pszText = "Customer Preferences";
    m_Tabs.InsertItem( 2, &TabCtrlItem );
    return TRUE;  // return TRUE  unless you set the focus to a
control
}
```

If you compile the program and run it you'll see a set of tabs, though they don't do much.

A tab control, based on the CTabCtrl class, works with a set of "tab control items" of the TC_ITEM structure. The structure member **mask** specifies which other member to retrieve or set. In our case, the mask TCIF_TEXT singles out the member *pszText* for work. *pszText* is the string of a tab's caption.

Once a tab caption is set you can include it in the tab control with its *InsertItem()* member function, which takes on the index of the tab starting with 0, and a pointer to the caption string.

After you have built the tab control you can use the member functions in Table 33.1 to work with it.

TABLE 33.1 Often-Used Tab Control Member Functions

Function	*Description*
DeleteAllItems()	Remove all the tab control items
DeleteItem(int nItem)	Remove an item at the specified index
int GetCurFocus()	Get the index of the tab item in focus

(Continues)

TABLE 33.1 Often-Used Tab Control Member Functions *(Continued)*

Function	Description
it GetCurSel()	Get the index of the tab item selected by the user (which may not yet be in focus)
GetItem(int nItem, TCITEM* pTabCtrlItem)	Get the TCITEM structure of the specified tab item
int GetItemCount()	Get the number of items in the control
int GetRowCount()	Get the number of tab rows in the tab control (if the TCS_MULTILINE property has been checked)
SetCurFocus(int nItem)	Sets the specified item in focus
SetItem(int nItem, TCITEM* pTabCtrlItem)	Sets the TCITEM structure of a specified item, such as to programmatically change its caption

However, these functions are useful only if they are coordinated with the user's actions, such as sensing when the user has clicked on a particular item. The tab control offers the event messages listed in Table 33.2.

TABLE 33.2 Tab Control Event Messages

Message	Description
TCN_SELCHANGE	The tab item selection has changed
TCN_SELCHANGING	The selection is about to change
TCN_KEYDOWN	A key has been pressed
TCN_GETOBJECT	An object has been dragged over the control

The difference between "changing" and "change" is that the former occurs before the target item is in focus, while the latter occurs after the item you're changing to is already in focus.

In programming a tab control, you generate a message handler function for the control and in the function implement the operation that you intend to accomplish under that circumstance.

Why are the property sheet and the tab control so similar? Because the former is actually wrapped around the latter. In other words, inside a property sheet is a tab control. In fact, while working with a property sheet if you ever need to work with the underlying tab control directly, use its *GetTabControl()* member function to get a pointer to the tab control.

When all is said and done, it is a lot more convenient to use the property sheet instead of the tab control directly.

COMMAND LINE PROCESSING

Another way a user can impart initialization information to an application is to provide it during program start-up via the command line, as in Figure 33.3, which shows starting the FormFiller.exe program at Windows' Start->Run with a parameter for the sales representative Sharon.

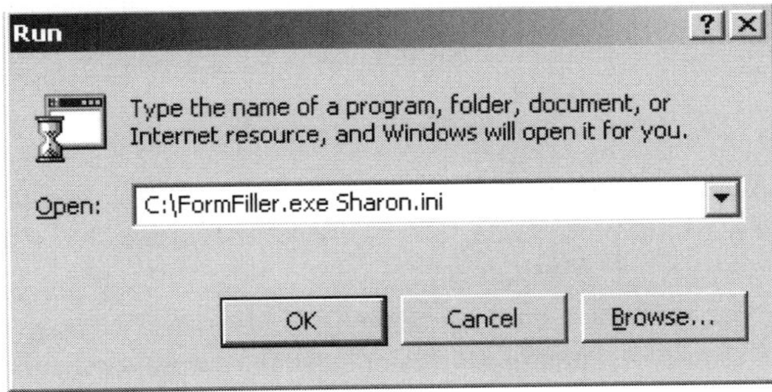

FIGURE 33.3 Command-line parameter.

If you open the FormFiller project once again and scroll down the *InitInstance()* function of the CFormFillerApp class you'll see the following code lines:

```
CCommandLineInfo cmdInfo;
ParseCommandLine(cmdInfo);
if (!ProcessShellCommand(cmdInfo))
     return FALSE;
```

These lines parse the command line and extract the parameters for you. It is up to us to make use of them. The parameters can range from none to a "filename" for opening, "/p filename" for printing a file, and so forth.

A popular use of this facility is to open an initialization file in which specific start-up settings are recorded. To obtain this information all you need to do is add the following code lines immediately after the command line parsing generated by AppWizard:

```
if (!ProcessShellCommand(cmdInfo))
     return FALSE;
CString     csIniFile;
csIniFile = cmdInfo.m_strFileName;
```

The string in **csIniFile** is the text file to open.
The parameters maintained in cmdInfo are listed in Table 33.3.

TABLE 33.3 Command Info Data Members

Data Member	Description
m_bRunAutomated = TRUE	Start up as an OLE automation server
m_bRunEmbedded = TRUE	Start up for editing an embedded OLE item
m_bShowSplash = TRUE	Display splash screen during startup if no file is opened
m_nShellCommand	Indicates the shell command for this instance of the application
m_strFileName	(1st non-flag on command line) The name of the file to open
m_strPrinterName	(2nd non-flag on command line) The name of the printer for a Print To shell command
m_strDriverName	(3rd non-flag on command line) The name of the printer driver for a Print To shell command
m_strPortName	(4th non-flag on command line) The name of the printer port for a Print To shell command

WINDOW AND OBJECT SIZING

Another more subtle form of initialization is the state of the application upon start up, which often is set to the state left behind upon the application's previous exit. A typical example is the placement of the application program window's overall geometry.

In previous chapters you already have learned how to size and reposition objects relative to the windows they are in with the *GetClientRect()* function. Here we are talking about the application's main dialog or window relative to the physical monitor screen. As it turns out, this geometry is easily obtained with the CWnd class's *GetWindowRect()* function.

Typically what you do is get this information from the MainFrame class right before the frame is destroyed and preserve it, then retrieve the information when the application is executed. For example:

```
void CMainFrame::OnDestroy()
{
	CFrameWnd::OnDestroy();

	// TODO: Add your message handler code here
	CRect	rect;
	GetWindowRect( rect );
}
```

To position the frame add the following code in CMainFrame's *OnCreate()* function:

```
SetWindowPos( &wndTop, rect.left, rect.top, rect.Width(),
rect.Height(), SWP_SHOWWINDOW );
```

The first parameter of the CWnd *SetWindowPos()* function &wndTop puts the application's window at the top of the *Z order*; that is, above every application that is currently open, which is where a new application should be.

Incidentally, an object's rectangular geometry obtained with the *GetClientRect()* function can be translated into screen coordinates with the CWnd *ClientToScreen(LPRect rect)* function.

With all the preferences and initialization data we now have, the only remaining question is where do we preserve them? Certainly we can use serialization from the Document class to do it almost effortlessly. We can utilize an initialization .ini file to do the trick, with or without the help of CCommandLineInfo. We can also do what many modern Windows applications do: make use of Windows' registry.

THE WINDOWS REGISTRY

The Windows Registry is a system-maintained hierarchical database. Let's return to the **FormFiller** project and examine the App class's *InitInstance()* function again. Not too far from the top you'll see the following code line:

```
SetRegistryKey(_T("Local AppWizard-Generated Applications"));
```

This CWinApp member function sets the application to transact with an entry in the Windows Registry called a *key* by the context of "Local AppWizard-Generated Applications."

1. Use Windows' Start->Run command to execute the Regedit.exe program and bring up Registry Editor's main window as in Figure 33.4.

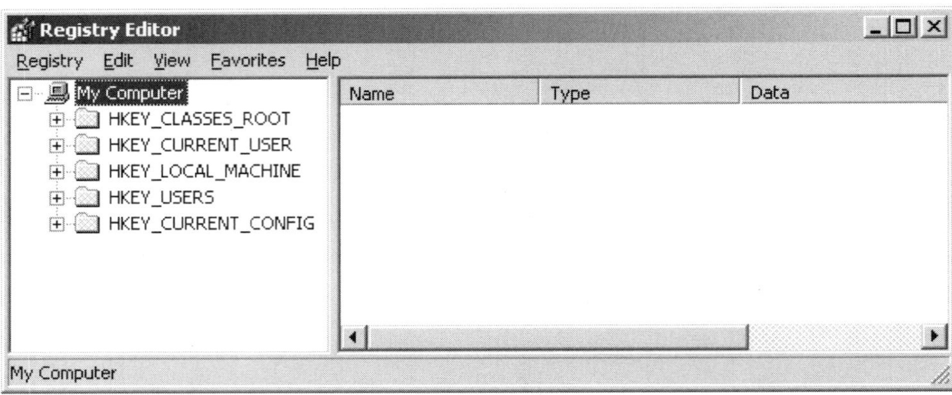

FIGURE 33.4 The RegEdit.exe utility.

2. In Registry Editor choose the Edit->Find command and search for the "Local AppWizard-Generated Applications" string.

When the string is found, you should see Figure 33.5.

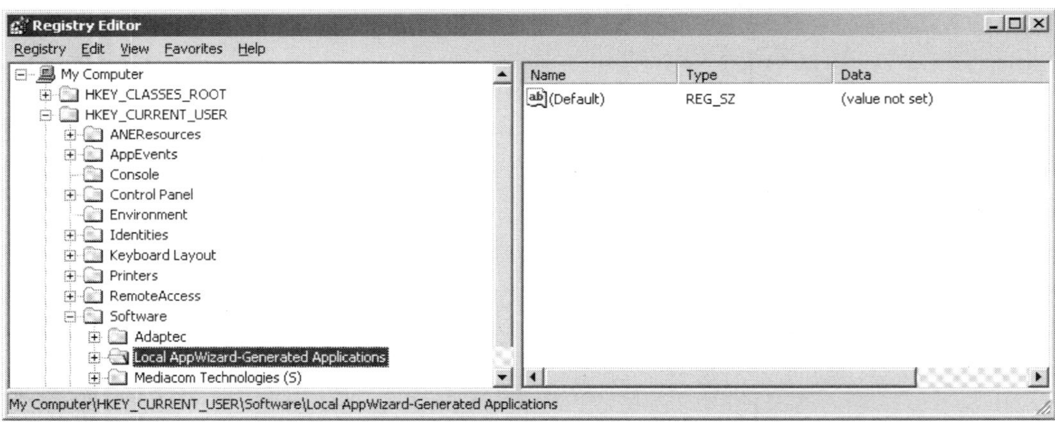

FIGURE 33.5 Locating a string in RegEdit.exe.

The folder our application belongs to is in the Software folder under the HKEY_CURRENT_USER and HKEY_USER folders.

If you expand any of the two folders you'll see FormFiller there.

Inside these folders you'll find subfolders, notably the Settings subfolder in which you can store settings. (The other subfolder is the Recent File List folder that maintains a list of the names of the most recently opened files.)

3. Terminate the Regedit.exe program.

In a real, non-exercise application you would certainly change the "Local App-Wizard-Generated Applications" string to something unique, such as your company's name, in which case the registry entries will belong to a folder bearing your company's name, such as Microsoft does with its applications and program settings.

Transacting with the Windows Registry at the application settings level using MFC is simple. You use the CWinApp class's *WriteProfileString()*, *WriteProfileInt()*, *GetProfileString()*, and *GetProfileInt()*, functions to write to and read from the registry.

The *WriteProfileString()* function takes on three LPCTSTR parameters: the registry section, the registry entry, and the string value. For example, the following function call writes the value "Sharon" to the registry under the FormFiller subfolder:

```
WriteProfileString( "Settings", "SalesRep", "Sharon" );
```

When the application is executed, preferably in the *InitInstance()* function you'll call *GetProfileString()* to read the registry entry, such as:

```
CString     m_csSalesRep = GetProfileString( "Settings", "SalesRep",
"No Name" );
```

In this example "Sharon" would be read back into the member variable **m_csSalesRep**. However, should the entry be absent, such as when the program is first used, a default value of "No Name" would be substituted.

The other two functions operate the same way, except with integer values. They are ideal to use with window geometries.

As a real example, the following is how you would save the MainFrame exit window geometry for the FormFiller application.

1. First, create member variables to hold the geometry values in the CWinApp class:

```
class CFormFillerApp : public CWinApp
{
public:
     CRect m_frmRect;
```

2. Next, capture the geometry in the MainFrame class's ON_DESTROY message handler:

```
extern      CFormFillerApp theApp;
void CMainFrame::OnDestroy()
{
      CFrameWnd::OnDestroy();

      // TODO: Add your message handler code here
      CRect     rect;
      GetWindowRect( rect );
      theApp.m_frmRect = rect;
}
```

The extern statement provides an access to the global variable **theApp**, which is generated by AppWizard close to the top of the CWinApp.cpp file. This way, the data are passed on to the App class object.

3. The App class then write the values out in the *ExitInstance()* virtual function override:

```
int CFormFillerApp::ExitInstance()
{
      // TODO: Add your specialized code here...
      WriteProfileInt( "Settings", "left", m_frmRect.left );
      WriteProfileInt( "Settings", "top", m_frmRect.top );
      WriteProfileInt( "Settings", "right", m_frmRect.right );
      WriteProfileInt( "Settings", "bottom", m_frmRect.bottom );
      return CWinApp::ExitInstance();
}
```

When the application executes, code in *InitInstance()* will read the data from the registry:

```
m_frmRect.left = GetProfileInt( "Settings", "left", 100 );
m_frmRect.top = GetProfileInt( "Settings", "top", 100 );
m_frmRect.right = GetProfileInt( "Settings", "right", 600 );
m_frmRect.bottom = GetProfileInt( "Settings", "bottom", 500 );
```

Then code in the MainFrame's *OnCreate()* will size and position the frame window:

```
CRect     rect = theApp.m_frmRect;
SetWindowPos( &wndTop, rect.left, rect.top, rect.Width(),
rect.Height(), SWP_SHOWWINDOW );
```

Although the Windows Registry isn't the main subject of this book, it figures prominently in any software dealing with Windows or run in the Windows environment. Therefore, it behooves the Windows software developer to be familiar with it.

34 Bells and Whistles

At this point, you have pretty much the essential MFC tool set to build most Windows applications with quality. Now we will go one step further and learn to make your programming products snazzy. We'll talk bells and whistles—those not-quite-essential features that will set your applications apart from the herd. Specifically, we'll go over the following features:

- Pop-up menus
- Tooltips
- System info
- Splash screen
- The hourglass
- Tip of the Day

POP-UP MENUS

Strictly speaking, pop-up menus shouldn't be considered bells and whistles—they are really substantive parts of a GUI-oriented application. However, because they are accessible via mouse clicks only, they violate the unofficial dual keyboard/mouse access requirements of a proper Windows application[1]. Also, usually pop-up menu commands are culled from existing menu commands; therefore, they aren't really primary access points to the operations. However, a pop-up menu does offer encapsulated access to key commands that are specifically designed for

[1] We must remember that not all users prefer to use the mouse or can use the mouse. For example, a traditional typist operates a computer strictly by the keyboard for typing efficiency.

quick access to operational features that are relevant to the application functions at hand, and which may have been handled by commands that are scattered among various menus because they have been arranged by category. Hence, pop-up menus are also called *context menus.*

Pop-up menus used to be a nightmare to code, but thanks to VC++ and wizards and controls, we can now implement them with just a couple of mouse clicks and a few keystrokes.

1. In the **FormFiller** project, choose the Project->Add To Project->Components and Controls command, and then the Visual C++ Components folder.
2. From the Components and Controls Gallery, select Pop-up Menu and click Insert.
3. When prompted to insert the component, click OK.

You're now presented with the choice of where to insert the pop-up menu as shown in Figure 34.1.

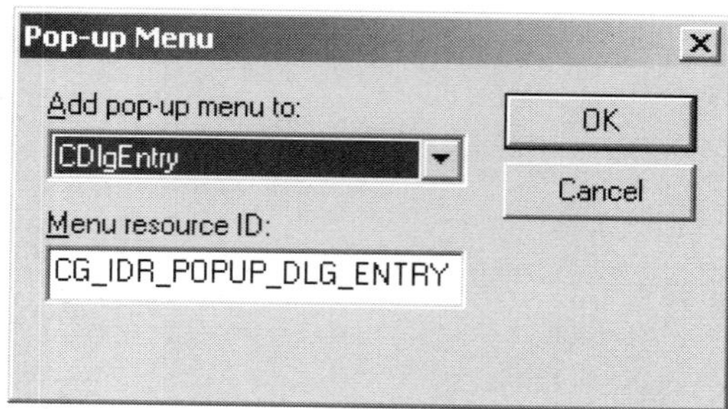

FIGURE 34.1 Inserting a pop-up menu in a project.

4. Select CDlgEntry for the target of the pop-up menu, and then click OK to exit the Gallery.

In ResourceView, you'll now find a new menu resource IDed CG_IDR_POPUP_DLG_ENTRY whose menu command is POPUP with preloaded cut, Copy, and Paste commands. It's up to you to decide if these commands should stay. If they're pertinent, they should; otherwise, you can remove them in the usual manner.

What we're interested here is to offer the View->Preferences, File->New, and File->Save commands.

5. Add new commands "New," "Save," and "Preferences" to the new pop-up menu resource and give them exactly the same IDs as those that already exist in the main menus.
6. Compile the program and test the new pop-up menu.

Let's now inspect what VC++ has done for us.

In ClassView, if you expand the CDlgEntry tree branch you'll see a new function *OnContextMenu()*. This is the new entry made by VC++ when it inserted the pop-up menu. The body of the function is at the end of the CDlgEntry.cpp file.

This function is actually the handler function for the WM_CONTEXTMENU message, and is called by the framework when the user clicks the right mouse button.

The function receives two parameters: a pointer to the window in which the mouse is clicked, and the position of the mouse pointer as a CPoint object.

As you can see, a CMenu object is created based on the new menu resource, which is the main entry of the pop-up menu. A call to *GetSubMenu(0)* points to the commands in the menu. It also checks to see if the owner window is the child window with *GetStyle()* ("GetStyle() & WS_CHILD" isolates the child flag bit and determines if it is non-zero). If the pop-up menu is installed in a child window, the owner is diverted to its parent window. Then, the *TrackPopupMenu()* function displays the floating pop-up menu at the specified location and tracks the selection of items on the pop-up menu.

Don't try to reason with the code logic too much and wonder why those functions are used. This is just the way the pop-up menu works by MFC design.

Note: If you noticed, the *OnContextMenu()* function inserted by VC++ may have an anomaly in it. In its declaration, the CWnd* parameter type is there but the variable is missing:

OnContextMenu(CWnd*, CPoint point)

You should restore it to:

OnContextMenu(CWnd* pWnd, CPoint point)

Make sure that you handle all the occurrences.

Also, if you already have previously generated a handler function for the WM_CONTEXTMENU message already, the Pop-up Menu insert won't work.

TOOLTIPS

Another useful Windows application feature is the tooltip—considered by many developers as pure bells and whistles, but deemed important because they help to make life as comfortable for the user as possible. A tooltip is that little yellow bubble that floats on top of an object and provides useful information on the object. It is a wonderful compact onscreen help of sorts.

Again, tooltips are easily implemented with the help of VC++.

1. In the **FormFiller** project, choose the Project->Add To Project->Components and Controls command, and then the Visual C++ Components folder.
2. From the Components and Controls Gallery, select ToolTip Support and click Insert.
3. When prompted to insert the component, click OK.
4. Select CDlgEntry for the target of the ToolTip Support insertion and click OK to exit the Gallery.
5. Open the CDlgEntry class's *OnInitDialog()* function. You should see the following code blocks added by VC++:

```
    // CG: The following block was added by the ToolTips component.
    {
        // Create the ToolTip control.
        m_tooltip.Create(this);
        m_tooltip.Activate(TRUE);
        // TODO: Use one of the following forms to:
        // m_tooltip.AddTool( GetDlgItem(IDC_<name>), <string-table-
id>);
        // m_tooltip.AddTool( GetDlgItem(IDC_<name>), "<text>");
    }
BOOL CDlgEntry::PreTranslateMessage(MSG* pMsg)
{
    // CG: The following block was added by the ToolTips component.
    {
        // Let the ToolTip process this message.
        m_tooltip.RelayEvent(pMsg);
    }
    return CDialog::PreTranslateMessage(pMsg);     // CG: This was
added by the ToolTips component.
}
```

Actually, a new entry has been added to the header file as well:

```
public:
    virtual BOOL PreTranslateMessage(MSG* pMsg);
// Implementation
protected:
    CToolTipCtrl m_tooltip;
```

The ToolTip code in *OnInitDialog()* creates the tooltip object with the simple *Create(this)* function that identifies the owner of the tooltip, and then activates it with *Activate(TRUE)*.

After that, it deposited two statements that have been commented out. These are the optional statements for providing tooltips to resourced objects. You can either directly provide a string constant for the tooltip's text or refer to an entry in the String Table, which is what you would do if you were to develop applications with switchable string resources.

6. Implement the following code and compile and test the tooltips:

```
m_tooltip.AddTool( GetDlgItem( IDC_EDIT_NAME ), "Subscriber name, last
  name first");
m_tooltip.AddTool( GetDlgItem( IDC_EDIT_ADDRESS ), "Subscriber billing
  address");
m_tooltip.AddTool( GetDlgItem( IDC_DATETIMEPICKER ), "Date of first
  delivery");
```

You can insert as many sets of tool tips in a project as you wish because the operation merely adds a CToolTipCtrl object and its associated member function calls. However, if you had been tipped off, you would have noticed that when inserting ToolTip Support from the Components Gallery, only classes that were based on dialogs were offered as insertion targets. How do we insert tool tips into non-dialog classes such as Views that may have resourced object members? Just use a surrogate dialog class to get the code, and then move them to the actual destination.

SYSTEM INFO

System Info is a bit of information about the client system that you often see in an About box. It can be helpful in informing the user of the resources available in the system when executing an application. However, with the accessibility of Task Manager and Windows disk drive property sheets, the usefulness of this little extra has diminished. Nevertheless, it is interesting to learn of the functions designed to implement this feature.

1. For any project with the Help->About feature turned on, choose the Project->Add To Project->Components and Controls command, and then the Visual C++ Components folder.
2. From the Components and Controls Gallery, select System Info for About Dlg. and proceed to complete the insertion process.

The inserted code is added to the CAboutDlg class's *OnInitDialog()* function. What is added to the project, however, is not MFC code but pre-MFC Windows API, or *Application Programming Interface* calls.

MFC is really a rough encapsulation of the Windows API, which has a much wider repertoire than MFC proper, which is why many developers still prefer to work with Windows API over MFC (their prior exposure to and familiarity with the API notwithstanding). For example, the API or SDK, Software Development Kit function *CopyFile()* copies a file, but the function does not exist in MFC. However, API being C++ functions, you can call these SDK functions from your VC++ programs.

Again, the logic is pretty much what it is; the code is simply what you need to do to obtain system information: available memory and free disk space. Our job is to present the information in the About dialog.

3. Add two static controls to the About dialog resource and give them the IDs of IDC_PHYSICAL_MEM and IDC_DISK_SPACE (as dictated by the inserted code).
4. Uncomment the following two statements, and then compile and test the About box:

```
SetDlgItemText(IDC_PHYSICAL_MEM, strFreeMemory);
SetDlgItemText(IDC_DISK_SPACE, strFreeDiskSpace);
```

SPLASH SCREEN

The splash screen is the dialog display that appears on the screen when an application loads itself. Again, it can be considered pure thrill if all it serves is to advertise for the application or the company that produced the application. However, especially when the application program loading process is lengthy, you can use the splash screen to display useful information, such as the status of the loading process or exceptions that have been encountered. For instance, you can inform the user that the .ini file is not found.

To implement a splash screen, again we use the "Add to project" feature of VC++. This time, we insert the "Splash screen" component. The default class suggested for the splash screen is CSplashWnd, and the picture for the splash screen is a bitmap named IDB_SPLASH. The bitmap is a simple, general picture that you can replace with your own design (by deleting the stock bitmap and inserting your own and identifying it with the same ID).

At this time, just compile the program and test it. You should see the splash screen appear. There is no coding required.

The magic of the splash screen is in the CSplashWnd class, which is derived from CWnd. This class has a public CBitMap member object that is based on the bitmap picture provided and is loaded into the object in the class's *OnCreate()* function: *m_bitmap.LoadBitmap(IDB_SPLASH)*. It then retrieves the bitmap information in a BITMAP structure that is required in the construction of a pop-up or child window with extended style by means of CWnd's *CreateEx()* function.

The crux of the splash screen's deployment, however, is in the *OnCreate()* function, in which you'll find the *SetTimer()* function, which controls the length for the splash screen's onscreen presence. Feel free to alter this time duration to make the splash screen stay for the duration to suit your purposes.

In addition, in the *OnTimer()* function you'll see that when the time is up, the splash screen is disposed of with the *HideSplashScreen()* function, which contains the following calls:

```
DestroyWindow();
AfxGetMainWnd()->UpdateWindow();
```

This tells you how you can implement your own splash screen control in case you prefer not to use a timer.

As a bonus, the CSplashWnd *OnPaint()* function will teach you how to load a bitmap into the window's device context.

Finally, the splash screen is launched in the App class's *InitInstance()* function. Note the addition of the CCommandLineInfo code preceding the splash screen launch. This is because if the application is executed with a filename parameter the splash screen will not deploy due to the linkage to the **m_bShowSplash** member of the CCommandInfoLine class being set to TRUE. If you want to sever this link, you need to modify the CSplashWnd's class's *EnableSplashScreen()* function so that the splash screen is displayed regardless of the **m_bShowSplash** value.

THE HOUR GLASS

One of the real purposes that a splash screen serves is to occupy the time that an application takes to start up, especially if the initialization process is extensive and otherwise would give a false impression that the computer is frozen.

Activities that take time but produce no visual evidence of work occur often in software applications. You have learned one way to break up such monotony: the progress bar. However, the coding of a progress bar isn't trivial, and often it can prove to be overkill for a small delay. In such situations, you can provide an hourglass on the screen to indicate that what is happening takes time.

The hourglass, a CWaitCursor class object, is easy to implement. All you need to do is instantiate it just before it appears:

```
CWaitCursor     wc;
```

You don't even have to maintain it, as it will be destroyed when the code block in which it is created goes out of scope.

In the case that an intervening event occurs and changes the shape of the cursor when the hourglass cursor is supposed to be active, just use the *Restore()* function after that event to bring back the hourglass:

```
wc.Restore();
```

TIP OF THE DAY

The last of the frill features we will explore is Tip of the Day, a display of paged information about the application that appears when the application is executed.

To implement this feature, use the Project menu's Add to Project command to select the "Tip of the day" component from the Visual C++ Components folder. Then, use a text editor to type up the daily tips one paragraph per day, and save the text file under the filename **tips.txt** in the application's source code folder. Compile the program and, voilà, you have tips of the day.

The bulk of the Tip of the Day logic is in the CTipDlg class's constructor, in which you'll see that crucial processing information is stored in Windows' registry; notably, the timestamp of the tip and that of the tip file are compared to determine which tip paragraph to use. The tip file is opened as a read-only text file, and the appropriate text paragraph (string) is read into the CString variable **m_strTip**.

The Tip of the Day dialog is initiated by the *ShowTipAtStartup()* function in the App class's *InitInstance()* function. In this function, you'll see that the dialog is displayed with its *DoModal()* function, if the display check box is checked. In addition, you see that this event is tied to the activation of the splash screen as well. Again, you can sever this dependency if you like.

Tip of the Day is an excellent example for many features that we have learned. It uses the Windows registry heavily. It also provides a strong dose of menu command manipulation in the MainFrame class's *OnInitMenu()* function, clearly showing us how the command menu can be worked to insert a Tip of the Day command at the top of the Help menu. Spend some time with the code to learn how to identify a submenu, locate its entries, add an entry if it is not there, and add new commands. It will reinforce everything we have learned about menus.

Finally, here you'll also find text file processing at work.

In conclusion, whereas Tip of the Day might not be something that you treasure highly, its programming educational value is immense.

35 Onscreen Help

We have now come to one of the most important topics toward a successful, professional application.

In this day and age, with applications getting increasingly complex, the user needs all the help he or she can get to be able to work with our software products, and onscreen help is an immediate resource when the user encounters a technical difficulty.

Onscreen help consists of a number of activities. Choosing the Help command from the program menu is one. Pressing the [F1] key when an object is in focus is another. MFC can help us in crafting supports for both, and we will learn how to do that in this chapter.

CONTEXT-SENSITIVE HELP

A Windows onscreen help system has many components. First, the onscreen help contents are provided by a .hlp help file apart from the program proper. This .hlp help file is actually compiled from a word processing *rich-text* (.rtf) file—the same one that can be edited using a Windows word processing program such as Microsoft's Word—with the help of linkage information that relates the help topics to their counterparts in the program. In fact, one of the most efficient ways to construct onscreen help contents is to use the Word program.

When you generate the framework of a new project using AppWizard and you elect to have context-sensitive help as we did in the **FormFiller** program, the essential component files needed to achieve onscreen help are generated for you. When you compile the application, instructions in the compiler automatically compile the help file for you as well. The files that are involved in the production of the help files are listed in Table 35.1.

TABLE 35.1 Help File Components

File	*Description*
*.rtf	Rich-text file containing the basic help contents plus reference code
*.hm	Mapping files that identify help topics with IDs
*.hpj	Help project file that organizes the related help components
*.cnt	Content file for the runtime onscreen help system

HELP ON MENU COMMANDS

ON THE CD

If you use Notepad to open the FormFiller.hm file in the hlp subfolder in the **FormFiller** project, you will see the following:

```
// Commands (ID_* and IDM_*)
HID_FORM                                    0x18003
HID_FORM_LABEL                              0x18004
HID_VIEW_PREFERENCES                        0x18005

// Prompts (IDP_*)

// Resources (IDR_*)
HIDR_MAINFRAME                              0x20080
HIDR_FORMFITYPE                             0x20081
```

etc.

These are the mapping code ID values used to uniquely identify the menu commands and dialog resources for the help files. In fact, they are all based on the original resource IDs. For example, HIDR_MAINFRAME is generated from the resource IDR_MAINFRAME. They are merely the resource IDs prefixed by an "H."

Use Word to open the AfxCore.rtf file in the hlp subfolder. If you display the file contents in Word's Layout view, you'll see the same Help IDs in the footnotes of the Help topic segments. These footnote entries are how the Help support items are matched up with the program items via the .hm mapping file.

As you develop your software program, it will take on more menu commands and dialogs. Their IDs will be converted into mapping Help IDs when you compile the program. This automatic activity is the result of a setting in the project.

Use the Project->Settings command to bring up the Project Settings dialog. Expand the Settings For tree branches and select the Resource.h file. You'll see the instructions for the generation of the .hm file based on the resource IDs in the program (Figure 35.1). As you can see, you don't have to worry about the generation of the menu command and dialog Help IDs.

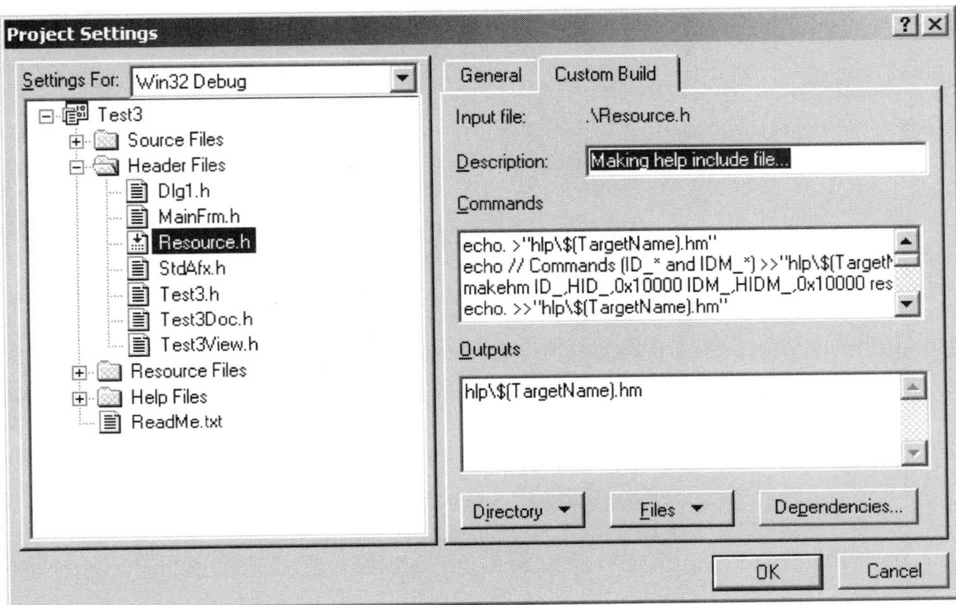

FIGURE 35.1 Project settings for .HM file generation,

PREPARING HELP CONTENTS

VC++ uses two rich-text files to support the Help system: AfxCore.rtf and, if the application is SDI or MDI based, AfxPrint.rtf. The second file contains general support for printing operations, and if your application does not provide printing support, this file can be ignored.

To understand the structure of the Help rich-text file, use Word to open the AfxCore.rtf file.

Go to any command segment, such as the Save command in the File menu, and you'll see the entry shown in Figure 35.2. The Help ID for context-sensitive help is footnoted by the # marker.

The entries under the $ footnote marker are topics for the Help Search feature. The K marker is used for the Index tab entries in the Help file.

#K $ **Save command (File menu)**

Use this command to save the active document to its current name and directory. When you save a document for the first time, <<YourApp>> displays the Save As dialog box so you can name your document. If you want to change the name and directory of an existing document before you save it, choose the Save As command.

Shortcuts
Toolbar: {bmc filesave.bmp}
Keys: CTRL+S

HID_FILE_SAVE
K files: managing
$ File Save command

FIGURE 35.2 A Help file entry.

The best approach to adding new Help segments in the rich-text file is to borrow from what is already there. For example, to add the Help support for the View-> Preferences command, first show the rich-text file in Normal View. Copy an entire segment from the topic, including the manual page break as shown in Figure 35.3. Then, promptly paste it in front of any topic segment. Once the copied segment is in place, edit the topic to reflect the new Help entry, and in Layout view, edit the

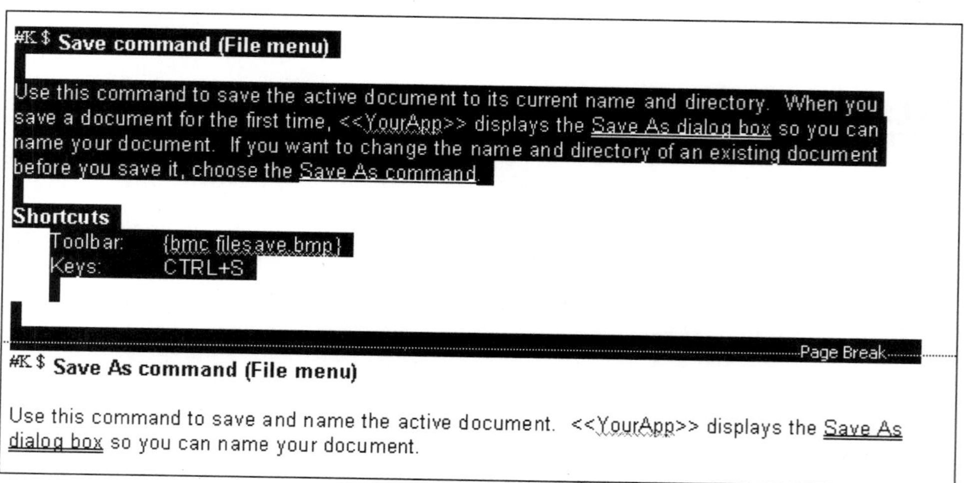
#K $ **Save command (File menu)**

Use this command to save the active document to its current name and directory. When you save a document for the first time, <<YourApp>> displays the Save As dialog box so you can name your document. If you want to change the name and directory of an existing document before you save it, choose the Save As command.

Shortcuts
Toolbar: {bmc filesave.bmp}
Keys: CTRL+S

Page Break

#K $ **Save As command (File menu)**

Use this command to save and name the active document. <<YourApp>> displays the Save As dialog box so you can name your document.

FIGURE 35.3 Selecting a Help entry.

footnote as well. You now have a functional entry in the Help file for the View->Preferences command.

Save the AfxCore.rtf file, close it, and then rebuild the entire application to ensure that all the components are fresh. To test your work, execute the application and use the keyboard to select (highlight) the View->Preferences command. When it is highlighted, press the [F1] key. You should see the Help topic for Preferences show up.

HELP WITH CONTROLS

To provide onscreen help for controls, the procedure is slightly more convoluted. This is because AppWizard hasn't built the Help message processing into the framework as it has with the menu commands and dialogs. However, the process of adding your own code is not at all daunting, just tedious. What follows is what you need to do.

First, we need Help IDs for the controls. We can define them ourselves in the code, but since VC++ has a built-in ID generator, why not use it?

The Help IDs are produced by a utility named MakeHm.exe as shown in Figure 35.1. There you see that ID_s are to be generated as HID_s, and IDM_s are to become HIDM_s. All we need to do is modify the command as shown here:

```
makehm ID_,HID_,0x10000 IDM_,HIDM_,0x10000 IDC_,HIDC_,0x10000
resource.h >>"hlp\$(TargetName).hm"
```

This way, control IDs with IDC_ prefixes in the Resource.h file would generate unique Help IDs with HIDC_s. Rebuild the project, and new Help IDs for controls will appear in the .hm file.

However, these Help IDs are unknown to the program, which needs to use them to coordinate with the Help system. Therefore, you need to copy these values and paste them into the control's source file.

As an example, in **FormFiller** we need to provide context-sensitive help for the controls in the CDlgEntry class. After producing Help IDs for the controls, copy those IDs from the FormFiller.hm file, paste them in the DlgEntry.cpp file, and precede the IDs with the "#define" meta command, such as:

```
#define     HIDC_EDIT_NAME          0x103E8
#define     HIDC_EDIT_ADDRESS       0x103E9
#define     HIDC_RADIO_WKDAYS       0x103EA
#define     HIDC_RADIO_WKENDS       0x103EB
#define     HIDC_RADIO_ALL          0x103EC
#define     HIDC_DATETIMEPICKER     0x103EF
#define     HIDC_EDIT_SALES_REP     0x103F0
```

For the CDlgEntry class, use ClassWizard to generate a handler function for the WM_HELPINFO Windows message, and then add code to it as follows:

```
static     DWORD  HelpID[] =
{
     IDC_EDIT_NAME,          HIDC_EDIT_NAME,
     IDC_EDIT_ADDRESS,       HIDC_EDIT_ADDRESS,
     IDC_RADIO_WKDAYS,       HIDC_RADIO_WKDAYS,
     IDC_RADIO_WKENDS,       HIDC_RADIO_WKENDS,
     IDC_RADIO_ALL,          HIDC_RADIO_ALL,
     IDC_DATETIMEPICKER,     HIDC_DATETIMEPICKER,
     IDC_EDIT_SALES_REP,     HIDC_EDIT_SALES_REP,
     0, 0,
};

extern     CFormFillerApp theApp;
BOOL CDlgEntry::OnHelpInfo(HELPINFO* pHelpInfo)
{
     // TODO: Add your message handler code here…
     ::WinHelp( (HWND) pHelpInfo->hItemHandle,
          theApp.m_pszHelpFilePath,
          HELP_WM_HELP,
          (DWORD) HelpID
          );
     return TRUE;
     // return CDialog::OnHelpInfo(pHelpInfo);
}
```

The DWORD array collects the ID translation pairs. In each pair, the first ID is the control resource ID. The second is the Help ID for the control. By rule, the last pair must be a pair of zeros.

In the *OnHelpInfo()* function, the SDK's *WinHelp()* function is called. Although MFC has its own CWinApp *WinHelp()* function, that function processes a single ID. Here we have one *OnHelpInfo()* function for all the controls in the Dialog class; we need to use the SDK version, which is signified by the "::" prefix.

The *::WinHelp()* function takes four parameters. The first is a handle to the window requesting help. The second is the path of the help file. The third is the type of help requested. HELP_WM_HELP asks for a display of the controls' help in a pop-up window. The fourth is the list of DWORD ID data.

When all is said and done, this is just the way it must be done.

If you have all the control help segments properly created in the AfxCore.rtf file and you rebuild the project, the [F1] key will work on all the controls in the data entry window.

Help Contents

The AfxCore.rtf file is a generic file containing general contents that will fit all applications generated through AppWizard. It is up to you to customize it to suit your application. As you have seen, you must add entries to support your program's custom commands and controls. Then, you should remember to do at least two more things.

First, you need to replace all the occurrences of the general text "<<Your App>>" with the name of your program. You also need to supply your own descriptions for all the text enclosed by "<<>>." The program will look silly if these generic markers are left in the Help system.

The second thing you should do is remove all the entries that don't apply to your program. For example, if your program does not offer the Window->New command, take it out of the Help system so it won't show up.

You can use these "deadbeat" entries to your advantage. Because the formatting is already in, simply edit them to support your program's special controls. However, you must be careful in handling the index and search items, as they are contextually sensitive. You don't want your users to search for things that have nothing to do with the system and find them.

Also, pay attention to the double-underscored entries in the .rtf files. These are links; that is, you can click on them and jump to target locations. Use Word's "show hidden text" option to show the targets and edit them appropriately. If you aren't familiar with the Word program, it won't take you long to find out what they do by trial and error or through simple experimentations.

THE CNT FILE

In Windows' Help system, there is a file with the extension .cnt. This is the contents file. Open the FormFiller.cnt file (by double-clicking the mouse on it) with Microsoft Help Workshop and you will see the Help system's "Table of Contents" presented as shown in Figure 35.4. The contents file contains the opening page that appears when the user chooses the Help->Help Topics command of your program.

On this page, you should find two major entries: Menus, and your own special content category.

The Menus section already has the major menu items in. All you need to do is select one such as File, click Edit, and you'll see that the topic target is "menu_file". By emulating what already has been constructed for you, you can implement your own Help categories. Even if you don't plan to offer anything extra or fancy, at the least you should delete all those items that don't apply.

Many developers prefer to use expensive commercial Help construction software packages to construct their Help files. These utility programs are loaded with

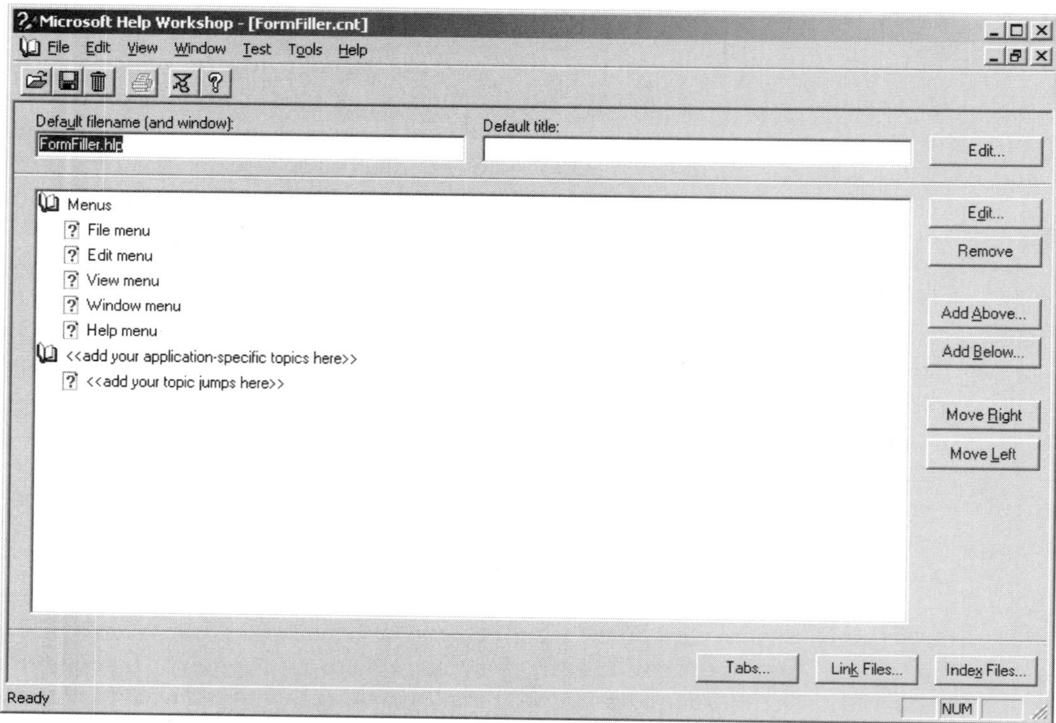

FIGURE 35.4 The Microsoft Help Workshop.

capabilities that can assist you in creating fanciful features, from pop-up windows to image maps. They also can be costly, ranging into the thousands of dollars. At any rate, at the end of the day, all the true bells and whistles don't count if the finished product isn't functional.

With all the lavish automation we put into our programs and Help support elements, the best Help facility that you can offer the users is a Help system that works, and that means more than just no program bugs. A good Help system is one in which pertinent program topics have entries built for them and they can actually be found. When they are found, the explanations are presented in simple English and are understandable to a typical user. The Word program is good enough to do all the real work required.

36 Program Installation and Distribution

At last, you have a viable, finished product. However, do realize that the product only works on *your* machine—the developmental platform. You now must make sure that the product works on a user's machine as well.

A commercial software product must be thoroughly tested and ultimately packaged for distribution. It is assumed that you have done your share of testing during your development effort, following standard procedures such as unit and stress testing, and that the application is free of bugs to the best of your knowledge. Therefore, the program is now ready for distribution.

Software distribution in the most general sense is nothing more than gathering all the pertinent files of the product and organizing them into a single unit that facilitates its physical delivery and installation on the user's machine.

The files can be compressed or not. File compression is but a means of compacting the delivery package. What is important is the management of the files so that none is missed when delivered and installed, that the files are installed in the correct locations, and that they execute as intended.

The installed files must not conflict with the client machine configuration as to create problem for the system. This means that the files from your product should be compatible with those on the user machine, and that older versions will not accidentally overwrite newer ones. This also means carefully entering information about your product in the client machine's Windows registry.

Although we can program all these activities—and we have the wherewithal to do so now—the task of preparing software product distribution from scratch can be overwhelming. There are commercial software installation packages for doing this, and you should use them to package your software.

One of the most prominent competitors in the software distribution and installation market is InstallShield®, and a version of the utility is bundled with VC++

Enterprise Edition. In the remainder of the chapter, we'll learn to use this special edition of InstallShield to prepare our software product for release.

RELEASE COMPILATION

Before you use InstallShield to create a distribution package, you must produce a final release version of your product. This is a simple matter of changing the compilation mode from debug to release as in Figure 36.1.

FIGURE 36.1 Setting the compilation mode.

However, if you have been modifying the project settings in the Debug environment during your program development, you must make sure that those same settings are applied to the release environment as well. This means that you need to go into Project->Settings and make sure that "Settings for" is set for "Release," and that all the settings therein are correct. Then, to ensure that you have not missed any module in recompiling, simply use Rebuild All to compile the program's release version.

The release version of the .exe product is much smaller than the debug version, because debugging information is excluded in the final binary code. You should find this version in the Release subfolder of the project.

USING INSTALLSHIELD

The InstallShield version that comes with VC++ is simple to use. The result, however, is very powerful. We'll package the finished **FormFiller** program for illustration using InstallShield.

1. Start up InstallShield.
2. When InstallShield is up, double-click on the Project Wizard icon (Figure 36.2) to execute it.

The Welcome dialog that appears (Figure 36.3) allows you to provide high-level information for the project. Under Application Name you should enter the

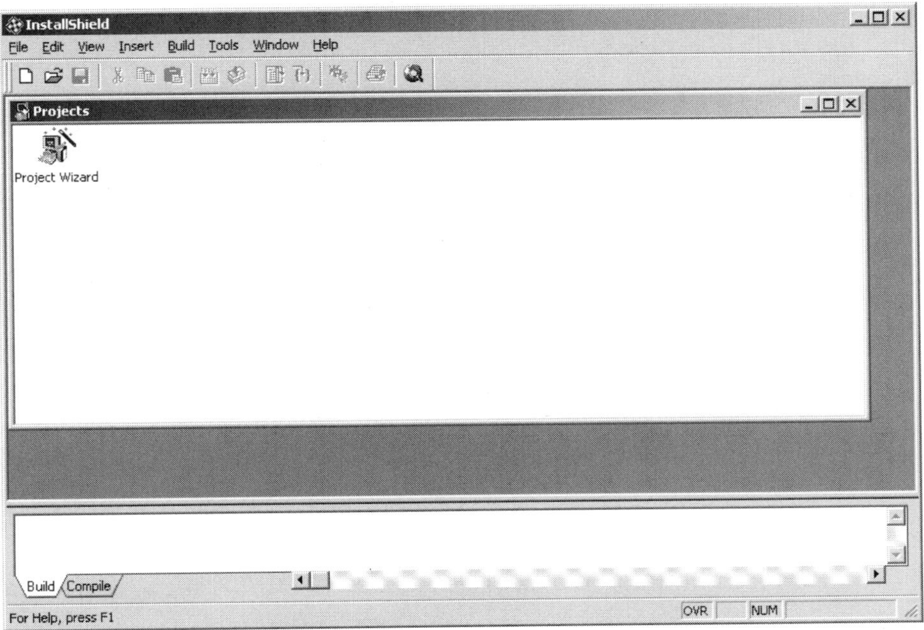

FIGURE 36.2 The InstallShield main window.

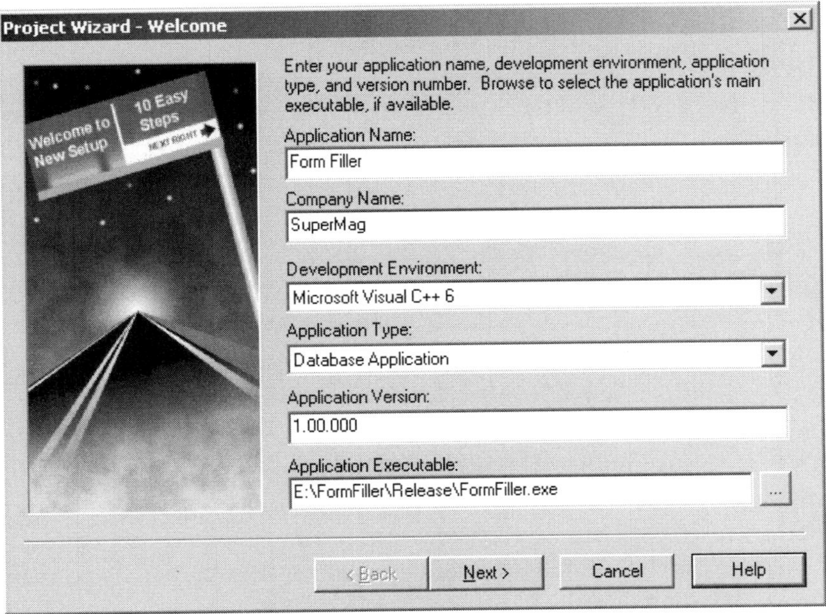

FIGURE 36.3 InstallShield project Welcome screen.

Windows registry key name for the software product. Under Application Executable, browse and select the main .exe file of your product. The remaining items are not important.

3. Fill in the Welcome form and move to the next step, in which you get to choose the installation screens and options that you want to provide the user (Figure 36.4).

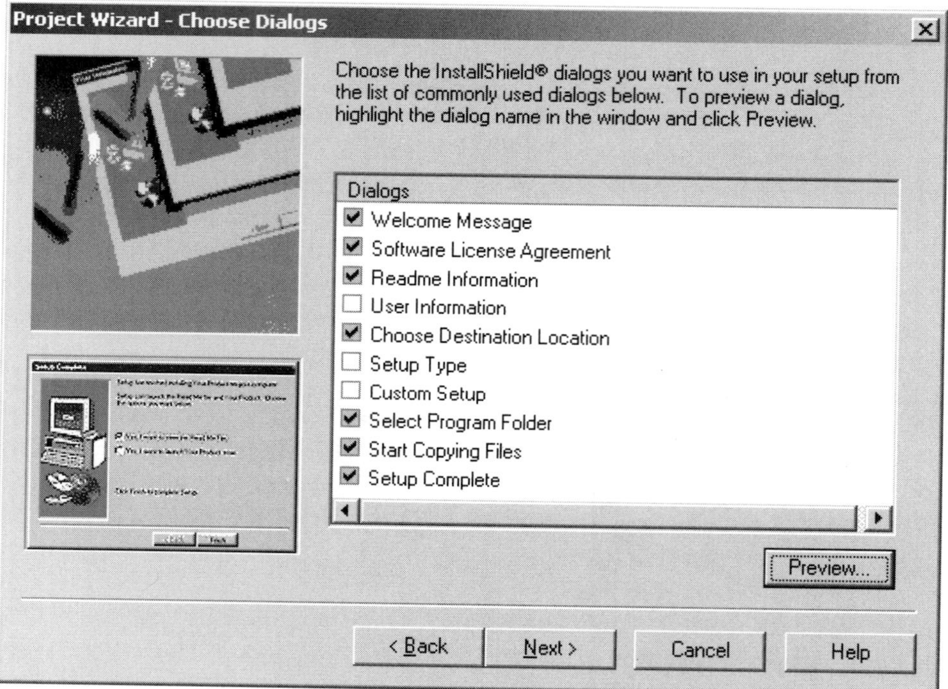

FIGURE 36.4 InstallShield project dialog selection.

Many of the information pages such as Welcome Message are stock and you don't have to do anything about them. You'll have to supply your custom documents for those that are specific to your product.

You don't have to use all the pages if they don't apply to you. For example, unless you will use the user's information in your software, there is no reason to ask for User Information.

The same goes for Setup Type. Don't include it if you're not providing different setups for different environments.

Custom Setup is another unnecessary option. In any case, for each page you can use the Review button to see what that page would look like.

4. Click Next to go to Target Platforms, which you can skip through. Also move past Languages and Setup Types.
5. In the Specify Components step, select and remove any component that you don't need. For example, we aren't providing any example files, so Example Files goes.
6. In Specify File Groups, remove Program DLLs and Example Files because our project doesn't use any of these.

The differences between components and file groups will be clear shortly.

7. After reviewing the summary, click Finish to complete the wizard steps to reach the InstallShield IDE (Figure 36.5).

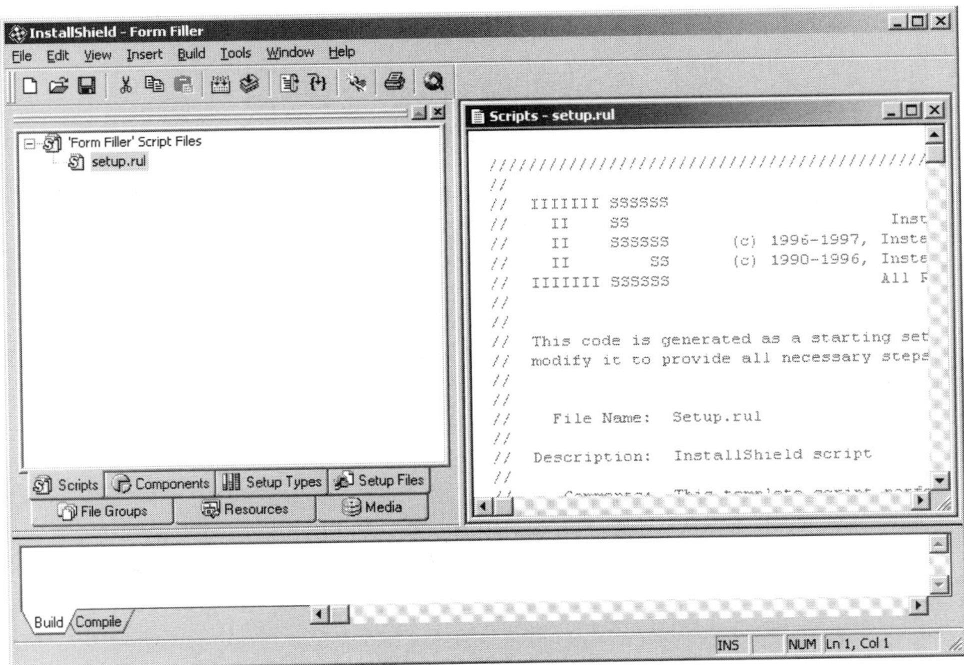

FIGURE 36.5 InstallShield IDE.

Resources

The first thing you do in customizing your installation project is to make certain that the basic resources used are correct.

1. Select the Resource tab and the entry for English under String Table (Figure 36.6). Edit the contents if necessary.

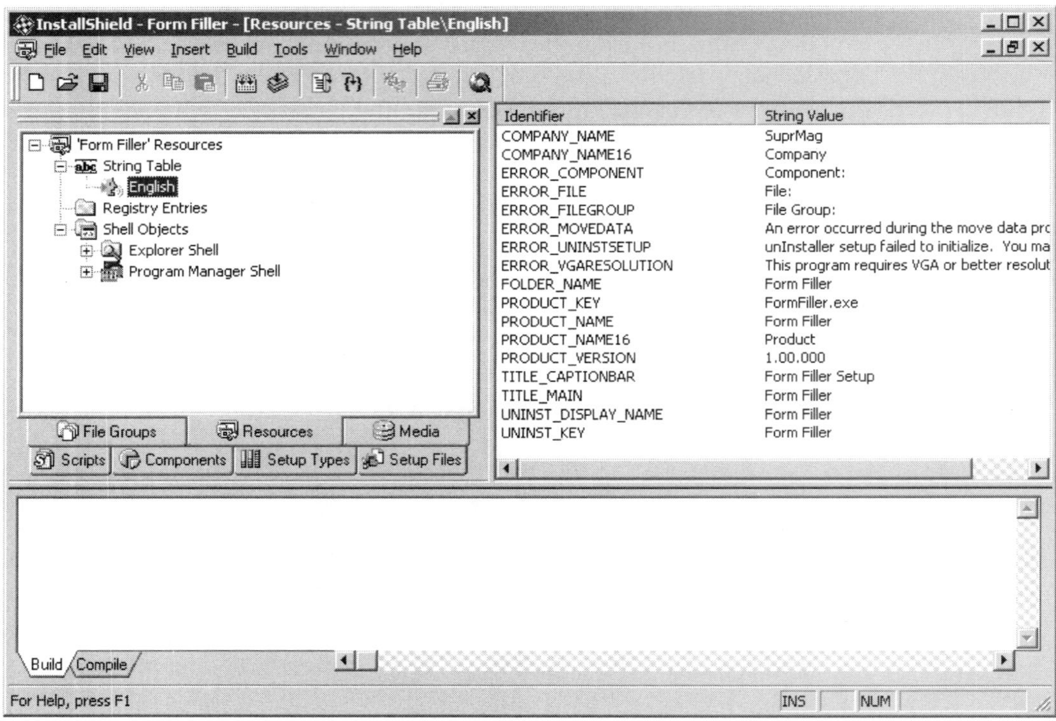

FIGURE 36.6 InstallShield project resources.

The Strings resources will be used in titles, messages, and other displays and identifications. The ones with the "16" suffix are for the 16-bit platforms such as Windows 3.1. Otherwise, errors in them will not have fatal impact.

Setup Types

The Setup Types pane lists the types of setup that you're providing. The categorization allows you to selectively install files. For example, in a compact installation you might not want to install the Help files to save disk space. Check and uncheck the file groups for each setup type as appropriate.

Setup Files

In the Setup Files pane, provide any auxiliary external files that might be needed for the installation.

Splash Screen

The installation process displays a splash screen, and here is where you can provide your own design.

In the Setup Files pane, you should find an entry named Splash Screen. In it are two versions, one for Language Independent and one for English. Select the one for Language Independent and there should be a file named setup.bmp. Use the right mouse button to bring up its Property page where you will find the setup.bmp file's physical location. Go there and replace it with your own splash screen file.

License

The installation license is listed under Operating System Independent, which is under Language Independent. Again, remove the generic version and provide your own.

Information

Likewise, update the Infolist.txt file to produce your own general information.

Components

Components are groupings that have unique installation criteria, such as destination directory and file-overwrite conditions.

1. Select the Components pane and fill in the values as shown in Figure 36.7. For each value, you can click the right mouse button and read about what it is used for.

In this pane, several values are important.

First, the Overwrite value should be set correctly to avoid writing over existing files. For example, if a user gets hold of an older software version of your program, do you want an existing, later version to be overwritten?

To set the Overwrite value, double-click on it to bring up the Property dialog (Figure 36.8) and select from it.

<TARGETDIR> stands for the directory where the program will be installed. During installation, the user will determine what this will be. This directory will be created if it does not exist, and you don't have to know at this time what it is.

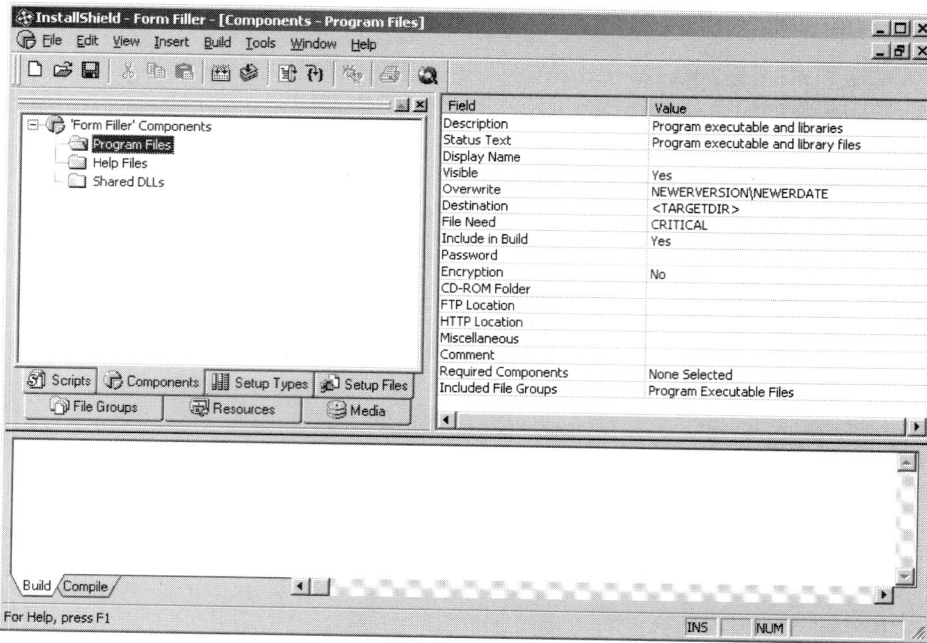

FIGURE 36.7 InstallShield components.

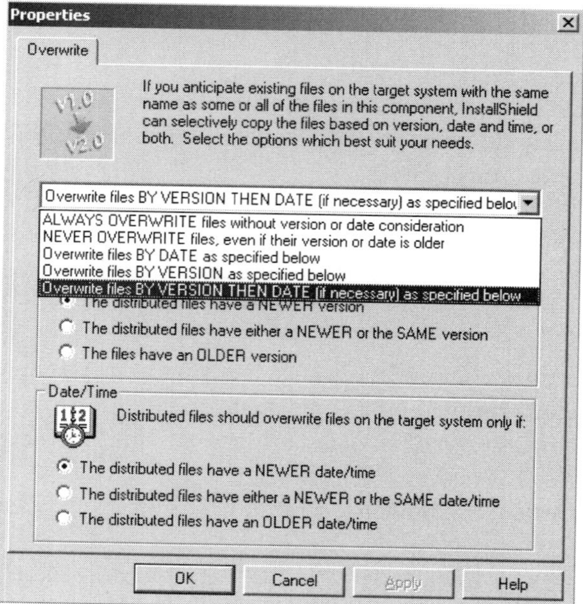

FIGURE 36.8 Setting overwrite criteria in InstallShield.

TABLE 36.1 Program Installation File Destinations

Components	***Destination***	***Include File Group***
Program Files	< TARGETDIR>	Program Executable
Help Files	< TARGETDIR >	Help files
Shared DLLs	< WINSYSDIR>	Shared DLLs

The values for Components destinations should be as summarized in Table 36.1.

To specify the Include File Groups, double-click on the value and click Add to select the file group to add.

File Groups

In File Groups, you collect files that should be installed as one unit into a group.

You might be wondering, if there are components, why should there be groups? The reason for the apparent dual classification is that they are not always in direct correspondence with each other. For example, although program executables and Help files go to the same place, in different installation types one might not be included, such as the Compact case described previously.

1. Switch to the Files Group pane and expand the Links as shown in Figure 36.9.

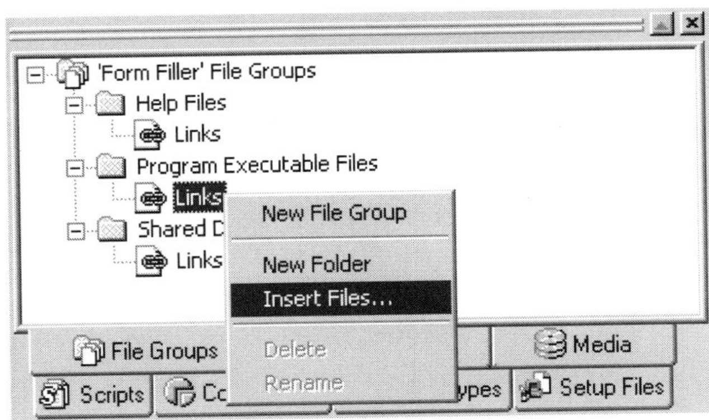

FIGURE 36.9 InstallShield file group links.

The Links are where you specify the files to be included in the file groups.

2. Select a Links entry, click the right mouse button to bring up the context menu (Figure 36.9), and choose Insert files. Select the appropriate files and insert them in the respective folders as specified in Table 36.1.

TABLE 36.1 FormFiller File Groups

Folder	*Files*
Program Executables	FormFiller.exe
Help files	FormFiller.hlp, FormFiller.cnt, Tips.txt
Shared DLLs	Msvcrt.dll, Mfc42.dll

The shared DLLs are on the VC++ installation CD-ROM. InstallShield also supplies them in its own program directory. If you don't have these sources, a simple file search should reveal the whereabouts of these files on your system. You should have working copies of these files in your Windows systems directory, such as C:\WINNT\system32.

Msvcrt.dll is the VC++ runtime library. Mfc42.dll is the MFC link library. You need these for your VC++ executables unless they have been statically linked to the finished program.

The Self-Registered field lets you specify whether the files in a group self-register in Windows registry. If the field is set to No, InstallShield will register them for you. Typically, OLE servers self-register. Other file types, including OCXs and DLLs, must be explicitly registered. In short, if a file needs to be registered but you mistakenly indicated that it self-registers, the installation will result in error. Generally speaking, set this field to No if you're unsure.

You should now understand that the Components specify the overwrite policy and file installation locations, while file Groups specify the files to be collected into groups for the components. Therefore, even if some files go into the same destination directory, if their overwrite policies are different, they should be organized as different groups.

Before you leave this pane, make sure that you have not missed anything, including any commercial OCXs that your application employs, and any associated license files that must be present.

At this time, we must address an issue that has plagued many a good developer: How do we know what files to include? The dilemma exists because the application uses controls, and the developer has no idea what the files are behind these controls.

There are three aspects to this matter.

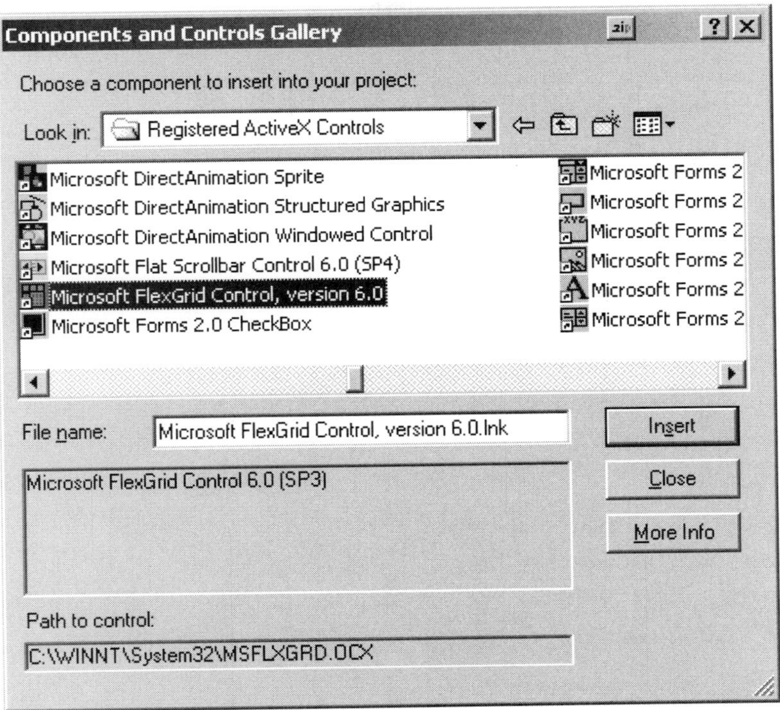

FIGURE 36.10 Identifying component file sources.

First, the developer should be responsible for the files involved in the application proper. In other words, you should know which .exe, .dll, .hlp, .cnt, .txt, and other files are directly used by the application. After all, you developed them.

Next, you should know which third-party tools you have employed in your project, and therefore what files must be included. If you have used commercial third-party software, its manuals should spell out what files (such as .ocx) should be included and stored where.

If you used one of the registered components offered by VC++ via the Project->Add to Project facility, you often can obtain information on the necessary files to include through the process itself. For example, Figure 36.10 shows you the location of the third-party software (pay attention to the "Path to control" caption).

Finally, there are support files that are normally "transparent" to the developer. Database support is a typical example. These files are documented to a certain extent in the VC++ language manuals, although they are not well organized. Fortunately, InstallShield has provided valuable assistance toward this end.

An alternate way to starting an InstallShield project is to build the project based on an applicable template. You do this by starting the project with File->New

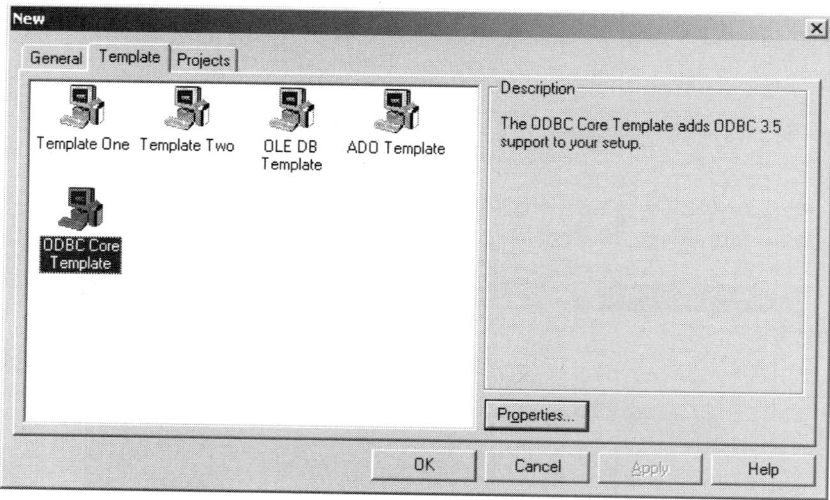

FIGURE 36.11 InstallShield templates.

rather than Project Wizard (Figure 36.11). When you start a project this way, the basic support files are already compiled for you (see Figures 36.12 and 36.13).

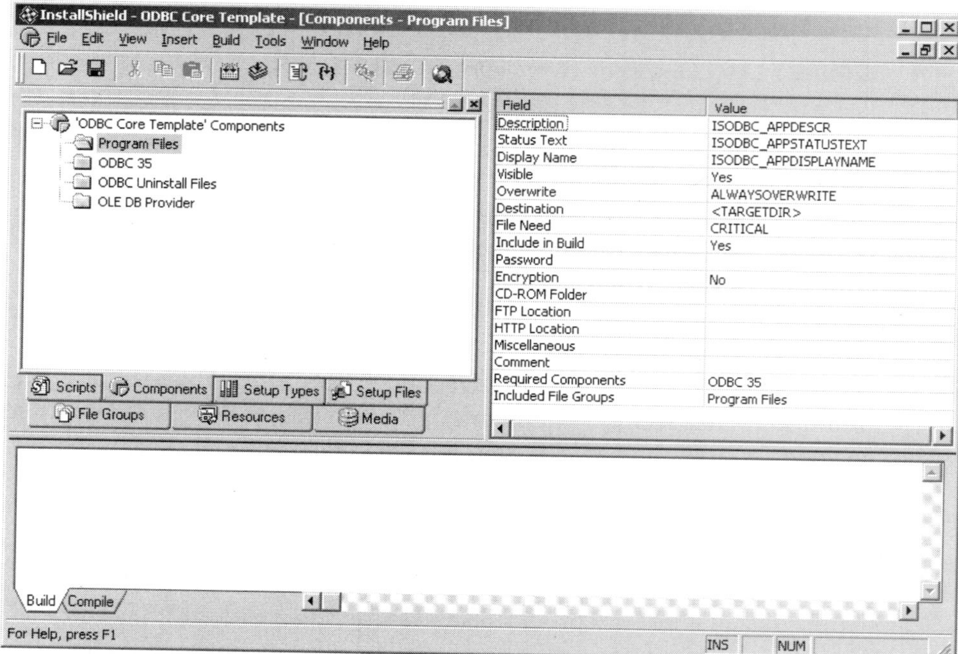

FIGURE 36.12 InstallShield-provided component settings.

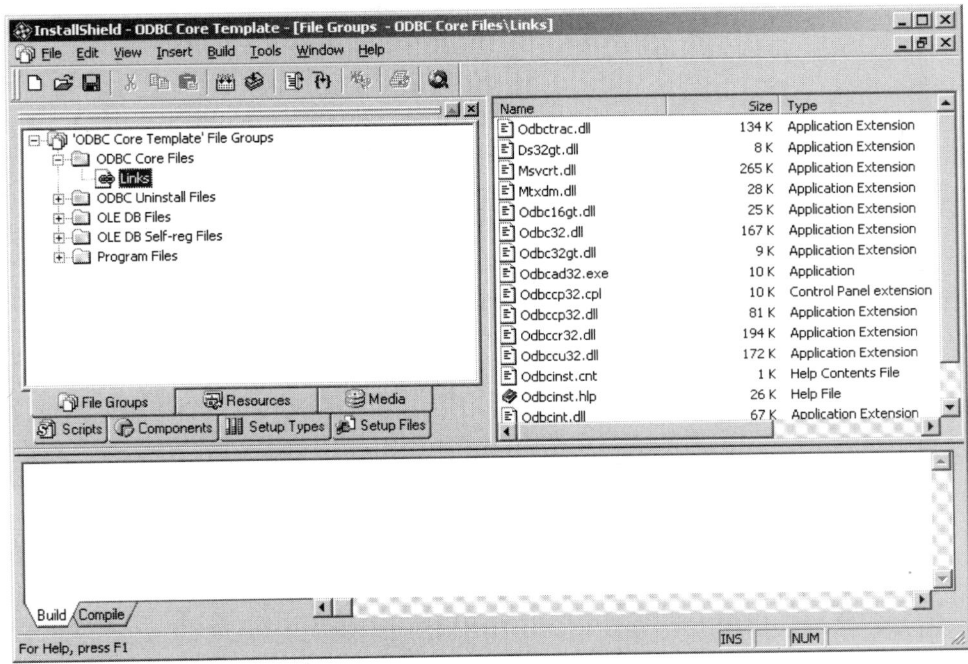

FIGURE 36.13 InstallShield-identified file components.

Ultimately, if you have missed a crucial file that would render the application dysfunctional, you will pick it up during the test runs after a trial installation. Run-time messages will inform you of the absent files.

Scripts

At last, let us turn to the Scripts pane in InstallShield's IDE (Figure 36.5).

If you browse through the scripts, you'll see immediately that InstallShield has its own programming language. It is outside the scope of this book to discuss InstallShield programming in any detail. However, with a little study you should be able to pick up on the logic, as the language syntax is similar to that of C and C++. For illustration, we'll demonstrate how you create a file folder for the application.[1]

[1] This step should be omitted if you're distributing an OCX or DLL, such as for an Internet server installation.

1. Locate the *SetupFolders()* function in Scripts and enter the following script:

```
function SetupFolders()
 NUMBER nResult;
 STRING szCommandLine;
 begin
  // TODO : Add all your folder (program group)…
  nResult = CreateShellObjects( “” );
  szCommandLine = TARGETDIR ^ “FormFiller.exe”;
  LongPathToQuote ( szCommandLine , TRUE );
  return nResult;
 end;
```

2. Immediately after the *LongPathToQuote()* function, use the right mouse button to bring up the context menu, and choose the Function Wizard command.
3. Select the **AddFolderIcon** function name and move to Step 2 of the Function wizard.
4. Fill in the parameter list as in Figure 36.14 and click Finish to complete the wizardry.

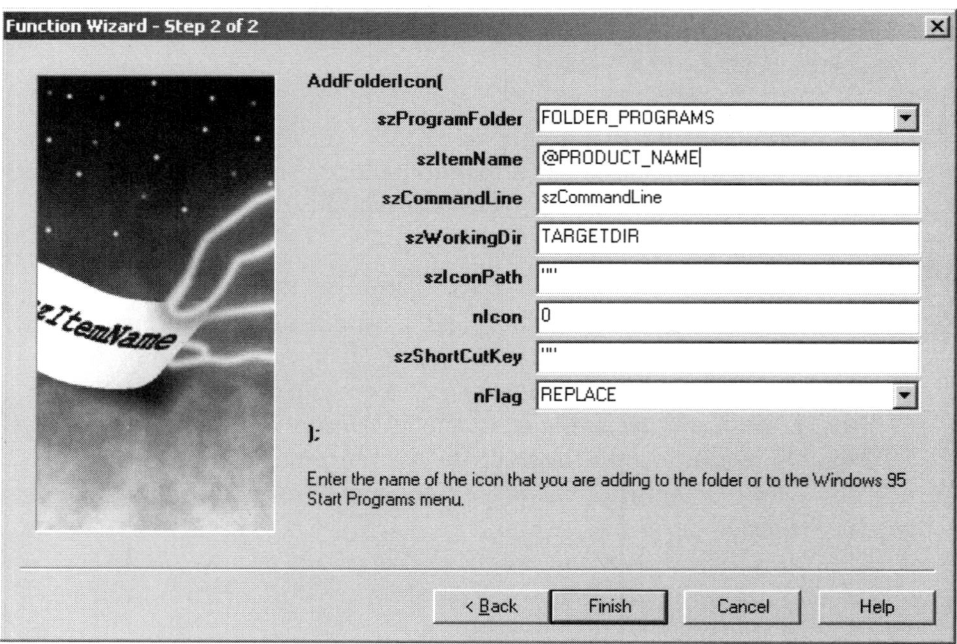

FIGURE 36.14 InstallShield Function wizard.

You should have the following code line:

```
AddFolderIcon ( FOLDER_PROGRAMS , @PRODUCT_NAME , szCommandLine ,
TARGETDIR , "" , 0 , "" , REPLACE );
```

This line will add a "Form Filler" entry to the Windows Start->Programs command listing.

If you want an icon for **FormFiller** on the desktop, duplicate the code line and change FOLDER_PROGRAMS to FOLDER_DESKTOP.

One last thing before proceeding to build the distribution files: use the Edit->Find command to locate the string "Place the summary here." Change it to say what you want to say in the "Start Copying File" step.

We're now ready to create the distribution media.

Building Distribution Files

When all is set, you can build the distribution media—the distribution disks—unless you're distributing via Internet.

1. Choose the Build->Media Build Wizard command.
2. Enter an appropriate Media Name such as "3.5 Inch Diskettes," and click Next.
3. Select the appropriate media type, and click Next.
4. Select the Full Build type, and click Next.
5. Perfect the contents for a tag file, which will be included in the distribution, and move to the next wizard step.
6. Check the platforms and go to the next step.
7. Review the summary and finish the wizard process.

Creating Distribution Media

When you're ready to distribute, you'll create the actual distribution media, which, in this case, are diskettes.

1. Choose the Build->Send Media To command to activate the Media Build wizard.
2. Select the "3.5 Inch Diskettes" media name and move to the next wizard step.
3. Select a destination, such as to the actual diskettes. (If you send the results to a hard disk folder, you can still copy the folder contents out to diskettes yourself.)
4. Follow through with the wizard until the distribution media is created.

Testing the Distribution Package

For the **FormFiller** project, you should have a disk1 in either a diskette or a directory on your hard disk at the end, depending on your option in the Send Media To operation.

In any case, use Windows' Start->Run command to execute the Setup.exe file and check the installation process, making sure everything you specified occurs, including the display messages and the folders and icons created.

Look in the program folder and see if all the program files are there. If anything is missing, return to InstallShield, correct it, recompile the setup, and regenerate the distribution media.

When all works correctly, use Windows' Settings->Control Panel->Add/Remove Programs utility to remove your installed application. Afterward, go into the registry (RegEdit.exe) and search for any remnants of the application to ensure that the uninstall operation is clean.

Finally, find a representative client machine and test install your application there. When the test passes, you can distribute your software product with confidence.

PART IX Beyond VC++ 6.0

In every sense of the word, the subjects of VC++ and MFC are formidable. Yes, at this point we have completed the subject matters set down for this book. We have run the gamut, ranging from using the VC++ rapid application development environment to quickly flesh out feature-rich application frameworks, to packaging and delivering professional-quality finished software products. We covered pivotal topics such as modal and modeless dialogs, and intricate issues such as constructing ActiveX controls and DLLs. While all are essential to application development in VC++ using MFC, much more have been excluded from the limiting scope of 600 pages by necessity.

As *foundation classes* for the Microsoft Windows products, MFC covers a lot of ground. Although this book attempts to explain those software development elements that form the core of any Windows applications—desktop, client-server, Internet, Web components, and otherwise—to excel in any particular area of specialization, much remains to be investigated.

MFC is a huge library. As the cornerstone of Microsoft products, it hosts resources that encompass virtually the entire requirement set of Windows software development. To address each and every aspect in every detail would require a book of literally tens of thousands of pages. The official reference materials span six volumes, each over 1000 pages in length. What this book provides is the scaffold, so to speak, on which the building of specialization can be erected.

For the aspiring software developer, where does one go after this book? You can approach the answer by specializing within VC++ or by taking what you have learned to new Microsoft technologies. In the remaining chapters, we'll attempt to map out the strategies.

37 Current VC++ and MFC Applications

Focusing on VC++ and MFC, your next step might be to look into those library supports that can enable a programmer to attain expert status in a particular field of specialization. For example, this book has stayed out of the realm of graphic data manipulation and mouse command processing, two important areas that are central to successfully coding computer games.

There is a reason for this omission: not all developers aspire to be game developers. If games programming is your primary field of interest, those member functions in the CDC class, such as *Chord()*, *MaskBlt()*, and *StretchBlt()*, and the CBitmap class, just to name a few, might be prime targets of your exploration. In fact, let a book dedicated to the particulars of electronic game programming be your guide.

Where you want to go is therefore purely a matter of personal choice.

VC++ AND CLIENT/SERVER SYSTEMS

One area of specialization that you might want to consider is client/server systems. This is because these systems are widely deployed in the business world, and from a career opportunity standpoint, they warrant serious attention.

Client/server systems range from desktop applications to networked enterprise solutions with or without database support. This is a huge area of study. If your main professional undertakings are desktop oriented, as most client systems are, you will likely be interested in OLE and all the COle classes that have been designed for it.

For the network specialist, those classes that have to do with communication, such as CAsyncSocket, will be fertile research grounds. In addition, don't ignore the software development kits for all the communicational protocols.

Database mavens will have a field day with the abundant entries that include CDao, ADO, and the many recordset classes. Of course, don't forget COM, DCOM, and Microsoft's Transaction Server either.

VC++ AND THE WEB

If your field of play is the Internet at large, you certainly want to treat yourself to the CFtp, CGopher, CHtml, CHttp, and CInternet classes. By the way, one View class that we didn't spend time on, the CHtmlView class, can get you a functional browser in less than half an hour.

Because the Internet increasingly uses *live* data, a componentized approach to database interaction might be a strong candidate for your attention. This means VC++'s handling of COM and DCOM objects, and the programming of Microsoft's Transaction Server.

Although the Internet community is predominantly preoccupied with VB-Script and JavaScript to augment or supplement HTML and XML, when it comes to efficiency, C++ is very much a workhorse to fall back on.

DEVICE DRIVERS AND ONBOARD APPLICATIONS

If you view the Microsoft school of technologies as your primary field of recreation, the possibilities are far and wide. C, C++, and VC++ and MFC are applied from the PC to hand-held devices and beyond.

You can become a whiz in device drivers and secure the next 10 years of your professional life. You can concentrate on embedded (onboard) software alone and will hardly find it lacking in challenges both professionally and academically.

In the summer of 2001, job requisitions for device driver programmers for printers dominate the opportunities for VC++ programmers in Orange County, California, the "Silicon Valley of the South."

WINDOWS SDK

During the early Windows days, there was no such a thing as MFC. Windows programmers relied on a software library called the SDK, or *Software Development Kit*, to design their applications. When OOP (*Object Oriented Programming*) came along, Microsoft decided to switch over to the new philosophy and began wrapping the SDK functions in an attempt to organize the functions into a class library. It was codenamed Afx.

In our study, we have come across many instances of the "Afx" prefix. In fact, if you were to refer to the online help references and turn to the Index pane, you would see all types of references to Afx-specific functions and topics (Figure 37.1). These functions number in the thousands, which is why you should hardly attempt to memorize them all, and why this book emphasizes a programming framework—state of mind, if you will—as opposed to learning by memorizing.

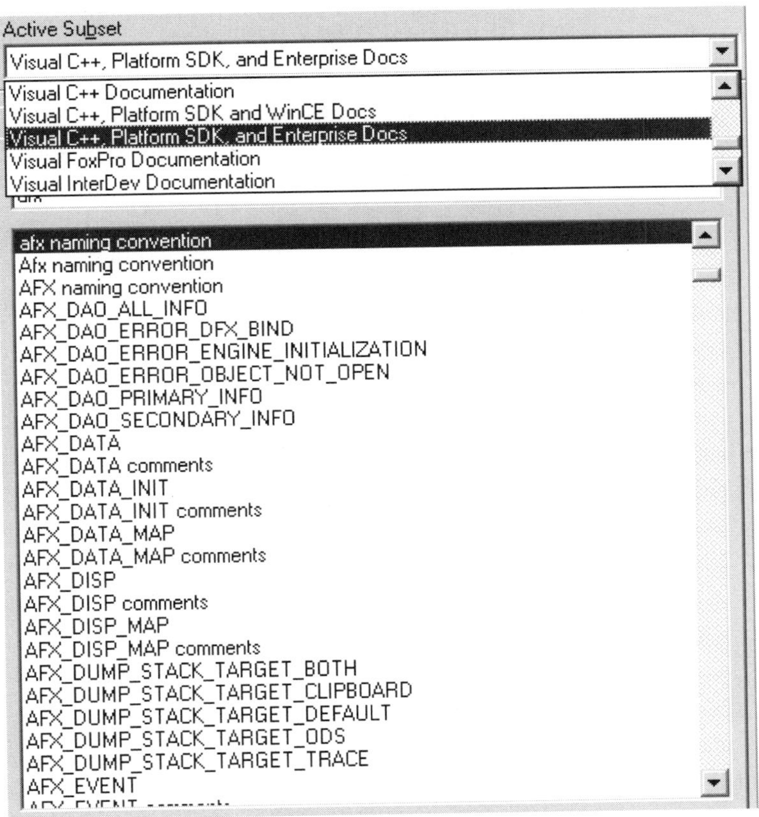

FIGURE 37.1 MSDN platform SDK references.

Not only are these functions numerous, many of them are not even in the current MFC, which is in a way why VC++ with MFC is difficult to learn. One must constantly return to the "old days" to find what is needed to get something done. For example, one of the first functions you learned in this book is the *MessageBox()* function. Well, good news to you: this function is a CWnd member function, and won't work in a non-CWnd derived class. So, how would you pop up a message box when you're in CWinApp? You use the *AfxMessageBox()* function instead.

If you're new to Windows C++ programming, there's a lot of work to do going back in time.

Along with the Windows SDK there are all sorts of "DKs" designed for different application purposes. These "kits" are constantly being developed, and hardly any of them are getting into MFC because of the sheer volume.

For instance, if you wish to cash in on the lucrative device driver development market, you'll need to understand DDK, or *Driver Development Kits*.

The different kits developed for different applications are just too numerous to cite. Your MSDN or Microsoft's Web site are good reference sources for them.

38 VisualStudio.NET

Yet another approach to specialization after learning VC++ and MFC is to look forward to new Microsoft technologies. After surveying the technologies of the past, we can ask ourselves, "What new frontiers lie ahead?" For this, we must mention .NET, the new software development initiative from Microsoft.

WHAT IS .NET?

In short, .NET is Microsoft's grand-scale effort to unify its software technologies.

Computer languages are developed to satisfy different computing needs. The result, unfortunately, can be overwhelming for developers—computer languages and platforms that are so numerous and diverse that virtually no one person can learn all that there is to learn, and enterprise solutions so non-homogeneous that hardly any one works effectively and smoothly. The implication of this on the computing industry is duplicated efforts and coding inefficiency.

With .NET, Microsoft attempts to create a common intermediate software layer that all languages get compiled to, resulting in a code base that transcends language barrier.

Imagine developing software in Visual Basic and compiling the source code to—instead of a final executable—a "semi" compiled version of a code library that, coincidentally, has the same format as one that might have been compiled from a VC++ source code. The inference is that one can now create code libraries that are language independent.

To achieve this, not only must the internal structures of the languages be reworked, but the classes behind them also must be reorganized. For the MFC student, this means there will be new classes and functions to explore, and new languages to learn.

THE .NET MICROSOFT DEVELOPMENT ENVIRONMENT

Besides language unification, .NET has promised a new, unified development environment as well. In the new VisualStudio.NET, one can select different languages to work with all in the same environment. Figure 38.1 shows what the opening window of the new VisualStudio.NET looks like.

In .NET, there also will be two new VC++ versions to support all these new features: a VC++ 7.0, which extends the current 6.0 version, and a "Managed" VC++ version, which will be compliant with the new .NET standards. Your continuing education therefore will include learning to work with a new IDE that is more like

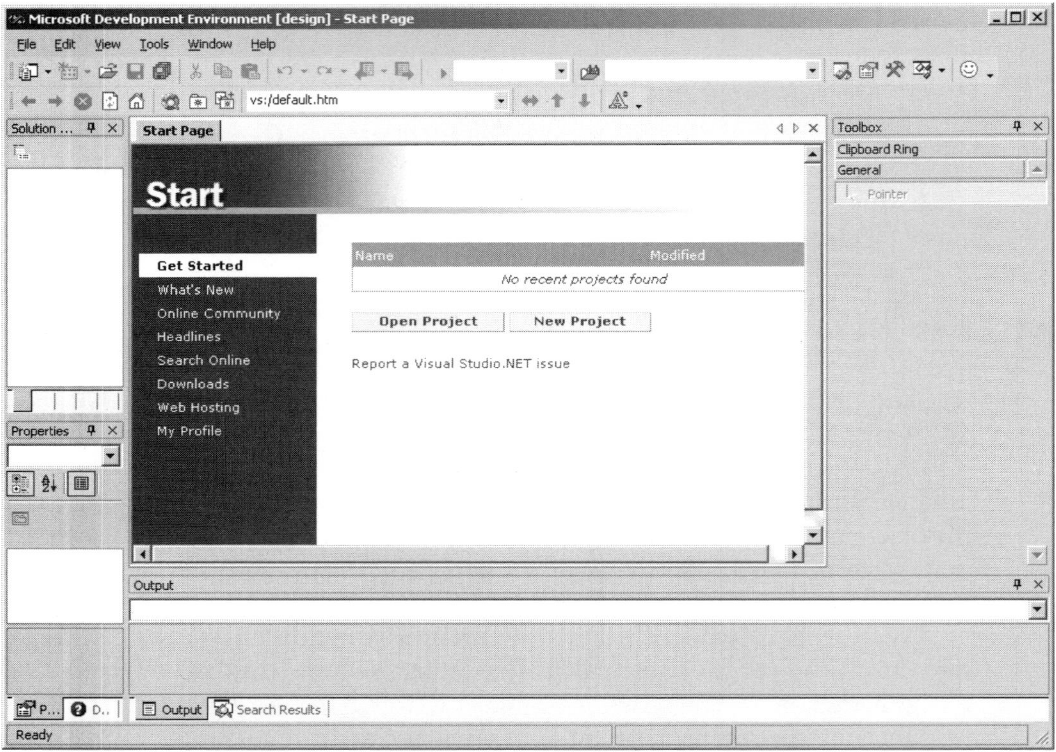

FIGURE 38.1 VisualStudio.NET start window.

the current VB IDE on top of the new features, and at least two new VC++ versions—and the new IDE is definitely different from the current one.

To begin, starting a new programming project now requires you to determine what language to use as in Figure 38.2, because you now have one integrated environment for all languages. Once you decide on the language, you select the template to use and assign a project name (Figure 38.3), and you're on your way to a new .NET project.

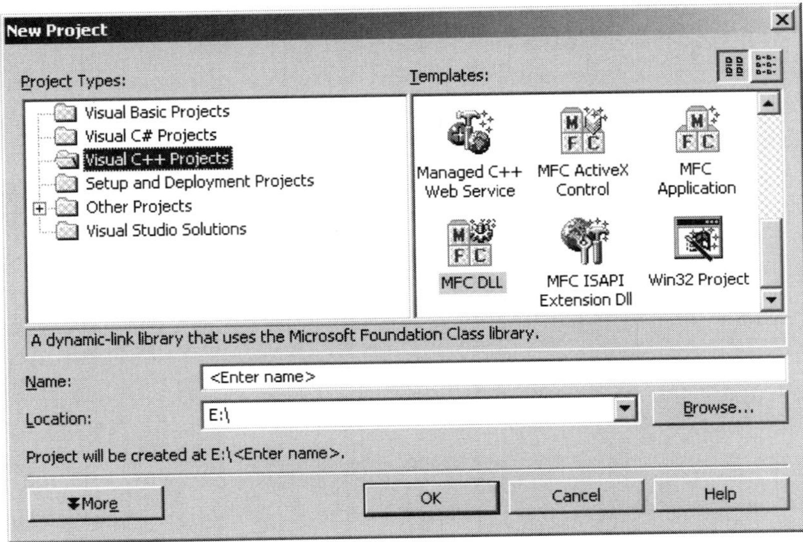

FIGURE 38.2 The .NET New Project window.

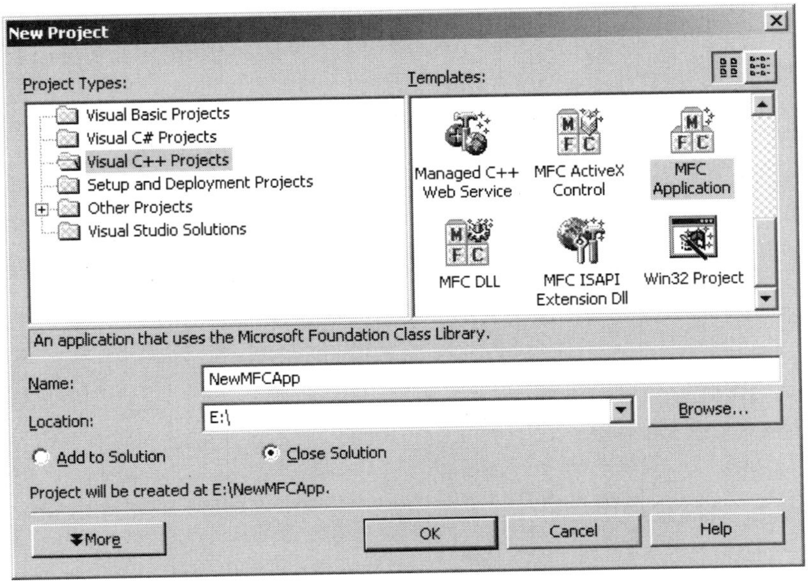

FIGURE 38.3 Selecting a .NET language and template.

VC++ 7.0 AND MANAGED VC++

If you decide to join the new .NET family, you will certainly want to look into the new "Managed" .NET version of VC++, or VC++.NET. The word "managed" refers to the initiative to make C++ more compliant with both OOP and the requirements of .NET to make the software products created using the new platform and its tools as robust as possible.

Take memory leak, for example. Memory leak refers to computer memory that is unclaimed after use, therefore becoming inaccessible for other applications. The result is ever-diminishing available system memory resources. When memory becomes scarce to the point that it can no longer support the execution of an application, the system needs to reboot.

Memory leak is an inherent problem with the C family of languages. First, it is a significant software development problem because the developer must be vigilant in allocating and de-allocating memory subscriptions. If the software developer misses, the result is memory leak. In fact, the memory leak problem with C, C++, and VC++ is so severe that commercial utility software has been crafted just to help identify memory leaks.

To be truthful, the C++ language has fixed the memory leak problem of C to a great extent. However, if the developer really tries, memory leak can still be achieved, such as by not deleting objects created with the "new" operator.

The "Managed" VC++ language will redefine many of the language syntax elements so that the .NET platform, which has new "garbage collection" mechanisms built-in, can help stem problems such as memory leak from taking place.

.NET's *Common Language Runtime* comes with a "garbage collector" that looks for objects that have gone out of scope yet have not been "released" from the computer's memory, much like what the Basic language does. When it finds them, it "deallocates" them and returns the recovered memory to the system.

On the other hand, if you will be continuing to develop applications for the current Windows platforms, you can advance to the VC++ 7.0 version, which promises many upgraded features. For example, VC++ 7.0 includes the following new classes:

CDHtmlDialog
CHtmlEditCtrl
CHtmlEditCtrlBase
CHtmlEditDoc
CHtmlEditView
CHttpArg
CHttpArgList

CMultiPageDHtmlDialog
COccManager
COleControlSite
CPrintDialogEx

This is exciting because these new classes promise so much more capability and productivity. However, the effect of overhauling MFC is unknown at this time. Will that mean that existing applications might not be compatible with the new environment? It is possible that some projects will have to be reworked. However, the initial study of the new MFC catalog indicated that, by and large, the classes have been preserved. Therefore, even if there are compatibility problems in porting in old projects, the impact should be minimal.

From the list of new classes, one can confidently conclude that the movement is to more intensive Internet-oriented undertakings.

In any case, at a minimum, just to continue to work in VC++, you'll have to get used to a new IDE—and a much improved and organized IDE it is. For example, when you start a new VC++ Win32 project in .NET, you'll first determine the project settings (Figure 38.4). Then, you'll specify the application type. For VC++,

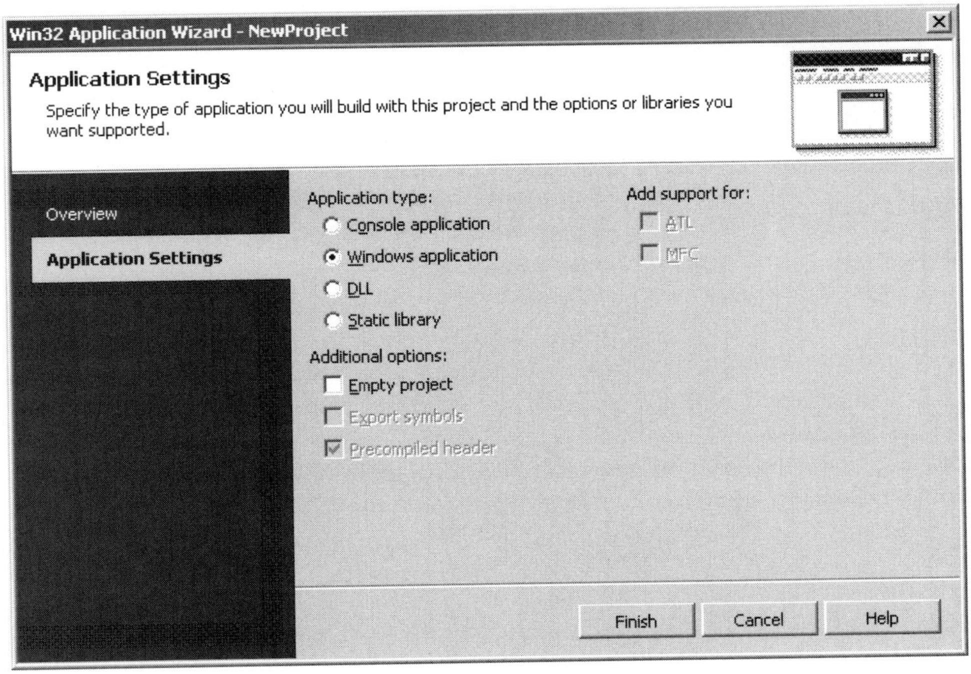

FIGURE 38.4 .NET application settings.

you'll find that there is a new type of application framework: the Multiple Top Level Documents model (Figure 38.5).

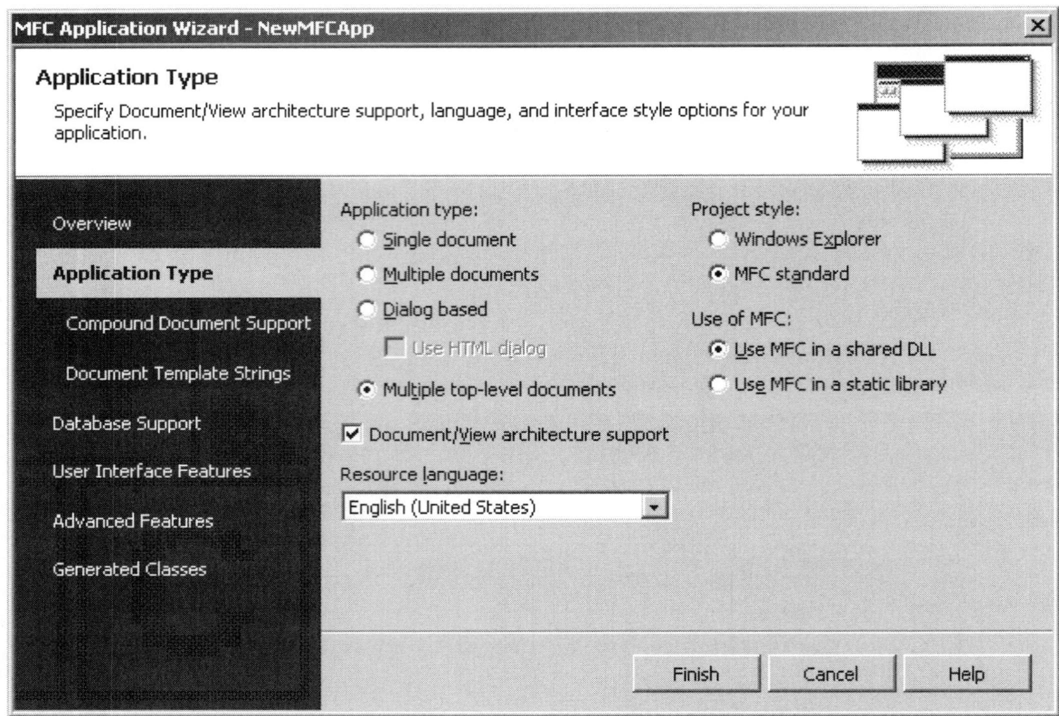

FIGURE 38.5 Selecting the application type in .NET.

A Multiple Top Level Documents application is one that has multiple frame windows (Figure 38.6), just as the MDI framework supports multiple child windows.

At any rate, the new project window looks like that in Figure 38.7. This window layout greatly resembles that of a VB 6.0 project. If you focus on the lower-left corner of the window you should see the properties of the default dialog resource presented in the same GUI as that of a VB project GUI. You now can set the properties

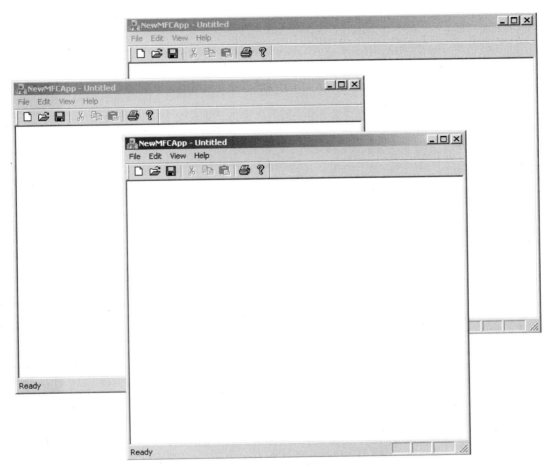

FIGURE 38.6 A Multiple Top-Level Documents application.

by selecting them in plain sight without having to bring up a separate Properties window.

In short, even if you continue to work in VC++ 7.0—"unmanaged"—you'll need to spend some time to assimilate the new and improved environment and classes.

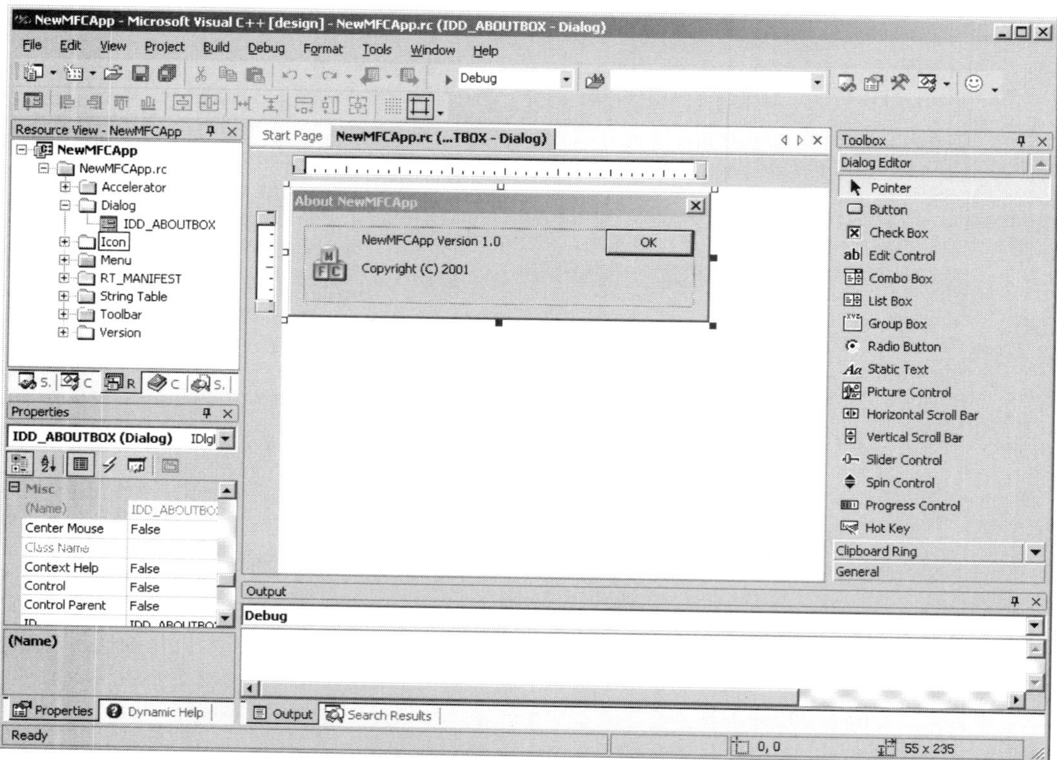

FIGURE 38.7 .NET project has VB-style layout.

C#

Of all the new features that will be introduced with .NET, the most interesting and most intriguing one is perhaps the new language C#. By its name, you can gather that it is somehow related to C and C++ and, in a sense, it is.

Although C++ is well known as an OOP "compliant" language (in contrast with a procedural language with which you develop logic line by line, and therefore are subject to the threat of unstructured consequences), it is not foolproof as pointed out earlier. Moreover, although it started out as a potentially platform independent, truly portable language, the innate ability to work with machine-level features quickly imbued the language with platform-specific elements (such as Windows-specific attributes).

Then came Java, designed to be platform independent by mandate. The way Java achieved its objective was to require the use of a virtual machine (an operating system software module) that bridged the language with the physical machine on which it was executed.

The new C# language will be a language with an opportunity to fulfill the requirements of portability (although not a stated goal), and achieve an even more robust language structure than C++ by including most of C++'s features and those high points of Java. Therefore, C# is a C++/Java-like language that will be more OOP compliant than C++.

Java, in many ways, was largely based on C++, with many parallel elements between the two languages. This is the reason why traditionally C++ programmers have little difficulty transitioning to Java.

It would be interesting for us to take a brief look at the C# language with reference to (V)C++ and Java, and observe their similarities and where they diverge, thus conceivably gaining an understanding of what the new C# language is attempting to achieve, and maybe confirming that C# is the next language for VC++ programmers to pursue.

The first things one looks at in a new language are the data types that it can handle and the logic constructs that it provides to manipulate them. We'll now look at just how C# deals with such language elements.

Data Types

C# uses two groups of data type: the *value* type and the *reference* type. Sound familiar to you? Value types are constructed in the computer's stack memory area, while reference types are placed on the heap, just as VC++ does.

Note that the C# *reference* type is not the same as the *pointer* type. Pointer types in C# are considered *unsafe*, and are outside the oversight of the garbage collection mechanism. In contrast, *reference* types, which are really pointers to objects, are managed.

Other than the predefined types, all other types, typically *reference* types, are derived from a master *object* class (just as the MFCs are mostly derived from a *CObject* class). Table 38.1 lists the predefined C# data types.

TABLE 38.1 C# Predefined Data Types

Type	*Description*
sbyte	8-bit signed integer
short	16-bit signed integer
int	32-bit signed integer
long	64-bit signed integer
byte	8-bit unsigned integer

(Continues)

TABLE 38.1 C# Predefined Data Types (*Continued*)

Type	*Description*
ushort	16-bit unsigned integer
uint	32-bit unsigned integer
ulong	64-bit unsigned integer
float	Single-precision floating point
double	Double-precision floating point
bool	Boolean
char	Unicode character
decimal	Decimal with 28 significant digits
object	Prototype of classes, reference type
string	String data of reference type

As a VC++ programmer, you should be familiar with most of the data types listed.

Note that the *char* data type is defined as Unicode (two bytes). This anticipates a world in which internationalization is inevitable.

Operators

Table 38.2 lists the C# operators.

TABLE 38.2 C# Operators

<table>
<tr><th>Category</th><th>Operators</th></tr>
<tr><td>Arithmetic</td><td>+ - * / %</td></tr>
<tr><td>Assignment</td><td>= += -= *= /= %= &= |= ^= <<= >>=</td></tr>
<tr><td>Increment/Decrement</td><td>++ --</td></tr>
<tr><td>Ternary</td><td>?:</td></tr>
<tr><td>Logical</td><td>& | ! ^ ~ && ||</td></tr>
<tr><td>Bit Shift</td><td><< >></td></tr>
<tr><td>Comparison</td><td>== != < > <= >=</td></tr>
</table>

TABLE 38.2 C# Operators (*Continued*)

Category	***Operators***
String Concatenation	+
Index (Subscript)	[]
Member Access	.
Cast	()
Object Creation	new
Delegate	+ -
Overflow Management	checked unchecked
Indirection/Addressing	* -> [] &

Again, mostly the operators agree with VC++ and Java, with a few new members introduced to perform tasks that have been neglected or mishandled in the earlier languages.

Note the absence of the *delete* operator. This is because C# vows to handle garbage collection for us, and will not rely on the *delete* directive to release computer memories. For that matter, objects in C# have no destructors for the same reason.

Another C# distinction that isn't obvious from the table is that, unlike C++ and Java, in C# even the basic data types are objects, which means that they can have member functions. We discussed this in Chapter 2 when explaining classes and objects, illustrating what a basic data type would have been had we thought of it as an object. This also illustrates Microsoft's conviction toward OOP.

The extension of this almost purely OOP approach is a major departure of C# from C++ (or even Java). In C#, arrays are objects, too. For example, you must use the *new* keyword to create arrays.

In C#, arrays are serious business, and come in many flavors. There are single-dimension arrays, and there are multidimensional arrays. In multidimensional arrays, there are rectangular arrays (like the traditional ones) and jagged arrays, which are single-dimensional arrays with uneven element lengths.

You can have some fun with arrays in C#.

Data Declaration

Data are declared in C# in the same way as in VC++ or Java. In fact, the basic program statement syntax is the same. For example, the following C# statement declares an integer variable and assigns it a value:

```
int     iValue = 100;
```

However, a floating point is declared as:

```
float     fCoeff = 2.874523F;
```

As you can see, the basic elements of C# are very similar to that of VC++, and even more so to Java.

Then, there are differences as well.

For example, in C++ the "#include" directive actually opens the target include file for inclusion in the current project. The counterpart in C#, the "using" directive, only provides unresolved class name information, and is similar to Java's "import" directive.

Moreover, in C#, structs are value data types; in C++, they are public classes.

Logic Controls

The C# language supports the logic controls listed in Table 38.3.

TABLE 38.3 C# Logic Controls

Control	*Description*
if-else (if)	Execution branching
for	Looping
do-while	Looping
foreach	Looping in array or collection
switch	Execution selection
break/continue	Looping control
goto	Directs program execution to label

Clearly, the *goto* mechanism is preserved here (although C and C++ have it, too) because of compatibility requirements with Visual Basic, which is also a .NET component.

Classes

Of course, there are classes in C#. You're familiar with classes by now; therefore, we won't spend too much time on it. Suffice it to say that classes are the backbone of

C# and .NET, and Microsoft has used every opportunity to make the most of classes to optimize programming efficiency, as evidenced in the use of classes and objects extensively in C#'s data definitions.

C# also has refined a few of the class's traditional implementation. For example, in C# you can specify a class function (method) parameter as of the *ref* type, thus allowing the parameter's actual data to be manipulated by the method.

There are other similarities between C# and its predecessors as well. Some are obvious, such as functions (methods) can be overloaded. Some are subtle, such as allowing operators to be overloaded to take on local meanings in classes, or limiting derived classes to inheriting implementation from only one parent class, as with classes in Java.

Exceptions are handled in the same ways as in C++ and Java. The major difference here, if you will, is the large library of exception classes that C# provides, helping the programming catch as many exceptions as possible.

C# emphasizes the use of *namespaces*, which are available in C and are by and large implemented as packages in Java. Namespaces are but names assigned to program scopes. For instance, in C, two program files File1.h and File.2 might contain classes of the same name: MyObject. When a program uses the MyObject class, which definition should the compiler use? If the two files are respectively assigned the namespaces of File1 and File2, their identifications would be unique, such as File1::MyObject.

In Java code, modules are organized into *packages*. When packages are imported and code modules are called upon, they are identified along with the package name, such as "package1.object1" and so on. The C# language promotes the use of namespace heavily.

These examples of C# emphases highlight Microsoft's redoubled effort to make the .NET platform as robust as possible.

A C# Project

Now we'll see what an actual C# project in .NET's Visual Studio looks like (Figure 38.8).

With the .NET's C# language, a new project may generate a default dialog, or form, just as VB 6.0 does (Figure 38.9). The default code that comes with the new project looks like that shown in Figure 38.10. As you can see, the syntax of the C# language is quite similar to that of C++.

First, you have a cluster of "using" statements. As discussed previously, these are call-out references to packaged library files and functions, resembling the Java "import" directive, and in a conceptual way, VC++'s "#includes."

The main program code is marked by a namespace that uniquely identifies the program code in case of conflicting program module names.

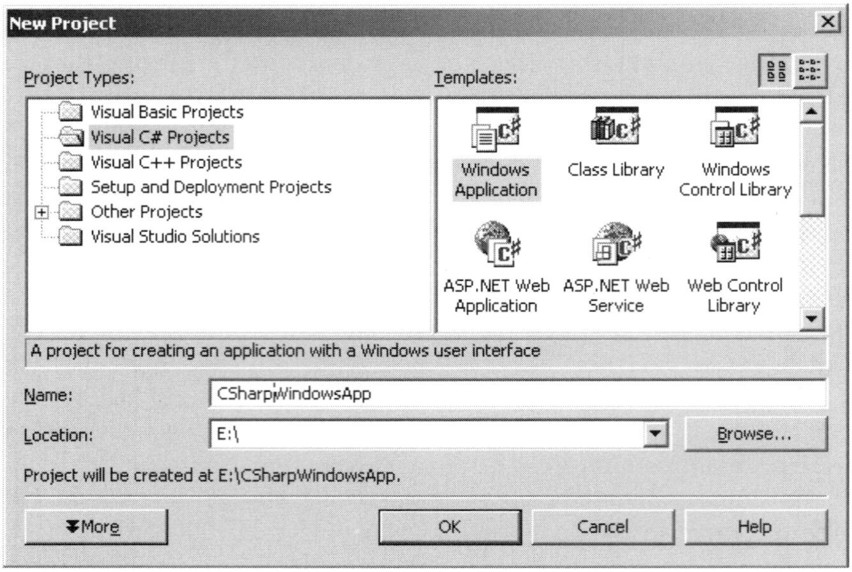

FIGURE 38.8 Initiating a C# project.

The rest is just code. Keywords such as "public," "private," function naming, object access using the "." symbol, and code syntax with statements ending in the semicolon are all familiar to you.

From this point on, it is just a matter of writing code and compiling it.

Why is C# so much like VC++, and even more like Java? The truth is, C# is Microsoft's alternative to Java, which is why it has language features such as *attributes*, *metadata*, and *reflection*, allowing you to obtain information about existing objects. These are concepts and features directly inherited from Java, and C++ programmers will have to learn them as new programming topics.

Microsoft has long sought to improve Java by adding Windows-specific features to the language to render the language more efficient for Windows than it was. This was at odds with the portability requirements of the Java language. To solve the problem and avoid violating the Java standard, Microsoft simply decided to introduce its own "Java" language. That language is C#.

Because of all the favorable settings for the invention of C# as we have discussed, the new language stands to achieve the goals of creating a robust software development environment. Therefore, not only is C# a natural candidate for new technologies to pursue for a VC++ student, it is virtually required that a practicing VC++ programmer become familiar with it.

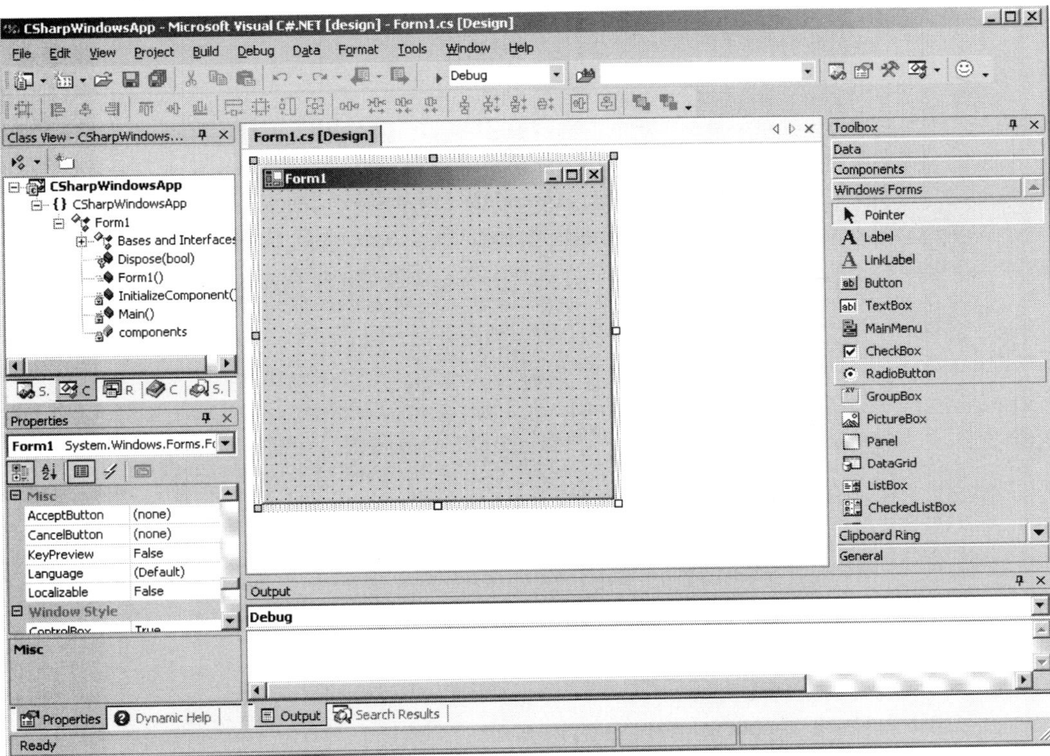

FIGURE 38.9 A new C# project main form.

MIGRATING TO VB

Finally, we must mention Visual Basic.

At first glance, the mentioning of a transition from C++ to VB might appear paradoxical. Isn't Basic supposed to be the unstructured language; therefore, any talk of transitioning should be from VB to C++ rather than the other way around? On its face it may seem so. However, since the introduction of Visual Basic (distinguishing itself from the predecessors that adhered pretty much to the Kemeny-Kurtz specifications), elements of OOP have already found their way in. For example, the existing VB version has a pseudo form of class. The new VB.NET will have true classes with inheritance and all.

This transformation of the VB language is actually necessary if the language is to share common classes with VC++ and C#. In short, VB will become a language in VB.NET that resembles the original Basic language pretty much in the statement syntax only. Virtually everything else will be OOP oriented. That will make the

```
using System;
using System.Drawing;
using System.Collections;
using System.ComponentModel;
using System.Windows.Forms;
using System.Data;

namespace CSharpWindowsApp
{
    /// <summary>
    /// Summary description for Form1.
    /// </summary>
    public class frmMain : System.Windows.Forms.Form
    {
        private System.Windows.Forms.Label lblLastname;
        private System.Windows.Forms.TextBox txtLastname;
        /// <summary>
        /// Required designer variable.
        /// </summary>
        private System.ComponentModel.Container components = null;

        public frmMain()
        {
```

FIGURE 38.10 Sample C# code.

new VB.NET a candidate of further education for current C and C++ developers because of the rich application features that it has, and the widespread adoption by the technology industries.

CONCLUSION

This book focuses on giving the core elements of the VC++ 6.0 language and MFC a thorough and structured presentation with the goal of engendering a programming culture in the reader. It is a culture because software development is not just code statement multiplied by x. It is indeed a mindset; a way of thinking that is unique to a language platform. A SmallTalk programmer "thinks" differently than a FoxPro programmer or VC++ programmer. With this programming *philosophy*, you, a VC++ developer, will have the fertile soil in which to grow and flourish.

Although the horizon is far and wide beyond this book, with many new possibilities, you may well remain with VC++ 6.0 for years to come and find the experience rewarding. Just because a new platform, a new language, and a new approach to product development begin to take life, doesn't mean that the current one will soon expire. In fact, experience has taught us that the opposite is true. While the new paradigm must gain acceptance and work out its many kinks and missteps, the vintage model gets more mature and reliable. Just look at Windows itself. While we are already at Windows 2000, many users still embrace Windows NT, '98, '95, and even in many cases, 3.1. Take note that many embedded systems are coded not with VC++ 6.0, 5.0, 4.2, or C++, but C.

Whichever path you take, your experience will be just as challenging.

Glossary

accelerator See **hot key**.

ActiveX Controls Microsoft code components that conform to the COM standard.

AppWizard VC++ feature that facilitates the development of complete applications or program modules through stepped feature selections.

array An orderly collection of data, usually occupying contiguous memory space and identified by a group name with indices.

C++ An OOP language that evolved from C; most notably, incorporating the concept of classes and objects.

child dialog A dialog box that exists as a component of another window.

class A template to a collection of code and data that can be used to engender objects with similar characteristics.

ClassWizard The VC++ IDE feature responsible for managing the classes used by a project.

collection A concept dealing with the scientific handling of data groups.

constructor The function that is automatically executed upon the construction of an object.

controls Visual objects that perform specific tasks; for example, an edit box control.

data abstraction Coding philosophy that advocates isolating program code from directly dealing with database data.

data aware A term referring to program code or controls' being inherently and directly connected to external data sources.

destructor The function that is automatically executed upon the destruction of an object.

device context An MFC class responsible for encapsulating the characteristics of an output device such as the screen, and provides operational functions for output.

dialog Abbreviation for dialog box, a screen window without toolbars, menus, and status bars.

dialog-based application A Windows application with a dialog box as its main window.

DLL, or **Dynamic Link Library** A collection of code components that exists as an individual file.

dynaset A life profile of a database that reflects the up-to-date states of the data.

event-driven A term describing program logic responding to events such as mouse clicking.

exporting Exposing a code element to an external user file.

FileView The windowpane in VC++ that displays the files of an application.

filtering Selection of database records.

function A named code block that produces a return value.

grid A visual device that uses rows and columns (thus forming cells) to present data.

GUI Graphical user interface.

handle A memory identification of an object.

helper function A function that takes over a common or significant portion of a higher-level function to help reduce the complexity of that function.

hot key A key-press combination that accesses a menu command directly. Also known as quick key or accelerator.

ID A mnemonic numeric value in VC++ used to uniquely identify a resource.

IDE, or **integrated development environment** The visual environment of the language compiler.

inheritance The attainment of characteristics as a result of an object being created based on an existing class.

instantiation The action of creating an object based on a class.

IntelliSense A VC++ IDE feature whereby a few keystrokes from the developer brings up possible code candidates by context.

invalidation A term referring to the action of updating the display on the screen (because the current display is outdated, it is therefore invalid).

key A database record field used to identify the record.

kit Software development tool set.

list A collection of data in which each data member points to its neighbor.

MainFrame A term applied to the portion of a screen window where the toolbar, status bar, and menus of an application are hosted.

mapping mode A coordinate system used by the device context to express output geometries.

MDI application A Windows application with a single-framed window supporting multiple child-framed windows.
member A code block or data that belongs to an object.
member function A function that is a part of a class.
member e A variable that is a part of a class.
MFC, or **Microsoft Foundation Classes** Library collection of classes used by Microsoft in the development of many of its software products.
Microsoft Foundation Classes See **MFC**.
modal dialog A dialog window that stays on the screen and remains in focus until it is closed explicitly.
modeless dialog A dialog window that does not remain in focus.
MSDN Library The Microsoft Software Developer's Network Library, reference materials for software developers.
null A C feature that indicates that an object has no existence.
object Functional code and data collection created based on specifications called a class.
Object-Oriented Programming See **OOP**.
OCX The filename extension of an ActiveX control.
ODBC Open Database Connectivity; a standard of interfacing with a diverse number of proprietary database structures that enables the structured accessing of data.
OLE Object Linking and Embedding; Microsoft's protocol for the interfacing of data, objects, or code of diverse characteristics.
OOP, or **Object-Oriented Programming** A programming approach that looks at code as objects dedicated to supporting an application objective as opposed to instruction lines.
paradigm An application model.
persistence The preservation of data by saving them to disk.
properties dialog box A dialog box that presents the properties of an object.
query The technical expression of a data record set selection.
quick key See **hot key**.
reference The memory address of a data item, object, or code.
ResourceView The windowpane in VC++ that displays the resources of an application.
SDI application A Windows application with a single-framed window.
serializing The sequential input or output of data.
snapshot An instance of a database; does not reflect the changing state of the data.
SQL Structured Query Language; a language used to selectively work with relational database records.
string table A VC++ resource used to collect and manage string data.

text metrics The description of a text object such as the character height, and so on.
title The textual display at the top of a screen window.
unhandled exception An error that had not been anticipated.
view The portion of a screen window, usually white, where displays take place.
Visual C++ Microsoft C++ compiler/application development software providing visual means to quickly develop application features.
workspace A named collection of pertinent projects and files.

Appendix: About the CD-ROM

The CD-ROM included with *Professional Software Development with Visual C++ 6.0 and MFC* contains files to assist you in learning VC++ and MFC. There are four primary folders: Figures, Source Code, Third Party Software, and Extras. The contents of these separate areas are listed below.

CD FOLDERS

Figures: Contains the full color version of all the figures in the book.

Source Code: Contains all the example files presented in the book, by chapter. Some applications require you to use the extra or supplemental utilities offered by VC++ Professional or Enterprise Edition only, such as InstallShield. If you use a lower edition of the compiler, you may not be able to execute some of the programs included. The Access database file (Books.mdb) used in many examples also can be found here.

Third Party Software: Demo versions of many useful software packages are included here to show the types of applications that you can develop with VC++ and to assist you in the development of your own VC++ projects.

- **CursorArts Company:** Several programs are available from this company. These are all useful development tools. For example, IconForge helps you create or change icons, cursors, animated cursors and icon libraries for Windows. Each program is a 30-day trial version.
    - *Trial version of IconForge, version 5.23*
    - *Trial version of ImageForge PRO 2.98a*

    - *Trial version of FileWrangler, version 5.22a*
    - *Freeware version of ActivIcons, version 3.13*

- **Dart Communications:** Several programs are available from this company. These tools, written in C++, perform many useful functions. For example, the Power-TCP Winsock tool contains controls to help you build Internet applications. The Emulation tool has controls that will help you build terminal emulation capabilities into your application. Each program is a 30-day trial version.
    - *PT-1510 PowerTCP Winsock Tool, version 2.2*
    - *PT-1520 PowerTCP Emulation Tool, version 1.1*
    - *PT-1530 PowerTCP FTP Tool, version 1.6.01*
    - *PT-1540 PowerTCP Mail Tool, version 2.2.0*
    - *PT-1550 PowerTCP SNMP Tool, version 2.0*
    - *PT-1560 PowerTCP Server Tool, version 3.0*
    - *PT-1570 PowerTCP Web Tool, version 1.0.43*
    - *PT-1580 PowerTCP Telnet Tool, version 1.1*
    - *PT-1590 PowerTCP WebServer Tool, version 1.5.0*
    - *PT-1600 PowerTCP SSL Tool, version 1.5.0*
    - *PT-1610 PowerTCP WebEnterprise Tool, version 1.5*
    - *Update.exe*

- **Goldstone Software:** *Super Color Picker 1.0 Free Version,* is a smart pick-color tool that can pick color from anywhere in the screen and then show you the color code in different formats.
- **Nitrobit Software:** *DevFriend, version 1.3,* is a tool that contains a comment generator for C++ source code.
- **Northwoods Software:** *GO++, version 3.0 Evaluation Kit,* is a set of classes built upon MFC that facilitates graphical object programming.
- **Palisand:** *DALC++, version 1.21,* is a C++ class library that makes connecting to a relational database effortless.
- **ParaSoft:** Several programs are available from this company. You will need to obtain a password from ParaSoft to use these programs. Instructions on how to do so are included in a readme file located in the folder. Each program is a 7-day trial version. The trial period begins upon receipt of password from ParaSoft.
    - *C++Test, version 1.3,* is a C/C++ testing tool that automatically tests any C/C++ class, function, or component. The program automatically performs both white-box, black-box, and regression testing.
    - *Insure++, version 4.0,* detects memory leaks in C/C++ applications. Insure++ thoroughly examines and tests C/C++ code from inside and out, then reports errors and pinpoints their exact location.

- *CodeWizard, version 6.0,* is a C/C++ source code analysis tool that uses coding guidelines to automatically identify dangerous coding constructs that compilers do not detect.

- **Teemu Lätti:** *CodeWiz (Developer Studio Add-In), version 1.31,* adds a new toolbar/menu to Visual Studio, providing extra code manipulation functions.
- **WordenWare:** *C++ Numerics Library, version 1.1,* is a collection of numerical and statistical computation routines that are commonly used in science and engineering (and other fields).

Extras: In this folder, you will find more illustrations and sample applications on the VC++ language and MFC that were not included in the book. These programs illustrate many topics and applications that may be of interest to you, such as an Internet browser. Although most of the programs do not include detached explanations, you can learn a lot from these programs just by studying their source code.

SYSTEM REQUIREMENTS

Microsoft Visual C++ 6.0, preferably the Enterprise Edition (with MSDN reference library)
Windows 95, 98, NT, or 2000 operating system
32 MB of RAM, 64 MB preferred
2 GB hard disk space
CD-ROM

INSTALLATION

The illustration programs contained on this CD were designed to work with the D drive. The presumption is that your computer has at least two hard drives: C for system and application files, and D for data, documents, and miscellaneous content files including exercises. If your system is set up differently, such as using drive C or drive E for example programs, simply copy the programs to your target drive by folder, search through the contents of the copied files in the folders for the "D:" drive spec, and replace them with the appropriate designation.

By nature of the medium, the files on the CD-ROM are write-protected. Make sure that after you copy the files onto your hard drive that you remove the read-only attribute from the files before you work with them.

Index